# Children
# With
# Learning
# Disabilities

## Theories, Diagnosis, and Teaching Strategies

**JANET W. LERNER**

**Northwestern University**

**HOUGHTON MIFFLIN COMPANY    BOSTON**
New York  Atlanta  Geneva, Illinois  Dallas  Palo Alto

Library of Congress Catalog Card Number: 77-142327

ISBN: 0-395-11229-X

**TO EUGENE**

# EDITOR'S INTRODUCTION

Learning disabilities in children are not new. What is new is the rapidly growing movement by parents, schools, state departments of education and the Federal government to offer services to children who are not developing adequately because of learning disabilities.

During the postwar period, special education concentrated on the expansion of services for children with previously identified disorders—the visually and auditorily handicapped, the mental deviates, the physically handicapped, the speech defective and the emotionally disturbed. After such programs were established in public and residential schools, it was discovered that there remained many children who were physically unimpaired and intellectually normal, but who failed to perceive visually, or to process auditory information, or to talk, read, spell or think adequately. A more thorough analysis of these children showed that they had central process dysfunctions which inhibited learning by ordinary methods. In response to these diverse problems a new discipline arose which borrowed and integrated insights from neurology, psychology, speech pathology and remedial reading. The subjects of this new field were given various names—brain-injured children, children with perceptual handicaps, children with minimal cerebral dysfunction or children with learning disabilities. The latter term, because it emphasizes the educational character of such disorders, has become the most acceptable for educational purposes. The field has now become sufficiently specialized to undertake the diagnosis and remediation of severe learning problems.

*Children With Learning Disabilities* presents the discipline from a broad point of view, without attempting to promote any single method or theory. Many teachers complain of the overly theoretical approach of much that is written on learning disabilities, and point out that very little information is available on how theory is implemented. Dr. Lerner has minimized that problem—the emphasis of her book is the development of teaching strategies for various disabilities.

*Children With Learning Disabilities* integrates theory, diagnosis and teaching strategies into a comprehensive guide for regular and special teachers of children with learning disabilities.

Samuel A. Kirk

# PREFACE

A typical school class includes two or three children who are destined to become educational discards unless their learning disabilities are recognized and diagnosed and ways are found to help them learn. Although children with learning disabilities are not blind, many cannot see as normal children do; although they are not deaf, many cannot listen or hear normally; although they are neither retarded in mental development nor deprived of educational opportunities, they cannot learn and many develop personality and social disturbances. Moreover, many of these youngsters exhibit other behavioral characteristics which make them disruptive in the classroom and at home.

Such children are the concern of this book.

*Children With Learning Disabilities* is intended as an introduction to the field of learning disabilities for the teacher, clinician, therapist, administrator, or other professional preparing to work with the learning-disabled child. Its approach is eclectic, to offer the reader a comprehensive view of the field. A teacher of children with learning disabilities should have an understanding of the theories and approaches to learning disabilities, knowledge of diagnostic methods, skill in the art of clinical teaching, and familiarity with teaching techniques and materials. This book deals with each of these essential areas.

Part I is an overview of the field of learning disabilities. Chapter 1 describes the multidisciplinary nature of the field; Chapter 2 offers an historical perspective; and Chapter 3 examines the contributions of medicine.

Part II deals with the diagnostic-teaching process. Diagnosis and clinical teaching are interrelated parts of a continuous process of trying to understand a child and help him learn; both are necessary if the child is to be effectively helped. Diagnosis that does not lead to teaching is a dead end, while teaching without a clear purpose may be wasteful and detrimental. Diagnosis is discussed in Chapter 4 and clinical teaching is the subject of Chapter 5.

Part III reviews the theories that provide a rationale for diagnostic and teaching decisions. The role of theory in the field of learning disabilities is discussed in Chapter 6. Theories related to sensory-motor and perceptual-motor development are the subject of Chapter 7. Theories of perception and memory are discussed in Chapter 8, language in Chapter 9, cognitive development in Chapter 10, and maturation and emotional development in Chapter 11. Chapters 8 through 11 include sections on the academic implications of the theories previously discussed, with examples of teaching strategies derived from theoretical approaches.

Part IV discusses the administration and organization of programs for children with learning disabilities. The implementation of such programs—usually undertaken within organizational settings such as schools, clinics, hospitals, or child guidance centers—is discussed in Chapter 12.

The appendices contain supplementary material useful to teachers and administrators.

*Children With Learning Disabilities* grew out of my experiences teaching an introductory course in learning disabilities over a number of years. It has been considerably influenced by feedback from college students and teachers enrolled in the course. The ideas set forth here have also evolved from many years of working with children who face difficulty in learning and with teachers and other professionals in clinical settings, as well as from writers in the field, lecturers at professional conferences, co-workers, and students.

I would like to express my appreciation to my colleagues at City College of the City University of New York, National College of Education, Northeastern Illinois State College, and Northwestern University for the opportunities they provided and for their friendship and confidence. I would like particularly to thank my colleagues at Northwestern University; Dr. Harold J. McGrady, Professor Doris J. Johnson, and Carol Sonnenschein, who have contributed to my thinking in many ways.

Dr. Samuel A. Kirk played a dual role in the making of this book: as my first college instructor in special education, he made the field exciting and challenging; as the editor of this book, he made many perceptive and discerning suggestions. Dr. Frank W. Lutz deserves a special note of gratitude for his help and guidance with my doctoral work. I would also like to thank my children, Susan, Laura, and Dean, for their cooperation and understanding. But my great debt is to my husband, Eugene, who provided the faith and encouragement needed to write this book.

Janet W. Lerner

# CONTENTS

# I

# OVERVIEW OF LEARNING DISABILITIES

# Chapter 1

# Learning Disabilities: An Interdisciplinary Field

Tony's parents have long been aware that their son has severe problems in learning. Even as an infant, he had difficulty in learning to suck and was a colicky baby. His early speech was so garbled that no one could understand him, and frequently his inability to communicate led to sudden temper tantrums. The kindergarten teacher reported that Tony was "immature"; his first-grade teacher said he "did not pay attention"; and succeeding teachers labeled him "lazy" and then "emotionally disturbed." In desperate attempts to find the source of Tony's learning problems and to alleviate his misery and theirs, Tony's parents followed suggestions from many sources and took their son to a number of specialists and clinics.

One clinic detected a visual problem, and as a result Tony received visual training exercises for several years. At another clinic, Tony's problem was diagnosed as a lack of neurological organization, and a lengthy series of motor exercises was instituted. An opinion of emotional disturbance at another agency led to years of psychotherapy for both Tony and his parents. A reading tutor analyzed the problem as a lack of instruction in phonics, and Tony received intensive phonics instruction for a period of time. Tony's family pediatrician advised that the boy was merely going through a stage and would grow out of it. Yet despite this wealth of diagnosis and treatment, Tony still cannot learn. He is unhappily failing in school, and understandably he has lost faith in himself.

The problems encountered by Tony and his parents are typical. Each specialist had viewed Tony's problem from his own perspective and therefore saw only part of the picture. What was needed, instead, was a unified interdisciplinary approach to the problem of Tony's learning disabilities—a coordinated effort, with each special field contributing its expertise to the analysis and treatment of the child. A unified procedure was required to mobilize the team and coordinate the efforts of the various contributing professions.

Without a coordinated effort, each field may see the child with learning disabilities in terms of its own perspective, much as the fabled blind men of India are said to have "seen" the elephant. The problem of fragmentation has been well stated by Bassler (1967, p. 3): Within our schools and community, we have untapped resources to help the underachieving child become an achiever. However, too many schools have failed to integrate the various professional services being used with an individual child.

> The reading consultant knows the child has a complex of reading problems. The teacher sees a phonics difficulty. The school nurse observes a hearing problem; the speech therapist, a lisp. The school psychologist, the family doctor, the optometrist, the ophthalmologist, the

parents each has a different view of the child and his constellation of problems. We have so segmented and fragmented the child, we have so atomized our approach to the educational problems that we have lost the child in the labyrinth of professions and techniques.

## Disciplines Contributing to the Study of Learning Disabilities

The major disciplines contributing to the study of learning disabilities can be grouped into five categories: *medicine, language, education, psychology,* and *other professions.* The mingling of professions brings a multi-disciplinary depth to the study of the child with learning disabilities.

### MEDICINE

The medical specialties (represented by both practioners and researchers) include pediatrics, neurology, ophthalmology, psychiatry, pharmacology, endocrinology, electroencephalography, and nursing. Medical specialists are, by training and experience, cause oriented—always searching for the source or etiology of a health problem. Once the cause of an illness is determined, a cure can be prescribed. Medical specialists tend to view a learning disability as a pathological

FIGURE 1.1 LEARNING DISABILITIES: AN INTERDISCIPLINARY FIELD

condition, and their terminology, which is frequently concerned with the cause of a learning disorder, is medical in origin. Many of the terms are adaptations of words used to describe various kinds of damage to the nervous system of the adult patient, e.g., a cerebral stroke. Terms such as brain impairment, cerebral insult, brain damage, brain injury, apraxia, agnosia, dyslexia, and aphasia are examples of medically oriented terminology.

## PSYCHOLOGY

Important contributions to the field of learning disabilities are being made by psychologists, particularly specialists in child development and learning theory. The psychologists observe, test, evaluate, and characterize the outward behavior of children. The psychological perspective also leads to the development of views concerning the psychodynamic concomitants of learning abnormalities. Psychology has contributed such terms as perceptual disorder, impulsivity, disinhibited behavior, perseveration, and hyperkinetic activity.

Specialists in child development focus on the developmental processes of the normal child, which become the basis for many concepts of the atypical child. The theory of maturational lag, for example, is rooted in the analysis of child growth patterns.

Learning theorists have contributed to the analysis of school-subject content areas in behavioral terms, identifying tasks to be taught and behaviors to be expected. Reinforcement theory, operant conditioning, and behavioral modification are among the contributions of learning theorists being incorporated in the learning disabilities research and teaching.

## LANGUAGE STUDY

Workers in the fields of speech and language pathology, language development, linguistics, and psycholinguistics have recently recognized that many of their interests and concerns overlap those of the field of learning disabilities. Since speech teachers and language pathologists have traditionally allied themselves closely with the medical profession, their thinking and terminology readily follow the viewpoint and concepts developed by the medical field. Terms from the fields of speech and communication disorders found in the literature on learning disabilities include aphasia, dyslexia, anomia, and expressive and receptive language disorders.

The science of linguistics is the study of human language in all its forms. Psycholinguistics is a recently developed area that combines psychology and linguistics. These fields are making important contributions to our understanding of the relationship of language development to the learning process. A renewed interest in the puzzle of language acquisition, kindled by recent work in linguistics, shows promise of contributing to our understanding of the child with learning disabilities. Knowledge of how the normal child learns language will be invaluable in developing the ability to diagnose and treat language difficulties in children. Conversely, perhaps an understanding of the normal child's language acquisition will come through the study of the language disorders of exceptional children. Psycholinguistics and linguistics have incorporated terms such as encoding, decoding, syntax, phonology, and morphology in the literature on learning disabilities.

## EDUCATION

The field of education has yet another framework. Kirk (1962, p. 30) has noted that "Education often begins where medicine stops." The training and experience of educators permit teachers, reading specialists, special educators, clinical teachers, psychoeducational diagnosticians, physical educators, and curriculum developers to focus on the learning behavior of the child. The educators' expertise includes knowledge about subject area sequences, an understanding of the relationship of curricular areas, an acquaintance with a variety of school organizational patterns, and knowledge of materials and methods. The very term *learning disabilities,* with its emphasis on the learning situation instead of the etiology of the disorder, is evidence of the impact of the educator in this field.

## OTHER PROFESSIONS

Many other specialists play important roles in the research and literature on learning disabilities. Optometrists, who are concerned with the visual function, have made key contributions. Many of the child's percepts and concepts come to him through the visual field. Visual acuity, visual perception, visual memory, and visual motor learning are discussed by optometrists.

Audiologists, who work in the field of hearing, have contributed important concepts concerning auditory perception and auditory training. Social workers, physical therapists, and guidance counselors have also made vital contributions to the growth of the field. In addition, research findings from fields such as genetics and biochemistry may provide additional important information.

## THE LEARNING DISABILITIES SPECIALIST

Kirk (1969, p. 4) foresees the emergence of the learning disabilities specialist as the agent who is responsible for coordinating the efforts of the contributing professions.

> A position for a person with interdisciplinary training will evolve in our schools, perhaps entitled "Diagnostic-Remedial Specialist." This individual will serve as the responsible agent for the child—responsible for adequate diagnosis, evaluation or assessment, and for the remediation or the organization of remediation for a child with a learning disability. All personnel involved in the assessment of the child—doctors, psychologists, and social workers—will report their findings and interpretations to this diagnostic-remedial specialist. She or he will be responsible for the collation and interpretation of information, for remediation, or for the prescription for remedial education. The diagnostic-remedial specialist will function somewhat as the family physician does—as the responsible agent for obtaining information from other specialists and for prescribing treatment.

One crucial role of the learning disabilities specialist within such a framework would be to build a cooperative interdisciplinary team that works together, rather than to permit team members to pursue a splintered and isolated approach that sometimes works at crosspurposes with the proposals of others. Although the learning disabilities specialist is not an expert in all of these contributing fields, his intensive interdisciplinary training should enable him to understand the vocabularies and basic concepts of the other specialists and to know something of what they can do. The learning disabilities specialist should not operate as an expert in the spheres of neurology or ophthalmology or psychoanalytic theory, but he may serve as a highly skilled co-worker and coordinator.

## The Definition of Learning Disabilities

The field of learning disabilities is relatively new, but it is growing at a phenomenally rapid rate. Through the intermingling of many professions, a multidisciplinary breadth is evolving. However, because so many diverse professions are concerned, a confusion of terminology and seemingly conflicting ideas pervade current discussions found in the literature.

In the various attempts to identify the population of children with learning disabilities, several dimensions of the problem have been considered. Discussions of these different approaches to the problem of definition follow:

1. *Neurological dysfunction or brain impairment.* Definitions that focus on this dimension of the problem attempt to identify organic etiology. For example, the concept of *psychoneurological learning disability* put forth by Johnson and Myklebust (1967, p. 8) implies a neurological dysfunction:

> . . . we refer to children as having a psychoneurological learning disability, meaning that behavior has been disturbed as a result of a dysfunction of the brain and that the problem is one of altered processes, not of a generalized incapacity to learn.

2. *Uneven growth pattern.* Another emphasis in the identification of the learning disability population is upon the irregular development of mental abilities. An examination of profiles of subskills reveals that growth in the various areas is uneven and inconsistent. Gallagher (1966, p. 28) focuses on such developmental imbalances in identifying the population:

> Children with developmental imbalances are those who reveal a developmental disparity in psychological processes related to education of such a degree (often four years or more) as to require the instructional programming of developmental tasks appropriate to the nature and level of the deviant developmental process.

3. *Difficulty in academic and learning tasks.* Another aspect of identifying the population of children with learning disabilities is that of considering the learning problems that such children encounter. Kirk's definition emphasizes this problem (Kirk 1962, p. 263):

> A learning disability refers to a retardation, disorder, or delayed development in one or more of the processes of speech, language, reading, spelling, writing, or arithmetic resulting from a possible cerebral dysfunction and/or emotional or behavioral disturbance and not from mental retardation, sensory deprivation, or cultural or instructional factors.

4. *Discrepancy between achievement and potentiality.* Yet another focus to define the population of learning-disabled children is the criterion of a significant discrepancy between what the child is potentially capable of learning and what in fact he has learned. Bateman (1965, p. 220), for example, defines children with specific learning disabilities as those who

> manifest an educationally significant discrepancy between their estimated intellectual potential and actual level of performance related to basic disorders in the learning processes, which may or may not be accompanied by demonstrable central nervous system dysfunction,

and which are not secondary to generalized mental retardation, educational or cultural deprivation, severe emotional disturbance, or sensory loss.

5. *Definition by exclusion.* Another dimension of many of the definitions is that the children under consideration do not primarily fit into any other area of exceptionality; that is, children with learning disabilities are not primarily mentally retarded, emotionally disturbed, culturally deprived, or sensorily handicapped. This dimension, among several others, is included in the definition by Johnson and Myklebust (1967, p. 9):

> In those having a psychoneurological learning disability, it is the fact of adequate motor ability, average to high intelligence, adequate hearing and vision, and adequate emotional adjustment together with a deficiency in learning that constitutes the basis for homogeneity.

The U.S. Office of Education recently attempted to channel these diverse perspectives by calling together a committee to formulate a definition of learning disabilities. This committee comprised individuals representing a variety of disciplines concerned with the handicap of learning disorders; they were charged with the task of formulating a definition that would be meaningful and acceptable to all professional groups involved. The definition resulting from the work of this committee is (Kass and Myklebust 1969, p. 399):

> Learning disability refers to one or more significant deficits in essential learning processes requiring special education techniques for remediation.
> Children with learning disability generally demonstrate a discrepancy between expected and actual achievement in one or more areas, such as spoken, read, or written language, mathematics, and spatial orientation.
> The learning disability referred to is not primarily the result of sensory, motor, intellectual, or emotional handicap, or lack of opportunity to learn.
> *Significant deficits* are defined in terms of accepted diagnostic procedures in education and psychology.
> *Essential learning processes* are those currently referred to in behavioral science as involving perception, integration, and expression either verbal or nonverbal.
> *Special education techniques for remediation* refers to educational planning based on the diagnostic procedures and results.

Finally, a concise definition was formulated by the National Advisory Committee on Handicapped Children in their annual report to Congress in 1968 (p. 4):

> Children with special learning disabilities exhibit a disorder in one or more of the basic psychological processes involved in understanding or using spoken or written languages. These may be manifested in disorders of listening, thinking, talking, reading, writing, spelling or arithmetic. They include conditions which have been referred to as perceptual handicaps, brain injury, minimal brain dysfunction, dyslexia, developmental aphasia, etc. They do not include learning problems which are due primarily to visual, hearing, or motor handicaps, to mental retardation, emotional disturbance, or to environmental disadvantage.

Congressional legislation concerning the child with learning disabilities incorporates the definition formulated by the National Advisory Committee on Handicapped Children (Children with Specific Learning Disabilities Act of 1969, PL 91–230, The Elementary and Secondary Amendments of 1969).

*N ACHC*
*1 - 3 %*

# Prevalence of Learning Disabilities

A variety of estimates of the prevalence of children who suffer from learning disabilities have been made, ranging from 1 percent to 30 percent of the school population, depending upon the criteria used to determine the disability. One estimate, for example, was the result of a recent screening of almost 2,800 children in the third and fourth grades in a public school population; this screening was conducted as part of a research project at Northwestern University (Myklebust and Boshes 1969). The identification criterion used in this study was based on an educational-discrepancy definition of learning disabilities: the entire public school population was initially screened by administering a battery of psychoeducational tests and deriving a ratio between achievement and expectancy for each child tested. The criterion of underachievement was a ratio or learning quotient of less than 90; by this standard, 15 percent of the research population were identified as underachievers. However, further study and more stringent criteria for identification revealed that approximately one half of those initially identified fell into the category of learning disabled. In this study, then, the prevalence of children with learning disabilities in the public school population examined was determined to be 7 to 8 percent.

A more conservative estimate of the prevalence of children with learning disabilities has been made by the National Advisory Committee on Handicapped Children (1968) in their report to Congress. They recommend that 1 to 3 percent of the school population be considered as a prevalence estimate, at least until research provides objective criteria by means of which these children may be more clearly identified.

Nevertheless, it is clear that we are talking about a tremendous number of children. It is interesting to compare these prevalence estimates with those of other areas of exceptionality, as shown in Table 1.1 (Mackie 1969, p. 61).

NOT LD

| Type of Exceptionality | Estimated Percentage |
| --- | --- |
| Mentally retarded | 2.3 percent |
| Deaf and hard-of-hearing<br>(deaf: 0.1 percent)<br>(hearing impaired: 0.5 percent) | 0.6 |
| Visually handicapped<br>(partially seeing: 0.07 percent)<br>(blind: 0.03 percent) | 0.1 |
| Crippled | 0.8 |
| Special health problems | 0.8 |
| Speech handicapped | 3.5 |
| Emotionally disturbed and<br>socially maladjusted | 2.0 |
| Gifted | 2.0 |
| Total | 12.1 |

**TABLE 1.1 ESTIMATED PREVALENCE OF HANDICAPPED CHILDREN IN THE SCHOOL-AGE POPULATION.**
Adapted from Romaine P. Mackie, *Special Education in the United States Statistics 1946–1949.* New York: Teachers College Press, 1969, p. 61.

The number of children with learning disabilities, as estimated by studies such as the Northwestern project (Myklebust and Boshes 1969), is much larger than the number of children with any other kind of handicap listed in the table. Whatever the prevalence is finally determined to be, there are likely to be at least several children in every classroom who can be identified as children with learning disabilities.

## REFERENCES

Bassler, John J. "Interdisciplinary Needs in Reading." *Illinois Journal of Education* 58 (December 1967): 3–4.

Bateman, Barbara. "An Educator's View of a Diagnostic Approach to Learning Disorders," pp. 219–236 in Jerome Hellmuth (ed.), *Learning Disorders*, Vol. I. Seattle: Special Child Publications, 1965.

Gallagher, James. "Children with Developmental Imbalances: A Psychoeducational Definition," pp. 21–34 in W. Cruickshank (ed.), *The Teacher of Brain-Injured Children: A Discussion of the Bases of Competency.* Syracuse, N.Y.: Syracuse University Press, 1966.

Johnson, Doris, and Helmer Myklebust. *Learning Disabilities: Educational Principles and Practices.* New York: Grune & Stratton, 1967.

Kass, Corrine, and H. Myklebust. "Learning Disabilities: An Educational Definition," *Journal of Learning Disabilities* 2 (July 1969): 377–379.

Kirk, Samuel. *Educating Exceptional Children.* Boston: Houghton Mifflin, 1962.

————. "Learning Disabilities: The View From Here," pp. 21–27 in *Progress in Parent Information, Professional Growth and Public Policy.* Selected papers, Association for Children with Learning Disabilities. San Rafael, Calif.: Academic Therapy Publications, 1969.

Mackie, Romaine P. *Special Education in the United States: Statistics 1946–1966.* New York: Teachers College Press, 1969.

Myklebust, Helmer, and Benjamin Boshes. *Minimal Brain Damage in Children.* Final report, U.S. Public Health Service Contract 108–65–142. U.S. Department of Health, Education and Welfare. Evanston, Ill.: Northwestern University Publications, June 1969.

National Advisory Committee on Handicapped Children. *Special Education for Handicapped Children.* First Annual Report. Washington, D.C.: U.S. Department of Health, Education, and Welfare, January 31, 1968.

# Chapter 2

# Historical Development of a New Profession

This chapter looks at the brief history of the field of learning disabilities. The enigma of the child who is unable to learn has been the concern of researchers for many years. In the late 1800's, Morgan (1896), an English ophthalmologist, reported on a condition he called "word blindness," which involved an inability to read. The concept of remedial reading began in the United States in the 1920's (Smith 1961). In the 1930's, Orton (1937), a neuro-pathologist, studied the relationship between cerebral dominance and developmental language disorders. Also during this period, McGinnis (1963), a speech pathologist, investigated and treated the problem of language disorders and aphasia. Learning disabilities as a comprehensive field of study in this country is generally considered to have begun in 1947, with the appearance of the book by Alfred A. Strauss and Laura E. Lehtinen, *Psychopathology and Education of the Brain-Injured Child.*

Since that time many have dedicated themselves to an intensive study of this problem. As new knowledge has accrued, the existing theories have often proved to be inadequate, and so have been treated as working hypotheses to be refined, modified, revised, and enlarged to encompass the new knowledge. The historic growth of any science is dependent upon such a continuum of inquiry. Indeed, this is the essence of the scientific method. According to John Dewey (1938, p. 246):

> That earlier conclusions have the function of preparing the way for later inquiries and judgments, and that the latter are dependent upon facts and conceptions instituted in earlier ones are commonplaces in the intellectual development of individuals and the historic growth of any science.

In the field of learning disabilities, one consequence of the modifications and refinements of the working hypotheses since 1947 has been an accompanying change in terminology. The early works of Strauss focused on a new category of exceptional child conceptualized as "brain-injured," but this view was soon questioned in the light of new knowledge and insights. Many new concepts and terms were introduced, such as brain damage, the Strauss syndrome, perceptual handicap, neurophrenia, "the other child," minimal brain dysfunction, and learning disabilities. The historical development of the field of learning disabilities has been a process of building toward systematic knowledge.

## The Brain-Injured Child

Educators and teachers have long been aware of children who have difficulty with school subjects or whose school achievement is far below

what they are believed to be capable of performing. However, the pioneering work in the field now called learning disabilities can be traced to the initial investigations in the late 1930's and early 1940's of Heinz Werner, a psychologist, and his associate, Alfred A. Strauss, a neuropsychiatrist. Their views were presented in the first volume of the now-classic work *Psychopathology and Education of the Brain-Injured Child* (Strauss and Lehtinen 1947).

Strauss and Werner perceived a common pattern in a group of children who had been previously classified in various exceptional categories such as mentally retarded, emotionally disturbed, autistic, behaviorally maladjusted, and aphasic. A new category of exceptional children was created—*brain-injured children.*

Strauss, a physician who had received his medical training in Germany, had emigrated to the United States prior to 1937 and joined the staff of the Wayne County Training School in Michigan. Later, in Wisconsin, he established the Cove Schools for brain-injured children. The subjects of Strauss' studies, most of whom exhibited such severe behavioral disturbances that they were excluded from the public schools, frequently had medical histories indicating that brain injury had occurred at some time.

Seeking a medical cause for the behavioral characteristics he observed, Strauss surmised that the behavior and learning patterns of these children were manifestations of brain injury. This hypothesis was unique in that the behavioral abnormalities of many such children had been explained by others as having emotional causes or as being psychogenic. Strauss further speculated that children who exhibited characteristics similar to those of the children in his study had also experienced an injury to the brain which produced the abnormal behavioral symptoms. Strauss concluded that the injury to the brain could have taken place in the prenatal stages, during the birth process, or at some point after birth. He defined the brain-injured child as follows (Strauss and Lehtinen 1947, p. 4):

> The brain-injured child is the child who before, during or after birth has received an injury to or suffered an infection of the brain. As a result of such organic impairment, defects of the neuromotor system may be present or absent; however, such a child may show disturbances in perception, thinking, and emotional behavior, either separately or in combination. This disturbance can be demonstrated by specific tests. These disturbances prevent or impede a normal learning process. Special educational methods have been devised to remedy these specific handicaps.

Strauss theorized that such brain injury was *exogenous* rather than *endogenous;* that is, the impairment was due not to an inherited pattern or the genetic structure of the brain, but to an injury that occurred outside of the genetic structure. An example of an exogenous cause of brain injury before birth is an infection such as German measles contracted by the mother early in pregnancy and affecting the fetus. An example of an exogenous cause of injury during birth is any condition that would seriously reduce the infant's supply of oxygen during the birth process. An example of exogenous brain injury after birth is a fall on the head or an excessively high fever in infancy or early childhood.

Among the characteristics Strauss noted in the children he categorized as brain-injured were the following:

## BEHAVIORAL CRITERIA

1. *Perceptual disorders.* When he looks at a picture, the child with perceptual disorders sees parts instead of wholes, or he sees figure-ground distortions and may confuse the background with the foreground. An example of seeing an object as a whole rather than as unrelated parts is the identification of a letter. When asked to identify the capital letter "A", the child with perceptual disorders may perceive three unrelated lines rather than a meaningful whole.

Figure-ground distortion refers to an inability to focus on an object without having its setting interfere with the perception. Looking at the picture in Figure 2.1, one child saw a room rather than the door. Consequently he answered that the initial consonant of the object in the picture was "r" instead of "d."

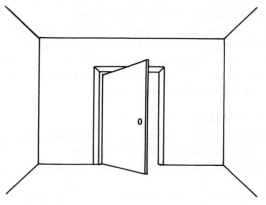

FIGURE 2.1

The classic illustration shown in Figure 2.2 illustrates the feelings of ambiguity that perceptual disorders present. This illustration contains a reversible figure-

FIGURE 2.2

ground pattern, and a confusion or a shifting of background and foreground is expected. The ambiguity in perception that the normal observer senses in this illustration can help him understand the unstable world of the child with a perceptual disorder.

2. *Perseveration.* A child with perseverative behavior continues an activity once it has been started and has difficulty in changing to another. For example, a child may not be able to stop after writing the letter "a" the three times required in a writing lesson. Instead, he continues this activity until the entire page is filled with a's. One such child continued the activity onto the desk and up the wall.

3. *Conceptual disorders.* A child with conceptual disorders is unable to organize materials and thoughts in a normal manner. This is a disturbance in the cognitive abilities, and it affects comprehension skills in reading and listening.

4. *Behavioral disorders.* Children with behavioral disorders may be hyperactive, explosive, erratic, or uninhibited in behavior. The child who is continually in motion, blows up easily, and is readily distracted from the task at hand by outside stimuli is exhibiting behavioral disorders.

## BIOLOGICAL CRITERIA

1. *Slight neurological signs.* This term refers to subtle, rather than obvious or severe, evidence of neurological abnormalities. An awkwardness in gait, for example, is considered a slight neurological sign. The inability to perform fine motor skills efficiently is also included in this category.

2. *A history of neurological impairment.* This refers to evidence in the medical history of brain injury that occurred before, during, or after birth.

3. *No history of mental retardation in the family.* Strauss felt that it was important to rule out endogenous or genetic abnormalities of the brain, such as familial mental retardation. His concern was with exogenous brain damage to a potentially normal brain. He did not include within his category of the brain-injured child endogenous abnormalities caused by inherited factors.

In Strauss' thinking, a child could be diagnosed as brain injured without hard evidence of any of the three biological signs. Strauss' original subjects were known to have had an injury to the brain. These groupings of brain-injured children included youngsters who fell within the normal and above-normal intelligence ranges as well as those who were classified as mentally retarded. Because these children known to be brain injured exhibited the appropriate behavioral characteristics, Strauss concluded that children who exhibited the same characteristic behavioral patterns could be presumed to have suffered a brain injury at some time.

One consequence of Strauss' initial work was that physicians were alerted to events that could be related to injury to the brain. An alarmingly large number of possibilities have been suggested as potential causes of exogenous brain injury. For instance, the mother's condition during pregnancy might be a possible cause of brain injury. Examples of such conditions include the RH factor, diseases during pregnancy such as rubella, and medication taken by the mother during pregnancy. Another area that can be related to possible brain injury is the birth process itself, including insufficient oxygen during the birth process; prematurity; a long, hard labor; difficult delivery; or a purposely delayed birth. Examples of severe childhood diseases and accidents that have been related to brain injury include encephalitis, meningitis, dehydration, extremely high fevers, and head injuries.

It must be remembered that these events are merely potential causes of injury to the brain. Many children with case histories of such events apparently escape injury to the brain, while other children who evidence clear symptoms of brain injury have no such events in their case histories. Even in cerebral palsy clinics, which deal with obviously grossly damaged brains, the causes of about one-third of the cases of cerebral palsy are obscure (Paine 1965).

In addition to the development of a theory of the brain-injured child, Strauss and Lehtinen presented a plan for teaching brain-injured children. Their suggested methods, materials, and settings were dramatically different from those of a regular classroom. For example, the learning environment was designed to reduce distraction and hyperactivity. All stimulating visual materials such as bulletin boards or pictures were to be removed and the windows were to be painted to conceal overstimulating outside views. Moreover, the teacher was to avoid jewelry and to dress in a manner that would reduce distractions still further. The children's desks were to be placed against a wall, behind a screen, or in a partitioned cubicle. Special materials were constructed to aid a child in perception of visual forms and in organization of space and form. The authors advised that many of the commercially prepared teaching materials designed for normal children were unsuitable for the brain-injured child.

Although the volume by Strauss and Lehtinen is still one of the best basic sources in the field, questions about the assumptions and implications of its framework arose soon after its publication. It should be remembered, however, that Strauss and his co-workers laid the foundation for the field of learning disabilities by (1) perceiving a homogeneity in a diverse group of children who had been misdiagnosed by specialists, misunderstood by parents, and often discarded by society; (2) devising diagnostic tests to specify and evaluate the characteristics of these children; (3) planning and implementing educational settings and procedures to teach such children successfully; and (4) alerting many professions to the existence of a new category of exceptional children.

Strauss' work filled a great void. There was finally another possible diagnosis for children who previously had been given many other labels, such as badly behaved, emotionally disturbed, lazy, careless, or stupid. For parents who had been blamed for causing psychological situations that created learning disorders in their children, for parents who had been told that their children did not fit into a public school setting, and for parents who had been vainly seeking a diagnosis, this framework was most welcome. It provided a meaningful, logical, and hopeful analytic view of their problem children.

## Objections to Strauss' Terminology

The terminology put forth by Strauss and his associates proved to be confusing. The terms exogenous and brain injury began to be consistently linked by some authors. Anomalies that were considered exogenous brain injuries by certain writers were viewed as endogenous by others (Doll 1951). For example, one condition that is difficult to place within either classification is the condition called phenylketonuria, a congenital defect that results in the lack of an enzyme needed to digest an amino acid in proteins. This lack leads, in turn, to deterioration of brain tissue. It is difficult to classify this biochemical disorder that results in brain injury as exogenous or as an inherited endogenous condition.

Further, it was observed that some children with brain injuries, for example, many with cerebral palsy, had no learning disorders. Some have even gone on to earn Ph.D. and M.D. degrees, while other brain-injured children have proved to be severe mental defectives. Kirk (1963) has stated that applying the term *brain injury* does not constitute a diagnosis that leads to methods of treatment or teaching.

The term *brain-injured,* then, was seen to have questionable value as a means of describing and categorizing or diagnosing and teaching children. This objection was stated by Wortis (1956):

> There is no "brain-injured child," but only a variety of brain-injured children whose problems are quite varied and whose condition calls for far more refined analysis than some of the current generalizations on the brain-injured child provide.

Educators and psychologists found the label *brain-injured child* a difficult one to use in communicating with parents, administrators, physicians, and others. If the diagnosis was based on behavior, there was frequently no medical evidence of brain injury. Since it was essentially a medical term, nonmedical personnel were reluctant to use it. Moreover, educators and others found the diagnosis of brain injury a difficult concept to communicate, and it appeared excessively condemning on the child's school record. Parents understandably reacted in a negative, traumatic, or guilt-ridden manner when told their child had a brain injury.

Four objections to the term *brain-injured child* were presented by Stevens and Birch (1957):

1. The term *brain-injured child* is a cause-oriented or etiological concept. It does not relate to the symptoms or behavioral aspects of the condition. However, the condition of brain injury is described in terms of symptoms rather than of causation.

2. The term can be associated with other conditions, such as cerebral palsy or epilepsy, and these conditions have no relation to the kind of child under consideration.

3. The term *brain-injured child* does not help in the development of a sound teaching approach.

4. The term is not suited for use as a descriptive concept because it is too broad in meaning and easily leads to over-simplification.

## THE STRAUSS SYNDROME

Stevens and Birch (1957) recommended, therefore, that the name "Strauss syndrome" be used instead of *brain-injured child* to describe the child who could not learn and did not easily fit into other classification schemes. The new label would focus on the collection of behavioral characteristics noted in these children, while having the additional virtue of paying tribute to an early pioneer and great worker in the field. The term "Strauss syndrome" was introduced to describe the child who exhibited several of the following behavior characteristics (Stevens and Birch 1957, p. 348):

1. Erratic and inappropriate behavior on mild provocation.
2. Increased motor activity disproportionate to the stimulus.
3. Poor organization of behavior.
4. Distractibility of more than ordinary degree under ordinary conditions.
5. Persistent faulty perceptions.
6. Persistent hyperactivity.
7. Awkwardness and consistently poor motor performance.

## Development of Other Nomenclature

Other authors or groups utilized different terminology to overcome the shortcomings of the term *brain-injured child.* Doll (1951) suggested *neurophrenia,* and Lewis (1960) used *the other child.* Others described this child as *perceptually handicapped,* which was actually one of the behavioral characteristics identified by Strauss.

Some researchers and clinicians noted that children exhibiting the Strauss syndrome were but a portion of the children with learning problems. For example, some children who were unable to learn readily did not exhibit hyperactive behavior, but instead were hypoactive: quiet, without excessive movement, and even withdrawn. Further, while some children exhibited perceptual disturbances along with the learning problems, many others did not.

### MINIMAL BRAIN DYSFUNCTION

Clements (1966) and others preferred the description *minimal brain dysfunction* or *minimal neurological impairment.* These authors placed children with various brain impairments along a scale that ranges from mild to severe. At the severe end of the scale are children with obvious brain damage, such as cerebral palsy or epilepsy. At the opposite end of such a scale are children with minimal impairments that affect behavior and learning in a more subtle way. In 1966, Clements concluded that the term *minimal brain dysfunction syndrome* was the best way to describe the child with near-average intelligence and with certain learning or behavioral disabilities associated with deviations or functions of the central nervous system. This term differentiated the minimally involved child from the child with major brain disorders. Table 2.1 illustrates this dichotomy.

| Minimal (minor, mild) | Major (severe) |
|---|---|
| 1. Impairment of fine movement or coordination. | 1. Cerebral palsies. |
| 2. Electroencephalographic abnormalities without actual seizures, or possibly subclinical seizures which may be associated with fluctuations in behavior or intellectual function. | 2. Epilepsies. |
| 3. Deviations in attention, activity level, impulse control, and affect. | 3. Autism and other gross disorders of mentation and behavior. |

4. Specific and circumscribed perceptual, intellectual, and memory deficits.
5. Nonperipheral impairments of vision, hearing, haptics, and speech.

4. Mental subnormalities.

5. Blindness, deafness, and severe aphasia.

**TABLE 2.1. CLASSIFICATION GUIDE OF BRAIN DYSFUNCTION SYNDROMES**
From Sam D. Clements, *Minimal Brain Dysfunction in Children.* Washington, D.C.: U.S. Department of Public Health Services, Publication #1415, 1966, p. 10.

## CENTRAL PROCESSING DYSFUNCTIONS

Chalfant and Scheffelin (1969) express an awareness of the need to formulate several definitions, each of which would have relevance and function for different users. Their Task Force III report focuses attention upon the deviant behaviors that arise from dysfunction of the central processing mechanisms. More specifically, the term *central processing dysfunctions* comprises disorders in the analysis, storage, synthesis, and symbolic use of information.

Some writers in the current literature prefer to keep the Strauss terminology of the brain-injured child. According to Cruickshank (1966), the inability of the diagnostician to be specific and to obtain positive proof of a brain injury does not imply that no injury to tissue exists. Cruickshank speculates that if diagnostic procedures were available to permit accurate evaluation of children possessing certain characteristic behaviors, tissue damage or injury would be demonstrated and thus the child would be accurately called brain-injured.

## LEARNING DISABILITIES

Still other authorities have noted that the so-called major brain injuries on the conceptualized brain-dysfunction scale may or may not be accompanied by difficulties in learning. While some individuals with obvious brain injury, such as cerebral palsy, have no learning difficulties, others exhibit conditions such as mental subnormalities, infantile autism, and childhood schizophrenia (Kirk 1967). Some educators have found that minimal brain dysfunction does not properly describe the behavior or learning characteristics of the child. Another question was: How much is minimal?

In many cases, the dysfunction of the brain has been inferred through observation of the behavior of the child, through analysis of the child's reactions to learning situations, or through the sampling of behavior through psychological tests. Since it is impossible to look at the physical brain injury inside the child's skull or to know for certain that specific cerebral tissue has been injured, guesses necessarily have been made on the basis of behavioral symptoms.

Some authorities therefore suggested the use of terminology that accurately and meaningfully describes the child's behavioral symptoms. One of the first writers to suggest the term *learning disabilities* was Kirk (1963) who used this term to describe a group of children who had disorders in the development of language, speech, reading, and associated communication skills needed for social interaction. Children who had sensory handicaps such as blindness or deafness and children who had generalized mental retardation were excluded from this group. Children whose learning failure was primarily caused by emotional disturbances or experience deprivation were also excluded from the learning disabilities group.

Johnson and Myklebust (1967) suggested a variation: *psychoneurological learning disabilities.* Implied in this term is the concept that the "psychology of learning" is disturbed because of an impairment of the central nervous system. Because of a neurological deficit, the learning process of these children is different. Although a dysfunction of the brain is often extremely difficult to establish diagnostically, the presumption of this concept is that learning disabilities are the result of a disturbance in the central nervous system. The term "psychoneurological learning disabilities" assumes the concern with learning and education as well as an acknowledgement of medical pathology or etiology.

At the present, then, the concept *learning disabilities* appears to be a satisfactory one. Rather than emphasizing a presumed cause, it focuses on the problem the child faces. It is still a blanket term in that it does not specify the areas in which the child has learning problems nor does it specify the learning processes in which the child is deficient. Although *learning disabilities* covers a wide range and diverse types of learning disorders, the term avoids the medical difficulties, focuses on the educational problem, and seems to be acceptable to parents as well as teachers.

There is evidence that the term is gaining general acceptance. For example, a separate division recently created within the Council for Exceptional Children is called the *Division for Children with Learning Disabilities* (DCLD); a national parent and professional organization has chosen the name *Association for Children with Learning Disabilities* (ACLD); and many states now use the term in their educational statutes and certification legislation. Finally, a Congressional bill entitled the *Children with Specific Learning Disabilities Act of 1969* was passed by both the Senate (1969) and House of Representatives (1969) and became law in 1970 as part of Public Law No. 91–230, the "Elementary and Secondary Educational Amendments of 1969." This legislation includes Special Programs for Children with Specific Learning Disabilities and authorizes provisions for the field of learning disabilities in the areas of research, training of educational personnel, development of model centers, and educational innovations.

Congress has officially accepted the term *learning disabilities,* and it probably will continue to be the term used to describe the children we are concerned about.

## Parent Groups

Parents who were convinced that Strauss' views perceptively described their children welcomed the theories of diagnosis and treatment presented by Strauss. However, these parents soon discovered that educators, physicians, and psychologists were generally unaware of the concepts that Strauss had evolved and of the educational treatment that he had suggested. These parents, believing that public schools should provide the special education required for their children, organized parent groups for the purpose of convincing schools that these exceptional children were educable and that it was the obligation of the schools to provide appropriate education. As has been typical within the history of special education, the pressure and impetus came from parent groups rather than from educators.

In the period 1950 to 1960, many parent groups were formed to bring the findings of this field to the attention of educators, physicians, legislators, other parents, and the lay public. Among the first such groups were the Fund for Perceptually Handicapped Children, in Evanston, Illinois, and the New York (state) Association for Brain-Injured Children, both organized in 1957. The California Association for Neurologically Handicapped Children was organized in 1960. The formulation of many other such local organizations and the increase in membership were rapid.

One outcome of the Conference on Exploration into the Problems of the Perceptually Handicapped Child (1963) was a decision to formulate a national association for children with learning disabilities. The general acceptance of the term *learning disabilities* probably can be traced to decisions made at this meeting. As a result, a national organization, the Association for Children with Learning Disabilities (ACLD), was formed to strengthen the thrust of these many local parent organizations. State chapters of ACLD were established in most states. These structures in turn have been the impetus for the establishment of additional local chapters. An illustration of the growth of these groups is the state of Illinois, which by 1970 had fourteen local chapters affiliated with the Illinois Association for Children with Learning Disabilities; in 1967 California had twenty-nine chapters affiliated with the California Association for Neurologically Handicapped Children (McCarthy and McCarthy 1969). The proceedings of ACLD's annual conferences are published by Academic Therapy Publications, 1543 Fifth Avenue, San Rafael, California 94901. An organizational newsletter is distributed from ACLD headquarters, P. O. Box 3303, Glenstone Station, Springfield, Missouri 65804. Membership in local chapters is open to any interested parent, professional, or student; and membership in the local chapter includes membership in the national ACLD.

## Other Professional Learning Disabilities Organizations

In 1968 the Council for Exceptional Children established its Division for Children with Learning Disabilities (DCLD). Membership is open to interested members of the Council for Exceptional Children. Membership information can be obtained from: Council for Exceptional Children, Jefferson Plaza Office Building One, Suite 900, 1411 South Jefferson Davis Highway, Arlington, Virginia 22202.

## REFERENCES

Chalfant, James C., and Margaret A. Scheffelin. *Central Processing Dysfunctions in Children: A Review of Research.* NINDS Monograph No. 9. Bethesda, Md.: U.S. Department of Health, Education and Welfare, 1969.

Clements, Sam D. *Minimal Brain Dysfunction in Children.* NINDB Monograph No. 3, Public Health Service Bulletin No. 1415. Washington, D.C.: U.S. Department of Health, Education and Welfare, 1966.

*Conference on Exploration in the Problems of the Perceptually Handicapped Child.* Evanston, Ill.: Fund for Perceptually Handicapped Children, 1963.

Cruickshank, William "An Introductory Overview," in W. Cruickshank (ed.), *The Teacher of Brain-Injured Children: A Discussion of the Bases of Competency.* Syracuse, N.Y.: Syracuse University Press, 1966.

Dewey, John. *Logic: The Theory of Inquiry.* N.Y.: Henry Holt, 1938.

Doll, Edgar A. "Neurophrenia," *American Journal of Psychiatry* 108 (1951): 50–53.

Johnson, Doris, and Helmer Myklebust. *Learning Disabilities: Educational Principles and Practices.* N.Y.: Grune & Stratton, 1967.

Kirk, Samuel A. "Behavioral Diagnosis and Remediation of Learning Disabilities," pp. 1–7 in *Conference on Exploration into the Problems of the Perceptually Handicapped Child.* Evanston, Ill.: Fund for Perceptually Handicapped Children, 1963.

————. "From Labels to Action," pp. 36–44 in *Interdisciplinary Approach to Learning Disabilities of Children and Youth.* Tulsa, Okla.: Association for Children with Learning Disabilities, 1967.

Lewis, Richard S., A. Strauss, and Laura Lehtinen. *The Other Child—The Brain-Injured Child.* New York: Grune & Stratton, 1960.

McCarthy, James, and Joan McCarthy. *Learning Disabilities.* Boston: Allyn & Bacon, 1969.

McGinnis, Mildred. *Aphasic Children: Identification and Education by the Association Method.* Washington, D.C.: Volta Bureau, 1963.

Morgan, W. P. "A Case of Congenital Word-Blindness," *British Medical Journal* 2 (1896): 1378.

Orton, Samuel T. *Reading, Writing and Speech Problems in Children.* New York: Norton, 1937.

Paine, R. S. "Organic Neurological Factors Related to Learning Disorders," pp. 1–29 in J. Hellmuth (ed.) *Learning Disorders,* Vol. 1. Seattle, Wash.: Special Child Publications, 1965.

Smith, Nila B. "What Have We Accomplished in Reading?—A Review of the Past Fifty Years," *Elementary English* 38 (March 1961): 141–150.

Stevens, Godfrey D., and Jack W. Birch. "A Proposal for Clarification of the Terminology Used to Describe Brain-Injured Children," *Exceptional Children* 23 (May 1957): 346–349.

Strauss, Alfred, and Laura Lehtinen. *Psychopathology and Education of the Brain-Injured Child.* New York: Grune & Stratton, 1947.

U.S. House of Representatives. *Children with Specific Learning Disabilities Act of 1969. Bill H.R. 11310. 91st Congress,* October 6, 1969.

U.S. Senate. *Children with Learning Disabilities Act of 1969.* Bill S. 1190. 91st Congress, February 28, 1969.

Wortis, Joseph. "A Note on the Concept of the 'Brain-Injured' Child," *American Journal of Mental Deficiency* 61 (July 1956): 204–206.

# Chapter 3

# Medicine
# and
# Learning Disabilities

The medical profession plays a crucial role in the field of learning disabilities. An underlying assumption, whether stated or implied, of many theories of learning disability is that the condition is an organically based problem. As educators, psychologists, and guidance counselors become aware that a learning problem may have pathological implications, children are being referred to pediatricians, neurologists, ophthalmologists, otologists, and psychiatrists for further diagnosis. Medical specialists are becoming key members of multidisciplinary teams treating learning disabilities.

This chapter looks at the way in which the various medical specialties view the child with learning disabilities and at the contributions these specialties are making to diagnosis, prognosis, and treatment. In addition certain physiological functions related to learning are discussed.

## Pediatrics

When a parent becomes concerned about his child's behavior at home or his poor performance in school, he often turns to the pediatrician for help. The parent might describe the child's behavior at home in the following terms: he overreacts to everything, is constantly in motion, is silly at inappropriate times, does not see the consequences of his actions, cannot control his behavior, is overly affectionate, indiscriminate, and gullible. He has poor relations with his peers, a low tolerance of frustration, and frequent temper tantrums. The child's performance in school might be reported in the following ways: he has a short attention span, is easily distracted, is disorganized in his work, varies in mood from day to day or even hour to hour, has problems in reading, and does not seem to understand numbers and arithmetic concepts.

Frequently, however, the medical training of pediatricians has not included the detection of those medical symptoms that indicate the likelihood of learning disabilities. If the symptoms are reported as school failures or emotional disturbances, the pediatrician may feel these areas are out of the realm of his specialty.

On the other hand, many pediatricians see their role as a central one in the total management of the child in matters of both physical and mental health. They consider themselves to be concerned with such areas as language development, school adjustment, and academic learning of the child. Many pediatricians have commented on the change in the types of problems faced by their profession. For example, while there has been a decline in serious infectious diseases in children, there has been an increase in emphasis on biochemical abnormalities. At the present time, pediatricians are increasingly being alerted to learning disabilities. They are frequently panel members at educational conferences dealing with such problems as dyslexia; they are often part of diagnostic teams in various clinical settings in which learning disabilities are encountered; and they are beginning to make referrals when a cluster of symptoms suggestive of learning disabilities is noted (Ong 1968).

The pediatrician who is concerned with the mental and emotional facets of the child's development and health can be extremely helpful to a parent. He can play a central and coordinating role in diagnosis and treatment, can become an important consultant and adviser in various treatment programs, and may be the key person to see the child over a long period of time.

## Neurology

The teacher who deals with learning disabilities must have some knowledge of the physiology and function of the brain and nervous system in order to evaluate new views and theories, to have a basis for meaningful diagnoses, to help plan sound therapeutic strategies, and to read the literature intelligently. Although it is often difficult to verify medical evidence of brain dysfunction, it is nevertheless important for the educator to have some familiarity with the current state of knowledge of the function of the brain and nervous system as it concerns learning and the language process.

### THE BRAIN

All human behavior is mediated by the nervous system and the brain. Thus, the behavior of learning, one of the most important activities of the brain, has a physiological basis within the nervous system and brain. Gaddes (1969, p. 89) describes the brain activity during the learning process:

> All of this mental activity is subserved by a rich and elaborated physiological excitation in the brain and the brain-stem, of millions of tiny neurons or nerve cells firing many times a second and causing minute electrochemical changes. The human cortex alone is believed to contain about nine billion nerve cells, and these are interconnected by millions of neural pathways or fibers. The possibility of activity between various parts of the brain staggers the imagination. However, it is known that relatively large areas of the human cortex are involved with certain sensory and motor activities, and new information is gradually emerging regarding the correlative action of these areas and mental imaginative functions.

Modern medical techniques such as refined neurosurgical procedures, electrical stimulation of the living brain tissues, and procedures in electroencephalography and neurophysiology are providing new data about the structure and function of the brain which appear to have much relevance for understanding learning disabilities.

Much of our knowledge of how the human brain deals with language-related skills and the learning process has been derived from studies of the adult brain, usually an adult brain that has incurred some tissue damage from disease or injury. Science, however, has at last begun to develop new tools to enable the scientist to observe the functioning brain. One consequence of improved techniques of observation is that we are beginning to realize how little is really known about the very complex brain mechanism for learning.

## The Cerebral Hemispheres

The brain of man is composed of two halves, the right hemisphere and the left hemisphere, which appear to be almost identical in construction and metabolism. Each hemisphere contains a frontal lobe, a temporal lobe, an occipital lobe, a parietal lobe, and a motor strip area. The motor area of each hemisphere controls the muscular activities of the opposite side of the body. Thus, the right hand and foot movements originate in the motor strip of the left hemisphere. Both of the eyes and ears are represented in both hemispheres.

Language function is thought to be located in one hemisphere of the brain. Research indicates that in over 90 percent of adults, language function originates in the left hemisphere, regardless of whether the individual is left-handed, right-handed, or mixed (Ketchum 1967). According to Geschwind (1968), the speech area is located in the left hemisphere in the majority of right-handed people; for left-handed people, the location for speech appears to occur with nearly equal frequency in each hemisphere. Similarly, Rossi and Rosadini (1967) found that about 98 percent of right-handed and 71 percent of left-handed patients had speech dominance in the left hemisphere.

Although the two halves of the brain appear to be almost identical in structure, they are quite different in function. Current research suggests that while the left hemisphere appears to react to and utilize language-related activities, the right hemisphere deals with nonverbal stimuli, including spatial perception, directional orientation, time sequences, and body awareness (Ketchum 1967; Teuber 1967). Thus, even though visual and auditory nerve impulses are carried to both cerebral hemispheres simultaneously, it is the left hemisphere that reacts to stimuli that are linguistic in nature, such as words, symbols, and thought. Consequently, adult stroke patients with brain injury in the left hemisphere often suffer language loss along with an impairment in the motor function of the right half of the body.

However, the two hemispheres of the brain do not function altogether independently; there are many interrelating elements and functions. Faulty efficiency in either hemisphere reduces the total effectiveness of the individual and also results in a reduction of his ability to deal with language and his environment (Teuber 1967, Mountcastle 1962).

## The Cerebral Dominance Controversy

Orton (1937), one of the early investigators of reading difficulties, concluded that reversal of letters and words (which he called *strephosymbolia,* or twisted symbols) was symptomatic of a failure to establish cerebral dominance in the left hemisphere, the location of the speech area. According to this view, the interference of the right hemisphere during language activities was the cause of language confusion. Orton's therapeutic reasoning was therefore as follows: Language function originates in the left cerebral hemisphere. The left cerebral hemisphere is also the center for motor movement on the right side of the body. Therefore, the language center in the left hemisphere could be strengthened and made dominant by strongly establishing the right-sided motor responses of the body. Right-handed and right-sided activities should be strongly encouraged and practiced, while left-sided activities should be discouraged or eliminated. This procedure, according to the Orton theory, would reduce the interference of the right cerebral hemisphere which causes the language problems.

Most researchers today find the concept of cerebral dominance as put forth by Orton untenable (Ketchum 1967). Current findings suggest that, although the left hemisphere usually does specialize largely in language functions while the right hemisphere services nonverbal areas, both hemispheres contribute to the learning process. Faulty efficiency in either hemisphere reduces the total effectiveness of the individual and the way he handles language. Concepts of cerebral dominance, mixed dominance, or nondominance have not proved to be useful in teaching language skills. The nondominant hemisphere does not retire to nonfunctional silence. According to Money (1966, p. 91): "A great deal of material about mixed dominance adds up to make sheer anatomical nonsense."

**Laterality.**   The laterality issue is a related controversial subject. The theory involved is that an individual's tendency to use either the right or left side of his body, or his preference in using one hand, foot, eye, or ear has a relationship to learning disorders. *Established laterality* refers to the tendency to perform all functions with one side of the body, while *mixed laterality* refers to the tendency to mix the right and left preference in the use of hand, feet, eyes, and ears. In a test of lateral preference designed by Harris (1958), the child is asked to perform such tasks as throwing a ball, kicking a stick, sighting with a tube, and listening to a watch. In each case the child's lateral preference is noted.

Recent research suggests there is no difference in reading ability between established and nonestablished laterality groups of public school children, and many research studies in reading conclude that the determination of laterality has dubious practical value as part of a reading diagnosis (Capobianco 1967, Belmont and Birch 1965). Spache (1968, p. 284) has come to a similar conclusion: "The tangential studies of the inter-relatedness of reading, [eye-preference,] cerebral dominance, and the like are gradually disappearing under the weight of accumulated research which indicates that these areas do not yield significant findings for reading instruction."

## THE NEUROLOGICAL EXAMINATION

If neurological impairment is suspected, the child may be referred to the neurologist, the medical specialist who evaluates the development and functioning of the central nervous system. Overt disturbances of motor function (such as cerebral palsy, epilepsies, and cortical blindness or deafness) and overt neurological abnormalities (such as the absence of certain reflexes or asymmetry of reflex responses) can be readily detected by the neurologist. However, children with learning disabilities rarely have such obvious impairments. They are more likely to manifest minimal, subtle, refined deviations called *soft signs* (Paine 1965).

The conventional neurological examination would not reveal many soft signs. Medical specialists carrying on research in the field of learning disabilities have noted that the conventional neurological examination often fails to find any abnormalities in patients whose primary complaint is the inability to learn (Vuckovich 1968). Many children receive negative neurological reports because the neurologist may not be looking for subtle symptoms (Paine 1965). Neurologists also face a number of further difficulties in interpreting neurological findings:

1. A wide range of soft signs of minimal neurological dysfunction occur among children who *are* learning satisfactorily.

2. Because the child's neurological system is not yet mature and is continually changing, it is often very difficult to differentiate between a lag in maturation and a dysfunction of the central nervous system.

3. Many of the tests for soft signs are psychological or behavioral rather than neurological tests.

For these reasons the value of the soft signs is open to question by some neurologists. Perhaps the best answer to these critical reservations has been suggested by Vuckovich (1968): the supreme test of healthy neurological function is efficient learning. The key difference between man and lower animals is man's unique ability to learn, which is attributable to the highly complex organization of his brain and nervous system. The well-functioning nervous system will facilitate learning.

The neurological examination has been described for educators by medical specialists and pediatric neurologists (Vuckovich 1968, Grossman 1966a). In the conventional neurological examination, the neurologist first obtains a careful, detailed *medical history* to provide specific information and to obtain clues to the causes of the problem. The information collected includes a family history (for clues of a genetic nature), the details of the mother's pregnancy, the birth process, and the neonatal development. The neurologist records information about all illnesses, injuries, and infections that the child has had. The developmental history of the child's motor behavior (the age at which he crawled, stood, walked) and language skills is also important. He collects further data on the child's hearing, vision, feeding, sleeping, toilet-training, and social and school experiences.

An *examination of the cranial nerves* gives information relating to vision, hearing, taste, facial expression, chewing, swallowing, vestibular function (equilibrium), and the ability to speak. Evaluation of the function of the various cranial nerves is derived by noting responses to certain stimuli, the condition of various organs, and the ability of the child to perform certain tasks.

Another area of the conventional neurological examination is the *assessment of all the components that control motor function.* A number of reflexes are tested in the neurological examination. Other aspects of the examination include an assessment of the sensory nerves through tests of perception, or tactile stimulation.

*Electroencephalography,* commonly called EEG, is a technical process of measuring the electrical activity of the brain. In this examination, electrodes are attached with a special paste to several locations on the head of the person being examined. The brain activity emanating from the various locations of the electrodes is represented on a chart by a graph-type pattern. The electroencephalographer reads the pattern that has been produced to determine if abnormalities in brain activity exists.

Abnormal or borderline EEG patterns are found in many children with learning disabilities. However, most investigators have concluded that at the present time a diagnosis with this instrument is rather unreliable. Research findings indicate that many children who are not learning efficiently have normal EEG patterns while some children without apparent learning problems seem to have abnormal

EEG patterns. One portion of a large-scale learning disabilities research project reported by Myklebust and Boshes (1969, p. 177) compared the EEG examination of normal children with that of children with learning disabilities. In this study 35 percent of the severe learning disabilities population of 99 children and 26 percent of the control or normal population of 99 children were found to have abnormal EEG readings. The difference between these two groups was not reported to be significant. The study also reported that among 101 children with a moderate degree of learning disabilities, 48 percent had abnormal EEG readings; while among a control population of 101 children without learning problems, 32 percent had abnormal EEG readings. The difference between these two groups was significant at the 5 percent level.

Moreover, at present, researchers are unable to correlate the location of electroencephalographic abnormalities with the nature of the child's difficulty in learning (Paine 1965). One example of the uncertainty of the interpretation of EEG patterns is the disagreement about the significance of the EEG pattern called "14 and 6 per second positive spike discharges." This pattern is found quite frequently, yet there is difference of opinion among electroencephalographers as to whether or not such a pattern indicates an abnormality of the neurological system. In the research reported by Myklebust and Boshes (1969, p. 178), the type of EEG abnormality found most frequently was positive spikes; however, the percent of children found to have such an EEG reading was reported to be essentially identical in the experimental learning disabilities group and in the control group of children without learning problems.

Although many authorities feel that, in the light of our present knowledge, the EEG has been overused and overemphasized in the determination of the source of learning disabilities (Grossman 1966a), other researchers predict that in the near future a relationship between EEG patterns and deficiencies in learning will be established and will be of importance in diagnosing and managing children with learning disabilities (Hughes 1968).

Other special medical procedures that might be requested by the neurologist include X rays of the skull and the blood vessels of the brain, biochemical studies, endocrinological studies and genetic examinations.

A neurological examination more complete than the conventional one will include *tests to detect soft neurological symptoms.* As previously noted, the neurological abnormalities most often seen in the child with learning disabilities are not the gross deviations, but rather the fine, subtle, and minor symptoms. Many of the tests used to detect these symptoms have been borrowed or adapted from psychological assessment procedures. The soft signs include mild coordination difficulties, minimal tremors, motor awkwardness, visual-motor disturbances, deficiencies or abnormal delay in speech development, and difficulties in reading and arithmetic skills.

Vuckovich (1968) discusses a number of tests used by neurologists to detect soft signs of central nervous system dysfunction:

## 1. Visual-motor Tests

*Bender Visual-Motor Gestalt Test* (Bender 1938): This test and others like it evaluate the child's visual-motor functioning by requiring him to copy various geometric forms. Following are some of the geometric forms used and the normal age at which the task can be performed (Ilg and Ames 1964):

| Figure | Age |
|--------|-----|
| circle | 3 |
| cross | 4 |
| square | 5 |
| triangle | 6–7 |
| diamond | 7 |

*Draw-a-Man Test* (Harris 1963): In this test the child is asked to draw a picture of a human figure. The scoring is dependent upon the body detail represented. This test is used by some diagnosticians to evaluate the child's awareness of his own body parts, as a measure of intelligence, or as a projective psychological test.

## 2. Gross Motor Tests (Vuckovich 1968)

Following are tests used to indicate postural skills, movement and balance, and the normal age at which the task can be performed:

| Task | Age |
|------|-----|
| Hopping on either foot | 5 |
| Standing on one foot | 6 |
| Tandem walking (heel-to-toe) | 9 |
| The child's walking gait is also observed. | |

Tests of crossing the midline in execution of movements:

A. Touching nose and left ear and then nose and right ear. Observers note the rapidity with which the automatic level of takeover of motor movements is introduced. B. Finger-nose test. The child is asked to touch his finger to his nose and to the examiner's finger repeatedly. Facility in alternating movement is observed.

## 3. Fine Sensory-motor Tests (Vuckovich 1968)

The finger-agnosia test: This test assesses the child's ability to recognize through a tactile sensation which of his fingers is being touched by the examiner. The child may be asked to close his eyes. Following are the tasks and the normal age at which each task can be performed.

| Task | Age |
|------|-----|
| Recognition of thumb | 4 |
| Recognition of index finger | 5–6 |

Other tests of tactile perception:

Recognition of objects by touch

Recognition of two simultaneous contacts as the examiner touches two parts of the child's body (such as his face and hand).

Recognition of letters or numbers by touch

Recognition of letters or numbers drawn in the palm of the hand

Tests of facility in moving the tongue (vertically and horizontally)

As noted earlier, many of these tests of soft signs of neurological dysfunction overlap with the evaluation techniques of the psychologists.

According to Vuckovich (1968), there is no domain in neurology more controversial than the area of learning disabilities. Although it seems reasonable to presume that neurological disturbances have a detrimental effect on the learning processes, the precise nature of the relationship between neurological abnormalities and learning disabilities is still not clear. In the learning disabilities study reported by Myklebust and Boshes (1969, p. 214), neurological examinations were given to children in the experimental groups (203 children with varying degrees of learning disabilities) and to a control population (203 children who did not evidence learning problems). In the experimental groups, 50 to 53 percent were classified as normal in the neurological examination, while in the control groups 63 percent were classified as normal. The difference between these two groups was not statistically significant. As more knowledge is gained in the fields of neurology and pediatric neurology, and as the parameters of normal neurological development in children become more precise, the relationship between the neurological system and learning will become clearer. Vuckovich (1968, p. 37) asserts:

> Knowledge of neurology as it relates to learning disabilities is still fragmentary. Parameters must be more clearly established so that the soft neurological signs can be more meaningful, not merely indications of a variation from the normal.

## Ophthalmology

Whereas the pediatrician is usually the first to be consulted by the parent when the child has problems at home, the eye specialist is often consulted when the child has difficulty in school, particularly when the problem is poor reading. In fact, one of the first published papers on reading problems (Morgan 1896) was written by an ophthalmologist. It seems axiomatic that ocular comfort and visual efficiency are desirable attributes for reading success. Because reading is so obviously related to vision, it is not surprising that the eye specialist is involved when the child fails to learn to read.

The ophthalmologist is the specialist in the medical field who is responsible for the health of the eye, while the optometrist is the nonmedical specialist concerned with vision and its measurement and correction. The medical background of the ophthalmologist enables him to consider the physiology of the eye, its organic aspects, diseases, and structure. The optometrist is more likely to stress the uses of the eye. There are differences in diagnosis and treatment procedures among eye specialists. While some treat deviations they consider significant by patching, lenses, and surgery, other specialists emphasize functional vision and the fact that visual skills are learned. Others treat weak or impaired visual skills by direct training procedures, as well as by lenses and other methods (Spache 1966).

Another way of presenting the contrast between these two views is to differentiate between an "eye problem" and a "visual problem." This point has been articulated well by Ilg and Ames (1955, p. 271) of the Gesell Institute of Child

Development:

> One reason for overlooking the child's vision problem has been a lack of understanding by some educators and even by some eye specialists as to what constitutes a *visual* problem, and how it may differ from an eye problem. Many children have a visual problem, but not an eye problem. That is to say, the interior and exterior parts of their eyes are healthy, they have the ability to see small letters clearly at twenty feet (20/20 vision), and there are no obvious errors in the optical systems of either eye. Therefore, the diagnosis is healthy eyes and no visual problem.
>
> In a proper visual examination, more than that is involved. In a visual examination, we should be concerned with the child's visual *abilities...*

The visual abilities to be examined are the following: (1) whether or not he can focus and point the eyes together as a team (fusional ability); (2) whether or not he can look from one object to another quickly and accurately (fixation ability); (3) whether or not he can keep his eyes on an object moving toward him (convergence ability); and (4) whether or not he can maintain a clear focus at reading distance (accommodation ability).

> When a child lacks some of these essential visual skills, he may find himself classed as a reading problem, a behavioral problem, or more often just as a lazy child who could do the work if he would only try. When we speak of vision, we must be concerned with the child's ability to get meaning and understanding from what he sees by the skillful and efficient use of both eyes (Ilg and Ames 1955, p. 271).

## OPHTHALMOLOGICAL FINDINGS AND READING

Since visual deficiency may be a factor in certain cases of reading disability, children with reading problems should have an eye examination as part of their diagnosis. Teachers should be alert to such symptoms as facial contortions, head thrust forward or tilted, tension during close work or when looking at a distant object, poor sitting posture, frequent rubbing of eyes, excessive head movements, avoidance of close work, and frequent losing of the place during reading (Knox 1953).

In the eye examination, the eye specialist checks for visual acuity, refractive errors, and binocular difficulties. *Visual acuity* refers to the ability to see forms or letters clearly from a certain distance. The Snellen chart, a visual screening test used in many schools, tests visual acuity at twenty feet from the chart. A 20/20 score means that the subject sees at twenty feet what the normal eye sees at twenty feet. A score of 20/40 indicates that the subject sees at twenty feet what the normal eye sees at forty feet.

*Refractive errors* are due to a defect of the lens and are of three types: (1) *myopia* (nearsightedness), (2) *hyperopia* (farsightedness), and (3) *astigmatism* (the blurring of vision due to an uneven curvature of the front of the eye). Research studies have revealed that myopia has little or no correlation with poor reading and, in fact, is found as often or more often in good readers than in poor readers (Bond and Tinker 1967). The visual screening devices that detect only the condition of myopia may not detect those children with visual defects that appear to be significantly related to reading difficulties. Reading requires visual acuity at "near-point," a distance of fourteen to sixteen inches, rather than at twenty feet. Astigmatism does not appear to be closely related to reading disability, either. In fact, Robinson found that in some cases it is associated with better-than-average reading (Bond and Tinker 1967). Poor readers, however, do seem to have a slightly higher occurrence of hyperopia (Bond and Tinker 1967).

*Binocular difficulties* occur because the two eyes are not functioning together. Three binocular conditions are (1) *strabismus* (lack of binocular coordination), (2) *inadequate fusion* (poor accommodation of focus of the eye lens to fuse the two images), and (3) *aniseikonia* (ocular images of an object fixated are unequal in size or shape in the two eyes). Some research studies have indicated that problems of binocular vision have more implications for reading than refractive errors do.

In summing up the research studies of visual adequacy and reading, Park (1968, p. 328) reached the following conclusions:

1. Many visual deficiencies occurring in cases of reading retardation can be considered nothing more than coincidental.

2. Although visual acuity or the occurrence of refractive errors probably is not related directly to reading ability, lack of adequate coordination in the functioning of the two eyes probably contribute to reading disorders.

3. Although reading ability and visual functioning are not related directly, the detection and correction of visual difficulties may improve comfort and effiency in reading.

Other ophthalmologists concur. According to Lawson (1968), the role of ocular factors as *the cause* of reading retardation has been refuted, but there is general agreement that eye defects can aggravate a learning disorder. Goldberg (1959) concluded that defective vision and eye muscle imbalance are not significant factors in problems of spatial confusion or poor visual memory. Further, he believes that poor ocular motility is not a causal factor in poor reading comprehension (Goldberg 1970). Finally, the research in reading has not revealed much difference between the visual characteristics of good readers and those of poor ones (Bond and Tinker 1967).

Probably of greater importance to learning and reading than visual acuity or refractive errors is the process of visual discrimination and visual perception—the interpretation of visual sensory stimulation. Disturbances in visual perception, however, are not due to organic ocular abnormalities but rather to psychological or central processing dysfunctions.

*Visual discrimination* is the process of detecting differences in objects, forms, letters, or words. *Visual perception* is the cognition and interpretation of a visual sensation and the mental association of the present visual stimuli with memories of past experiences. The mechanisms of visual discrimination and visual perception are not strictly within the realm of the medical aspects of vision. They are, therefore, discussed more fully in a later chapter (Chapter 8) dealing with perceptual skills.

## EYE MOVEMENTS DURING THE READING PROCESS

The eye movements of readers have been photographed and plotted with an instrument, made especially for this purpose, called an *ophthalmograph*. In visual terms, Spache (1966) describes the events that occur during the reading act: As the individual reads, his eyes do not make a continuous sweep across the page; instead they make a series of jumps and pauses from left to right, across the line of print, and then make a return sweep to the beginning of the next line. Observers of the eyes of readers through a peephole in a page have likened the movement of the eyes to that of a typewriter. Each pause is called a *fixation*. The reader reads only when the eyes are at rest during a fixation. During the *interfixation movement*, from one fixation to the next, vision is blurred and the reader sees nothing clearly. The fixations are the heart of the visual reading act, accounting for about 90 percent of the reading time, while interfixation movements and return sweeps account for the balance. During the entire process the two eyes must focus, relax, and move together. A backward movement and fixation called a *regression* is made when the reader fails to recognize or understand the material seen during the fixation.

The good reader has fewer, shorter, and more regular fixations than the poor reader, as well as fewer regressions. Inefficient eye movements, however, are symptoms rather than causes of poor reading. A recent research study with the eye camera (Taylor 1966) revealed that the average first-grade reader makes 240 fixations per 100 words and that the average college student, reading at 340 words per minute, has 75 fixations per 100 words. The first-grader makes over two stops per word, the sixth-grader sees less than one word per fixation, and the college student sees about 1.3 words per fixation. The implication of these findings makes questionable the methods, materials, and machines that are designed to increase the span of recognition, the amount of material the eye takes in during a fixation. Accumulating research on eye movements during reading supports the following statement by Lawson (1968, p. 155):

> The average child cannot be expected to see several words in a single fixation. The individual has little voluntary control of his visual apparatus in reading. He cannot increase the rapidity of his eye movements automatically and expect his comprehension to remain the same or to increase. The brain controls the way the eyes work when various types of material are read; it must do the organizing and comprehending after perception takes place.
>
> The average reader cannot be trained to read at high speed. Those who obtain excessive speeds generally are superior readers before they take special training and usually have better than average vocabulary.

**Eye dominance and reading.** As we saw earlier, the relationship of eye dominance and eye laterality to reading has been controversial and findings are still not precise. However, it appears that there is not a significant relationship between eye preference and reading achievement (Belmont and Birch 1965, Balow and Balow 1964). Neither eye dominance nor the preference for one eye with the opposite hand seems to be a significant factor in differentiating good from poor readers (Tinker 1965).

## Otology

The ability to hear the sounds and language in the environment is a crucial factor in a child's learning. Language, for example, is learned largely through his sense of hearing. The medical specialist responsible for the diagnosis and treatment of auditory disorders is the otologist, and the branch of medicine dealing with the ear is called otology. A slightly broader area of medical specialization, otolaryngology, deals with the ear, nose, and throat.

The nonmedical specialist who is concerned with normal and abnormal aspects of hearing is called an audiologist. Audiology spans a number of functions, including the testing and measurement of hearing, the diagnosis and rehabilitation of the deaf and hard-of-hearing, the scientific study of the physical process of hearing, and the broadening of knowledge and understanding of the hearing process.

Hearing is most frequently measured with an electronic device called a pure-tone audiometer. Pure tones are produced near the outer ear and the subject states whether or not a sound is heard. A second method of assessing hearing is through a bone conduction test. This method measures hearing in certain types of hearing loss by conducting sound waves that lead directly to the inner ear by way of the bones of the ear. In testing for auditory disorders, two dimensions of hearing are considered—intensity and frequency.

*Intensity* refers to the relative loudness of the sound and is measured in decibels (db). The louder the sound, the higher the decibel measure. Ordinary conversation measures at 50 to 60 decibels. Silverman (1960) estimates a hearing threshold of 30 decibels as the minimum level at which children begin to encounter problems in school. *Frequency* refers to the pitch or vibrations of a given sound wave and is measured in cycles per second (cps). A person may have a hearing loss at one frequency but be able to hear well at another. In speech, consonant sounds such as *s, sh, z,* are high-frequency sounds; vowels, such as *o* and *u,* are low-frequency sounds.

A person's *hearing level* is the intensity level in decibels at which he begins to detect sounds in various frequency levels. When screening children for hearing loss, the audiometer may be set at an intensity of 15 to 20 decibels. In a comprehensive sweep check test, the child is tested at frequencies of 250, 500, 1000, 2,000 and 8,000 cycles per second.

Wooden (1963) suggests that a prevalence estimate of slightly more than one-half percent (0.6 percent) is probably a fair approximation of children in the school population with hearing loss. In addition, many children suffer temporary hearing losses due to infected adenoids or tonsils, wax in the ears, or other abnormalities which can be corrected. When such a temporary impairment occurs during certain developmental stages in early childhood, it may have a detrimental effect on learning, particularly language learning.

A sensory hearing impairment, then, is an important consideration in diagnosing and treating a child with learning disabilities. Occurring with greater frequency than impairments in auditory acuity, however, are deficits in auditory perception and auditory discrimination. A disability in auditory perception is not related to organic abnormalities of the ear. The subject of auditory perception is discussed in greater detail in Chapter 8.

## Pharmacology

Many children with learning disabilities are given drugs intended to control behavior. It is hoped that an improvement in behavior will enhance the child's ability to learn. Although drug therapy is a medical problem, the teacher plays an important role in improving the effectiveness of the therapy. To accomplish this, the teacher should be aware of the specific drug program a child is under so that he can provide feedback to the doctors and parents concerning the effect of the drug on the child in school. With such feedback, the physician can gauge the effectiveness of the drug and make appropriate modifications.

Children with volatile behavior symptoms are most likely to receive drugs to aid in the management of behavior both at home and at school. The drug may decrease the child's hyperactivity and increase the length of his attention span so that learning can take place.

The child with learning disabilities has been noted to have an unpredictable reaction to a particular drug or combination of drugs. Certain stimulants, used by adults as antidepressants and energizers, seem to have the effect of calming the behavior of children who are hyperactive, impulsive, and distractible (Grossman 1966b). On the other hand, sedatives such as phenobarbital have been reported to increase activity in the lethargic and hyperactive child (Paine 1965). There are many exceptions to these generalizations; Millichap (1968) therefore cautions that no specific treatment is available for pediatric patients who have been diagnosed as having learning disabilities or minimal brain dysfunction because the causes and manifestations are so diverse.

Since these children often have an abnormal reaction to certain drugs, some physicians have suggested that trial of a drug can be a useful diagnostic tool to indicate the presence of a neurological abnormality. An atypical reaction to a drug such as Dexedrine or Ritalin could serve as part of the data in making a diagnosis. Normal use of such drugs is as an energizer, so a calming-down reaction to the drug could be a diagnostic indication of central nervous system dysfunction.

Some physicians have questioned the effectiveness of drugs as a means of improving learning or even of affecting behavior. Parents often report that their child's behavior and learning have improved after he was given a placebo. Thus, a harmless substance given to a patient to humor him may have a beneficial psychological effect, but this result raises doubts concerning the effectiveness of genuine drugs. Many experimental studies on the effectiveness of drugs have been criticized because they have been poorly designed and inadequately controlled. For example, there is frequently little assurance that subjects actually follow the precise directions of the research design. In one two-year study designed partly to test the effect of a particular drug, the authors reported that this portion of the research had to be abandoned because it proved impossible to control administration of the drug to the subjects (Abrams and Belmont 1969).

Grossman (1966) concluded that drugs appear to be of considerable value in certain instances, but are of little or dubious help in other cases. Drug therapy is only part of the management picture and should be considered an adjunct to the educational procedure.

Among the drugs currently being used alone or in combination to treat learning-disabled children are Ritalin, Dexedrine, Benadryl, Dilantin, phenobarbital, Librium, and Thorazine. Griffin (1969) grouped the commonly used drugs into three categories: (1) *anticonvulsant drugs* (Dilantin, phenobarbital); (2) *central nervous system drugs* (Dexedrine, Ritalin); and (3) *tranquilizers* (Librium, Thorazine). Baldwin (1967) adds a fourth category, *antihistamines* (Benadryl).

Baldwin (1967, p. 118) reached the following conclusions as a result of a study of children's response to medication:

First, several cautions were stressed in the use of drugs:

> 1. Patience and understanding of the parents, teachers and others in contact with the child are of importance, since in some cases repeated changes in medication must be made before a medicine is found which helps to improve the condition.
> 2. In some cases counseling or psychiatric therapy must be given along with the medical management for the best results.

A summary of the findings of this study were:

> 1. The response to medication is an individualized proposition, and a process of trial and error is necessary to find the proper drug.
> 2. There is a group of drugs including (a) stimulants, (b) anticonvulsants, (c) tranquilizers, and (d) antihistamines that are generally useful in controlling behavior manifestations of brain damage.
> 3. The younger the child is when brought in for treatment, the better the overall results. The more complications in the environment, the more difficult the case is to treat successfully. The more complications in the child's medical or physical condition—such as hearing or visual difficulties, paralysis, seizures, retardation, etc.—the more difficult the condition is to treat.
> 4. Further study involving larger groups is necessary to attempt to find more explicit results.

**The future.** The field of drug therapy is a relatively new field, still not accepted by many medical specialists. Others feel that the future shows great promise and that in years to come discoveries in biochemistry may enable us to alter not only the behavior but also the intellectual capacity of children. For example, who knows what the impact of ribonucleic acid (RNA) will be on the improvement of long-term and short-term memory? Biochemical experimentation has shown that rats given a memory drug containing RNA improved their learning capacity up to 500 percent (Smith 1968). Will we someday be able to substitute administration of a memory pill for long and difficult sessions of remedial therapy?

## Other Medical Specialties

The discussion in this chapter does not exhaust the medical specialties concerned with or contributing to the field of learning disabilities. Practitioners and researchers in the fields of psychiatry, endocrinology, biochemistry, and genetics are very much involved with the problems of the child who cannot learn in a normal fashion. They are treating such children, are members of diagnostic teams, and are contributing important findings to the literature. The future may hold important breakthroughs from these disciplines.

## Summary

This chapter has presented an overview of the contributions of a number of specialties within the medical profession to the field of learning disabilities. Because of the nature of the medical profession, the medical specialists involved in learning disabilities are largely engaged in seeking the cause of the problem. While the medical members of the learning disabilities team may perform an important function in aiding in the identification of children with learning disabilities, the task of treatment falls primarily to educators and psychologists. Experience within the general field of exceptional children shows that the most far-reaching contributions of the medical field have been in prevention rather than treatment. It is hoped that the outcome of medical research will eventually lead to the prevention of learning disabilities in children.

## REFERENCES

Abrams, Jules C., and Herman S. Belmont. "Different Approaches to the Remediation of Severe Reading Disabilities in Children," *Journal of Learning Disabilities* 2 (March 1969): 136–141.

Baldwin, Ruth. "The Treatment of Behavioral Disorders with Medication," pp. 111–121 in *International Approach to Learning Disabilities of Children and Youth*. Tulsa, Okla.: Association for Children with Learning Disabilities, 1967.

Balow, I. H., and B. Balow. "Lateral Dominance and Reading Achievement in the Second Grade," *American Educational Research Journal* 1 (1964): 139–143.

Belmont, Lillian, and H. G. Birch. "Lateral Dominance, Lateral Awareness, and Reading Disability," *Child Development* 34 (March 1965): 57–71.

Bender, Loretta. *A Visual-Motor Gestalt Test and Its Clinical Uses*. Research Monograph No. 3. New York: American Orthopsychiatric Association, 1938.

Bond, Guy L., and Miles A. Tinker. *Reading Difficulties: Their Diagnosis and Correction*, 2nd ed. New York: Appleton-Century-Crofts, 1967.

Capobianco, R. J. "Ocular-Manual Laterality and Reading Achievement in Children with Special Learning Disabilities," *American Educational Research Journal* (March 1967): 133–138.

Gaddes, William H. "A Neurological Approach to Learning Disorders," pp. 88–102 in *Successful Programming: Many Points of View*. Association for Children with Learning Disabilities. San Rafael, Calif.: Academic Therapy Publications, 1969.

Geschwind, Norman. "Neurological Foundations of Language," pp. 182–199 in H. Myklebust (ed.), *Progress in Learning Disabilities*, Vol. I. New York: Grune & Stratton, 1968.

Griffin, Mary. "RX for Learning Disabilities," speech delivered at the Workshop on Learning Disabilities. Wilmette, Ill.: Northern Suburban Special Education District, April 23, 1969.

Goldberg, Herman. "The Ophthalmologist Looks at the Reading Problem," *American Journal of Ophthalmology* 47 (1959): 67–74.

————. "Ocular Motility in Learning Disabilities," *Journal of Learning Disabilities* 3 (March 1970): 40–42.

Grossman, Herbert J. "The Child, the Teacher, and the Physician," pp. 57–68 in W. Cruickshank (ed.), *The Teacher of Brain-Injured Children*. Syracuse, N.Y.: Syracuse University Press, 1966.

————. "Psychopharmacology," pp. 245–254 in W. Cruickshank (ed.), *The Teacher of Brain-Injured Children*. Syracuse, N.Y.: Syracuse University Press, 1966.

Harris, Albert. *Harris Test of Lateral Dominance*, rev. 3rd ed. New York: Psychological Corporation, 1958.

Harris, Dale. *Children's Drawings as Measures of Intellectual Maturity*. New York: Harcourt, Brace & World, 1963.

Hughes, John R. "Electroencephalography and Learning," pp. 113–146 in H. Myklebust (ed.), *Progress in Learning Disabilities*, Vol. I. New York: Grune & Stratton, 1968.

Ilg, Frances, and Louise B. Ames. *Child Behavior*. New York: Harper & Row, 1955.

————. *School Readiness; Behavior Tests Used at the Gesell Institute*. New York: Harper & Row, 1964.

Ketchum, E. Gillet. "Neurological and/or Emotional Factors in Reading Disabilities," pp. 521–525 in J. Figurel (ed.), *Vistas in Reading*. Newark, Del.: International Reading Association, 1967.

Knox, Gertrude E. "Classroom Symptoms of Visual Difficulty," in *Clinical Studies in Reading*. Supplementary Education Monograph No. 77. Chicago: University of Chicago Press, 1953.

Lawson, Lawrence J. "Ophthalmological Factors in Learning Disabilities," pp. 147–181 in H. Myklebust (ed.), *Progress in Learning Disabilities*. New York: Grune & Stratton, 1968.

Millichap, J. Gordon. "Drugs in Management of Hyperkinetic and Perceptually Handicapped Children," *Journal of the American Medical Association* 206 (Nov. 11, 1968): 1527–1530.

Money, John. "The Laws of Constancy and Learning to Read," pp. 80—99 in *International Approach to Learning Disabilities of Children and Youth*, Tulsa, Okla.: Association for Children with Learning Disabilities, 1966.

Morgan, W. P. "A Case of Congenital Word Blindness," *British Medical Journal* 2 (November 1896): 1375–1379.

Mountcastle, V. B., ed. *Interhemispheric Relationships and Cerebral Dominance*. Baltimore: Johns Hopkins Press, 1962.

Myklebust, Helmer R., and Benjamin Boshes. *Minimal Brain Damage in Children*. Final Report. U.S.P.H.S. Contract 108–65–142. U.S. Public Health Service; Neurological and Sensory Disease Control Program. U.S. Department of Health, Education and Welfare. Evanston, Ill.: Northwestern University Publications, June 1969.

Ong, Beale H. "The Pediatrician's Role in Learning Disabilities," pp. 98–112 in H. Myklebust (ed.), *Progress in Learning Disabilities*. New York: Grune & Stratton, 1968.

Orton, Samuel T. *Reading, Writing, and Speech Problems in Children*. New York: W. W. Norton, 1937.

Paine, Richmond S. "Organic Factors Related to Learning Disorders," pp. 1–29 in J. Hellmuth (ed.), *Learning Disorders*, Vol. I. Seattle, Wash.: Special Child Publications, 1965.

Park, George E. "The Etiology of Reading Disabilities: An Historical Perspective," *The Journal of Learning Disabilities* 1 (May 1968): 328.

Rossi, Gian F., and G. Rosadini. "Experimental Analysis of Cerebral Dominance in Man," pp. 167–175 in C. Millikan (ch.) and F. L. Darley (ed.), *Brain Mechanisms Underlying Speech and Language*. New York: Grune & Stratton, 1967.

Silverman, S. R. "Hard of Hearing Children," pp. 452–458 in Davis, Hallowell, and S. R. Silverman (eds.), *Hearing and Deafness*, 2nd ed. New York: Holt, Rinehart & Winston, 1960.

Smith, Nila B. "Perspectives in Reading Instruction: Past Perfect? Future Tense?" *Elementary English* (April 1968): 440–445.

Spache, George. "Contributions of Allied Fields to the Teaching of Reading," pp. 237–290 in Helen Robinson (ed.), *Innovation and Change in Reading Instruction*. National Society for the Study of Education Yearbook, Part II. Chicago: University of Chicago Press, 1968.

———. "What Teachers Should Know About Vision and Reading," *The Optometric Weekly*, October 20, 1966.

Taylor, E. *The Fundamental Reading Skill as Related to Eye-Movement Photography and Visual Anomalies*. Springfield, Ill.: Charles C Thomas, 1966.

Teuber, Hans-Lukas. "Lacunae and Research Approaches to Them, I," pp. 204–216 in C. Millikan (ch.) and F. Darley (ed.), *Brain Mechanisms Underlying Speech and Language*. New York: Grune & Stratton, 1967.

Tinker, Karen J. "The Role of Laterality in Reading Disability," pp. 300–303 in *Reading and Inquiry*. Newark, Del.: International Reading Association, 1965.

Vuckovich, D. Michael. "Pediatric Neurology and Learning Disabilities," pp. 16–38 in H. Myklebust (ed.), *Progress in Learning Disabilities*, Vol. I. New York: Grune & Stratton, 1968.

Wooden, Harley Z. "Deaf and Hard-of-Hearing Children," pp. 339–412 in Lloyd M. Dunn (ed.), *Exceptional Children in the Schools*. New York: Holt, Rinehart & Winston, 1963.

# II

# THE
# DIAGNOSIS–
# TEACHING PROCESS

# Chapter 4

# The Diagnosis of Learning Disabilities

This chapter presents the first of the two parts of the diagnosis-teaching process: the diagnosis of learning disabilities. This chapter looks at the stages of diagnosis, case study or interview techniques, clinical observation and informal and formal standardized tests. The second part of the diagnosis-teaching process, clinical teaching, is examined in Chapter 5.

Diagnosis and teaching should be interrelated parts of a continuous process of trying to understand a child and to help him learn. The instructional program that consists merely of the routine teaching of skills or the blind use of methods and materials without regard to diagnostic information about the child and his unique problem may not only waste time and effort but may also prove detrimental to the child. A diagnosis that culminates in merely attaching a label such as dyslexia, or that names the presumed cause of the learning problem (such as a lesion in the angular gyrus, or perhaps an overindulgent mother) is not operational because it provides insufficient guidelines for devising strategies to help the child learn. Terminology that has recently appeared in the literature emphasizes the inter-relatedness of diagnosis and teaching as a total process: for example, *diagnostic teaching, remedial diagnosis,* and *psychoeducational remedial diagnostician.*

It must be remembered that both diagnosis and teaching activities are shaped in large part by the perspective and theoretical framework of the diagnostician and teacher. The various theories of learning disabilities that might affect this perspective are discussed in Part III.

## The Diagnostic Process

Children with learning disabilities are a heterogeneous group. The wide range of both degree and type of learning disorders requires a diversity of approaches and techniques of diagnosis. While a child with a severe and complex disorder may need a complete, intensive diagnosis provided by an entire interdisciplinary team of specialists, a child with milder problems may be helped with a less thorough examination given by a psychoeducational or learning disabilities specialist. Sometimes the learning disabilities specialist receives a child after the child has had a diagnostic evaluation by specialists in other disciplines. In that case some diagnostic data accompany the referral. If the learning disabilities specialist is the first professional to see the child, he may need diagnostic information from other disciplines and will then take the initiative in making referrals.

The purpose of the diagnosis is to collect information that will help in planning an educational program to improve the child's learning. The steps in the process of diagnostic evaluation have been described by Kirk (1962), Bateman (1965), and others. Depending upon many variables, a specialist in each of the contributing disciplines could provide data and information at any of these stages; the learning disabilities specialist has the responsibility of bringing the information together. Most authorities agree that the following steps are essential in making the diagnosis:

1. *Determine whether the child has a learning disability.* Implicit in most definitions of learning disability is a discrepancy between what a child is actually learning and what he ought to be learning. His actual learning is determined by measurement of his present achievement, while what he ought to be learning is estimated through measures of his capacity to learn. A number of ways of measuring this discrepancy are discussed later in this chapter under "Quantifying the Learning Disability."

Another kind of discrepancy which may indicate a learning disability can be detected by an analysis of the relationship of various subskills of the child's mental functioning. An uneven pattern (sometimes referred to as *developmental imbalances*) suggests that a weakness in specific areas of mental functioning is preventing the child from reaching his full learning potential. A profile of subtest scores on certain tests is useful in determining whether the child does have an uneven pattern of mental functioning.[1]

2. *Measure the child's present achievement* to detect in what specific areas he is failing and at what levels he appears to be blocked. For example, to determine his present achievement level in reading, a reading test is given. Another approach to this diagnostic step is to determine the developmental level of his learning problem—is his learning disorder a motor problem, a perceptual problem, a memory problem, a language problem, or a cognitive problem? Evaluations of performance in these areas of learning should be made. Clinical observations, informal tests, and standardized instruments can all provide useful data and information.

3. *Analyze how the child learns.* What are his approaches to processing information? The framework of theory within which the diagnostician views the child will have an important impact on his analysis of how the child learns.[2] Questions that might be asked at this stage include: Is the child's problem one of receiving information, expressing information, or processing and associating information? What are his strengths and weaknesses in learning visually, auditorily, and in intersensory tasks? What behavior characteristics does he display? How does he attack a learning problem? For example, how does he attack new words in reading, and what kinds of errors does he make? Data for such analysis can be obtained through both informal observations and standardized tests.

4. *Explore why he is not learning.* It is difficult to establish clear cause-effect-correlates, and these may not always be directly relevant to therapeutic planning. Nevertheless, it is useful to note all the possible causes of the learning problem, as well as contributing factors. Emotional, environmental, and psycho-

---

[1] The concept of developmental imbalances is also discussed in chapter 10.
[2] The various theories of learning disabilities with which the diagnostician may approach the child's problem are discussed in Part III.

logical factors should be considered. Data from various sources, the case history, informal tests and observations, and standardized formal tests can help identify these factors.

Clusters of factors and characteristics revealed in the diagnosis sometimes constitute a syndrome that leads to a useful analysis and a practical teaching plan. For example, one such cluster of organic factors might include soft signs of neurological dysfunction, motor awkwardness, poor performance in motor tests, and low scores on subtests related to spatial orientation. Another set of correlates might point to a deficiency in auditory processing. This set might include slow language development, articulation substitutions, poor performance in auditory discrimination and sound-blending tests, poor auditory memory, poor reading, and an inability to learn phonics.

5. Collate and interpret data and *formulate a diagnostic hypothesis*. This hypothesis sums up all that has gone before and points the way for educational planning. Technical terminology should be avoided where possible. An opinion about any specific area of disability should be substantiated by several objective measures plus clinical observations. A single random shortcoming revealed by one subtest score is insufficient evidence for a diagnostic decision. Further, any single isolated area of disability should be examined for possible relatedness to a larger syndrome of characteristics. The formulation of the hypothesis will obviously be affected by the theoretical outlook of the diagnostician.

6. Develop a *plan for teaching* in the light of the hypothesis that has been formulated. This plan should specify areas of the child's strengths and weaknesses and should suggest approaches that take these into account. Most authorities feel that strategies for teaching should include plans to teach through areas of strength while helping to develop and build deficient areas. Planning such strategies requires that the diagnostician have a broad knowledge of methods, materials, approaches, curriculum areas, child development, and, most important, children themselves. Since the earlier steps of the diagnostic process were shaped in part by a framework of theory, teaching plans similarly will be affected by such views.

The diagnosis is continuous and must be revised and modified as more knowledge of the child is acquired through teaching, and as the child himself changes through learning. It involves continuous reappraisal. In order to accomplish each step of the diagnostic process just outlined, data must be obtained to provide the basis for decisions. The next section discusses methods and techniques of data collection.

## Obtaining Data for the Diagnosis

Data for the diagnosis can be obtained in four major ways: (1) a case history or interview, (2) clinical observation, (3) informal testing, and (4) formal standardized testing. In practice these four methods are not separated, but are often accomplished simultaneously. One procedure may suggest the others. As a result of astute clinical observation, specific formal tests may be selected. For example, speech misarticulation, along with frequent misunderstanding of the examiner's conversation, could suggest an auditory difficulty and lead to a decision to administer formal tests of auditory acuity and discrimination. For purposes of discussion, however, it is useful to separate these four areas of data-gathering.

In an interdisciplinary approach, any of the various specialists could contribute to the diagnostic information obtained through any of these techniques. For example, the physician could obtain a medical history, observe the child during the medical examination, and give standardized medical tests.

## THE CASE HISTORY

The case history provides information, insights, and clues about the child's background and development. The following kinds of information are obtained, usually from the parents: learning problems of other members of the family (indicating possible genetic traits); the child's prenatal history, birth conditions, and neonatal development; age of the child when he reached developmental milestones such as sitting, walking, toilet training, and talking; and the child's health history, including illnesses (particularly those with high fevers) and accidents. Additional information, such as the school history, can be obtained from parents, from files, and from school personnel, including teachers, nurses, and guidance counselors.

It requires a skillful interviewer to obtain a maximum amount of useful data. He must try to establish a feeling of mutual trust with the persons being interviewed. He must be careful not to alarm parents by his questions nor to make them defensive because they suspect his disapproval of their actions. His attitude should convey a spirit of cooperation and acceptance. Though he should show empathy for problems, he must maintain a degree of professional objectivity so that he does not become emotionally involved and consequently ineffective.

If the history-taking is to be useful in making a diagnosis, it must go beyond routine questions and gather more information and impressions than the questions themselves ask. The skillful interviewer is able to gather information in a smooth, conversation-like manner while fulfilling all the other requirements of case study technique. The data and impressions thus gained are integrated with information obtained through clinical observation and formal testing procedures.

Many school systems have designed screening interviews or questionnaires that are used with the parents of all incoming kindergarten children. Questions are designed to detect those children who are likely to have learning difficulty. The hope is that early detection of high-risk cases will permit plans to be made to help prevent the development of learning disabilities. Below are some questions that might be used in such a screening interview:

*Questions concerning general background and health:*
How old is the child in years and months?
Was there anything unusual in his birth history?
How is the child's general health?
Has he had any periods of illness or hospitalization?
Have you ever suspected that the child has poor eyesight? If he had a visual examination, what were the results?
Have you ever suspected that the child has poor hearing? If an examination was given, what were the results?

*Questions concerning development:*
   At what age did the child sit up, crawl, walk?
   At what age did he say his first word?
   At what age did the child begin to use sentences?

*Questions concerning present activities:*
   Can the child use pencils, crayons, scissors? Can he ride a bicycle? Can he write his name?
   Does the child have any nervous tendencies such as bed-wetting, unusual fears, extreme moods of depression, anxiety, temper tantrums?
   Is he overly active or restless?
   Can the child use language to express himself intelligently?
   Does he like to listen to stories?
   What responsibilities or independent activities does he accept and perform with some regularity?
   How does he spend his time at home?

A variety of forms designed to obtain information about the case history by means of an interview have been developed. Some are quite lengthy and complete, procuring information in many categories. Working somewhat like a detective, the diagnostician must gather enough information to analyze the child's learning failure and to design an appropriate treatment procedure. Not all cases require all the information found on some forms. It should be further noted that information obtained from a case history is thought to be unimportant by those who approach assessment from a behavioral approach based on the theories of Skinner (1953) and others. Evaluation from this perspective is not based on events from the case history but rather on the child's present performance and symptoms of learning failure.
   Case history forms generally contain questions in the following categories:

1. Identifying Information
   Child: name, address, telephone, date of birth, school, grade
   Parents: father's name and occupation; mother's name and occupation
   Family: siblings' names and ages; others in the home
   Clinic: date of interview, referral agency; name of examiner

2. Birth History
   Pregnancy: length, condition of mother, unusual factors
   Birth conditions: mature or premature, duration of labor, weight, unusual
                     circumstances
   Conditions following birth

3. Physical and Development Data
   Health history: accidents, high fevers, other illnesses
   Present health: habits of eating and sleeping, energy and activity level
   Developmental history: age of sitting, walking, first words, first sentences,
                     language difficulties, motor difficulties

4. Social and Personal Factors
   Friends
   Sibling relationships

Hobbies, interests, recreational activities
Home and parent attitudes
Acceptance of responsibilities
Attitude toward learning problem

4. Educational Factors
   School experiences: skipped or repeated grades, moving, change of teachers
   Preschool education: kindergarten, nursery school
   Special help previously received
   Teachers' reports
   Child's attitude toward school

No one case history form will be entirely suitable without revision and modification from one clinical setting to another. Each diagnostic center must develop a form that meets its own needs and provides the information it desires.


## CLINICAL OBSERVATION

Many attributes of the child are inadequately identified through either standardized test instruments or the interview. The skillful diagnostician, however, is able to detect many of these characteristics through astute observation of the child's behavior and through the proficient use of informal tests. Further, informal tests and observation of behavior provide an opportunity to corroborate findings of the other two areas of assessment. For example, the skillful observer can determine whether the behavior of a child who appears to be deaf is characteristic of children with actual deafness or of children with other types of problems such as aphasia, emotional disturbance, or mental retardation.

Norman, who was being diagnosed because of poor reading, was overheard by the diagnostician to warn another child that for his bad behavior he would no doubt get "H-A-L-L." The diagnostician perceptively inferred that Norman's incorrect spelling might be related to a deficit in auditory processing. A formal test of auditory discrimination was subsequently given, and Norman's poor performance substantiated that hypothesis.

An assessment of the child's general *personal adjustment* can be made through observation techniques. For example, in the testing situation the examiner observes that when the work becomes difficult, Ricky gives up completely and simply fills in the blank spaces with any answer; Jane tenses up and refuses to continue the work; and Pat, refusing to guess and afraid to make a mistake, struggles with a single item for as long a time as he is permitted. Through such observations, questions such as the following should be probed: How does the child react to new situations and people? What is his attitude toward his learning problem? Has his school problem interfered with other aspects of his life? Has it drained his energy? How does he seem to feel about himself? Is his attitude one of interest or of indifference?

A child's *motor coordination and development* can be at least partially assessed by observing his movements and his gait. How does he attack a writing task? Does he contort his entire body while writing? What is the general appearance of his handwriting? How does he hold a pencil? Is he hyperactive during the sessions, engaging in continuous movement?

One can also informally assess his *use of language*. Is there evidence of infantile speech articulation? Does he have difficulty finding words he wants to use? Does he have an adequate vocabulary for his age? Doe he speak easily or haltingly or perhaps excessively? Does he use complete sentences or single words and short partial phrases? Is the sequence of sounds correct in words? Does he commit major errors of grammar and syntax?

Games, toys, and informal activities are useful to the diagnostician both as a means of building rapport with the child and as an aid in making informal clinical observations. Materials that the child might view as toys or games can give information about his functioning. For example, the child's ability to zip a zipper, tie a shoelace, button clothing, or lock a padlock gives clues to his *fine motor coordination* and *eye-hand relationships*. Games such as phonic rummy or phonic bingo give clues to the child's *auditory skills*.

The concept of observation takes on a very specific meaning within the behavior modification approach to teaching children with learning disabilities, since quantified observational data are required. Direct and structured observational techniques are used in this approach to provide data for measuring the child's behavior over a long period of time, to determine a base line of initial behavior, and to determine and measure those events that appear to modify behavior. The data obtained through these detailed quantitative observations provide the basis for planning ways to teach such explicit behavioral goals as reading, computing, and speaking. Behavioral modification theory and techniques are discussed further in Chapter 11.

## Pupil Rating Scales

Teachers' observations of children can be captured in a pupil rating scale. These scales record the teacher's judgment or impression of the child in a measurable fashion. For example, the teacher is asked to judge the child's ability to follow directions on a five-point scale. A rating at level one indicates that the teacher judges the child as being unable to follow directions while a rating at level five indicates that the child is skillful at following directions.

A Northwestern University research project (Myklebust and Boshes, 1969) tested many identification procedures for selecting children with learning disabilities. The findings of this five-year study, funded by the Neurological and Sensory Disease Control Program of the U.S. Public Health Service and involving 2176 children, indicated that teachers' judgment of certain behavioral characteristics of the children was a more reliable technique for identifying children with learning disabilities than any of the other measures used in the study— more reliable than the neurological, electroencephalographic, ophthalmological, or psychological tests that were given.

Teachers involved in the research project were asked to judge 24 behavioral characteristics of the children by rating them on a five-point scale. A score of *one* represented the lowest area of function and a score of *five* represented the highest, while a score of *three* was considered average. Teachers were prepared to use the rating instrument in meetings at which the scale was explained, items were defined, and suggestions for objectivity in judgment were given. The following behavioral categories were rated:

*Auditory Comprehension*
1. Ability to follow oral directions
2. Comprehension of class discussion
3. Ability to retain auditory information
4. Comprehension of word meaning

*Spoken Language*
5. Complete and accurate expression
6. Vocabulary ability
7. Ability to recall words
8. Ability to relate experience
9. Ability to formulate ideas

*Orientation*
10. Promptness
11. Spatial orientation
12. Judgment of relationships
13. Learning directions

*Behavior*
14. Cooperation
15. Attention
16. Ability to organize
17. Ability to cope with new situations
18. Social acceptance
19. Acceptance of responsibility
20. Completion of assignments
21. Tactfulness

*Motor*
22. General coordination
23. Balance
24. Ability to manipulate equipment

Since five was the highest possible rating on any one factor, the highest total possible score was 120. The mean score of children identified as normal was 81, while the mean score of the learning disabilities group was 61 (Myklebust and Boshes 1969, p. 274).

## INFORMAL TESTS

A number of informal nonstandardized tests are extremely useful in diagnosis:

**Informal reading inventory.** The *Informal Reading Inventory* can be quickly and easily administered, yet it provides a wealth of information concerning reading skills, reading levels (independent, instructional, and frustration), types of errors, the child's techniques of attacking unknown words, and related behavioral characteristics (Johnson and Kress 1965).

Briefly, the technique of the informal reading inventory is as follows: the examiner chooses selections approximately one hundred words in length from various graded reading levels. To assure that the selections represent the difficulty level desired, their readability may be checked using such procedures as the Spache (1953), Dale and Chall (1948), or "cloze" readability methods (Bormuth 1968).

The child is asked to read aloud from several graded levels, and his errors are recorded in a systematic manner. If more than five errors per hundred words are made, the child is given progressively easier selections until a level is found at which he makes no more than two errors per hundred words. The child is asked approximately four questions about each selection to check his comprehension. Using the following criteria, three reading levels can be determined through the use of an informal reading inventory:

(1) *Independent reading level.* Criteria: The child is able to recognize about 98 percent of the words and is able to answer all of the comprehension questions correctly. This is the level at which the child is able to read on his own in library books or do self work.

(2) *Instructional reading level.* Criteria: The child is able to recognize about 95 percent of the words in the selection and his comprehension score is about 75 percent. This is the reading level at which the child will profit from directed reading instruction.

(3) *Frustration reading level.* Criteria: The child is able to recognize less than 90 percent of the words and his comprehension score is 50 percent or less. This reading level is too difficult for the child. He does not understand the material and it should not be used for instruction.

**Informal graded word recognition test.**  This sort of test can be used as a quick method to determine the child's approximate reading level. Such a test is also useful in detecting the child's errors in word analysis. The informal graded word recognition test can be constructed by selecting words at random from graded basal reader glossaries. The list below illustrates the informal graded word recognition test. Words from the pre-primer through third-grade levels were selected from several basal reader series. Words from grades four through six were selected from the Durrell-Sullivan reading vocabularies for grades four, five, and six (Durrell 1956).

*Informal Graded Word Reading List*

| Pre-primer | Primer | Grade 1 | Grade 2 |
|---|---|---|---|
| see | day | about | hungry |
| run | from | sang | loud |
| me | all | guess | stones |
| dog | under | catch | trick |
| at | little | across | chair |
| come | house | live | hopped |
| down | ready | boats | himself |
| you | came | hard | color |
| said | your | longer | straight |
| boy | blue | hold | leading |

| Grade 3 | Grade 4 | Grade 5 | Grade 6 |
|---|---|---|---|
| arrow | brilliant | career | buoyant |
| wrist | credit | cultivate | determination |
| bottom | examine | essential | gauntlet |
| castle | grammar | grieve | incubator |

| | | | |
|---|---|---|---|
| learned | jingle | jostle | ludicrous |
| washed | ruby | obscure | offensive |
| safety | terrify | procession | prophesy |
| yesterday | wrench | sociable | sanctuary |
| delight | mayor | triangular | tapestry |
| happiness | agent | volcano | vague |

The informal graded word list test can be given as follows: (1) type the list of words selected for each grade on separate cards; (2) duplicate the entire test on a single sheet; (3) have the child read the words from the cards while the examiner marks the errors on the sheet, noting the child's method of analyzing and pronouncing difficult words; and (4) have the child read from increasingly difficult lists until he misses three words. The level at which he misses two words suggests the instructional level at which he is able to read with help. The level at which he misses one word suggests his independent reading level—that at which he can read alone. The level at which he misses three words suggests a frustration level and is probably too difficult for him.

**Trial lessons.** Trial lessons provide a means of informally assessing the way a child responds and learns through several teaching methods. In contrast to standardized testing requirements, the informal testing situation can engender a free and spontaneous atmosphere permitting the clinician to enlist the student's participation in the search for ways to overcome his learning problem. Roswell and Natchez (1964) describe the technique of trial lessons used as informal tests. This technique consists of giving small sample lessons using various approaches to help both teacher and pupil find the student's best style of learning. These authors have described trial lesson techniques for reading levels ranging from grade 1 to grade 12. In addition, the Learning Methods Test by Mills (1956) is designed for this purpose.

The procedures suggested by Roswell and Natchez for trial lessons for reading levels 1 to 3 are described below. For the nonreader or the reader who has a minimum of word analysis techniques, the following major word recognition approaches are tried: (1) visual, (2) phonic, (3) visual-motor, and, if all of these are unsuccessful, (4) kinesthetic. At the conclusion of the trial lessons, the teacher and pupil should both have a clear picture of the methods that can be used most successfully.

In the visual method, the teacher selects about five words not known by the child, such as pencil, lady, sock, and prints each of them on a separate card. (The examiner first tests the child to make sure he does not already know the words.) He then writes each word on another card, along with the picture of the object denoted. The examiner points to the word on the picture card, pronounces it, and then asks the child to look at the word and say it several times. After a lapse of time, the child is tested on the nonillustrated cards.

The phonics trial lesson consists of several parts. First, the teacher asks the child to make new words by substituting beginning consonants: change run to sun, fun, bun, and so on. Then the teacher pronounces single phonemes in one-syllable words slowly and distinctly and asks the child to combine the sounds to make a word: k-a-t blends to cat. The teacher next asks the child to substitute final consonants in short-vowel words using sounds taught in the first part: *fat* to *fan, cat* to *can, run* to *rub.* Finally, the teacher asks the child to read in mixed order the words learned through the phonic approach: *run, cat, rub, man.*

In the *visual-motor* trial lesson, the teacher chooses three unknown words five to seven letters in length; for example, *fight, missile, horse.* He presents each word separately on a card and asks the pupil to look carefully, to shut his eyes and try to visualize the word, to open his eyes and check his visual image by looking at the word, and finally to say the word. Then the card is removed and the child writes the word from memory.

The *kinesthetic* trial lesson is attempted if all the other methods have failed. The teacher writes or prints an unfamiliar word on unlined paper. Each letter is made approximately two inches high. The child is told that he will learn a new way to read through his fingers. The child looks at the word and traces it with his index finger while simultaneously pronouncing it very slowly. This trace-and-say process is repeated several times, and the child is then asked to write the word without reference to the model.

Other trial lesson techniques are suggested by Roswell and Natchez for older students reading at higher grade levels. Again, at the conclusion of the trial lesson session both teacher and student have a better idea of how to begin and where to go. Roswell and Natchez state:

> In this way, trial lessons at all levels are extremely helpful in preparing the pupil for remedial instruction. Instead of leaving the examination with a vague feeling of "something is wrong with my reading," he knows what is wrong. He has been shown in which areas he needs help. . . . As the pupil recognizes his problem and understands what he can do about it, he becomes more hopeful. His anxiety is lessened and the foundation is laid for effective remedial treatment.

Another informal test to determine what processes the child is using in learning situations is the analysis of the kinds of *spelling errors* the child makes (Boder 1968). Such an analysis might give clues about whether the child is relying on auditory or visual processes to spell the words. The child who is strong in auditory perception and in the ability to remember the sounds of words but poor in visual memory and visual learning may misspell the words, but his errors follow some kind of phonic generalization. He may spell *attention* as *atenchen,* or *peace* as *pese,* or *almost* as *olmoste.* In contrast, the child who is strong in visual learning and visual memory but low in auditory perception and learning makes spelling errors that do not follow any phonic generalization. He may remember the correct letters, but they may be in the wrong order. He may spell *mark* as *mrak, eat* as *aet, orange* as *ronaeg.* As in the trial lesson technique, spelling pattern errors are analyzed to discover how the child is learning.

## FORMAL STANDARDIZED TESTS

Formal standardized tests are used in the diagnosis to sample performance in particular aspects of learning. Norms for these tests have been standardized on large populations, and reliability and validity statistics are available from the publishers.

Differing kinds of standardized tests are given by psychologists, by medical specialists, remedial specialists, physical educators, and classroom teachers. The learning disabilities specialists might serve in a role that incorporates the diagnostic responsibilities of several of these professional people.

The examiner should have a sound foundation in the techniques of using and interpreting tests in general, and he should be thoroughly familiar with the specific test being used. Frequently the value of a test may not be so much in the final test score as in the measurement of a particular subtest performance or in the profile of all the subtest scores. As the diagnostician gains experience with a test, he may find that some parts used alone yield the necessary information.

Finally, caution must be exercised in the interpretation of test scores. The score indicates only a small sample of the child's performance at one moment in time. All tests, by their very nature, give only a limited measurement of a child's abilities.

Formal tests can be viewed as a means of providing two levels of information about the child: (1) *General tests* sample general or global areas of functioning. Such tests determine whether a child is performing at, above, or below his age level in some area. (2) *Diagnostic tests* provide a microscopic view of the component elements of some area of performance. Such tests enable the diagnostician to analyze the child's functioning within specific subskill areas and supply direction for remediation. Some commonly used formal tests of both types are discussed below. A listing of these tests and their publishers is presented in Appendix C; many are discussed in greater detail in Part III.

### Mental Tests and Tests of Mental Processes

The purpose of the general intelligence tests is to assess the global aspects of intelligence, usually for classification or categorization. The most commonly used individual general intelligence tests are: the *Wechsler Intelligence Scale for Children* (WISC), and the *Stanford-Binet Intelligence Scale*. While the Stanford-Binet yields a single score of general intelligence, the WISC provides a verbal IQ and a performance IQ in addition to the full scale score. Such global tests provide initial data for classifying a child as high, average, or low in general mental abilities.[3] The global nature of such tests limits their usefulness in analyzing the characteristics of a child's learning problems and in designing suitable treatment procedures.

While intelligence tests provide an overall estimate of general intelligence, other tests are required to examine specific mental processes. A second stage in diagnosis, then, is the use of tests to analyze mental processing and specific intellectual, perceptual, and/or cognitive factors (Kirk and Kirk 1971). One test designed expressly for analysis of the subskills of intellectual function is the *Illinois Test of Psycholinguistic Abilities* (ITPA). The stated purpose of the ITPA is to provide an instrument that will aid in diagnosis by identifying specific areas of learning difficulty. ITPA subtests attempt to measure certain perceptual and cognitive abilities which seem to bear a relationship to intellectual development and academic learning. The ITPA yields a global psycholinguistic age, a psycholinguistic quotient, as well as scores indicating at what level the child is functioning in twelve specific areas of mental processing. The ITPA yields an age score and a scaled score for each of the twelve areas tested so that the diagnos-

[3] Interpretation of the WISC subscore tests is discussed in a later section of this chapter.

cian has a profile of the child's abilities and disabilities. Interpretation of the TPA is discussed in greater detail in a later section of this chapter.

Another diagnostic test battery that assesses several subareas of mental processes is the *Detroit Tests of Learning Aptitude*. This test yields an overall age score as well as specific age scores in nineteen areas of mental functioning. There are also a number of other diagnostic tests that sample only one or a few of the subareas of mental processing. Tests of visual motor perception include: the *Bender Visual Motor Gestalt Test for Children*, the *Developmental Test of Visual-Motor Integration*, the *Marianne Frostig Developmental Test of Visual Perception*, and the *Monroe Reading Aptitude Tests*. A test that estimates visual perception development and intelligence is the *Goodenough-Harris Drawing Test*. Auditory perception tests include the *Wepman Test of Auditory Discrimination* and the *Roswell-Chall Auditory Blending Test*.

## Reading Tests

There are many global or general survey-type tests of reading. Among them are the *Gates-MacGinitie Reading Tests;* the *Stanford Achievement Test: Reading; California Reading Test; Metropolitan Achievement Tests: Reading; SRA Achievement Series: Reading*. These tests yield a general score of silent reading, and they give an indication of the level at which a child reads.

A diagnostic reading test differs from a general reading test in that it analyzes the processes by which the child attempts to read—it gives information on *how* the child reads rather than only indicating his reading level. Analysis of specific errors, for example, might indicate poor word attack skills, a lack of familiarity with certain phonic elements (vowels, consonant blends, diphthongs), inadequate sight vocabulary, or a slow reading rate. Some of the useful diagnostic reading tests include: *Gates-McKillop Reading Diagnostic Tests*, the *Durrell Analysis of Reading Difficulty; Roswell-Chall Diagnostic Reading Test of Word Analysis Skills, Gray Oral Reading Tests, Spache Diagnostic Reading Scales*.

## Tests of Other Academic Skills

Some of the general tests that measure performance in academic subjects such as arithmetic, spelling, and grammar are: the *Iowa Every-Pupil Tests of Basic Skills*, the *California Achievement Test*, the *Metropolitan Achievement Tests*, *SRA Achievement Test*, and the *Stanford Achievement Test*. Fewer tests of a diagnostic nature are available for academic areas other than reading. Some of them are: *Diagnostic Tests and Self-Helps in Arithmetic*, the *Gates-Russell Spelling Diagnostic Tests*, and the *Stanford Diagnostic Arithmetic Test*.

## Motor Tests

A general assessment of motor skill can be made with the *Heath Railwalking Test*. Examples of diagnostic tests that examine the component parts of motor performance are the *Lincoln-Oseretsky Motor Development Scale, Purdue Perceptual Motor Survey* and the *Southern California Perceptual-Motor Tests*.

## Language Tests

In the area of language tests it is important to differentiate between speech assessment and language assessment. A speech test evaluates the child's skills in articulation and his voice quality. A language test evaluates his linguistic abilities. Many of the tests previously listed in this section (such as the ITPA) have subtests of language abilities.

A speech screening test of articulation is the *Templin-Darley Screening and Diagnostic Tests of Articulation*. Two tests of the child's ability to understand words are the *Peabody Picture Vocabulary Test* and the *Ammons Full-Range Picture Vocabulary Test*. A measure of syntax development is made by the *Northwestern Syntax Screening Test*. Several linguistic categories are measured by the *Houston Test for Language Development*. The *Mecham Verbal Language Development Scale* uses the informant-interview method to estimate language development. A test of written language is the *Picture Story Language Test*, in which the child writes a story.

### Measure of Social Maturity

The *Vineland Social Maturity Scale* is an instrument that uses the technique of interviewing an informant to assess several areas of social maturity.

### Sensory Acuity Screening

Defects in vision or hearing may adversely affect the learning processes, so it is important for children with learning disabilities to be checked for such sensory deficits. Vision and hearing screening tests may be given by the learning disabilities specialist if he has been trained in the administration of these tests, or sensory screening may be conducted by the school nurse or some other member of the interdisciplinary team. Those children who fail the screening tests are referred to an eye or ear specialist for a thorough and intensive professional examination.

There are several vision screening instruments that are useful in detecting children who require further testing. Among them are the telebinocular of the *Keystone Visual-Survey Service for Schools* and the *Ortho-Rater*. These instruments use stereoscopic slides to screen for near vision and far vision acuity, eye-muscle balance, and fusion.

The *audiometer* is an auditory screening instrument for detecting children who should be referred for a more thorough and intensive hearing examination. Two attributes of the child's ability to hear sound are measured: *frequency* and *intensity*. The frequency of a sound is measured by the number of vibrations that occur per second; as the frequency of sound increases, the pitch of the sound becomes higher. The intensity of a sound wave refers to the strength (or loudness) measured in decibels. If in a threshold audiometric examination a child exhibits hearing levels of 20 decibels or greater at any two frequencies in either ear, he should be referred for an otological examination (Newby 1964, p. 233). Considerable training in audiology is required before a diagnostician is able to use an audiometer and interpret the findings of an audiometric test.

## Interpreting Test Scores

In using test scores, the examiner should be aware of the test's reliability and validity. Moreover, a child's performance on any one day is subject to many factors such as fatigue, interest, and motivation. Tests have limitations and any single test score must be viewed with caution.

## The Wechsler Intelligence Scale for Children

One of the most widely used tests of general intelligence for children aged five to fifteen is the Wechsler Intelligence Scale for Children, (WISC, 1949). The complete test, which is administered by a trained psychological examiner, consists of five verbal and five performance subtests, plus two optional tests. The test yields a full-scale IQ, a verbal IQ, and a performance IQ. Although it was designed as a measure of general intelligence, some clinicians use it as a diagnostic instrument by analyzing the subtest patterns. Other investigators caution that there is little empirical evidence to support such diagnostic use of the WISC subtest patterns (Anastasi 1968; Glasser and Zimmerman 1967).

The WISC is designed so that a scaled or standard score of 10 indicates average ability for age in the particular subtest. A general idea of the kinds of abilities sampled in each of the subtests is given below:

*Verbal Tests.* These tests use oral language for administration and responses of the subject.

*Information*—a test of how much general knowledge the child has acquired through living in his environment.

*Comprehension*—an assessment of a child's ability to make judgments about social situations.

*Arithmetic*—a test of ability to do arithmetic reasoning problems within a time limit.

*Similarities*—a test of a child's skill at detecting analogies or similar elements in different objects.

*Vocabulary*—a test of the child's ability to describe selected spoken words.

*Digit span*—an optional test measuring the child's ability to remember and repeat a series of digits after the examiner says them.

*Performance Tests.* These tests are presented in a visual manner and the subject responds by performing some task.

*Picture completion*—this test requires the child to detect missing elements in pictures.

*Picture arrangement*—in this test the child must rearrange a set of pictures so that they relate a sequential story.

*Block design*—in this test the subject must arrange small colored blocks to copy a geometric design.

*Object assembly*—in this test the child must assemble the parts of a puzzle that represents an object.

*Coding*—in this test the child must remember associations between numbers and geometric symbols and quickly record these associations.

*Mazes*—an optional test requiring the child to find his way out of a maze.

Clements (1964) has isolated three WISC patterns that occur in the subtest performance of children with learning disabilities:

*Pattern 1.* The verbal score is 15 to 40 or more points higher than the performance score. Children displaying this pattern have difficulty in perceptual-motor areas, but they are strong in language areas.

*Pattern 2.* A scatter is evidenced in both the verbal and performance scores, with a wide range between high and low scores of 7 to 12 points. Such a pattern suggests specific deficits in certain mental processes.

*Pattern 3.* The performance score is 10 to 30 points higher than the verbal score. Children with this pattern are likely to have difficulty in expressing themselves verbally.

Bannatyne (1968) has suggested another technique for analyzing the WISC subscore patterns by grouping them as follows:

*Spatial score* = sum of scaled scores of picture completion + block design + object assembly.

*Conceptualization score* = sum of scaled scores of comprehension + similarities + vocabulary.

*Sequencing score* = sum of scaled scores of digit span + picture arrangement + coding.

Since the average scaled score is 10, the composite standardized scaled score expected for each for these three groups of subtests is 30. By comparing a child's spatial score, conceptualization score, and sequencing score, Bannatyne suggests that the diagnostician can obtain information about areas of deficits and strengths.

## Illinois Test of Psycholinguistic Abilities

The ITPA (Kirk, McCarthy, and Kirk 1968) was designed to diagnose problems of learning by assessing specific and discrete underlying psychological functions of young children. In designing the test the authors attempted to consider mental functioning in three ways (Paraskevopoulos and Kirk 1969): (1) They wanted to consider *levels of organization* or the degree to which habits of communication have developed within the child. The representational level requires the mediating process of utilizing symbols which carry the meaning of an object; while the automatic level reflects the more habitual, less voluntary, but highly organized and integrated functions. (2) Another consideration was *channels of communication* or the input and output routes through which communication flows: auditory-vocal, auditory-motor, visual-motor, visual-vocal. (3) *Psycholinguistic processes* were the third consideration involving the acquisition and use of language—the receptive process, the expressive process, the associative process.

There are twelve subtests in the ITPA designed to sample various components of mental processing. They are:

*REPRESENTATIONAL LEVEL*

    *THE RECEPTIVE PROCESS*

        **Auditory Reception Test.** This test samples the child's ability to understand what is said to him The child responds by answering *yes* or *no*. For example, "Do birds fly?"

**Visual Reception Test.** This test assesses the child's ability to derive meaning from pictures that he looks at. He responds by pointing.

### THE ASSOCIATIVE PROCESS

**Auditory Association.** This test assesses the child's ability to relate concepts that are presented orally. The child supplies the missing word in verbal analogies. For example "I cut with a saw; I pound with a _____."

**Visual Association.** In this test the child must associate concepts that are presented visually through pictures. The child responds to the question "What goes with this?" by pointing to the appropriate picture from four options.

### THE EXPRESSIVE PROCESS

**Verbal Expression.** This test examines the child's ability to express himself vocally about objects he sees and touches. The child is asked to tell about familiar objects he is shown. For example, he is shown a ball and asked, "Tell me all about this."

**Manual Expression.** In this test the child must express ideas by gesture. He is asked to show what we do with various objects—for example, a telephone.

## AUTOMATIC LEVEL

### CLOSURE

**Grammatic Closure.** This test measures how well the child has learned automatic habits for handling linguistic constructs of grammar and syntax of the English language. He is asked to supply the missing grammatical elements in incomplete sentences. For example, "Here is a dog; here are two _____."

**Auditory Closure.** This test measures the child's ability to complete a word by filling in missing parts that are deleted when the word, with certain sounds omitted, is spoken by the examiner. For example, the examiner might say "tele/one" and the child is to respond "telephone."

**Sound blending.** This test taps the child's ability to blend or synthesize the isolated phoneme sounds of a word. Thus, the examiner says "C—a—t." The child is to respond: "Cat."

**Visual Closure.** This test measures the ability of the child to identify common objects in pictures from an incomplete visual presentation. Objects are partially hidden in pictures shown to the child.

### SEQUENTIAL MEMORY

**Auditory Sequential Memory.** This test measures the child's ability to remember and reproduce sequences of numbers or digits that are spoken to him. For example, he might be asked to repeat the sequence "4—7—2."

**Visual Sequential Memory.** This test measures the child's ability to remember sequences of nonmeaningful figures.

The ITPA is designed to permit a comparison of an individual child's specific and discrete areas of development. Thus, while the normal child exhibits a relatively flat profile of performance on the twelve subtests with little deviation between a single area of development and the average of all his scores, the child with learning disabilities is likely to show discrepant growth patterns with large deviations of individual subtest scores from the average of all subtest scores. Data on the deviation patterns of normal children on whom the ITPA was standardized is provided by Paraskevopoulos and Kirk (1969). In addition, these authors describe a technique to evaluate the likelihood that the difference between two ITPA subtest scores is a statistically significant difference (Paraskevopoulos and Kirk 1969, pp. 113–120).

The twelve subtests each yield both age scores and scaled scores. Figure 4.1 illustrates the profile of a child's scaled scores on the ITPA. His mean scaled score was 33. Since one standard deviation is 6, one standard deviation above the mean is 39 while one standard deviation below the mean is 27. In this way it is easy to note individual high scores and low scores at a glance (Kirk and Kirk 1971).

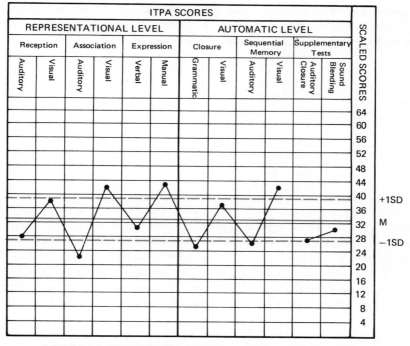

**FIGURE 4.1. A CHILD'S PROFILE OF SCALED SCORES ON THE ILLINOIS TEST OF PSYCHOLINGUISTIC ABILITIES**
From Samuel A. Kirk and Winifred D. Kirk. *Psycholinguistic Learning Disabilities: Diagnosis and Remediation.* Urbana, Ill.: University of Illinois Press, 1971.

Further analysis may be made by combing the subscores to discover various factors of mental functioning. To determine the existence of significant discrepancies in areas of mental functioning, the subscores can be combined to evaluate the child in each of the three dimensions of the ITPA: levels of organization, channels of communication, and psycholinguistic processes (Kirk and Kirk 1971).

*Levels of organization.* The mean score of tests at the representational level can be compared to the mean score of the tests at the automatic level. Such an examination would compare the child's abilities in habitual but highly organized and integrated responses (automatic level) with responses requiring the more complex mediating processes that utilize symbols which carry the meaning of an object (representational level).

*Channels of communication.* Scores on tests in the auditory-vocal channel may be compared to scores in the visual-motor channel. The child's performance in tasks in which he listens to language and speaks (auditory-vocal) is compared to tasks in which he looks and performs motor action (visual-motor).

*Psycholinguistic processes.* Scores on the three processes of receiving information, associating it, and expressing it can be compared. Thus the child's ability to recognize and/or understand what is seen or heard (receptive process); his ability to relate and organize what is seen or heard (association process); and his skill in expressing ideas verbally or by gesture (expressive process) are compared.

Analysis of the three dimensions of the ITPA for the scores of the child in Figure 4.1 is shown below (Kirk and Kirk 1971). The table shows the child's age scores as well as the scaled scores pictured in the profile in Figure 4.1.

|  | Age Scores | Scaled Scores |
|---|---|---|
| Levels of Organization | | |
| Representational | 6–4 | 34 |
| Automatic | 5–11 | 33 |
| Channels of Communication | | |
| Auditory-vocal | 4–9 | 26 |
| Visual-motor | 7–5 | 40 |
| Psycholinguistic Processes | | |
| Reception | 5–9 | 33 |
| Association | 6–2 | 32 |
| Expression | 6–11 | 37 |

Analysis of scores classified this way indicates that (a) there are no significant differences between the representational and automatic levels of organization, (b) there are no significant differences among the psycholinguistic processes, but (c) there is a significant difference between the visual-motor and auditory-vocal channels. Further analysis and testing did substantiate the diagnostic hypothesis that for this child the auditory-vocal channel was the weak area of functioning. A treatment plan based on this diagnosis was thereby designed (Kirk and Kirk 1971).

## Quantifying the Learning Disability

Most definitions of learning disability state that a significant discrepancy exists between what the child has actually learned and what he is potentially capable of learning. Three difficult questions are implied in this statement: (1) What has the child actually learned and what is his present achievement level? (2) What is the child potentially capable of learning and how can this potential best be measured? (3) What amount of discrepancy between achievement and potential should be considered significant?

The first question involves the difficulty of determining the child's present achievement level. Because of the problem of measurement error, it is never certain that a test score actually represents the child's present ability. The second question, concerning assessment of the child's potential capacity, is difficult because of the problems inherent in judging intelligence. Group tests, individual tests, verbal and nonverbal tests—all give vastly different measures of intelligence; and the relationship between various factors of intelligence and learning capacity is still not clear. Further, the entire concept of IQ and mental age as an accurate means of judging intelligence is under severe attack on a number of grounds. The third question deals with the amount of discrepancy between potential and achievement which is to be considered significant. This amount differs from grade to grade and age to age. A child with a six-month discrepancy in reading in the first grade has a much greater learning problem than an eleventh-grader with a six-month discrepancy.

In spite of the difficulties raised by these questions, it is necessary for the practitioner to make decisions using the quantitative data that is available. Several methods of measuring the learning disability have been suggested; three of these are discussed here: the mental grade method, the years-in-school method, and the learning quotient method. Still another recommended procedure is the computation of differential indices (Woodbury 1963).

**The mental grade method** (Harris 1961).   This is the simplest method. It uses the child's mental age to assess his reading expectancy. To determine reading expectancy grade, the examiner subtracts five years from the child's mental age.

$$RE \text{ (reading expectancy grade)} = MA \text{ (mental age)} - 5$$

Thus, a child with a mental age of thirteen is expected to read as well as the average thirteen-year-old or average eighth-grade student. An MA of seven suggests a reading expectancy of the average seven-year-old or second-grade child.

A comparison is made between the expected reading level and the child's present reading level to determine whether a discrepancy exists. For example, Tony is 10 years 0 months old and has an IQ of 120. Using the mental grade method, his reading expectancy grade is grade 7.0. If he reads at 4.0 grade level, he has a three-year discrepancy in reading.

$$7.0 \text{ (RE)} = 12(MA) - 5$$

**The years-in-school method.**   Bond and Tinker (1967, pp. 198–203) suggest that the mental grade method does not take into account the years of teaching exposure and therefore gives an inaccurate expectancy in some cases, especially when the IQ is particularly high or particularly low. In the first case it overestimates expectancy, while in the second it underestimates it. These authors suggest calculating expectancy grade with the formula

$$RE \text{ (reading expectancy grade)} = \frac{\text{years in school} \times IQ}{100} + 1.0$$

Ten-year-old Tony is in the middle of the fifth grade and therefore has been in school for 4.5 years. Using this formula with his IQ of 120, his reading expectancy is grade 6.4.

$$RE = \frac{4.5 \times 120}{100} + 1.0 = 6.4$$

If he reads at 4.0 grade level, the discrepancy between his expectancy and achievement levels is 2.4 years.

**The learning quotient method.** Another method that has been suggested to quantify a learning disability first takes three factors into consideration: mental age (MA), chronological age (CA), and grade age (GA) (Myklebust 1968). Since each factor contains certain errors, an average of the three—called expectancy age (EA)—tends to minimize error. In this method the MA is considered separately as a verbal MA and as a performance MA, as measured by the *Wechsler Intelligence Scale for Children*.

$$\text{EA (expectancy age)} = \frac{MA + CA + GA}{3}$$

The learning quotient is then the ratio between present achievement level (achievement age, or AA) and the expectancy age (EA).

$$\text{LQ (learning quotient)} = \frac{AA \text{ (achievement age)}}{EA \text{ (expectancy age)}}$$

A learning quotient (LQ) of 89 or below is one basis for classifying a child as having a learning disability.

An estimate of verbal mental age (MA) is obtained by multiplying verbal IQ by chronological age and dividing by 100:

$$\frac{\text{Verbal IQ} \times CA}{100}$$

Similarly with performance MA:

$$\frac{\text{Performance IQ} \times CA}{100}$$

An estimate of grade age (GA) is made by adding 5.2 to present grade placement (Grade + 5.2).

We can look at Tony using this method. He is 10.0 years old, is in grade 5.5, and has a WISC IQ of 120. His verbal IQ is 110 and his performance IQ is 130. His reading achievement score was 4.0 which gives him a reading achievement age of approximately 9.2.

$$\text{Verbal MA} \quad \frac{11(MA) + 10 \ (CA) + 10.7 \ (GA)}{3} = 10.6 \ (EA)$$

$$\frac{9.2 \ (AA)}{10.6 \ (EA)} = .87 \ (LQ)$$

$$\text{Performance MA} \quad \frac{13(MA) + 10(CA) + 10.7 \ (GA)}{3} = 11.2 \ (EA)$$

$$\frac{9.2 \ (AA)}{11.2 \ (EA)} = .82 \ (LQ)$$

By using the learning quotient method, Tony would be designated as having a learning disability because on the basis of his verbal mental age he has a learning quotient of 87 and in his performance mental age he has a learning quotient of 82. These quotients suggest that he has learned 87 percent of what he is capable of in one case and 82 percent of what he is capable of in the other. Both are below the cutoff point of 89.

Another technique of estimating expectancy age is suggested by Harris (1970). This method, which gives priority to intelligence but also gives weight to experience, involves giving mental age twice the weight of chronological age. Thus:

$$EA \text{ (expectancy age)} = \frac{2 \text{ MA} + \text{CA}}{3}$$

This calculation can be substituted for step one of the Learning Quotient Method. However, Harris suggests subsequent calculations for estimating a reading expectancy quotient and a reading quotient (Harris 1970, pp. 212–214).

A similar method of measuring reading proficiency has been suggested by Monroe (1932), using a reading index in which an expected reading age is obtained by averaging chronological age, mental age, and arithmetic computation age. The reading index is then obtained by dividing the reading achievement age by the expected reading age.

These methods of quantifying a learning disability may be useful in deciding whether a child is learning disabled and in making decisions concerning school programs. However, it must be noted that a number of flaws are inherent in these techniques (Spache 1969). The use of MA as a measure of expectancy has been questioned. Can a nine-year-old with an MA of 13 be expected to perform like a thirteen-year-old? Further, the techniques are not useful for the preschool youngster or the first-grade child who has not yet learned to read, since an achievement score is required by the formula. Such techniques have also been criticized because they neglect many important variables such as background, environment, language, motivation, and psychodynamics. Nevertheless, there are many times when such methods are helpful in making decisions.

## REFERENCES

Anastasi, Anne. *Psychological Testing,* 3rd ed. New York: Macmillan, 1968.

Bannatyne, Alex. "Diagnosing Learning Disabilities and Writing Remedial Prescriptions," *Journal of Learning Disabilities* 1 (April 1968): 28–34.

Bateman, Barbara. "An Educator's View of a Diagnostic Approach to Learning Disorders," pp. 219–237 in J. Hellmuth (ed.), *Learning Disorders,* Vol. I. Seattle, Wash.: Special Child Publications, 1965.

Boder, Elena. "Developmental Dyslexia: Diagnostic Screening Patterns Based on Three Characteristic Patterns of Reading and Spelling," *Claremont Reading Conference,* 1968.

Bond, Guy, and Miles Tinker. *Reading Difficulties: Their Diagnosis and Correction,* 2nd ed. New York: Appleton-Century-Crofts, 1967.

Bormuth, John R. "The Cloze Readability Procedure," *Elementary English* 45 (April 1968): 429–436.

Clements, Sam D., Laura E. Lehtinen, and Jean Lukens. *Children with Minimal Brain Injury.* Chicago: National Society for Crippled Children and Adults, 1964.

Dale, Edgar, and Jeanne S. Chall. *A Formula for Predicting Readability.* Columbus, Ohio: Ohio State University, Bureau of Educational Research, 1948.

Durrell, Donald D. *Improving Reading Instruction.* New York: Harcourt, Brace & World, 1956.

Glasser, A. J., and I. L. Zimmerman. *Clinical Interpretation of the Wechsler Intelligence Scale for Children.* New York: Grune & Stratton, 1967.

Harris, Albert. *How to Increase Reading Ability,* 4th ed. New York: David McKay, 1961; 5th ed., 1970.

Johnson, Margorie, and Roy Kress. *Informal Reading Inventories.* Newark, Del.: International Reading Association, 1965.

Kirk, Samuel A. *Educating Exceptional Children*. Boston: Houghton Mifflin, 1962.

Kirk, Samuel A., and Winifred D. Kirk. *Psycholinguistic Learning Disabilities: Diagnosis and Remediation*. Urbana, Ill.: University of Illinois, 1971.

Kirk, Samuel A., James P. McCarthy, and Winifred D. Kirk. *The Illinois Test of Psycholinguistic Abilities*, rev. ed. Urbana, Ill.: University of Illinois Press, 1968.

Lovitt, Thomas C. "Assessment of Children with Learning Disabilities," *Exceptional Children* 34 (December 1967): 233–240.

Mills, Robert E. *Learning Methods Test*. Fort Lauderdale, Fla.: 1612 E. Broward Boulevard, 1956.

Monroe, Marion. *Children Who Cannot Read*. Chicago: University of Chicago Press, 1932.

Myklebust, Helmer. "Learning Disabilities: Definition and Overview," in *Progress in Learning Disabilities,* Vol. I. New York: Grune & Stratton, 1968.

Myklebust, H., and B. Boshes. *Minimal Brain Damage in Children: Final Report*. U.S. Public Health Service Contract 108–65–142. Department of Health, Education, and Welfare. Evanston, Ill.: Northwestern University Press, June 1969, pp. 293–301.

Newby, Hayes A. *Audiology*. New York: Appleton-Century-Crofts, 1964.

Paraskevopoulos, John N., and Samuel A. Kirk. *The Development and Psychometric Characteristics of the Revised Illinois Test of Psycholinguistic Abilities*. Urbana, Ill.: University of Illinois Press, 1969.

Roswell, Florence, and Gladys Natchez. *Reading Disability: Diagnosis and Treatment*. New York: Basic Books, 1964.

Skinner, B. F. *Science and Human Behavior*. New York: Macmillan, 1953.

Spache, George. "A New Readability Formula for Primary-Grade Reading Materials," *Elementary School Journal* 53 (March 1953): 410–413.

———. "Review of *Progress in Learning Disabilities*," *Journal of Reading Behavior* 1 (Summer 1969): 93–97.

Wechsler, David. *Wechsler Intelligence Scale for Children*. New York: Psychological Corporation, 1949.

Woodbury, Charles A. "The Identification of Underachieving Readers," *Reading Teacher* 16 (January 1963): 218–223.

# Chapter 5

# Clinical Teaching

In successful clinical teaching the diagnosis provides only a starting point. This chapter reviews the teaching portion of the diagnosis-teaching process. A special kind of teaching is required to help children who are handicapped by learning disabilities; to differentiate it from regular classroom teaching and other kinds of special help, it is called *clinical teaching*.

## What Is Clinical Teaching?

The goal of clinical teaching is to tailor learning experiences to the unique needs of a particular child. Using all the information gained in the diagnosis and through the hypothesis of the child's learning disabilities, a specific teaching program is designed. In clinical teaching, diagnosis does not stop when treatment procedures begin, and, in fact, continuous diagnosis and treatment become the essence of clinical teaching. This means that the teacher modifies his teaching procedures and plans as new needs become apparent.

A clinical teacher is a child-watcher. Instead of concentrating only on what the child *cannot* do, such a teacher observes in detail what the child *does* do. Knowing what kinds of errors he makes is as important as knowing about his successes. Errors provide clues about the child's mental processes and present level of development.

Clinical teaching can be viewed as an alternating teach-test-teach-test process with the teacher alternating his role between teacher and tester. First the child is tested; a unit of work based on the resulting information is then taught to the child. Then he is again tested to determine what he has in fact learned. If the child passes the test, the clinical teacher is informed that the teaching has been successful and plans the next stage of learning. If the child fails the test, analysis of his errors is valuable for determining why he failed and for planning subsequent teaching.

For example, a clinical teacher might make use of oral reading errors. Kenneth Goodman's studies (1969) of the analysis of errors (or miscues) in oral reading show that such errors provide excellent clues to the child's mental processes underlying reading. According to Yetta Goodman (1970), oral reading miscues should not be viewed as mistakes which must be eradicated, but as overt behavior which may reveal aspects of intellectual processing.

One child, Mike, read, "I saw a large white house," as "I saw a large white horse." The teacher might respond by concluding that Mike is wrong and his error must be corrected. The clinical teacher would respond by thinking, "That's an interesting error. I wonder what caused that behavior? What is involved in Mike's mental functioning that caused him to do that?" The teaching that followed, then, would depend upon analysis of this error—whether it is related to a deficiency in visual perception, in visual-motor processes, a poor sight vocabulary, inadequate visual memory, or lack of word attack skills. Subsequent teaching and testing would evaluate the analysis.

John read "Now he had been caught" as "Now he had been catched." Again, teaching will depend upon whether the clinical teacher analyzes such an error as lack of phonics skills, not paying attention to word endings, or an underlying linguistic difference between the reader and the text.

In another area of academic performance, Debby failed the arithmetic story problems in the testing situation. Observation revealed that though she could read the words of the story and perform the arithmetic calculations required, she could not visualize the story's setting. She could not picture in her mind's eye the items to be calculated. The clinical teacher speculated that Debby's arithmetic failures were related to her problems in spatial orientation and visualization. This hunch was supported by the observation that Debby could not remember how to get to school, the store, or a friend's house from her home and that she constantly lost her way in the hall outside the clinic. The teaching in this case was directed toward strengthening Debby's formulation of space and improving her skills of visualization.

Clinical teaching, then, implies a concept about teaching. It does require flexibility and continuous probing by the teacher, but it does not require any one particular organizational pattern, setting, form, or style of teaching. The concept of clinical teaching can be applied to teaching an individual child in many settings: for instance, in an individual tutorial arrangement, a small group, or even a whole classroom. Moreover, clinical teaching can be used in a variety of organizational patterns such as the resource room plan, the itinerant plan, or the self-contained classroom.[1] In many ways, clinical teaching is similar to what has been called individualized teaching but there is a difference in the way the child's disability is analyzed.

## The Clinical Teaching Cycle

Clinical teaching requires continual decision-making by the person doing the planning and teaching. The complete clinical teaching process can be viewed as a cycle, with each stage of the process as a point along a circle, as diagrammed in Figure 5.1. The phases of the clinical teaching process are (1) diagnosis, (2) planning, (3) implementation, and (4) evaluation, leading to (5) a modification of the diagnosis, and then to new planning, new forms of implementation, and a continuing cycle of clinical teaching (Lerner 1967).

Clinical teaching differs from regular teaching in several ways. First, while in clinical teaching continual decision-making is required, in the regular classroom the routine often appears to be designed to minimize decision-making points. For example, in the regular classroom, curriculum procedures are often deter-

[1] These organizational patterns will be discussed more fully in Chapter 12.

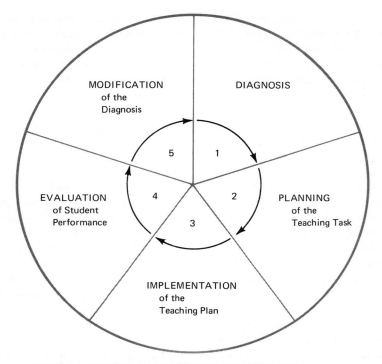

**FIGURE 5.1. DIAGRAM OF THE CLINICAL TEACHING CYCLE**

mined not by the teacher but by the materials being used. The search for the "perfect package" to teach academic skills and "foolproof" programmed materials can be viewed as an attempt to minimize the teacher's need to make decisions. One example of classroom methods that tend to reduce decision-making is the widespread use of a highly planned basal reader, the predominant instrumental tool in reading in 90 to 95 percent of the classrooms in the country. Once the choice of which basal reader should be adopted has been made, the implementation of the decision is largely formed by the nature of the basal reader itself. The initial decision can stand for five years or more. The rapid implementation of modern math programs is partly due to the minimizing of decision-making made possible by the materials. Step-by-step and day-by-day directions are laid down in the mathematics series. Even if grade-level materials are merely given to each classroom teacher without further explanation, the workbook, textbook, and teacher's manual become the decision-makers.

Another difference between clinical teaching and regular teaching is that while clinical teaching is designed for a unique child, lessons and materials in the regular class are designed for the "average" child of a given grade level or classroom. Educational research is frequently designed for the average child when its goal is to find the *best* method to teach a subject area. Such research is intended to measure the average or mean achievement level that results from the use of various methods or materials, rather than to study appropriate methods for teaching a unique child with a highly individualized learning style.

To summarize, clinical teaching differs from regular teaching because it is planned for an individual child rather than for an entire class; for an atypical child rather than for the mythical "average" child. The child may be taught within a group setting, but even so clinical teaching implies that the teacher is fully aware of the individual student, his learning style, his interests, his short-comings and areas of strengths, his levels of development and tolerance in many areas, his feelings, and his adjustment to the world. With such knowledge, a clinical teaching plan that meets the needs of a particular child can be designed and implemented.

## Manipulating Variables in Clinical Teaching

The teacher and the school are able to do relatively little about many factors related to learning disabilities. The home situation or the genetic or biological makeup of the child may be key elements producing the learning problem, but frequently such variables are not open to modification by the teacher. Some variables, however, can be changed or manipulated by the school, and these should be carefully analyzed for optimum effect.

Barsch (1965) has suggested six factors in learning that can be readjusted by the clinical teacher: space, time, multiplicity, difficulty level, language, and interpersonal relationships.

1. *Space* refers to the physical setting, which should be conducive to learning. Among the ways to modify space are the use of partitions, cubicles, screens, special rooms, and quiet corners, and the removal of distracting stimuli. Other areas to be considered in space are the actual work area, the size of the paper, and the desk surface. Strauss and Lehtinen (1947), as noted earlier, and Cruickshank (1961), suggest that a nondistracting school environment be provided. Translucent rather than transparent windows are advised to reduce the visible space and minimize distractions. Another recommendation is that the teacher's clothing be plain and free from distracting ornaments.

The goal of space control is to slowly increase the amount of space the child must contend with. Gradually the child must internalize his own controls so that he can get along in an unmodified space environment.

2. There are a number of ways to control *time* in the clinical teaching setting. For the child with a very short attention span, lessons can be designed to be completed in a shorter time. For example, one row of mathematics problems can be assigned instead of an entire page. The work page can be cut into squares or strips to shorten the time required to complete one section. In timed exercises, the time can be increased. Time can be broken into shorter units by varying the type of activities so that quiet ones are followed by more active ones. Planned interruptions of long lessons, such as having the child come to the teacher's desk or walk to a shelf to get supplies, can be useful.

3. The *multiplicity* variable refers to the number of factors the child must manipulate in a task. The teacher can control the factors the child must contend with and avoid overloading the child by limiting (1) the number of pieces of work to be dealt with, (2) the environment, or extraneous stimuli, and (3) the modality channels of various teaching methods.

The number of pieces of work can be reduced by giving the child fewer pages to complete or fewer spelling words to learn. The teacher can limit the number of pictures on walls and bulletin boards, can control the lighting and the color of the room or furnishings, and can reduce his own verbalization. Cruickshank (1961) urged that the elimination of unnecessary visual and auditory environmental stimuli is essential when creating a good teaching environment for brain-injured and hyperactive children.

For some children the modalities stimulated during learning should be limited because the multisensory approach may actually disturb their learning. That is, stimulation of the auditory, visual, tactile, and kinesthetic sensory modalities all at the same time may prevent rather than enhance learning. Many authorities advise teaching first through the sensory modalities that are intact or strong, and then in separate teaching sessions building up the weaker modalities, without placing undue stress on the disability itself. For example, the child who cannot discriminate between auditory differences in phonemes might be taught reading through a visual approach while building up his auditory skills of discriminating nonverbal sounds.

4. The *difficulty level* of material used can be modified to the tolerance level of the child. The concept of readiness applies here. Many children are failing tasks simply because the tasks are too difficult and the level of performance required is far beyond their present ability. Expecting a child to perform a task far beyond his tolerance level can result in a complete breakdown in learning. Strauss recognized such a reaction, calling it a "catastrophic response."

Another factor to be considered is the developmental hierarchy of the subject area. Certain tasks normally precede others. The child who has not learned to handle the oral language will probably do poorly in written language tasks of reading and writing. The child with poor word recognition skills cannot be expected to succeed in reading-comprehension exercises.

Some skills or responses must be overlearned so that they become automatic. If skills are to be utilized or transferred to new situations, they must be internalized. This internalization permits a shift from the representational level (the conscious, cognitive level) to the automatic response level (the subconscious, habitual level). For example, in reading, the child may initially use phonic skills in a conscious, deliberate way to decode words, but later the process should become automatic (at a subconscious level) for effective reading. The conscious sounding out of words may actually interfere with reading. Syntax and grammar must become automatic if the child is to understand and use language effectively.

5. *Language* can also be modified to enhance the child's learning. To assure that language clarifies rather than disturbs, clinical teachers should examine the wording of directions. They should plan communication so that the language used does not exceed the child's level of understanding. For some children, particularly those youngsters with auditory language disorders, language quantity must be reduced to the simplest statements. Barsch (1965) has suggested the following techniques to simplify language: reduce directions to "telegraphic speech," using only essential words; maintain visual contact with the learner; avoid ambiguous words and emphasize meaning with gesture; speak in a slow tempo; touch the child before talking to him; and avoid complex sentence struc-

ture, particularly negative constructions. In summary, do not overload a child beyond his capacity to handle language.

6. The *interpersonal relationship factor,* the rapport between the pupil and teacher, is of paramount importance. Without it, learning is not likely to take place, while with it, learning frequently occurs in spite of inappropriate techniques, materials, or other shortcomings. Both the pupil's concept of himself and his concept of the teacher must be considered. The importance of the pupil-teacher relationship is discussed in greater detail in this chapter under the heading "Establishing Therapeutic Relations in Clinical Teaching."

## Task Analysis

The first three sections of this chapter considered clinical teaching in terms of analysis of the student and his environment. This section considers ways to analyze the task itself.

### THE BEHAVIORAL APPROACH

This approach to task analysis concentrates on operational analysis of a task to state specific behavioral objectives so that learning experiences can be designed to direct a child to reach these objectives. Bateman (1967) describes this approach as one that places relatively little emphasis on discovering abilities or disabilities within the child, while it places major emphasis on the specific educational tasks to be taught. The important questions behind curriculum planning with this approach are: (1) What specific educational tasks are important for the child to learn? (2) What are the sequential steps in learning this task? and (3) What specific behaviors does the child need to perform this task?

In other words, an educational objective is operationally determined. For example, reading may be the objective which is operationally defined as pronouncing certain words. The desired educational task is broken up into small component parts or sequential steps: i.e., learning certain initial consonants, short vowels, blending certain sounds into words. Finally, specific desired behaviors of the child are determined for each step.

Several curriculum plans are purported to be built on a behavioral approach to task analysis. Valett (1969) specified 53 operationally defined tasks that are developmentally grouped into six learning areas: gross motor development, sensory-motor integration, perceptual-motor skills, language development, conceptual skills, and social skills. The Distar programs for reading, arithmetic, and language (Engelmann and others 1969) are built upon this view of teaching.

The basic philosophy of the behavioral approach to task analysis is summed up in a set of principles formulated by Engelmann (1969, p. 37):

1. Educational objectives must be stated as a series of specific tasks.
2. Everything that follows—the analysis, the development of specific teaching presentations, and the teacher's behavior—must derive from the objective tasks.
3. The analysis must be made by noting every concept needed for successful performance of the tasks.
4. Tasks that teach these concepts must be specified.

5. Each presentation designed to teach a given concept must admit of one and only one interpretation.

6. For clarity and maximum feedback of information from the performance of children, the program should be designed so that the child learns one new concept at a time.

7. The teacher must infer from the children's performance whether they have mastered a concept; she must provide appropriate remedies for children who have developed misconceptions or inadequate formulations of a given concept. She must recognize that she deals only in concepts and that the child's responses must be interpreted in terms of concepts.

8. The program must be evaluated in terms of whether the children meet the various criteria of performance specified by the objectives.

While this behavioral approach to task analysis is one outgrowth of behavioristic psychology (Skinner 1963), there are other applications of behavioristic psychology in the field of learning disabilities. Another related area, that of behavioral modification, is discussed further in Chapter 11.

## ANALYSIS OF TASK PRESENTATION AND RESPONSE

Another approach to task analysis has been suggested by Johnson (1967). Two aspects of the task the child is expected to accomplish are analyzed: the manner of the *presentation* of the task and the expected mode of *response*. These two aspects are then considered in relationship to the child's success or failure in performing the task.

The task can be analyzed in a number of ways: (1) What *perceptual channels* are required in order to receive the presentation and perform the task? These channels could be auditory, visual, kinesthetic, or tactile in nature. (2) Is a *single sensory-perceptual* system needed, or is a *cross-modal* shifting from one sensory system to another required? (3) Is the task primarily *verbal* or *nonverbal* in nature? (4) Does the task require *social* or *nonsocial* judgments? (5) What *skills and levels of involvement* (perception, memory, symbolization, conceptualization) are required?

If a child fails a task, then, the teacher analyzes whether failure is due to the manner of presentation or to the mode of response expected, and the teacher probes for the factor that accounts for the failure.

For example, two spelling tasks might differ significantly in presentation and mode of response: one spelling test might require the pupil to underline the correct spelling from among four choices, and another might require the child to spell orally a word spoken to him. The visual-memory, language, and motor requirements of these two spelling tasks are quite different.

As another example, two pictures in a workbook exercise represent a *ball* and a *rake*. The teacher orally asks the child to circle the one that rhymes with *bake*. If the child fails, one can analyze the task to discover why he failed. The manner of presentation was verbal and auditory (from the teacher) and visual (from the page). The child had to understand language, including the meaning of *rhyme* and *circle*, follow directions, and have good visual perception of the two-dimensional graphic representation of objects on the page. The mode of response was motor. Prerequisites for performing the task included previous knowledge of and experience with the items represented by the pictures, an adequate auditory memory of the sounds of the words represented by the pictures and the words spoken by the teacher, the skill to compare words and identify rhymes, and the motor ability to draw a circle. Failure to complete the task could have been due to a lack of any of these requirements.

In another task, the child is required to match a printed geometrical form with one of three choices by circling the matching form. This task, a common one in readiness tests and exercises, can be analyzed as being on the perceptual level, nonverbal, and nonsocial. The presentation is visual, and the response is motor.

The use of such task analysis in examining workbooks and test materials often reveals that the name of the exercise has little to do with the skills required to understand and perform the task. Clinical teaching requires the ability to understand the elements of the task and to compare these with the abilities of the child.

## Establishing Therapeutic Relationships in Clinical Teaching

Clinical teaching does not imply a mechanistic or unsympathetic view of the child. Clinical teaching does demand objective analysis of the child's mode of processing information and objective implementation of specific teaching plans, but it also requires subjective understanding of the pupil as a child—as a whole child with feelings, emotions, and attitudes. Abrams (1970) refers to this emotional dimension of the child with learning disabilities as "ego status," while Strang (1968) puts it within the framework of the child's self-concept.

Within such a framework a sensitive and empathetic description of the feelings of the child with learning disabilities has been made by Roswell and Natchez (1964). They emphasize that a pupil with a learning disability is one who has suffered years of despair, discouragement, and frustration. Feelings of rejection, failure, and hopelessness about the future are always present, and he is a lost and frightened person. The wider the discrepancy between achievement and ability, the more seriously he will be affected. He is usually affected in every subject in school.

> For twelve long years of school and after, he contends with a situation for which he can find no satisfactory solution. When schoolwork becomes insurmountable, the child has no resources from which to fortify himself. An adult dissatisfied with his job may seek a position elsewhere, find solace outside of his work, or be able to tolerate the difficulties because of a high salary or other compensations. For a child who fails, however, there is no escape. He is subjected to anything from degradation to long-suffering tolerance. Optimum conditions may lessen the child's misery, but proof of his inadequacies appears daily in the classroom. In the end, he is held in low esteem, not only by his classmates, but also by his family, on whom he depends for love and comfort (Roswell and Natchez 1964, p. 2).

The clinical teacher should realize that a learning disability may influence every aspect of the child's world. Deploring such statements as "There's no point in trying to teach him until his emotional problems are cured," Roswell and Natchez note that clinical teaching can provide therapeutic results. Experience has shown that success in learning has a beneficial effect on personality, improves feelings of self-worth, and rekindles an interest in learning. In fact, these authors refer to teaching that results in such changes as "psychotherapeutic." In addition to knowledge and skill in the use of clinical teaching techniques, the clinical teacher must understand the emotional impact of failure upon the child. The following description of the child who is failing in school reveals such an understanding attitude:

> A child who does not succeed in school incurs the displeasure of his parents and teachers, to say nothing of losing status with his classmates. Not only are his parents and teachers displeased with him, but their anxiety often becomes uncontrollable. The parents wonder whether their child is retarded or just plain lazy. If they are assured that his intelligence is normal even the most loving parents can become so alarmed at their child's inability to learn that they tend to punish, scold and threaten, or even reward with the hope of producing the desired results. Teachers also feel frustrated by their inability to reach the child.
>
> It is under such adverse conditions that the child tries his best to function. When he continues to fail, he can become overwhelmed and devastated. These feelings linger with him after school and on weekends. The notion that he does not measure up hangs over him relentlessly (Roswell and Natchez 1964, p. 64).

An important goal of clinical teaching, therefore, is to motivate the child who has been failing, to build his self-concept, and to interest him in learning. To accomplish such ends, Roswell and Natchez suggest consideration of the following "psychotherapeutic principles" of teaching.

**Rapport.** A good relationship between the teacher and student is an essential first step in educational therapy. In fact, it has been said that much of the success in clinical teaching depends upon the establishment of rapport. There must be total acceptance of the child as a human being worthy of respect in spite of his failure to learn. A good relationship implies compassion without overinvolvement, understanding without indulgence, and a genuine concern for the child's development. Since the child lives in a continuing atmosphere of rejection and failure, his relationship with the clinical teacher should provide a new atmosphere of confidence and acceptance.

One reason that it is so difficult for parents to remediate their own child is that it is extremely difficult for a parent to retain an accepting yet objective attitude, and the child becomes very sensitive to the parent's disappointment in his performance. Parents are often unaware of the child's reaction to their efforts. For example, one well-intentioned father, who was observed in a public library helping his son pick out a book and listening to him read, was overheard to say, "I'll tell you that word one more time, and then I don't want you to forget it for the rest of your life." This hardly reflects an attitude conducive to learning.

**Collaboration.** Involvement of both the pupil and the teacher in their joint task provides another step toward psychotherapeutic treatment. The pupil should be involved in both analysis of his problem and evaluation of his performance. In the same collaborative spirit, the child should take an active role in designing lessons and choosing materials.

**Structure.** Both structure and limits are important elements in teaching children with learning disorders because they introduce order into the children's chaotic lives. Many of these children need such order and welcome it. Structure can be provided in many aspects of clinical teaching—in the physical environment, in the routine sequence of activities, and in the manner in which lessons are taught.

**Sincerity.** Children are skillful at detecting insincerity. Honest appraisal is necessary. The child soon detects dishonesty if he is told he is doing well when he knows he is not. Instead, the teacher might try to minimize his anxiety about errors by telling him that many children have similar difficulties and by conveying a confidence that together they will find ways to overcome them.

**Success.** Achieving goals in learning and acquiring a feeling of success are of prime importance for the child with learning disabilities. This means that the materials selected must be at a difficulty level that will permit success.

The popularity of reading material printed on cardboard and packaged in boxes (instead of on pages bound into books), such as that published by Science Research Associates (SRA), is partly due to the fact that such programs are designed to assure success. Learning-disabled children are reluctant to read books at the appropriate difficulty level for them if the books are obviously labeled for a grade level lower than their own. Rather than identifying difficulty level by a grade level, the publishers of some new materials have identified difficulty levels by color-cuing the reading selections. The fourth-grader who would refuse to read a second-grade book can now meet success because he doesn't hesitate to read material at the purple level.

In addition to carefully selecting the level of difficulty of teaching materials, the teacher can also make the child conscious of success and progress by praising good work, by using extrinsic rewards as reinforcement, and by developing visual records of progress through charts and graphs.

**Interest.** The chance of successful achievement is greatly increased when materials based on the child's special interests are provided. Such interests can be determined through conversations with the pupil or by administering interest inventories. If reading material can be found in the child's area of interest, this may prove to be a strong motivation for learning. However, it is frequently difficult to find material in the child's area of interest which is also written at the appropriate difficulty level, particularly if his knowledge of the subject is quite advanced. In that situation, the child will find that books written on his difficulty level are too simple in content and therefore not interesting to him.

Middle-grade boys with an interest in Greek and Roman mythology have been observed to improve their reading skills greatly by devouring all the myths. The first real interest in reading shown by some junior high school students is stimulated by the necessity of passing a written test in order to get a driver's license. Utilizing this interest, some teachers have successfully used the driver's manual to teach reading. Series books have been the impetus for other youngsters to become readers. An interest in a series such as the Freddy books, Landmark books, or Nancy Drew mysteries, or an interest in an author, television series, or movie based on a book can spark reading if the clinical teacher can capture this interest. Once a real interest is tapped, great progress can be made. One eighth-grade boy found the first book he ever read from cover to cover, *The Incredible Journey,* so fascinating that he was completely oblivious to class changes, ringing bells, and classroom incidents from the time he started the book until it was completed.

One teacher reported as follows about a boy with a reading disability who became interested in the simplified Dolch version of *Robinson Crusoe:*

> He became so immersed in the story that he would grab the book as soon as he entered the room for our daily session. At first he couldn't allow me to read any part of the story, even trying phonetically to read new words. But as the story became more exciting, he'd ask me to tell him the words because he did not want to lose the thread of the plot while seeking the correct word.

Once in a while dramatic changes occur in the attitude and outlook of a child because of clinical teaching. When such changes occur because of a book the child has read, it is sometimes called *bibliotherapy.* Learning about the experiences of others fosters release and insight, as well as hope and encouragement. Fairy tales, for example, have great appeal for many children and primary teachers are aware of the sheer delight and excitement of children when they read a simple version of the classic themes in their reading books. Children with personal problems (for example, children who are short, fat, unpopular, or physically or academically handicapped) identify with characters in books suffering similar problems and are helped by the characters' resolution of them.

One boy in a learning disabilities group in seventh grade, who was without goals, direction, or adult identification, was able to identify with Houdini, the great escape artist. He read all the books he could find on Houdini in the school library and in the public library. At the same time, personality and attitude changes as well as tremendous improvement in reading were observed by his teachers. The boy who found an interest in *Robinson Crusoe* identified with the chief character and his predicaments. His teacher reported:

> Many times he would tell what he thought he would do if he were in a particular situation that Crusoe was in, and then he would be so delighted that the main character had done similarly. If Crusoe had taken another course of action, we would have to decide whose plan was better.

The right book can be a powerful tool to build interest, provide motivation, and improve reading.

## Summary

This chapter reviewed the clinical teaching portion of the diagnosis-teaching process. It examined the clinical teaching process, discussed the variables that can be manipulated in clinical teaching, reviewed ways of motivating the child, and discussed methods of analyzing the tasks the child is asked to perform so that they can be closely fitted to his individual needs. The direction of clinical teaching must be derived from the diagnosis, and is a continuous process in which teaching leads to evaluation and a subsequent revised diagnosis.

At many stages within the diagnostic-teaching process decisions must be made. These decisions will be colored, in large measure, by the theoretical framework of those making the decisions. In Part III, the various theories of learning disabilities, along with teaching strategies evolving from these theories, are reviewed.

## REFERENCES

Abrams, Jules C. "Learning Disabilities: A Complex Phenomenon," *Reading Teacher* 23 (January 1970): 299–303.

Barsch, Ray. "Six Factors in Learning," pp. 329–343 in J. Hellmuth (ed.), *Learning Disorders,* Vol. 1. Seattle, Wash.: Special Child Publications, 1965.

Bateman, Barbara. "Three Approaches to Diagnosis and Educational Planning for Children with Learning Disabilities," *Academic Therapy Quarterly* 2 (1967): 215–222.

Cruickshank, W. A., and others. *A Teaching Method for Brain-Injured and Hyperactive Children.* Syracuse, N.Y.: Syracuse University Press, 1961.

Engelmann, Siegfried. *Preventing Failure in the Primary Grades.* Chicago: Science Research Associates, 1969.

Engelmann, Siegfried, and others. *Distar Reading; Distar Arithmetic; Distar Language.* Chicago: Science Research Associates, 1969.

Goodman, Kenneth S. "Analysis of Oral Reading Miscues: Applied Psycholinguistics," *Reading Research Quarterly* 5 (Fall 1969): 9–30.

Goodman, Yetta M. "Using Children's Reading Miscues for New Teaching Strategies," *Reading Teacher* 23 (February 1970): 455–459.

Johnson, Doris. "Educational Principles for Children with Learning Disabilities," *Rehabilitation Literature* 28 (October 1967): 317–322.

Lerner, Janet W. "A New Focus for Reading Research—The Decision-Making Process," *Elementary English* 44 (March 1967): 236–242.

Roswell, Florence, and Gladys Natchez. *Reading Disability: Diagnosis and Treatment.* New York: Basic Books, 1964.

Skinner, B. F. "Operant Behavior," *American Psychologist* 18 (1963): 505–515.

Strang, Ruth. *Reading Diagnosis and Remediation.* Newark, Del.: International Reading Association, ERIC–CRIER, 1968.

Strauss, Alıred A., and Laura Lehtinen. *Psychopathology and Education of the Brain-Injured Child,* Vol. 1. New York: Grune & Stratton, 1947.

Valett, Robert E. *Programming Learning Disabilities.* Palo Alto, Calif.: Fearon Publishers, 1969.

# III

# THEORIES AND TEACHING STRATEGIES

# Chapter 6

# The Role
# of Theory

"If you don't know where you are going, any road will take you there." This statement is as true in learning disabilities as in other facets of life. Theory is needed to understand the learning problem encountered by the child and to provide a basis for development of the methodology that will be used. Teaching without theory may follow the road that leads nowhere.

In a visit to a hypothetical classroom, we might see all the children in a room, or in a school district, or even in an entire city, using the latest in educational technology—"Mother Hubbard's Cure-all," enticingly packaged material composed of colorful boxes, machines, and supplementary items. This program, which the publisher assures the user is based on extensive research and the most recent scientific evidence, is purported to cure children with learning disabilities and to improve children without learning disabilities. The program contains all teaching media: films, tapes, ditto sheets, workbooks, computers, muscle exercises, and even books. It also has a teacher's manual which describes the fool-proof step-by-step directions on *how* to use the equipment. Everything is carefully described except *why* a particular activity is to be used. The theoretical basis for the method has been eclipsed by the latest educational technology. The answer to the question of *why* a particular activity is being performed may be that the teacher's manual specified that this activity is to be completed two times a day for a period of three weeks before Book Three can be used with the audio-visual-motor-computer machine.

The point of this somewhat cynical view of children engulfed in orderly technology without a theoretical basis is that such activity may be wasteful. In their enthusiasm to "do something," education students often question the need to study theory. What is needed, they imply, are "practical" methods and techniques to help children. Knowledge of methods and techniques is indispensable, but one must inquire, "Techniques to do *what* and *why*." In many classrooms and clinics across the country, teachers are busily engaged in neat, orderly techniques, completing page after page or step after step in sequential fashion without knowing why. As a result, much of the work is probably wasteful of all resources—time, effort, money—and most important, children. There has been too great an emphasis in some classes on practical arts and practical academics, with a neglect of the theory underlying the methodology.

An understanding of the theories and concepts contributing to the field of learning disabilities seems a basic requirement for people in the profession. Theory provides perspective for viewing the various splintering branches of the field. A knowledge of theory also helps to sort and evaluate the bewildering deluge of new materials, techniques, machines and gadgets, methods and mediums confronting the educator (Lerner 1968).

Theories in this context are meant to be working statements. As John Dewey (1946) expressed it, "They are not meant to be ideas frozen into absolute standards masquerading as eternal truth or programs rigidly adhered to; rather, theory is to serve as a guide in systematizing knowledge and as a working concept to be modified in the light of new knowledge." This process of theory-building can be useful in separating what we know from what we believe or infer. Dewey contended that theory is the most practical of all things.

The purpose of theory, then, is to bring form, coherence, and meaning to what we observe in the real world. Theory is practical in that it provides a guide for action, it creates a catalyst for further research and theory-building, and it clarifies and structures the processes of thought. Without a theoretical basis for diagnosis and treatment, decisions are based on faith in what the experts say, homilies or principles based on intuition, or the bandwagon approach to decisions in education—the use of materials or techniques that appear to be popular at the moment.

## Theory and Learning Disabilities

In a recent position paper on special education, Dunn (1968) recommended that what is needed in special education—if it is to continue as a dynamic and growing field of study—is the development of conceptual models upon which to build treatment. He warned that progress in special education has been hampered by practices whereby children have been diagnosed only for the purpose of classifying them within a certain educational category and finally removing such children from the mainstream of general education to isolated special education classes and schools. The process of diagnosis in the past has been a search for an appropriate label, such as mentally retarded, perceptually impaired, emotionally disturbed, minimally brain-injured, or some other such term which would permit the child to be enrolled in some special group. Once the goal of placement was achieved, the diagnostic process was thought to be completed. Research studies have revealed that such isolation has not, in fact, been the best kind of treatment for these children.

The practice of special classification and educational placement has been acceptable to those in general education, since it did succeed in removing pressures on regular teachers and pupils, although often at the expense of the handicapped child. Kirk (1964) and others state that special education research strongly indicates that such procedures have not been successful. Indeed, in the case of mentally retarded pupils, children who stayed in the regular grades made as much or more progress as those who were placed in special education classes. Dunn concludes from such findings that special education as it has operated in the past is obsolete.

Instead of emphasizing procedures of identification, classification, and special education placement, Dunn recommends concentrating on the specific areas of learning difficulties found in children who are not progressing in school as expected. Those responsible for special education should stop trying to squeeze every child who has a learning problem into one of the existing categories of special education programs by fitting him with a label that makes him eligible for a special class. Rather, these children can all be viewed under a broad generic term, and Dunn suggests the term "school learning disorders." To help children with school learning disorders, we must recognize, diagnose, and treat these special areas of learning difficulty. Conceptual models and frameworks are needed to analyze each of these areas of learning difficulty and to develop teaching strategies that will help children improve in each of these areas.

The role of theory in the field of learning disabilities, then, is to develop conceptual frameworks for approaching each of the broad areas in which children have difficulty learning. The conceptual models discussed as theories of learning disabilities in Part III are organized within the following broad areas: sensory-motor and perceptual-motor development, perception and memory, language skills, cognitive skills, and personality and behavioral development. These areas are adapted from the taxonomy suggested by Dunn (1968). For each of these broad areas, several theories or conceptual models are presented.

## Learning Disabilities and Special and General Education

If the field of learning disabilities is viewed as the study of learning disturbances, it acts as a core for all areas of special education, since all children in special education categories have problems in learning. Thus knowledge of the field of learning disabilities enhances the skill of anyone involved in special education.

The field of learning disabilities also provides a way of bridging the gap between special education and general education, which currently seem to be moving closer together. As stated earlier, special educators realize that problems in special education will not be solved by isolating exceptional children and that there are many benefits to be obtained from placement in a regular classroom. At the same time changes are occurring in general education. The present philosophy of general education makes it more adaptable to the problems of the atypical child; and schools today are more concerned with individual differences. Moreover, schools have developed more flexible organizational patterns, there are better trained teachers and more ancillary school personnel available, the curriculum is more flexible, and a greater variety of teaching materials and media are to be found in the regular schools and classrooms. There remains a need to close the gap that still exists between general education and special education; and specialists in learning disabilities are in a unique position to fulfill this role. The training, knowledge, and philosophy of the learning disabilities specialist should prepare him to serve this function.

## Theory and Teaching Strategies

Emerging from the theories within each of the broad areas of learning disabilities are the teaching methods that are presumed to be appropriate for that area of disability. Strang (1968) and others acknowledge that compared to diagnosis and testing, remediation and treatment have received relatively little attention. There has been more work on theory than on remedial procedures.

The gap between theory and practice is very wide in this field. There is still little evidence of a clear-cut relationship between theoretical discussions of problem areas and remedial methods or therapeutic treatment to resolve these learning difficulties. Teachers, however, cannot wait for researchers to close the gap and to verify teaching methods. Teachers must face children with problems every day and must take some action to help them. Therefore, in spite of the lack of definitive evidence relating theory to methods, teaching strategies are presented here.

Part III presents the major theories, developed at a number of different research centers, about each of the learning areas in which learning disabilities occur: motor skills; perception and memory; language; cognitive skills; and maturational, psychological, and social factors. The second part of each of the chapters deals with teaching strategies which have been developed to improve skills in that area. These activities are gathered from many sources, and they are designed to serve as springboards for teaching ideas and plans. They are not meant to be a specific or structured way to teach any particular skill.

As stated earlier, Dunn (1968) suggests that a first step in establishing specialized programs of study for children with school learning disorders is to evolve conceptual models upon which to build treatment. The organization of this section builds upon Dunn's taxonomy of broad areas to be considered. The broad areas, roughly following the hierarchy of developmental stages of human growth and learning, discussed in the balance of Part III include: sensory-motor and perceptual-motor development, perception, memory, language, cognition, social and emotional development. Such a hierarchy of development has a long tradition in scholarly studies. For example, Aristotle in his treatise on the Soul (the ancient Greek equivalent of psychology) uses a very similar hierarchy in his analysis and discussion of the development of the human mind and man's state of knowing (McKeon, 1944).

## Overview of Part III

Chapter 7 presents models of *sensory-motor* and *perceptual-motor* development, and teaching strategies for sensory-motor and peceptual-motor development are suggested. In Chapter 8, theories of *perception* and *memory* are discussed, with related teaching strategies. In Chapter 9, various theories of *language* that have an impact on learning disabilities are discussed; followed by suggestions for teaching strategies in three language categories: *listening and speaking, reading,* and *writing and spelling*. Chapter 10 is a discussion of *cognitive development* with teaching strategies for developing these skills in arithmetic and reading comprehension. Theories of *maturation, psychological and social factors* are discussed in Chapter 11, with teaching strategies for development of social perception.

Although these somewhat arbitrary categories are useful for an organized presentation, the theories of learning disabilities presented by various writers do not always fit the abstraction. The concepts often relate to several of the categories and the boundaries merge and overlap. However, for the purpose of presentation and discussion, these groupings appear to be useful.

## REFERENCES

Dewey, John. *The Public and Its Problems*. Chicago: Gateway Books, 1946.

Dunn, Lloyd M. "Special Education for the Mildly Retarded—Is Much of It Justifiable?" *Exceptional Children* 35 (September 1968): 5–22.

Kirk, S. A. "Research in Education," in H. A. Stevens and R. Heber (eds.), *Mental Retardation*. Chicago: University of Chicago Press, 1964.

Lerner, Janet. "A Global Theory of Reading—and Linguistics," *Reading Teacher* 21 (February 1968): 416–421.

McKeon, Richard (ed.). *The Basic Works of Aristotle*. New York: Random House, 1941.

Strang, Ruth. *Reading Diagnosis and Remediation*. Newark, Del.: International Reading Association, ERIC–CRIER, 1968.

# Chapter 7

# Sensory-Motor and Perceptual-Motor Development

# THEORY

Philosophers and educators since the beginning of Western civilization have realized the important relationship that exists between motor development and learning. Plato places gymnastics at the first level of education in the training of the philosopher-king. Aristotle writes that man's soul is characterized by two faculties: sense and mind, and originating local movement. Spinoza advises: "Teach the body to do many things; this will help you to perfect the mind and to come to the intellectual level of thought." Piaget (1936) emphasizes the importance of early sensory-motor learnings as fundamental building blocks for later, more complex perceptual and cognitive development. From the neuropsychological focus, Hebb (1949) stresses the importance of early motor learnings as an integral part of the buildup of cortical cell assemblies. Interest in the relationship between motor learning and language and cognitive development is evident in the work of Russian scholars such as Luria (1966). It is not surprising, therefore, to find a number of theory approaches to learning disabilities which focus on sensory-motor and perceptual-motor development of the child.

*Sensory-motor* refers to a combination of the input of sensations and output of motor activity. It reflects what is happening in the child's central nervous system. Man has six sensitivity systems serving as intake channels for obtaining raw data about the world. They are: the visual (sight), auditory (sound), tactual (touch), kinesthetic (muscle feeling), olfactory (smell), and gustatory (taste).

Some writers prefer the term *perceptual-motor* development. The process of organizing the raw data obtained through the senses and interpreting its meaning is called *perception*. Perceptual information, then, is a refinement of sensory information; and perceptual-motor refers to the interaction of the various channels of perception with motor activity.

In the motor learning process, several input channels of sensation or perception are integrated with each other and correlated with motor activity, which in turn provide feedback information to correct the perceptions. Thus, in performing a motor activity such as a somersault the child *feels* the surface of the floor; has a body *awareness* of space, changing body position, and balance; *sees* the floor and other objects in relation to his changing positions; *hears* the thump of his body on the floor; and *moves* his body in a certain fashion. In education, emphasis is usually placed on the visual, auditory, kinesthetic, and tactile systems as the most practical approaches to sensory-motor and perceptual-motor development.

Medical terms are frequently used in discussions of sensory or motor disturbances. The inability to obtain information through one of the input channels or senses when the sense organ is not significantly defective is called *agnosia* (lack of knowledge). To illustrate, auditory agnosia is the inability to recognize or interpret sound even though it is heard; thus an individual might hear but not recognize the ring of a telephone. Difficulty in motor output in performing purposeful movements is called *apraxia*. For example, the person who cannot produce the motor movements required to speak, in spite of the fact that he knows the word and does not have a paralysis, is subject to apraxia. *Dysgraphia,* a condition in which the person has difficulty performing the motor act of writing, is another type of apraxia.

Professionals from various disciplines when working with learning disabled children investigate motor skills as they are related to their specialties. The physician, the psychologist, the language pathologist, and the educator—all realize the importance of obtaining information on motor functioning as an indicator of learning disability, since sensory-motor and perceptual-motor skills reflect the condition of the child's nervous system, past motor learning experiences, and the present stage of motor development.

Our present concern for sensory-motor and perceptual-motor development is derived from a rich background of educational and experimental literature including contributions from Itard (1801), Sequin (1894), Montessori (1912), Piaget (1936), and Gesell (1943). The concern for motor development is a recurring theme throughout the history of special education. In this section four schools of theory representative of current sensory-motor and perceptual-motor approaches to learning disabilities are presented. They are: the *visuomotor theory* of Getman, the *perceptual-motor theory* of Kephart, the *movigenic theory* of Barsch, and the *patterning theory of neurological organization* of Doman and Delacato. These statements are not the only motor theories of learning disabilities, but they serve as a vehicle for discussion of the key concepts of motor development and its relationship to learning disabilities.

## The Visuomotor Theory: Getman

A model of the development of the motor system and its interaction with learning has been devised by Getman (1965). Because Getman is an optometrist, the approach reflects his prime interest in the development of vision, which is equated in this model to perception. Vision is defined as the learned ability to understand things that cannot be touched, tasted, smelled, or heard, and is the process whereby space is perceived as a whole. Vision is differentiated from both sight and acuity; sight is simply response to light, and acuity refers to the clarity of the light pattern striking the retina. Vision, within this framework, is learned and refers to the child's ability to interpret the world and his relationship to the world.

### THE VISUOMOTOR MODEL

The visuomotor model of Getman in Figure 7.1 attempts to illustrate the developmental sequences of a child's performance in acquiring motor and perceptual skills. The model is designed to illustrate the dependence of each successive stage of development upon an earlier level. Each level or row is composed of a number of separate activities. The rows or levels of learning diagrammed in the model are described below.

**The innate response system: row A.** The infant begins life with the innate response system, represented by row A. This system, which the child brings with him at birth, is the beginning of all learning. The motor responses within this system are unlearned and must be reasonably intact and operable at birth. They include: the *tonic neck reflex,* which is the basic position or starting point from which the child moves; the *startle reflex,* which is a bodily reaction to a sudden

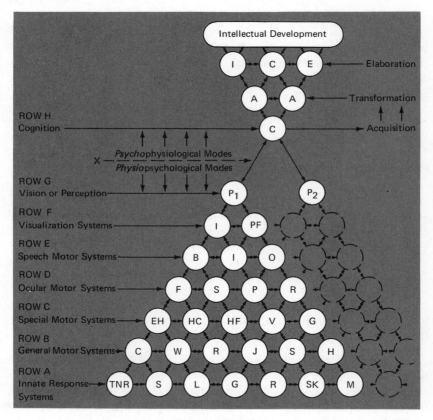

**FIGURE 7.1. THE VISUOMOTOR COMPLEX**
From G. N. Getman. "The Visuomotor Complex in the Acquisition of Learning Skills," in J. Hellmuth (ed.), *Learning Disorders, Vol. I.* Seattle, Wash.: Special Child Publications, 1965, p. 60.

loud noise and sudden flash of light; the *light reflex,* at first as a tightening of the eyelids and later as a reduction in the size of the pupil during exposure to bright light; the *grasp reflex,* which is a grasping of objects and is related to attention span; the *reciprocal reflex,* which refers to the facility of thrust and counter-thrust of bodily movements; the *stato-kinetic reflex,* the state of relaxed attentive-ness or a readiness to act; and the *myotatic reflex,* a stretch reflex system that provides the body with information concerning its own status. The innate response system becomes the basis, then, for all further learning.

**The general motor system: row B.** The next level of learning is called by Getman the general motor system. Row B of the model represents the general motor system of locomotion or mobility skills: *creeping, walking, running, jumping, skipping, hopping*. Through such activities the child is able to build upon information obtained in the innate response system. Now he acquires skills of mobility, reciprocity, and coordination. The child who does not master the skills of row B may be awkward and lacking in coordination. Moreover, the child who does not perfect the general motor skills at this level will not be able to build the solid base needed to continue building the pyramid of learning. For this reason, children need the physical activities that will permit the development of general or gross motor skills.

**Special motor system: row C.** Row C represents special motor systems and builds upon the first two levels. Skills of this system are more selective and elaborate combinations of motor skills: *eye-hand* relationships, *combinations of two hands* working together, *hand-foot* relationships, *voice,* and *gesture* relationships. Children are too often required to perform these fine motor tasks before they have facility with earlier and more basic skills. Getman observes that the child who cannot color a square or cut corners may not have learned to manipulate himself or move around corners using his entire motor system.

**Ocular motor system: row D.** Row D represents the ocular motor system. The movement of the eyes must be developed and controlled in a special manner for success in classroom tasks. The ocular system has two information receiving, processing, and effector circuits—one for each eye—that have to be constantly matched and balanced. Getman contends that skills of eye movement are often taken for granted. Children may test out with perfect 20/20 eyesight, yet have an inadequacy of the bilateral relationships, creating stress or even double vision when doing close academic work. The child must learn to control and team his eyes across the lines of print. The ocular skills include: *fixation,* the ability to visually locate a target; *saccadics,* the visual movement from one target to another; *pursuits,* the ability to have both eyes follow a moving target; and *rotation,* free movement of both eyes in any and all directions.

**The speech-motor system: row E.** Row E of this model refers to the speech-motor and the auditory integration system. The skills included at this level are *babbling, imitative speech,* and *original speech*. Getman sees an interplay at this level between vision and language processes. As an optometrist, he believes that skill in the speech-motor system is dependent upon efficient and intact visual and ocular systems.

**The visualization system: row F.** The term *visualization* refers to the ability to recall or remember not only what has previously been seen by the eye, but also what has been heard, touched, or felt. Row F refers to the ability to visualize, recall, or picture in one's mind a response when the original sensory stimulus is not present. All senses (tactile, auditory, sight, kinesthetic, etc.) contribute to this ability. This level of learning is sometimes called imagery.

Two kinds of visualization are considered: *immediate* whereby one can "see" a coin as he feels it in his pocket; and *past-future* whereby one can review an event that happened yesterday or preview an event which will occur tomorrow.

**Vision or perception: row G.**  Row G represents vision or the perceptual event, used in this model as synonymous terms. All the experiences, skills, and systems represented by the underlying levels or rows contribute to vision or the perceptual event. In this model, then, vision or perception is dependent upon and the result of intact and complete learning in the supporting development levels. Vision or perception is learned through the development of earlier motor skills.

$P_2$.  All of these experiences lead to $P_1$, a single perceptual event. $P_2$ signifies another perceptual event reached through a comparable pyramid of experiences. The letter C on the model represents cognition, which is reached through the process of integrating many perceptions. The three levels above cognition represent the higher symbolic and more abstract mental processes leading to intellectual development.

**Cognition: row H.**  Row H represents cognition, and the portion of the model above this point refers to abstractions and elaborations of intellectual development. Cognition and concepts are derived from many interrelating perceptions. The development of cognition and intellectual thought as presented in this model is the result of a solid base of the various levels of motor learning.

## IMPLICATIONS OF THE VISUOMOTOR MODEL

The Getman model of learning is one of visual development and learning. The pyramid shape indicates that a solid base of learning is required at each level before the next level can be added with security. Each level of motor learning is more precise and exacting than the preceding system. Getman believes that many learning programs being utilized today approach the child as if he had successfully achieved the motor and perceptual levels and was moving toward the cognitive levels. Such programs may not succeed if the foundation is not solidly built, because cognitive learning will then be insecure and shaky. The implication is that many children need more experience in the base levels of motor development.

What is the implication of this framework in the case of Tony? Tony is unable to read; but he also never learned to skip, he is awkward in running, and he cannot keep his balance while hopping on one foot. In the light of this model, Tony's problem in reading can be traced back to an inadequate development of the general motor system. The view suggests that Tony needs more practice and experience in perfecting motor skills.

Several teaching programs based on this model have been designed. One, *Developing Learning Readiness: A Visual-Motor Tactile Skills Program* (Getman et al. 1968), has activities for six areas of development: general coordination, practice in balance, practice in eye-hand coordination, practice in eye movement, practice in form recognition, and practice in visual memory.

The visuomotor model has been criticized for presenting an overly simplified picture of the development of learning, for overextending the role of vision and for overemphasizing the role of visual perception (Myers and Hammill 1969). The fact that Getman is an optometrist is reflected in the key role that vision plays while the role of language and speech in the learning process is relatively neglected. An inference can be drawn from this model that the blind or crippled child who could not experience the hierarchy would be unable to achieve skills of cognition or abstraction. Such children, of course, are not necessarily severely limited in mental growth. Further, the model does not clarify how the child moves from motor and physical development to the cognitive stages of learning. The complex role of feedback for providing information and another mode for learning is omitted from the model. Finally, empirical evidence to support the theoretical framework is lacking.

## The Perceptual-Motor Theory: Kephart

The perceptual-motor theory of learning disabilities put forth by Kephart (1960, 1963, 1967) postulates that normal perceptual-motor development helps a child establish a solid and reliable concept of the world about him. In Kephart's terms, the child establishes a stable *perceptual-motor world*. This approach examines the normal sequential development of motor patterns and motor generalizations and compares the motor development of children with learning problems to that of normal children.

The normal child is able to develop a rather stable perceptual-motor world by the time he encounters academic work in school at the age of six. For many children with learning disabilities, however, their perceptual-motor world is unstable and unreliable. These children encounter problems when confronted with symbolic materials because they have an inadequate orientation to what Kephart calls the basic realities of the universe which surrounds them—specifically the dimensions of space and time. To deal with symbolic materials the child must learn to make some rather precise observations about space and time and relate them to objects and events.

Most educational approaches assume these relationships have already been established and therefore build upon presumed competencies in programs designed to develop conceptual and cognitive abilities. The perceptual-motor theory suggests that for many children such assumptions cannot be made, for these children have not had the necessary experiences to internalize a comprehensive and consistent scheme of the world. These children have been unable to adequately organize their information-processing systems to the degree necessary to benefit from such a curriculum. As a consequence, they are disorganized motorically, perceptually, and cognitively.

### DEVELOPMENT OF MOTOR PATTERNS

An individual's first learnings are motor learnings—muscular and motor responses. Through motor behavior the child interacts with and learns about the world. According to Kephart, learning difficulty may begin at this stage because the child's motor responses do not evolve into motor patterns. The differentiation between a *motor skill* and a *motor pattern* is an important element of this frame-work.

A *motor skill* is a motor act which may have a high degree of precision, but it has a purpose of performing a specific act or the accomplishment of a certain end. The *motor pattern* may have less precision, but it has more variability. The purpose of the motor pattern is broader, beyond mere performance; it provides feedback and more information to the individual. For example, throwing a ball at a target may be a motor skill, but the ability to utilize this skill as part of a base-ball game may be called a motor pattern. Another illustration is Kephart's use of the trampoline. He is not trying to develop expert trampoline jumpers, but rather using the activity to develop certain motor patterns.

When outside pressure is exerted upon the child to perform a certain motor act that is not within his current sequential development, such a skill may be acquired; but it becomes a *splinter skill*. Splinter skills are not an integral part of the orderly sequential development. Kephart illustrates a splinter skill with the example of a child who was required to learn to write even though he had not developed the physiological readiness to perform this act. The child acquired a splinter skill permitting him to write his name by memorizing a series of fine finger movements that were unrelated to the wrist or other parts of the arm or of the body (Kephart 1963). Some people dance as though it were a splinter skill, and the movement of their legs seems unrelated to the rest of their bodies. Barsch (1966) takes a similar approach in his discussion of movement training: "Movement training is not for the arms and legs; it is for alignment and balance. Movement training is not for muscle development but rather for kinesthetic awareness."

## MOTOR GENERALIZATIONS

Extensions and combinations of motor patterns lead to motor generalizations. *Motor generalizations* are the integration and incorporation of motor patterns into broader motor tasks. In the realm of intellectual development, generaliza-tions are formed by combining concepts into higher abstractions of thought. Similarly, in motor learning, motor generalizations are the result of combining and integrating many motor patterns.

Four motor generalizations are discussed by Kephart as important to success in school: balance and maintenance of posture, contact, locomotion, and receipt and propulsion. The relationship of each of these generalizations to learning is discussed in the following sections.

**Balance and maintenance of posture.** This motor generalization involves those activities by which the child becomes aware of and maintains his relation-ship to the force of gravity. Gravity is a basic force and the point of origin for all learning, so it is very important that the child learn to be aware of the pull of gravity and learn to manipulate his body accordingly. The child gropes with gravitational forces in almost all situations—for example, when he first lifts his head against the gravitational pull; when he stands in an erect position; or when he keeps his balance in walking, going across a balance beam, or tandem (heel-to-toe) walking.

**Contact.** Through the motor generalization of contact the child obtains information about things in the world by manipulating objects. The activities of reaching for, grasping, and releasing objects enables him to investigate the objects via many sensory avenues, including looking, tasting, mouthing, listening, feeling, and even smelling. Through such extensive sensory-motor activities, he observes the attributes and characteristics of objects and eventually develops skill in form perception, figure-ground relationships, and others.

**Locomotion.** A third kind of motor generalization is locomotion, which enables the child to observe relationships between one object and another in space. The motor patterns of crawling, walking, running, jumping, and hopping permit the child to move through space to investigate the properties of surrounding space and the relationships between objects. He now moves his body to explore "out there."

**Receipt and propulsion.** The first three generalizations were static; objects remained in a place in space. *Receipt and propulsion* are dynamic; now the child learns about the movement of objects in space through motor activities such as catching, pushing, pulling, throwing, and batting. According to Kephart, the child is at first egocentric, seeing his own body as the center of the universe. He is the point of origin, and all directions are interpreted in terms of movements away from or toward himself. A ball rolling past him at first appears to be approaching him; but as it crosses the midline or center of his body, it appears to be going away from him. The concept of the midline plays an important part in Kephart's framework of laterality and directionality. He suggests the child must learn to deal with three midline planes within his body: (1) the lateral or side to side midline; (2) the forward and backward midline; and (3) the vertical or upper to lower midline.

*Receipt* refers to those activities in which the child makes observations of objects coming towards him; *propulsion* refers to activities and observations concerning objects being pushed away from his body. By combining these movements and observations, he also investigates movements lateral to himself, up and down, back and forth, and left and right.

It is through the four motor generalizations that the child gains information about space and comes to know about the space structure of the world he lives in.

## PERCEPTUAL-MOTOR MATCH

As the child gains information through motor generalizations, he also begins to note perceptual information. Since he cannot investigate all objects in motor fashion, he begins to learn to investigate them perceptually. Perceptual data only becomes meaningful when it is correlated with previously learned motor information; thus, perceptual information must be matched or aligned with the built-up body of motor information. The process of comparing and collating the two kinds of input data is termed *perceptual-motor match* by Kephart.

We know that the perceptual world is one of many seeming distortions. For example, when a circle is seen from an angle, it looks like an ellipse, or from certain angles the circle may appear to be a straight line. A rectangle from an angle may look like a trapezoid. This distortion of perception is utilized by the artist in creating perspective. In the process of perceptual-motor match, the distorted perceptions are equated to the stored information developed through motor generalizations; and the distorted perceptions are thereby adjusted.

If the perceptual-motor match is not properly made, the child lives in two conflicting worlds—a perceptual world and a motor world. The child cannot trust the information being received because the two kinds do not match and cannot be collated. The world for such a child is indeed an uncomfortable, inconsistent and unreliable place, and because he is not sure of what reality is, his behavior frequently becomes bizarre. The child who constantly touches objects may do so because he is not sure what he is seeing. One teacher of children with learning disabilities reported that whenever she wore a certain polka-dot dress, the children wanted to touch the dots because they did not understand what they saw. Figure 7.2 illustrates the match that must be made between the motor information of what a tabletop looks like and the perceptual information of what one actually views. The perceptual view of the table is distorted and must be matched to the motor information.

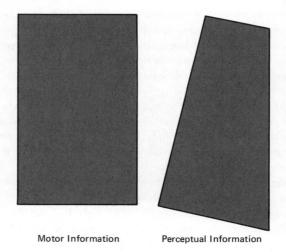

Motor Information          Perceptual Information

FIGURE 7.2. TWO VIEWS OF A TABLETOP

Another illustration of a motor-perceptual match that must be made is the apparent equal height of two unequal structures. From a certain perspective, the 555-foot Washington Monument in Washington, D.C., appears to be equal to the height of a 74-foot national Christmas tree when the President lights it during the holiday season. The child who has not developed perception of shapes like squares or rectangles will have many difficulties in school subjects that assume such perceptual ability.

Vision, according to this view, is the sensory avenue which gives the greatest amount of information since the child learns to explore objects by eye that previously had to be explored by hand. Ocular control, therefore, is important in the establishment of perceptual-motor match.

## THE TIME STRUCTURE

The preceding discussion of the Kephart framework was largely in terms of a space structure; but the development of a time structure also begins with motor responses, continues with perceptual information, and then develops into conceptual information. Kephart identifies three aspects of time important to learning: *synchrony,* or the concept of simultaneity—things happening at the same time; *rhythm,* or equal time intervals; and *sequence,* or the ordering of events on the temporal scale.

As with the dimension of space, many children with learning disabilities have an unstable world of time. One example of timing *synchrony* in motor movement is the changing of direction in running. All parts of the body involved in running must be ready for the change at a simultaneous moment in time or running movement will be awkward and clumsy. Another example of synchrony of timing is an activity that requires two parts of the body to perform a movement at the same time; for example, in cutting food two simultaneous hand movements are required.

Through *rhythm* the development of a temporal scale of the world is acquired. Motor activities such as walking, running, skipping, and talking require a sense of rhythm. Another function related to the temporal scale is awareness of time units. Some children cannot estimate time and cannot differentiate between a minute and an hour. Other children with a rhythm disorder cannot imitate tapped-out rhythm patterns.

*Sequence* is the third aspect of time. The child learns that events have an order in time. To perform activities, certain body movements must follow others. For example, in playing jacks the girl who tries to pick up the jacks before throwing the ball has a sequence problem. The child who confuses the order of sounds in talking and says *pusghetti* instead of *spaghetti,* or *cimmanon* instead of *cinnamon,* or *flutterby* for *butterfly* may have a time sequencing problem.

A concept of time, then, in addition to space, is established through perceptual-motor learning. The rhythm of speech, the timing of movement, the temporal sequence of steps in an activity are dimensions of time in perceptual-motor learning.

## IMPLICATIONS OF THE PERCEPTUAL-MOTOR FRAMEWORK

In analyzing the case of Tony, a child with learning disabilities, the perceptual-motor approach suggests that the basis of Tony's academic difficulties may be a more fundamental disturbance than an inability to deal with abstract symbols. The theory implies that children like Tony have a disturbed orientation to the physical universe that surrounds them. Further, by helping such children establish a more secure orientation to the physical universe, many of their academic problems could be alleviated.

One test built upon this framework is the *Purdue Perceptual-Motor Survey* (Roach and Kephart 1966); while a teaching program developed from this theory described by Kephart (1960) includes the following skills: walking board or balance beam, jumping and hopping, identification of body parts, imitation of movement, ability to move through an obstacle course, movement of arms and legs (angels in the snow), steppingstones, chalkboard drawing, ocular pursuits, and visual achievement forms (copying geometric shapes).

The perceptual-motor theory of learning disabilities concentrates on perceptual and motor development with relatively little emphasis on the transition from this development to academic and cognitive development, and, consequently, the framework neglects to formulate guidelines for helping the child bridge this gap. The role of speech and language in the learning process is not clearly incorporated within the theory. There has thus far been little research evidence to indicate that practice in motor training directly results in increased academic achievement.

## The Movigenic Theory: Barsch

The movigenic theory of learning difficulties, developed by Barsch (1965, 1967, 1968), proposes that difficulties in learning are related to the learner's inefficient interaction with space. In developing the movigenic framework, Barsch deals with three dimensions of the concept: the *theory* of movigenics, the *teacher* of movigenics, and the goals of the movigenic *curriculum*. Barsch's views toward each of these dimensions are discussed in this section.

### THEORY OF MOVIGENICS

Movigenics is defined as a theory of movement as it relates to learning; it is the study of the origin and development of patterns of movement in man and the relationship of these movements to his learning efficiency. The concept of movigenics is based upon Barsch's premise that human learning is highly related to motor efficiency—to the individual's performance of basic movement patterns.

> Perception is movement and movement is perception. According to this view, any effort to enrich perception and cognition must be initiated as a frank approach to attaining the highest possible state of efficiency in the fundamental patterns of physical movement (Barsch 1968, p. 299).

Barsch (1967) has formulated ten theses that provide the foundation of the movigenic theory:

1. *Man is designed for movement.* Movement is the key to life. The human being is designed to move and he is in constant motion in all of his activities.

2. *The objective of movement is survival.* Just as the history of mankind has been a story of survival, so each individual must learn to survive in the world. Survival is dependent upon the individual's ability to move efficiently. There are many kinds of survival: physiological, psychological, and environmental.

3. *Movement occurs in an energy surround.* Man is a constant and active seeker of information. His survival depends upon skill in attaining it, for it is essential to life.

4. *Man acquires information through his percepto-cognitive system.* The human being is capable of converting energy forms into information. The six systems of sensitivity for obtaining information are taste, touch, muscle feeling, smell, sight, and hearing.

5. *The terrain of movement is space.* Movement occurs within space; therefore, in learning to move efficiently, man must learn to cope with space.

6. *Developmental momentum thrusts the learner toward maturity.* Developmental momentum is a continuous and compelling force that moves an individual toward a peak of growth.

7. *Movement occurs in a climate of stress.* Man lives in a climate of stress. A certain level of stress is essential for learning and is part of life. However, each individual has a stress threshold beyond which he can no longer function.

8. *Feedback is essential for efficiency.* The human organism can be viewed as a homeostatic system seeking a steady state of equilibrium. An individual's "feedback system" provides the organism with information that enables him to make corrections in movement to maintain a steady state.

9. *Development occurs in segments of sequential expansion.* Each segment of development in a human being develops in a sequential, orderly fashion from the simple to the highly complex. However, since all types of behavior may not develop at the same rate, there may be an imbalance in the development of various segments of behavior.

10. *Communication of efficiency is derived from the visual spatial phenomenon called language.* An individual's language or symbol system is a reflection of his background of experience. Movement efficiency is thus a crucial variable in the development of language efficiency.

## ATTITUDES OF THE MOVIGENIC TEACHER

While these constructs set forth the basic framework of the movigenic theory, Barsch (1968) proposes that certain attitudes toward learning are essential for the teacher of such a program. The following are described as desirable orientations for the teacher:

*A firm belief in the importance of movement and space to learning.* The teacher should have a space-oriented approach to learning. He should recognize the child as a mobile, information-seeking organism trying to acquire movement efficiency.

*Ability to flexibly regulate space for instruction.* The teacher should move his position in the instructional setting as required. The traditional desk seating arrangement of children and teacher is not appropriate for the movigenic approach. Depending upon the objective of the lesson, the teacher may need to change his position in relation to the learner to emphasize front, back, left, right, up, down, near, mid-far, or some other spatial orientation.

*An awareness of developmental growth.* In contrast to clinical or remedial perspectives that attempt to diagnose and treat specific areas of difficulty, the movigenic approach concentrates on providing the child with a developmental hierarchy of motor activities. The presumption is that when the basic motor patterns have been established and the individual achieves movement efficiency, the academic content will be easily accomplished.

*Understanding of the importance of posture.* An individual's posture reflects his physical, psychological, and physiological experiences. The movigenic approach is directed toward "big muscle work" in positions which will facilitate and improve postural alignment.

*Realization that efficiency of movement is a primary goal.* The long-range goal of the movigenic approach is that the child should not only successfully perform a task, but he should be able to do so with efficiency of movement. There should be no evidence of wasted motion or wasted effort in his performance.

*Acceptance of a coordinate axis frame of reference.* A program of movement activities should concentrate on the development of three axes or planes: the vertical axis, the horizontal axis, and the depth axis.

*Utilization of the infant motor sequence as a basic model.* The teacher should understand that the infant's early motor activities have a purposefulness; they should not be viewed merely as a series of developmental motor performances. Rather, each activity should be searched for its teleological meaning—for its physiological purposes. Further, each of these activities becomes the foundation for subsequent motor activities. The omission of certain motor learnings during the infant stages may result in some later difficulty in motor movement or learning.

## GOALS OF THE MOVIGENIC CURRICULUM

The implementation of the theory of movigenics results in a curriculum designed to improve motor efficiency. There are several goals that Barsch views as paramount in constructing such an educational program, including:

*Developing a state of proprioceptive awareness in the child.* A major goal in planning the motor curriculum is to establish a state of awareness in the child about his surroundings and his movement in relation to these surroundings. Techniques that help pupils develop such awareness include: touching elements in the environment; locating and moving body parts.

*Developing flexibility in movement or spatial diversity.* To accomplish the goal of flexibility in methods of reaching certain ends, the child is advised to "try as many different ways to do it as possible." For example, he is urged to write in many diverse ways including sideways, upside down, with both hands simultaneously. The goal of such activities is to clarify the directional orientation of the learner.

*Using diverse positions in relation to gravity.* The curriculum should be planned to enable the child to move his body in relation to the pull of gravity from various positions. Six gravitational positions are suggested in planning activities: recumbent, kneeling, sitting, sitting on a chair, standing, and walking.

*Learning movement synchrony.* After the mechanics of movement are learned, the child should learn the relationship of time to movement. Three dimensions of time considered are *sequence, rate,* and *timing.* Sequence refers to the order of movements in an action, as well as the counterbalancing of other parts of the body during the movement. Rate is the rhythm involved in activities such as walking, clapping, and jumping. Timing is the final quality added to the movement that makes it efficient. It is the quality readily observed in professionals in their performance.

*Developing shifting capacity in rate and pattern.* The curriculum is designed to help pupils learn to shift easily and readily from one motor movement to another. Activities that require children to shift movement patterns are used in the curriculum. For example, the child is directed to shift from walking to skipping, or to continue walking but add a clap on every fourth step.

## IMPLICATIONS OF THE MOVIGENIC FRAMEWORK

A motor curriculum has evolved from movigenic theory and constructs. The specific activities of such a planned developmental motor program are described by Barsch (1965, 1967, 1968). He separates the two fields of learning disabilities and motor training, stating that it is by chance that their development coincided. He contends that although children with learning disabilities need motor training, such training is also required by a much larger population than those identified as children with learning disabilities (Barsch 1968).

As with the previous motor models of learning presented in this chapter, the roles that language development and auditory skills play in learning are relatively neglected. Moreover, guidelines to help the teacher bridge the gap from motor skill development to academic skills are not clearly specified.

# The Patterning Theory of Neurological Organization: Doman and Delacato

The "patterning" theory of neurological organization developed by a physical therapist, Glenn Doman, and an educator, Carl Delacato, in their work at the Institute of the Achievement of Human Potential in Philadelphia (Delacato 1966) has been among the most controversial of the motor approaches to learning problems. The method, which has been used with more than ten thousand children, has been one of the most widely publicized theories and treatment approaches. The goal of this framework, according to its authors, is to establish in brain-injured, mentally retarded, and reading disabled children the neurological developmental stages observed in normal children. The authors also suggest that the procedures are beneficial with normal children as well.

The concept providing the basis for the methods advocated is that the well-functioning child develops what the authors call full neurological organization. The theory assumes that the "ontogeny recapitulates the phylogeny," or that the process that an individual member of the human species goes through in maturing follows the same developmental stages as the entire species did in the long process of evolution. Thus, in the progression toward full neurological organization, man proceeds in an orderly way anatomically in the central nervous system, progressing sequentially through higher levels of the nervous system: 1) spinal cord medulla, 2) the pons, 3) the midbrain, 4) the cortex, and finally 5) full neurological organization or the establishment of cortical hemispherical dominance.

Doman and Delacato maintain that there are six functional attainments of man: motor skills (mobility in walking upright and in cross-pattern fashion), speech, writing, reading (visual skills), understanding speech (auditory), and stereognosis (tactile). The attainment of these six skills is related to and dependent upon the individual's anatomical progress toward neurological organization.

The failure to pass through a certain sequence of development at any stage indicates poor neurological organization and will result in problems in mobility or communication. Proponents of the theory maintain that by measuring the level of neurological organization, it becomes theoretically possible to prescribe activities that will improve neurological development and thereby eliminate or prevent learning disorders. Following are the kinds of behavior that are evaluated to determine the child's level of neurological development (Delacato 1963).

*Spinal cord medulla level.* Normal reflex movements of the infant indicate good neurological organization at this level.

*Pons level.* Good neurological development at the pons level is evaluated through the child's sleeping position. It should be appropriate to the child's laterality.

*Midbrain level.* Good neurological organization at this level is indicated by the child's creeping pattern; it should be smooth, rhythmical cross-pattern creeping.

*Early cortex level.* Good neurological organization at this level is indicated with walking that is cross-patterned and that has good balance and is smooth and rhythmical.

*Cortical hemispheric dominance.* The highest level of neurological organization is achieved with cortical hemispheric dominance. This is indicated with a clear dominance of one side of the body; the dominant hand, eye, and foot are all on the same side of the body and consistent with the dominant hemisphere of the brain.

Those neurological stages that are found to be underdeveloped are overcome by engaging the child in activities designed to develop those levels of neurological growth. For children who are physically unable to perform the prescribed motor activities, the activities are passively imposed upon their nervous systems by moving their limbs. According to the theory, when the neurological organization is completed, the problem in learning is overcome. The sequence of stages toward the attainment of mobility are (Doman *et al.* 1967): 1) rolling over, 2) crawling in a circle or backwards, 3) crawling without a pattern, 4) crawling homologous, 5) crawling homolaterally, 6) crawling cross-pattern, 7) creeping without pattern, 8) creeping homologous, 9) creeping homolaterally, 10) creeping cross-pattern, 11) cruising (walking holding), 12) walking without pattern, 13) walking cross-pattern.

The treatment requires children to pass through the above sequential stages to develop neurological organization. In severe cases of brain damage, the patterning is imposed by adults who manipulate the limbs and head of the child in prescribed positions determined by the authors. This "patterning" is to be carried out in strict observance to the plan for five minutes at least four times each day, seven days per week (Doman 1967). Other techniques include sensory stimulation; breathing exercises; restriction of fluids, salt, and sugar; early teaching of reading; sleeping in prescribed body positions; elimination of exposure to music; and training of eye and hand use. The goal of all of these activities is the establishment of hemispheric dominance and thereby full neurological organization.

## IMPLICATIONS OF THE PATTERNING THEORY OF NEUROLOGICAL ORGANIZATION

The approach and techniques suggested in this program have been used with many types of children, including individual therapy with severely retarded and brain-injured youngsters, as well as group classroom instruction with normal children. A number of reports of the success of the method have been presented in the literature (Delacato 1966). However, other writers, including educators (Robbins 1966), researchers (Glass and Robbins 1967), and medical and health specialists (Freeman 1967) have found the theory, approach, treatment, and research to be lacking.

Ten medical, health, and educational organizations have jointly expressed concern about the Doman-Delacato treatment of neurologically handicapped children in an official statement (Cruickshank 1968), for the following reasons:

1. Promotional methods appear to put parents in a position where they cannot refuse such treatment without calling into question their adequacy and motivation as parents;

2. The regimens prescribed are so demanding and inflexible that they may lead to neglect of other family members' needs;

3. It is asserted that if therapy is not carried out as rigidly prescribed, the child's potential will be damaged and that anything less than 100 percent effort is useless.

4. Restrictions are often placed upon age-appropriate activities of which the child is capable, such as walking or listening to music, though unwarranted by any supportive data and knowledge of long-term results published to date;

5. Claims are made for rapid and conclusive diagnosis according to a "Developmental Profile" of no known validity. No data on which construction of the Profile has been based has ever been published, nor do we know of any attempt to cross-validate it against any accepted methods;

6. Undocumented claims are made for cures in a substantial number of cases, extending even beyond disease states to making normal children superior, easing world tensions, and possibly "hastening the evolutionary process";

7. Without supporting data, Doman and Delacato have indicated many typical child-rearing practices as limiting a child's potential, increasing thereby the anxiety of already burdened and confused parents.

In spite of strong opposition from doctors and educators to the patterning method, many parents have become ardent advocates of the theory and techniques. In severe cases where all other professionals had counseled parents that there was no hope, patterning was the one avenue of action open. Many of these parents claim the method was successful and are enthusiastic supporters of the technique. The question is whether improvement is due to the techniques or to other factors.

## Summary of motor theories

A number of theories of learning disabilities have focused on sensory-motor and perceptual-motor development of children. Theorists who stress the importance of motor learning conclude that when the various sensory-motor and perceptual-motor systems have been fully developed and integrated, the child is ready for the next stage of development—concept formation. Concept formation depends upon intact perception, which in turn depends upon sound motor development. The authors of the motor theories of learning disabilities caution that a preoccupation with conceptual and cognitive learning may lead to a neglect of the base foundation of motor learning. As a consequence, there may be gaps in the developmental sequence which will affect all future learning by either limiting or distorting it. In this view the study of human movement is inseparable from the study of learning because as man moves, he learns. An understanding of the dynamics of learning thereby necessarily involves the understanding of movement. Movement and learning are reciprocal elements throughout the life of the individual.

Research with exercises to develop motor skills and thereby improve academic learning is currently in progress, but thus far there is little conclusive evidence to indicate that motor programs result in significant academic gains. As a group, children who have difficulty learning appear also to have difficulty with motor performance. One hypothesis for this high correlation is that the motor problem is not the direct cause of the learning problem, but rather a concomitant difficulty that children are likely to have. According to this hypothesis, training in motor skills leads to improvement in motor learning, but it does not necessarily lead to improvement in academic ability and learning. A further consideration is that the role of language development in learning is relatively neglected in most motor theories. Finally, the correspondence between motor growth and learning can be questioned by the observation that some children with superior motor skills are unable to learn to read or succeed in other academic areas, while some children with excellent academic skills are inferior in motor performance and physical activities.

**Motor assessment.** Among the available tests to measure motor development and to screen for motor deficits are the following: *Purdue Perceptual Motor Survey* (Roach 1960), *Heath Railwalking Test* (Goetzinger 1961), *Lincoln-Oseretsky Motor Development Scale* (1965), and the *Southern California Test Battery for Assessment of Dysfunction: Southern California Motor Accuracy Test* (Ayres 1969).

# TEACHING STRATEGIES

Jim is an example of the children with academic learning problems who also show indications of immature motor development, laterality confusion, and poor awareness of their own bodies. Jim was brought to a learning disabilities clinic at age twelve for a diagnosis because he was doing badly in school, particularly in reading and arithmetic. An individual intelligence test indicated that Jim's intelligence was normal, and a screening test for auditory and visual acuity showed no abnormalities. His oral language skills seemed good for his age. At first Jim's posture gave the impression of being unusually straight, almost military in bearing. During the motor testing, however, it was evident that this seemingly straight posture was actually rigidity. When a change in balance occurred because of a required movement, he was unable to make the correction within his body position and his relationship to gravity. He fell off the balance beam after the first few steps. When a ball was thrown to him, he was unable to catch it, losing his balance in the attempt. His trials at catching the ball were similar to those of a child of four or five. Jim was noted to work at times with his left hand, and at other times with his right hand; he had not yet established hand preference. Although he had been given swimming lessons several times, he still was unable to swim. All the boys in his neighborhood played baseball after school and on weekends, and Jim could not participate in this sport with boys of his age. Consequently he had no friends, and his teacher identified him as a loner. Evidence of poor motor skills appeared in many academic activities. For example, his handwriting was almost illegible, reflecting his perceptual-motor dysfunction. Jim's father, who had excelled in athletics and had won several championships in high school and college, had little patience for working or playing with a son who did not catch on quickly. In fact, because of Jim's abysmal failure in sports, his father was convinced his son was mentally retarded and not "a real boy." Looking at Jim as a totality, reading was but one part of the difficulty Jim had in relating to the world; a diagnosis should take into account his poorly developed motor skills, and a treatment plan should help Jim establish himself motorically within the world.

Many children with learning disabilities show motor behavior which is typical of a much younger child. Examples are overflow movements (when the child wishes to perform a movement with the right arm, the left arm involuntarily performs a shadow movement), poor coordination in motor activities, difficulty in fine-motor coordination, poor body image, lack of directionality, and confused laterality. These children are easily spotted in gym class, since they are poor in the physical education activities for their age level. Such children frequently disturb others in the classroom by bumping into objects, falling off chairs, dropping pencils and books, and appearing generally clumsy.

**Limitations of motor training.**   Deficiencies and lags in basic motor development may lead to subsequent difficulties in other areas of learning. However, not all children with learning disabilities have a deficiency in motor development, and a routine recommendation of motor training for all children with learning disabilities should be avoided. For many youngsters, the break in learning developed at some other point in the developmental process.

Moreover, if a deficit in sensory-motor function is diagnosed, this does not mean that the teaching of academic material is necessarily to be delayed (Frostig 1968). Motor training alone will not teach a child to read, any more than eyeglasses alone will instantly transform a nonreader into a bookworm. Simultaneous work in motor development and academic skills can be designed to reinforce and enhance each other. For example, in one summer camping and academic program for children with learning disabilities, children were noted to have a breakthrough in reading and other academic work at the same time they learned to swim (Lerner et al. 1971).

In spite of the apparent reasonableness of the current interest in motor readiness for learning, there is at present little hard evidence to support the theories that recommend development of motor skills before tackling the more complex academic tasks. Two reading authorities, for example, Spache (1968) and Harris (1968), are doubtful about the success of motor-training programs as a means to improve reading performance. In two recent experimental studies on the relationship between motor training and reading achievement, neither the Grattan and Matin (1965) research nor the Roach (1967) experiment found a significant relationship between motor training and reading achievement.

# Activities for Motor Development

The balance of this chapter lists some representative activities for teaching sensory-motor and perceptual-motor functions. These activities are not organized to implement any particular motor theory nor do they represent any particular curriculum program. They are simply a representative collection of motor activities designed to give the reader an idea of the kinds of activities used for motor development.[1]

It is readily noted that many of these activities are similar to what is done in the physical education program. When the learning disabilities specialists have been able to obtain the cooperation of the physical educators in the school, these specialists become ardent team members, taking the responsibility of developing and implementing a motor development curriculum for children with learning disabilities. Utilization of such personnel has proved beneficial to both the academic and physical education programs.

[1]Detailed and rather specific programs for motor training have been developed by a number of persons. Below is a partial list of sources for motor development programs.

Barsch, Ray. *Perceptual Motor Curriculum,* Vol. 1. Seattle, Wash.: Special Child Publications, 1967.

———. *Enriching Perception and Cognition.* Vol. 2. Seattle, Wash.: Special Child Publications, 1968.

Braley, William T., G. Konicki, and C. Leedy. *Daily Sensorimotor Activities.* Freeport, N.Y.: Educational Activities, Inc., 1968.

Cratty, J. S. *Developmental Sequences of Perceptual Motor Tasks,* Freeport, N.Y.: Educational Activities, Inc., 1967.

Delacato, Carl. *Neurological Organization in the Classroom.* Chicago: Systems for Education, Inc.

Getman, G. N., E. R. Kane, M. R. Halgren, and G. W. McKee. *The Physiology of Readiness Programs.* Chicago: Lyons and Carnahan, 1966.

Getman, G. N., E. R. Kane, and G. W. McKee. *Developing Learning Readiness Program.* Manchester, Mo.: Webster Division, McGraw-Hill, 1968.

Hackett, Layne C., and Robert C. Jenson. *A Guide to Movement Exploration.* Palo Alto, Calif.: Peek Publications, 1967.

Kephart, N. C. *The Slow Learner in the Classroom.* Columbus, Ohio: E. Merrill, 1960. *Manual of Perceptual-Motor Activities.* Johnstown, Penna.: Mafex Associates.

O'Donnell, Patrick. *Motor and Haptic Learning.* San Rafael, Calif.: Dimension Publishing Co., 1969.

Radler, D. H., and N. C. Kephart. *Success Through Play.* New York: Harper, 1960.

Raven, Betty. *Learning Through Movement.* New York: Teachers College, Columbia University Press, 1963.

*Teaching Through Sensory-Motor Experiences.* San Rafael, Calif.: Academic Therapy Publications, 1969.

Valett, Robert E. *The Remediation of Learning Disabilities.* Palo Alto, Calif.: Fearon Publishers, 1967.

Van Witsen, Betty. *Perceptual Training Activities Handbook.* New York: Teachers College, Columbia University Press, 1967.

Teaching strategies are subdivided into three areas: gross-motor skills, body awareness and body image development, and fine motor skills.

## GROSS MOTOR ACTIVITIES

Gross motor activities involve the total musculature of the body and the ability to move various parts of the body on command, controlling body movements in relationship to various outer and inner elements such as gravity, laterality, and body midlines. The purpose of these activities is to develop smoother, more effective body movements and also to add to the child's sense of spatial orientation and body consciousness. Activities of gross motor movement are grouped as walking activities, floor activities, balance beam activities, and other gross motor activities.

## Walking Activities

1. *Forward walk.* Have the child walk through a straight or curved path marked on the floor to a target goal. The path may be wide or narrow, but the more narrow the path, the more difficult the task. A single line requiring tandem walking (heel-to-toe) is more difficult than a widely spaced walk. A slow pace is more difficult than a running pace. Walking without shoes and socks is more difficult than walking with shoes.

2. *Backward walk.* Walk through the same course backwards.

3. *Sideways walk.* Walk a predetermined course sideways to the right one step at a time; then to the left one step at a time; finally walk sideways with one foot crossing over the other.

4. *Variations.* Walk the above with arms in different positions carrying objects, dropping objects along the way such as balls into containers, or with eyes focused on various parts of the room.

5. *Animal walks.* Imitate the walks of various animals: Elephant walk (bend forward at the waist, allowing arms to hang down, taking big steps while swaying from side to side; rabbit hop (placing hands on the floor, do deep knee bends, and move feet together between hands); crab walk (crawl forward and backward face up); duck walk (walk with hands on knees while doing a deep knee bend); worm walk (with hands and feet on the floor, take small steps first with feet, then with hands).

6. *Moon walk.* Imitate the leaping kangaroo-like steps of the astronauts on the moon.

7. *Cross-pattern walking.* Step off with one foot and the opposite hand pointed to the foot. Eyes and head follow the hand.

8. *Steppingstones.* Place objects on the floor for steppingstones identifying placement for right foot and the left foot by color or the letters R and L. Child is to follow course by placing the correct foot on each steppingstone.

9. *Box game.* The child has two boxes (the size of shoe boxes), one behind and one in front of him. He steps into the front box with both feet, moves rear box from behind to front and then steps into that. He can use different hands to move boxes and use alternating feet. Move toward a finish line.

10. *Line walks.* Draw lines in colors on the floor. Lines can be curved, angular, or spiral. Also use a rope placed on the floor and have child walk along the side of the rope.

11. *Ladder walk.* Place ladder flat on the ground. Have the child walk between rungs forward, backward, hopping.

## Floor Activities

12. *Angels in the snow.* Have the child lie down on the floor on his back and move limbs on command. Begin with bilateral commands: i.e., move feet apart as far as possible, move arms along ground until they meet above the head. Follow with unilateral commands: move left arm only, move left leg only; finally give cross-lateral commands: move left arm and right leg out.

13. *Crawling.* Since the child's first developmental motor activities are on the floor, some authorities feel it is important to have the child re-experience such movements. Creeping (creep with stomach touching the floor); unilateral crawl (moving arm and leg on one side of the body together); cross-lateral crawl (moving left arm with right leg and right arm with the left leg while crawling).

14. *Obstacle crawl.* Create an obstacle course with boxes, hoops, tables, barrels, chairs, etc. and have the child cover a pre-determined course, going *through, under, over* and *around* various objects.

## BALANCE BEAM ACTIVITIES

The balance beam can be a flat board, commercially purchased, or made from a two-by-four. It can be of various widths; the narrower the width, the more difficult the activities. Kephart (1960) suggests a section of two-by-four measuring eight to twelve feet long. Each end of the board is fitted into a bracket which serves as a brace and prevents the board from tipping over. The board can be set flat with the wide surface up or set in its edge with the narrow surface up.

15. *Walking forward.* Have the child walk forward slowly across the board. He can walk with a normal stride or a tandem walk (heel-to-toe). The task is more difficult with bare feet than with shoes on.

16. *Walking backward.* Walk backward while keeping balance.

17. *Sideways walking.* Walk across board sideways starting with the left foot, then with the right. One foot could slide to the other or cross over the other.

18. *Variations.* Variations and more complex activities for the balance beam can be devised by adding activities such as turning, picking up objects on the board, kneeling, dropping objects such as balls or beanbags into containers while going across, following oral or recorded commands while on the board, walking while blindfolded or with eyes focused on an object.

### Other Gross Motor Activities

19. *Skateboard.* The skateboard provides another technique for gross body movement activities. This can be done lying on the stomach, kneeling, or standing; and the surface can be flat or on a downhill slope. The *balance board* is another variation. This is a square board placed on a block-shaped piece of wood. Unless the weight of the body is correctly distributed, the board will tilt to one side.

20. *Stand-up.* Have the children sit on the floor with their knees bent and feet on the floor. Ask them to get up and sit down again. Vary this exercise by having them do it with or without the use of their hands, with the eyes closed, and with the eyes open.

21. *Jumping jacks.* Jump, putting feet wide apart, while clapping hands above the head. Variations of this can be made by asking the child to make quarter-turns, half turns, and full-turns, or by asking him to jump to the left, right, north, or south.

22. *Hopping.* Hop on one foot at a time. Alternate feet while hopping. Hop in rhythmical patterns: left, left, right, right; or left, left, right—right, right, left.

23. *Bouncing* activities and other variations can be accomplished on a trampoline, bedsprings, mattress, or on a large truck tire tube.

24. *Galloping steps*. These can be done to the accompaniment of rhythmic clapping or music. The speed can be regulated and changed from fast to slow.

25. *Skipping*. This is a difficult activity for children with poor motor coordination. It combines rhythm, balance, body movement, and coordination. Many children need help to learn to skip.

26. *Hopscotch games*. Hopscotch games can be made on the concrete outdoors, or put on plastic or oilcloth for indoor use.

27. *Hoop games*. Hoops of various sizes from the hoola hoop down can be used to develop motor skills. Twist them around the arms, legs, waist; bounce balls in them; toss beanbags in them, step in and out of them.

29. *The "Stegel."* The stegel is a flexible multi-use piece of equipment for outdoors. It is made up of a balance board, a ladder, a springboard, and sawhorses. This apparatus, adapted from Germany, has been found to be adaptable for a wide variety of motor activities. Some exercises to use with the stegel are to have children weave in and out of the ladder rungs, reverse the direction of an exercise, jump off the springboard, go forward and backward on the individual beams.

30. *Rope skills*. A length of rope can be used to perform a variety of exercises. Have the child put the rope around designated parts of his body (knees, ankles, hips) to teach body image. Have the child follow directions, put the rope around chairs, under a table, through a lampshade, jump back and forth or sideways over the rope, or make shapes, letters, or numbers with the rope.

## BODY IMAGE AND BODY AWARENESS ACTIVITIES

The purpose of these activities is to help the child develop accurate images of the location of the parts of his body and the function of these body parts.

1. *Point to body parts*. Ask the child to point to the various parts of his body: i.e., nose, right elbow, left ankle, etc. This activity is more difficult with the eyes closed. Children can also lie down on the floor and be asked to touch various parts of their bodies. This activity is more difficult if done in a rhythmic pattern —use a metronome, for example.

2. *The robot man*. A man made from cardboard, held together at the joints with fasteners, can be moved into various positions. The children can move the limbs of the robot on command and match the positions with their own body movements.

3. *Simon Says*. This game can be played with eyes open and with eyes closed.

4. *Puzzles*. Puzzles of people, animals, objects, etc., can be cut to show functional portions of the body.

5. *What is missing?* Use pictures with body parts missing. Have the child tell or draw what is missing.

6. *Life-sized drawings*. This can be made of the child by having him lie down on a large sheet of paper and tracing an outline around him. He fills in and colors the clothes and the details of the face and body.

7. *Awareness of the body parts through touch*. Touch various parts of the child's body while his eyes are closed and ask him which part was touched.

8. *Games*. Games such as Lobby Loo, Hokey-Pokey, Did You Ever See a Lassie, help develop concepts of left, right, and body image.

9. *Pantomime.* The children pantomime actions that are characteristic of a particular occupation, such as bus driver driving a bus, a policeman directing traffic, housewife cooking, or a mailman delivering a letter.

10. *Following instructions.* Instruct child to put his left hand on his right ear, and right hand on his left shoulder. Other instructions might be to put his right hand in front of his left hand; turn right, walk two steps, and turn left.

11. *Twister.* Make rows of colored circles on the floor, or use an oilcloth or plastic sheet, or use the commercial game. Make instruction cards: put left foot on green circle and right foot on red circle.

12. *Estimating.* Have the child estimate the number of steps it will take him to get to a goal.

13. *Facial expression.* Have the child look at pictures of people and tell if a person is happy, sad, or surprised. Tell a story and ask the child to match the appropriate facial expression to the story. How does the person in the story feel?

14. *Water activities.* Gross motor movements done in a pool or lake allow the child some freedom from the force of gravity. Some activities are easier for the child to learn in the water, since it affords greater control and can be done at a slower pace. Swimming is also an excellent activity to strengthen general motor functioning.

## FINE MOTOR ACTIVITIES

While some children may do well at gross motor activities, their performance is poor when it comes to fine motor activities. Teaching strategies in this section are grouped as: (a) throwing and catching activities, (b) eye-hand coordination activities, (c) chalkboard activities, and (d) eye movement.

### Throwing and Catching Activities

1. *Throwing.* Throwing objects at targets or to the teacher or other children can be performed with balloons, wet sponges, beanbags, yarn balls, and rubber balls of various sizes.

2. *Catching.* Catching is a more difficult skill than throwing, and the child can practice catching the above objects thrown by the teacher or other children.

3. *Ball games.* Many ball games help in the development of motor coordination. Balloon volleyball, rolling ball games, bouncing balls on the ground, and throwing balls against the wall are some examples.

4. *Tire tube games.* Old tire tubes provide good objects for games of rolling and catching.

### Eye-hand Coordination Activities

5. *Tracing.* Trace lines, pictures, designs, letters, or numbers on onionskin paper, plastic, or stencils. Use directional arrows, color cues, and numbers to help the child trace the figures.

6. *Water control.* Carrying and pouring water into measured buckets from pitchers to specified levels. Use smaller amounts and finer measurements to make the task more difficult. Use of colored water makes the activity more interesting.

7. *Cutting with scissors.* Have the child cut with scissors, choosing activities appropriate to his needs. Easiest are straight short lines marked near the edges of the paper. Then cut along straight lines across the paper. Some children might

need a cardboard attached to the paper to help guide the scissors. Cut out marked geometric shapes, such as squares, rectangles, and triangles. Draw a different color line to indicate change of direction in cutting. Cut out curving lines and circles. Cut out pictures. Cut out patterns made with dots and faint lines. Lazarus (1965) has additional specific suggestions for methods of using scissors.

8. *Stencils or templates.* Have the child draw outlines of patterns of geometric shapes. Templates can be made from cardboard, wood, plastic, old X-ray films or containers for packaged meat. Two styles can be made: a solid shape or frames with the shape cut out.

9. *Lacing.* A cardboard punched with holes or a pegboard can be used for this activity. A design or picture is made on the board and the child weaves or sews with a heavy shoelace, yarn, or similar cord through the holes to follow the pattern.

10. *Rolling pin game.* Place colored strips on a rolling pin. Hang a ball from a string at eye height and place a cardboard with stripes behind it. The ball is hit with a rolling pin at a place of a particular color and aimed to hit a designated color stripe on the cardboard. For example, hit the ball with the red stripe of the rolling pin and have the ball hit the cardboard on the green stripe.

11. *Primary games.* Many primary and preschool games and toys such as pounding pegs with a hammer, hammer and nail games, and dropping forms into slots can be useful to practice fine motor control.

12. *Paper and pencil activities.* Coloring books, readiness books, dot-to-dot books, and kindergarten books frequently provide good paper and pencil activities for fine motor and eye-hand development. The materials published by Continental Press and Marianne Frostig (1964) are useful.

13. *Jacks.* The game of jacks provides opportunity for development of eye-hand coordination, rhythmical movements, and fine finger and hand movements.

14. *Clipping clothespins.* Clothespins can be clipped onto a line or a box. Children can be timed in this activity by counting the number of clothespins clipped in a specified time.

15. *Copying designs.* Children look at a geometric design and copy it onto a piece of paper.

16. *Paper folding or Japanese origami.* Simple paper folding activities are useful for the development of eye-hand coordination following directions, and fine motor control. The appendix in the *Perceptual Training Activities Handbook* by Van Witsen (1967) illustrates the steps to follow to make a number of objects.

## Chalkboard Activities

Kephart (1960) suggests that chalkboard activities should be tackled before paper and pencil work. Chalkboard work encourages a freer use of large muscles of the shoulder and elbow rather than the tight, restricted "splintered" movement of the fingers that children often develop in paper and pencil tasks.

17. *Dot-to-dot.* The child connects two dots on the chalkboard with a line. Dots can be placed in various positions and in varying numbers and the child must plan the lines of connection.

18. *Circles.* The child can practice making large circles on the board with one hand, two hands, clockwise and counterclockwise.

19. *Geometric shapes.* Do similar activities to those described above with lines (horizontal, vertical, and diagonal), triangles, squares, rectangles, and diamonds. At first the child can use templates to make these shapes at the board; later he can copy the shapes from models.

20. *Letters and numbers.* The child can practice making letters and numbers on the chalkboard. Letters can be written in either manuscript or cursive style.

### Eye Movement Activities

One of the most controversial areas of motor training is that of eye-movement training. While some eye specialists discount it entirely, others believe it to be beneficial in certain cases. Kephart (1960) states that children must have a reasonably solid motor functioning and eye-movement pattern before training in ocular control can improve the child's ability to gain spatial and orientational information. Therefore, ocular pursuit training should be started only after the child has developed sufficient laterality and directionality to form the basis for adequate matching. Activities for eye-movement training are presented in detail by Kephart (1960) and Getman, Kane, and McKee (1968).

21. *Ocular-pursuit training.* In this activity the child is to follow a moving target with his eyes. The target could be the eraser end of a pencil, a penlight, or the examiner's finger. The target is moved in a horizontal arc, eighteen inches to the left and to the right; the target is moved in a vertical arc up and down; it is moved in a diagonal movement and in a rotating movement. Similar activities can be done with one eye covered.

22. *Finger and penlight.* The child can follow the light of a penlight or flashlight with his eyes, and with his finger and eyes. He can also try to follow the teacher's light with his own.

23. *Moving ball.* Have the child follow the motions of a ball. The teacher can hold a large ball, then smaller balls, or a ball can be hung from a hook in the ceiling or wall.

24. *Quick focus.* Have the child look at a pencil about a foot in front of him, and then look to a target on the wall as quickly as possible, then back to the pencil, then to the target. Repeat a dozen times. Change targets, using other points of reference in the room.

25. *Visual tracking.* Have students trace pathways on paper using crayon, then the finger, finger above the paper, and follow the line with only the eye. These pathways can become increasingly complex as they cross and overlap each other and change directions.

## Summary of Teaching Strategies

This section presented teaching strategies for the development of sensory-motor and sensory-perceptual skills. The suggestions were not designed as a specific motor curriculum but merely as a collection of activities that are representative of those used in motor programs. The activities were organized in the following categories: gross motor skills, body awareness and body image development, and fine motor skills.

# REFERENCES

Ayers, Jean A. *Southern California Test Battery for Assessment of Dysfunction (Southern California Motor Accuracy Test. Southern California Perceptual Motor Tests. Southern California Figure-Ground Visual Perception Test. Southern California Kinesthesia and Tactile Perception Tests. Ayres Space Test)*. Los Angeles: Western Psychological Services, 1969.

Barsch, Ray H. *Achieving Perceptual-Motor Efficiency*, Vol. 1. Seattle, Wash.: Special Child Publications, 1967.

———. *Enriching Perception and Cognition*, Vol. 2. Seattle, Wash.: Special Child Publications, 1968.

———. *A Movigenic Curriculum*. Bulletin No. 25. Madison, Wis.: Department of Public Instruction, Bureau for the Handicapped, 1965.

———. "Teacher Needs Motor Training," pp. 183–195 in William Cruickshank (ed.), *The Teacher of Brain-Injured Children: A Discussion of the Bases of Competency*. Syracuse, N.Y.: Syracuse University Press, 1966.

Cruickshank, William M. "To the Editor," *Exceptional Children* 35 (September 1968): 93–94.

Delacato, Carl H. *The Diagnosis and Treatment of Speech and Reading Problems*. Springfield, Ill.: Charles C Thomas, 1963.

———. *Neurological Organization and Reading*. Springfield, Ill.: Charles C Thomas, 1966.

Doman, Robert J., et al. "Children with Severe Brain Injuries: Neurological Organization in Terms of Mobility," pp. 363–386 in Frierson and Barbe (eds.), *Educating Children with Learning Disabilities*. New York: Appleton-Century-Crofts, 1967.

Freeman, Roger D. "Controversy over 'Patterning' as a Treatment for Brain Damage in Children," *Journal of the American Medical Association* 202 (October 1967): 385–388.

Frostig, Marianne. "Education for Children with Learning Disabilities," pp. 234–266 in H. Myklebust (ed.), *Progress in Learning Disabilities*, Vol. 1. New York: Grune & Stratton, 1968.

Frostig, Marianne, and David Horne. *The Frostig Program for the Development of Visual Perception*. Chicago: Follett Publication Co., 1964.

Gesell, A., and F. Ilg. *Infant and Child in the Culture of Today*. New York: Harper, 1943.

Getman, Gerald N. "The Visuomotor Complex in the Acquisition of Learning Skills," pp. 49–76 in J. Hellmuth (ed.), *Learning Disorders*, Vol. 1. Seattle, Wash.: Special Child Publications, 1965.

Getman, Gerald N., E. R. Kane, and G. W. McKee. *Developing Learning Readiness: A Visual-Motor Tactile Skills Program*. Manchester, Mo.: Webster Division, McGraw-Hill, 1968.

Glass, Gene V., and Melvyn P. Robbins. "A Critique of Experiments on the Role of Neurological Organization in Reading Performance," *Reading Research Quarterly* 3 (Fall 1967): 5–52.

Goetzinger, C. "A Re-evaluation of the Heath Railwalking Test," *Journal of Educational Research* 54 (1961): 187–191.

Grattan, Paul E., and Milton B. Matin. "Neuro-muscular Coordination Versus Reading Ability," *American Journal of Optometry and Archives of the American Academy of Optometry* 42 (August 1965): 450–458.

Harris, Albert J. "Diagnosis and Remedial Instruction in Reading," in Helen Robinson (ed.), *Innovation and Change in Reading Instruction*, Part 2. Chicago: University of Chicago Press, 1968.

Harris, Dale. *Children's Drawings as Measures of Intellectual Maturity*. New York: Harcourt, Brace & World, 1963.

Hebb, D. O. *The Organization of Behavior*. New York: Wiley, 1949.

Itard, J. M. G. *De l'education de l'homme sauvage*. Paris, 1801.

———. *The Wild Boy of Aveyron*. New York: Appleton-Century-Crofts, 1962.

Johnson, Doris, and H. Myklebust. *Learning Disabilities: Educational Principles and Practices*. New York: Grune & Stratton, 1967.

Kephart, Newell C. *The Brain-Injured Child in the Classroom*. Chicago: National Society for Crippled Children and Adults, 1963.

———. "Perceptual-Motor Aspects of Learning Disabilities," pp. 405–413 in Frierson and Barbe (eds.), *Educating Children with Learning Disabilities*. New York: Appleton-Century-Crofts, 1967.

———. *The Slow Learner in the Classroom*. Columbus, Ohio: Charles E. Merrill, 1960.

Kraus, H. "Kraus-Weber Test for Minimum Muscular Fitness," in *Therapeutic Exercises*. Springfield, Ill.: Charles C Thomas, 1963.

Lazarus, Phoebe, and Harriet Carlin. "Cutting: A Kinesthetic Tool for Learning," *Exceptional Children* 31 (1965): 361–364.

Lerner, Janet, Dorothy Bernstein, Lillian Stevenson, and Anne Rubin. "Bridging the Gap in Teacher Education: A Camping-Academic Program for Children with School Learning Disorders." *Academic Therapy Quarterly*, in press.

*Lincoln-Oseretsky Developmental Scale.* Los Angeles: Western Psychological Services, 1965.

Luria, A. R. *Higher Cortical Functions in Man.* New York: Basic Books, 1966.

_____. *Human Brain and Psychological Processes.* New York: Harper & Row, 1966.

Myers, Patricia, and Donald Hammill. *Methods for Learning Disorders.* New York: John Wiley & Sons, 1969.

Montessori, M. *The Montessori Method,* A. E. George, translator. New York: Frederick Stokes, 1912.

O'Donnell, Patrick. *Motor and Haptic Learning.* San Rafael, Calif.: Dimensions Publishing Co., 1968.

Piaget, J. *The Origins of Intelligence in Children,* M. Cook, translator. Originally published 1936. New York: International Universities Press, 1952.

*Reading Readiness Series.* Elizabethtown, Pa.: The Continental Press.

Roach, C., and N. Kephart. *The Purdue Perceptual-Motor Survey Test.* Columbus, Ohio: Charles E. Merrill, 1966.

Roach, Eugene C. "Evaluation of an Experimental Program of Perceptual Motor Training with Slow Readers," pp. 446–450 in *Vistas in Reading.* Newark, Del.: International Reading Association, 1967.

Robbins, Melvyn P. "A Study of the Validity of Delacato's Theory of Neurological Organization," *Exceptional Children* 32 (April 1966): 517–523.

Sequin, E. *Idiocy: and Its Treatment by the Physiological Method.* New York: Columbia University Press, 1907 (originally published in 1864).

Spache, George D. "Contributions of Allied Fields to the Teaching of Reading," pp. 237–290 in Helen Robinson (ed.), *Innovation and Change in Reading Instruction,* Part 2. Chicago: University of Chicago Press, 1968.

Van Witsen, B. *Perceptual Training Activities Handbook.* New York: Teachers College Press, Columbia University, 1967.

# Chapter 8

# Perception
# and Memory

# THEORY

This chapter examines the relationship of various views of of perception to learning disabilities and the role of memory and imagery in learning disabilities.

## Perception

Perception is used to mean recognition of sensory information, or the mechanism by which the intellect recognizes and makes sense out of sensory stimulation. Several constructs of perception have implications for learning disabilities, specifically, the perceptual modality concept, the semiautonomous systems concept of brain function, whole and part perception, visual perception, auditory perception, haptic perception, cross-modal perception, form and directional perception, and social perception.

For the teacher of children with learning disabilities, it is important to know that perception is a learned skill. This implies that the teaching process can have a direct impact on the child's perceptual skills. Once an evaluation of perceptual abilities is made, appropriate teaching procedures can improve various subskills of perception or modify the learning process in the light of perceptual deficits.

## THE PERCEPTUAL MODALITY CONCEPT

Major differences exist in the way children learn. Some children learn best by listening; some learn best by looking; and some learn best by touching or performing an action. Each of these ways of learning and receiving information is called a *perceptual modality.* Many children with learning problems have a much greater facility in using one perceptual modality than in using another. Further, a particular perceptual modality may be so inefficient for some children that it is an unproductive pathway for learning (Wepman 1968).

Children appear to have one optimal perceptual modality for learning. While some children learn most efficiently through their ears or by listening (auditory modality), others learn best through their eyes (visual modality), and a few children seem to learn best by touch (tactile modality), or even by muscle feeling (kinesthetic modality).

Adults too have individual learning styles. Some learn best by listening to an explanation; others know that to learn something they must read about it or watch it being done; while still other individuals learn best by writing it down or going through the action themselves.

As early as 1886, the clinical observation that individuals have a predilection for one perceptual input avenue over others was made by Charcot (1953), who categorized people as "audile," "visile," and "tactile" learners. Contemporary Russian scholars have also developed constructs of the typology preferences of perceptual modalities that individuals exhibit in learning (Luria 1966).

To choose the optimum method of teaching, the teacher should know a child's learning type—his best modality for learning. Before the appropriate approach to learning can be determined for a child, his strengths and weaknesses in learning through visual, auditory, and tactile modes need to be evaluated.

To illustrate the point, Sandra, age 8, failed many tasks that involved learning through the auditory modality. She could not learn nursery rhymes; she was unable to get messages straight over the telephone; she forgot spoken instructions; she could not discriminate between pairs of spoken words with minimal contrast or a single phoneme difference (cat-cap); she found phonics instruction baffling. Sandra was failing in reading; yet she had passed the reading readiness test with ease because it tested performance requiring skills within the visual modality. At first Sandra could not remember the arithmetic facts, but there was a sudden spurt in arithmetic achievement during the second half of first grade. She explained that she solved her arithmetic problems by putting the classroom clock in her head. By "looking" at the minute marks on the clock to perform arithmetic tasks, Sandra was using her superior visual modality to compensate for her deficit in auditory processing.

In contrast, John, at age 8, performed several years above his age level on tasks requiring auditory processing. He had easily learned to say the alphabet letters in sequence, he learned poems and nursery rhymes, he remembered series of digits and phone numbers, he remembered verbal instructions, and he quickly learned to detect phoneme differences in words. Visual tasks, however, were difficult for John. He had trouble putting puzzles together, seeing and remembering forms in designs, doing block arrangements, remembering the sequence and order of things he saw, and recalling what words looked like in print.

Once an evaluation of a child's modalities of strength and weakness is made, several alternative approaches are possible for teaching (Wepman 1964):

1. *Teach through the intact modality.* In this approach, once the modality of strength is determined, materials and methods that utilize the intact modality are selected. For example, if the child is high in auditory but low in visual perception, then an auditory teaching method would be selected.

2. *Strengthen the modality of deficit.* In this approach, the teaching procedure is designed to improve performance in the poor modality. The goal of this approach is to build the ineffective modality so that it can become a productive pathway for learning. The child who manifests a deficit in auditory perception would be taught with methods designed to improve his auditory processing.

3. *Combination approach.* This is a two-pronged approach to teaching; the stronger modality is initially used, but meanwhile separate lessons are also used to build the deficit modality. Care must be taken so the child is not overtaxed in the tasks that require processing within the weak modality. Johnson suggests such an approach in treating dyslexia (Johnson and Myklebust 1967). For example, in the case of a child who has a strong visual but weak auditory modality,

the clinical teacher might teach him to read using a visual method, while strengthening his auditory skills in separate lessons.

## THE SEMIAUTONOMOUS SYSTEMS CONCEPT

A similar view of perception is presented in the semiautonomous systems model of brain function and organization (Johnson and Myklebust 1967). Briefly, this view conceptualizes the brain as made up of semi-independent modality systems such as the auditory system, a visual system, a tactile system, and a kinesthetic system. A given modality system can function in three ways: (1) semi-independently of the other modalities; (2) in a supplementary way with another system, or (3) with all systems contributing as a unit. The following terms are used to refer to these three types of brain system functions: (1) intraneurosensory, (2) interneurosensory, and (3) integrative.

The *intraneurosensory system* refers to learning that takes place predominantly through one sense modality; that is, learning that takes place through one input pathway which functions relatively independently. Using this abstraction, one can state that certain learning tasks are primarily auditory, while others may be primarily visual. For example, during a hearing test the auditory modality functions relatively independently, and this represents an intraneurosensory task. An implication of this model is that a disability may be found in only one modality and this disability may not be disrupting to the other systems. Conceptually, then, there may be an impairment in the auditory system without involvement of the visual system. The intraneurosensory system concept is similar to the perceptual modality concept.

The *interneurosensory system* refers to learning that results from the interrelated function of two or more systems in combination. The brain serves as a mechanism for converting one type of information to another, such as visual to auditory, or auditory to motor. The interneurosensory system includes the inner processes where one type of neurosensory information is converted into another within the brain.

An illustration of an interneurosensory task is copying a circle. The child looks at the circle using the visual modality, and the visual information must then be converted to the kinesthetic modality or motor movement. If the child cannot perform the act, the disturbance may lie in the interneurosensory system, the ability to convert information from one modality to another.

*Integrative learning* is the third system of the semiautonomous concept of brain function. In this type of learning all of the systems function simultaneously, working together as a unit. Many learning difficulties are in the area of integration. It is speculated that deficiencies in nonverbal learning, social perception, conceptualization, or comprehension may be due to an impairment in the integrative system.

The view of integrative processing as a factor in learning disabilities is supported by Ketchum (1967) who observed that there is a segment of the population whose reading disorders appear to be some form of dysfunction within or between hemispheres of the cerebral cortex.

Similarly, Eisenberg (1957) has stated:

> The central nervous system is not to be regarded as a network of telephone circuits, but rather as a complex of transient electrical fields

whose reciprocal interrelations is the essence of normal function. . . . Any distortion in the felt-work of the cortex will alter the social adaptability of the organism.

**Overloading of the modality systems.**  The semiautonomous systems framework has also given rise to the concept of overloading of the brain. The reception of information through one input modality could interfere with the reception of information coming from another input modality. The child with learning disabilities may have a lower tolerance than the normal child for receiving and integrating information from several input systems at the same time. An analogy might be made to an overloaded fuse which blows out when it cannot handle any more electrical energy. Unable to accept and process an excess of data, the brain becomes overloaded and breaks down. Symptoms of such overloading include confusion, poor recall, retrogression, refusal of the task, poor attention, temper tantrums, or even seizures (Johnson and Myklebust 1967). Such reactions were noted by Strauss and called ''catastrophic responses.''

Many implications for teaching are implied in the concept of overloading. One recommendation stemming from such a view is that teachers be cautious in the use of multisensory techniques and that they evaluate the child before selecting methods that stimulate particular perceptual modalities. Such recommendations differ substantially from teaching plans stemming from certain other theories of learning disabilities. Some theoretical approaches suggest a simultaneous stimulation of all input modalities to reinforce learning (Fernald 1943; Gillingham and Stillman 1966). Such methods advocate that in learning to read a word, stimulating the eye, ear, touch, and motor avenues simultaneously will aid in the learning of the word. The child will hear the word, say the word, see the word, feel the word, write the word, and perhaps spell the word. In contrast, the semiautonomous systems approach cautions that for certain children such a procedure may cause a breakdown of learning by overloading the brain.

Wepman (1964) has also advised that indiscriminate multisensory approaches to teaching be used with caution. He suggests that two modalities should be trained quite independently since combining the two approaches before the child is capable of utilizing both often leads to confusion.

Children sometimes learn by themselves to adapt their behavior to avoid overloading perceptual modality input. One boy was observed to avoid looking at an individual's face whenever he was engaged in conversation. When asked about this behavior, the boy explained that he found he could not understand what was being said if he watched a person's face while listening to him. The visual stimuli, in effect, interfered with the ability to comprehend through the auditory modality.

## WHOLE AND PART PERCEPTION

In addition to differences in perceptual modalities of learning, another difference in perceptual styles has been observed—''whole perceivers'' and ''part perceivers'' (Goins 1958). Some children apparently perceive an object in its entirety—its entire gestalt; while others tend to focus on minute details, missing the gestalt. This perceptual characteristic is similar to the background-foreground confusion Strauss and Lehtinen (1947) noted in some brain-injured children. Both the ability to see the whole and the ability to see parts are needed for effective learning. In a task such as reading, children must be able to move flexibly from whole to parts as their purpose dictates. At times they must see the word in its entirety, and at other times see a small detail that differentiates it from another word. For example, to differentiate between *house* and *horse* the child must be able to note details in words. The word *elephant,* however, is likely to be recognized as a whole or as a sight word. Children who rely on only one of these perceptual styles appear to have difficulty learning to read.

Children with learning disabilities often manifest this characteristic in their coloring of pictures. The sleeve may be colored red, while the body of the shirt is blue, and the other sleeve is yellow. One girl colored each side of the crease in the trousers a different color. She saw the parts but not the whole. Jerry, another child who was a "part perceiver," identified a tiny difference that the artist had made in two illustrations of an automobile that accompanied a story. Jerry was so concerned with the suspicion that it was a different automobile that he could no longer concentrate on the story. Children with such atypical styles of perception may be noted by teachers, but frequently such behavior is misinterpreted. One kindergarten teacher described a child who was subsequently found to have severe learning and perception problems as follows: "Paul has a good deal of ability; he shows originality; and he has a knack for describing in detail. He is unusually perceptive."

## VISUAL PERCEPTION

Visual perception plays a significant role in school learning—particularly in reading. Some children have difficulty in tasks requiring the visual discrimination of geometric designs and pictures. Other children succeed at this task, but fail in the visual discrimination of letters and words.

Within the broad scope of visual perception, several component skills of visual perception can be identified. Chalfant and Scheffelin (1969) identify the following components:

*Spatial relations* refers to perception of the position of objects in space. This dimension of visual functioning implies the perception of the placement of an object or a symbol (pictures, letters, numbers) and the spatial relation of that entity to others surrounding it. In reading, words must be seen as separate entities surrounded by space.

*Visual discrimination* refers to the ability to differentiate one object from another. In a readiness test, for example, the child may be asked to find a rabbit that is different—he is to discover the rabbit with one ear from a row of rabbits with two ears. When the child is asked to visually distinguish between the letters *m* and *n,* he must perceive the number of humps in each letter. The skill of matching identical pictures, designs, shapes, letters, and words is another visual discrimination task. Objects may be discriminated by color, shape, pattern, size, position, or brightness. The ability to visually discriminate letters and words becomes essential in learning to read (Barrett 1965).

*Figure-ground discrimination* refers to the ability to distinguish an object from the background surrounding it. The child with a deficit in this area cannot focus on the item in question apart from the visual background. Consequently, he is distracted by irrelevant stimuli.

Visual closure is a task in which the subject is asked to recognize or identify an object, despite the fact that the total stimulus is not presented. For example, in a picture of a man the leg may be missing; yet the picture can be identified. A competent reader can read a line of print when the top half of the print is covered. There are enough letter clues in the remaining bottom portion for the reader to provide visual closure to read the line.

Object recognition refers to the ability to recognize the nature of objects when viewing them. This includes recognition of geometric shapes, such as a square; of objects, such as a cat, a face, or a toy; of alphabetic letters and numbers; and of words. The kindergartener's ability to recognize geometric patterns, letters, and numbers has been found to be a good predictor of reading achievement (Barrett 1965).

**Tests of visual perception.** Frostig (1964) has designed a test that samples the child's ability in visual perception. The five subskills evaluated in the Frostig Development Test of Visual Perception are:

1. Visual-motor coordination (the ability to coordinate vision with the movements of the body or parts of the body).

2. Figure-ground perception (the ability to attend to one aspect of the visual field while perceiving it in relation to the rest of the field).

3. Perceptual constancy (the ability to perceive objects possessing invariant properties such as shape, position, size, etc., in spite of the variability of the impression on the sensory surface).

4. Perception of position (the perception in space of an object in relation to the observer).

5. Perception of spacial relationships (the ability to perceive the positions of two or more objects in relation to each other).

The ITPA has several subtests that assess aspects of visual perception: Visual Reception, Visual Association, Visual Closure, and Visual Sequential Memory (Kirk, McCarthy, and Kirk 1968). Subtests of the Detroit Test of Learning Aptitude that sample aspects of visual perception include: Pictorial Opposites, Visual Attention Span for Objects, Memory for Designs, Visual Attention Span for Letters (Baker and Leland 1935).

Other tests of visual perception are: the Bender Visual-Motor Gestalt Test (Koppitz 1964; Bender 1938); the Developmental Test of Visual-Motor Integration (Beery and Buktenica 1967); Southern California Figure-Ground Perception Test (Ayers 1969); and A Perceptual Testing and Training Handbook for First-Grade Teachers (Sutphin 1964). Clues of the child's skills in visual perception tasks can be obtained from subtests of the Wechsler Intelligence Scale for Children (WISC); Picture Arrangement, Block Design, Object Assembly and Coding (Weschler 1949). Some informal tests of visual perception of letters and words are suggested by Durrell (1956).

Several illustrative items used in exercises to test or improve visual perception are shown in Figure 8.1.

## AUDITORY PERCEPTION

Dysfunction of the auditory modality as a pathway for learning has been relatively neglected by researchers. At present more tests and teaching materials have been designed for evaluating or improving visual perception than for auditory perception. Many of the children who have difficulty learning phonics are found to have poor auditory processing skills. This is not a problem of hearing or auditory acuity, but a disability in auditory perception—the ability to recognize or interpret what is heard. The auditory mode of perception can be divided into the following subskills to differentiate more specific auditory functions: (1) auditory discrimination, (2) auditory memory, (3) auditory sequencing, and (4) auditory blending.

*Auditory discrimination* refers to the ability to recognize a difference between phoneme sounds and to identify words that are the same and words that are different. In the *Wepman Test of Auditory Discrimination* (1958), the child must decide whether a pair of words are the same or different. The different words have a minimal sound difference or contrast of a single phoneme sound. The child is faced away from the examiner so he does not have the visual cue of watching the speaker's mouth and is asked whether a pair of words is the same or different: i.e., "mit—mat" or "big—pig." Ability to discriminate between long and short vowels and between initial consonants and consonant blends is assessed in the STAP (Kimmell and Wahl 1969).

*Auditory memory* is the ability to store and recall what one has heard. For example, the child could be asked to do three activities such as: "Close the window, open the door, and place the book on the desk." Is he able to store and retrieve through listening to such directions? Two subtests of the *Detroit Tests of Learning Aptitude—Oral Directions* and *Oral Commissions* (Baker and Leland 1935)—are designed to assess such functions. The STAP (Kimmell and Wahl 1969) has a section on the ability to remember and identify rhymes.

*Auditory sequencing* is the ability to remember the order of items given orally in a sequential list. For example, the sequences "A, B, C . . ." and "January, February, March . . ." are examples of the importance of sequence. Tests of auditory sequencing are found in the ITPA, *Auditory Sequential Memory* (Kirk, McCarthy, and Kirk 1968); WISC, *Digit Span* (Wechsler 1949); *Detroit Tests of Learning Aptitude, Auditory Attention Span for Unrelated Words* (Baker and Leland 1935); tests of the ability to remember a rhythmic pattern, STAP (Kimmell and Wahl 1969).

*Auditory blending* is the ability to blend single phonic elements or phonemes into a complete word. Children with such disabilities are not able to blend the phonemes "m—a—n" to form the word *man*. Tests of this auditory skill include the ITPA subtests, *Sound Blending* and *Auditory Closure* (Kirk, McCarthy, and Kirk 1968); and the *Roswell-Chall Auditory Blending Test* (Roswell and Chall 1963).

All of the auditory subskills can be sampled through clinical observations during teaching sessions, through informal tests, or through formally designed standardized tests. Durrell (1956) has many suggestions for informal tests of auditory perception of sounds and words.

## HAPTIC PERCEPTION

Haptic perception refers to information received through two modalities—tactile and kinesthetic. The term *haptic* is used to refer to both systems.

Tactile perception is obtained through the sense of touch via the fingers and skin surfaces. The ability to recognize an object by touching it, to identify a

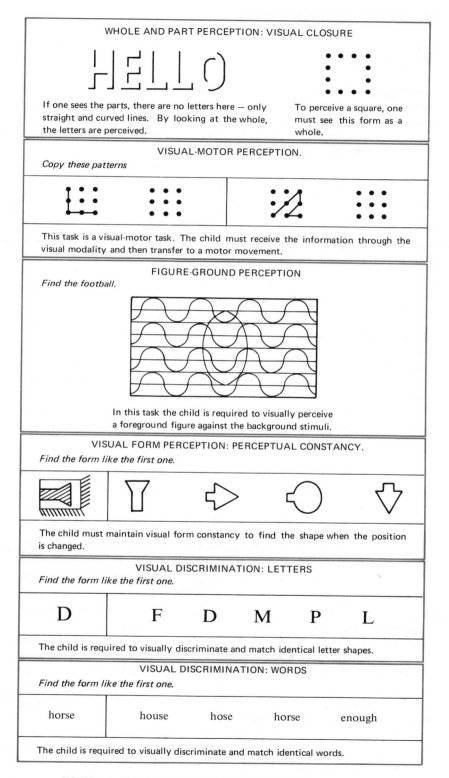

**WHOLE AND PART PERCEPTION: VISUAL CLOSURE**

If one sees the parts, there are no letters here — only straight and curved lines. By looking at the whole, the letters are perceived.

To perceive a square, one must see this form as a whole.

**VISUAL-MOTOR PERCEPTION.**

*Copy these patterns*

This task is a visual-motor task. The child must receive the information through the visual modality and then transfer to a motor movement.

**FIGURE-GROUND PERCEPTION**

*Find the football.*

In this task the child is required to visually perceive a foreground figure against the background stimuli.

**VISUAL FORM PERCEPTION: PERCEPTUAL CONSTANCY.**

*Find the form like the first one.*

The child must maintain visual form constancy to find the shape when the position is changed.

**VISUAL DISCRIMINATION: LETTERS**

*Find the form like the first one.*

D          F     D     M     P     L

The child is required to visually discriminate and match identical letter shapes.

**VISUAL DISCRIMINATION: WORDS**

*Find the form like the first one.*

horse          house     hose     horse     enough

The child is required to visually discriminate and match identical words.

**FIGURE 8.1. EXAMPLES OF VISUAL PERCEPTION TASKS**

numeral that is drawn on one's back or arm, to discriminate between smooth and rough surfaces, to identify which finger is being touched—all are examples of tactile perception.

Kinesthetic perception is obtained through body movements and muscle feeling. The awareness of positions taken by different parts of the body, bodily feelings of muscular contraction, tension, and relaxation are examples of kinesthetic perception. The discussion of body image and motor information in the previous chapter provides a broader view of the kinesthetic system.

It is sometimes difficult to conceptualize the difference between the two types of haptic perception. Perhaps the features distinguishing tactile perception from kinesthetic can be clarified with the illustration of shopping for mattresses. Both the tactile and kinesthetic modalities provide perceptual information about an innerspring mattress and a foam rubber mattress. By simply touching the covering on the two mattresses (tactile perception) it is difficult to tell the innerspring from the foam rubber. However, the body feeling received by sitting on each mattress differs considerably (kinesthetic perception). With such kinesthetic perceptual information, one can easily differentiate the innerspring mattress from the foam rubber one.

Both dimensions of the haptic system are important for obtaining information about object qualities, bodily movement, and their interrelationships. Most school tasks, as well as most acts in everyday life, require both touch and body movement. Chalfant and Scheffelin (1969) point out that in comparison to visual and auditory perception, little information is available concerning tactile and kinesthetic perception in the educational journals. Yet these authors emphasize that tactile and kinesthetic perception play important roles in learning. There is a need to know more about dysfunction in the haptic areas and their relationship to other areas of learning.

One test designed to assess haptic functions is the *Southern California Kinesthetic and Tactile Perception Test* (Ayres 1969). Several informal tests of tactile and kinesthetic perception are described by Chalfant and Scheffelin (1969, Chapter 4).

## CROSS-MODAL PERCEPTION

There is growing evidence that a major difficulty in learning is the inability to integrate one modality of function with another modality (Chalfant and Scheffelin 1969). The neurological process of converting information within the brain from one modality to another has been referred to as *cross-modality perception*. This process is also termed "intersensory integration," "intermodal transfer," and "transducing" in the literature (Johnson and Myklebust 1967).

In many types of learning, information received through one sensory input system must be transferred or integrated with another perceptual system; and the learner must be able to shift or cross from one to the other, integrating the two systems. Some children appear quite adequate in both visual and auditory systems when they are viewed alone, but the deficit appears when a task requires the integration of the two systems.

An example of cross-modal perception is found in the reading process, where the reader must integrate visual symbols with their auditory equivalents. Johnson and Myklebust (1967) propose that some reading disorders are due to an inability to make such conversions within the neurosensory system. Thus the child who cannot convert from the visual modality to the auditory modality is able to learn what letters look like, but he cannot associate these visual images with their sound equivalents. Conversely, the child who cannot convert from the auditory modality to the visual learns what letters sound like but cannot associate it with the visual form of the letters.

Ayres (1968) believes that integration of other perceptual modalities is also required in reading. She proposes that intersensory integration of the modalities of visual, tactile, and kinesthetic perception is essential for reading. Another illustration of a deficit in cross-modal perception is the child who has difficulty planning and executing motor movements. For example, to talk the child must convert an auditory memory of a word by implementing a motor plan in order to say the word (auditory system to motor system). The inability to plan and execute the proper motor action, to convert the auditory input into motor output, is sometimes called *apraxia*. Ayres (1968) notes that such children are characterized by poor tactile and kinesthetic perception.

Although there is as yet little information concerning the growth and development of the integration of perceptual systems, researchers believe that the appearance of higher and more complex learning is dependent upon the gradual integration of the modality systems. Research studies of cross-modality integration that have been conducted thus far suggest that there are differences in intersensory integrative ability between normal children and neurologically impaired children. Further, there is evidence that some individuals who apparently function normally with a task requiring a single perceptual modality have difficulty when the task involves simultaneous or successive functioning of several modalities. The breakdown occurs in tasks requiring cross-modal perception, and has been referred to as an integrative disorder (Chalfant and Scheffelin 1969).

Frostig (1965, 1968) advocates exercises in cross-modality associations for children found to have difficulty with the cross-modal process. Examples of such activities are: following spoken directions (auditory-verbal to motor); describing a picture (visual to auditory-verbal); finding certain objects in pictures (auditory-verbal to visual); feeling objects through a curtain and drawing their shapes on paper (tactile to visual-motor); determining whether two objects are the same or different when one is touched while the other is seen (tactile to visual); determining whether two patterns are the same or different when one is touched and the other heard—i.e., *dot–dot–dash* patterns (tactile to auditory). Activities designed to have the child perform cross-modal functions are suggested later in this chapter.

Probably many tests that purport to be testing a single perceptual modality actually require the integration of two or more perceptual modalities. That is, a visual perception test may actually require integration of the visual, motor and auditory functions. While many tests require cross-modal functions in performance, few tests, if any, at the present time are available that have been designed specifically to assess cross-modal perception. Certain researchers who are actively investigating this area of performance have developed tests of cross-modal processing designed to investigate their research problem. These include the studies of Birch and Belmont (1964), Birch and Lefford (1963), and Belmont, Birch, and Karp (1965).

## FORM AND DIRECTIONAL PERCEPTION

An interesting analysis of perception has been made by Money (1966), in regard to the relationship of perceptual world of objects and the perceptual world of letters and words. A perceptual generalization made by children in the pre-reading stage of development is the "law of object constancy." A child concludes that an object retains the same name or meaning regardless of the position it happens to be in, the direction it faces, or the modification of slight additions or subtractions. A chair, for example, is a chair regardless of whether it faces left or right, back or front, upside down or right side up, of whether it is uphol-stered or has additional cushions, or even if it has a leg missing. It is still called a chair. The child has made similar generalizations about dogs; no matter what its position, size, color, or quantity of hair, it is still called a dog.

When he begins to deal with letters and words, however, the child finds that this perceptual generalization no longer holds true. The placement of a circle on a stick from left to right, or top to bottom, changes the name of the letter from b to d to p to q, and the addition of a small line changes c to e. The direction the word is facing changes it from *was* to *saw*, or *no* to *on*, or *top* to *pot*. One incident of such confusion happened during a teachers' strike. A boy with directional per-ception difficulties looked at the picket signs and asked why they were picketing if the strike was called off. The sign, lettered *ON STRIKE*, was read by the young-ster as *NO STRIKE*.

The implication, then, is that some children with reading disabilities fail to make the necessary amendments to an earlier perceptual generalization they have formulated. An instrument that Money found useful in assessing such space-form-direction perceptual difficulties in children is the *Road Map Test* (Money, Alexander, and Walker 1965). Another instrument to evaluate space and direc-tion ability is the *Ayres Space Test* (Ayres 1969).

## SOCIAL PERCEPTION

The preceding sections of this chapter considered disturbances in the perception of physical objects and events. Psychologists have recently turned their attention to another dimension of perception—that of social perception (Hochberg 1964). The skill of interpreting stimuli in the social environment and appropriately relating such interpretations to the social situation is called *social perception*. Compared to the quantity of research on the perception of physical phenomena, the area of social perception is relatively unexplored. Certain children appear to have difficulty perceiving social data, and consequently they have trouble learn-ing how to make social judgments and how to adapt their behavior to the social situation (Johnson and Myklebust 1967).

Jimmy, nine and one-half years old, is an example of a child with a disability in social perception. On the Stanford-Binet Intelligence Test, Jimmy received an IQ score of 127, putting him in a high intelligence classification. He did par-ticularly well on the sections that required verbal and language responses. Yet on the Goodenough-Harris Drawing Test (Harris 1963), his drawing ranked at the sixth percentile for his age (Figure 8.2).

Jimmy had many problems in the area of social perception. While he per-formed satisfactorily in many academic subjects, his teachers consistently re-

**FIGURE 8.2. DRAWING OF A MAN MADE BY A BOY, AGE 9 YEARS, 8 MONTHS, WITH A DISABILITY IN SOCIAL PERCEPTION**

ported that his social behavior in school was both strange and disturbing. The speech teacher dismissed him because of his abnormal delight and hilarity when others in the class made mistakes. Another teacher reported that he seemed unconscious of wrongdoing, that he made odd statements totally out of context, and that he was not well accepted by other children. Another report commented that Jimmy had not developed skills in social situations. Although he wanted to be accepted by others and have friends, he did not seem to know the appropriate manner of gaining friends, and instead tended to antagonize other children. As seems to be true of some other children with a disability in social perception, Jimmy also did poorly in perceptual-motor tasks and seemed to have a poor understanding of space relationships. The psychologist reported poor performance in perceptual-motor and coordination activities on the Bender *Visual-Motor Gestalt Test.*

Problems of social development and teaching strategies for social development are discussed further in Chapter 11.

## SUMMARY

There are many components of perception that contribute to learning, and a deficit or disturbance in any one may be a key factor in a particular child's learning disability. Since perception is a learned skill, environmental influences including teaching procedures can modify and strengthen perceptual learnings. Teaching strategies designed to build perceptual modalities are presented in the second part of this chapter.

# Memory

Sensation and perception take place when the stimulus is present; they are ongoing activities. Memory pertains to sensations and data *already* received and perceived. The ability to store and retrieve previously experienced sensations and perceptions when the stimulus that originally evoked them is no longer present is called memory, imagery, recall, or sometimes "the mind's eye." Memory is a developmental phenomenon built upon the stages of motor and perceptual learning (Piaget 1968).

Examples of sensations and perceptions that occur only in the mind are the musician "listening" to music that he has actually played at an earlier time; the cook "tasting" the sourness of a lemon she is going to use; the carpenter "feeling" the roughness of sandpaper used yesterday in a job; the gardener "smelling" the sweetness of lilacs as he looks at the buds on the tree. McCarthy (1968) described how she helped her 3-year-old understand the qualities of memory. She explained the word "mind" by asking the youngster to close her eyes and think about a peanut butter and jelly sandwich. Yes, the child could "see" the jelly dripping down the sides of the bread; she could "smell" the peanut butter; and she could even "taste" the first bite. Where was this sandwich that had become so vivid? It was, so went the explanation, in the same place her mind was.

Children with learning disabilities frequently have difficulty recalling what things looked like or sounded like. Memory of past experiences must be retained and compared in order to organize and interpret experience. Otherwise each experience is unique, with no connection to previous experience and learning. Memory refers to the recall of nonverbal as well as verbal experiences—for example, the inability to recall the meanings of sounds made by dogs, horns, bells, and certain voice qualities, or to recall the meanings conveyed by facial expressions. The inability to remember words, directions, and explanations are examples of disabilities of remembering language. Memory problems can also be related to a specific perceptual modality; e.g., visual-memory, or auditory memory. There are other categories of memory that can be differentiated, such as rote memory, immediate or short-term memory, sequential or serial memory, and long-term memory.

*Rote memory* connotes repetition carried out mechanically without understanding. Thus a child who through rote memory learned to repeat the alphabet without realizing the meaning of the letters came home to ask his mother what an "elemenopee" was.

*Short-term* or *immediate memory* is required in tasks in which the subject is expected to hold information in his mind for a relatively short period of time before retrieval. Tasks such as repeating digits, repeating a string of words, following a short series of instructions, remembering and reproducing designs, or spelling a word for a test are examples of tasks requiring short-term memory. Research findings using the ITPA indicate that reading disability cases tend to perform poorly on auditory and visual short-term memory tests (Paraskevopoulos and Kirk 1969). Carroll (1967) found that people who had a poor aptitude for learning foreign language were also poor at the task of repeating nonsense syllables after a short time delay, while people with high language aptitude had no trouble with this task.

*Serial* or *sequential memory* is another type of automatic response requiring a specified order to the items being recalled. For example, in saying the days of the week or in the act of counting, the order of the elements is of paramount importance. The order of the words in a sentence is crucial, particularly in the English language. The child who formulates a sentence in the order of object–verb–subject, "milk want Baby," may be exhibiting a disturbance in sequential memory.

In *long-term memory* knowledge must be retained and stored for a long period of time before retrieval of the information is required. There is some physiological evidence to suggest that long-term and short-term memories are located within different structures of the brain (Magoun 1967). The phenomenon of memorizing material shortly before an examination and forgetting the bulk of it shortly thereafter is well known to most students. Long-term memory requires the ability to assimilate, store, and retrieve information when it is needed. It is dependent upon the learner's skill in seeing the relevancy of the material and relating it to past knowledge.

For efficient learning, an individual's memory in many areas of performance must become an automatic, habitual response to a stimulus. Examples of such automatic responses include remembering words when speaking, inserting the proper syntactic word form in a sentence, and remembering a word by sight when reading. Many factors have an effect on memory: the child's intensity of attention, meaningfulness of the material, interest in the subject, and the amount of drill and overlearning. Research indicates that appropriate environmental factors and teaching can help children improve in what they can remember (Vergason 1968; Wiseman 1965).

Some of the tests previously listed as useful in determining skills in perception also assess elements of memory. The *Benton Visual Retention Test* (Benton 1963); several subtests of the ITPA—*Grammatic Closure, Auditory Sequential Memory,* and *Visual Sequential Memory* (Kirk, McCarthy, and Kirk 1968); several subtests of the *Detroit Tests of Learning Aptitude—Memory for Designs* and *Oral Directions* (Baker and Leland 1935); and the *Memory-for-Designs Test* (Graham and Kendall 1960) are useful instruments for evaluating memory.

## Summary of Theories of Perception and Memory

We have reviewed perception and memory, which for some children are areas of disturbance that interfere with learning.

Several constructs of perception were examined, including the perceptual modality concept, the semiautonomous systems concept of brain function, the theory of whole and part perception, visual perception, auditory perception, haptic perception, cross-modal perception, form and directional perception, and social perception. The implications of each of these for children with learning disabilities was analyzed. The impact of memory and memory disorders on learning was considered. An important conclusion is that learning in these areas can be improved with appropriate teaching and environmental modifications.

One implication of the perceptual and memory problems that children face in learning is clear: the search for *the* best method to teach a subject such as reading to all children in the nation, the school, or even a classroom is a fruitless search. A method that is good for one child in the class may not provide a satisfactory learning medium for another. Just as each child is unique in appearance, personality, intelligence, and motor development, so too he is different from others in how he learns. A phonics approach, for example, may not be successful with the child who has a serious deficit in the auditory modality. In fact, continuous use of such an approach with a child who "cannot listen" or cannot hear the phoneme sounds may lead to such undesirable consequences as frustration, failure, and a dislike of school, reading, and the teacher. For such a child a method that teaches through his optimal perceptual modality may prove more successful. If he learns better through a visual or tactile pathway, methods that utilize such approaches should be used. While learning takes place through the stronger modality, instruction should also be planned to build up the area of deficit. The impaired system is strengthened so that eventually it can be a functional pathway for learning.

# TEACHING STRATEGIES

This second part of the chapter presents teaching strategies to help the child in two areas of learning: perception and memory. The ideas presented are merely representative of activities that can be used to improve each subskill. These activities, which represent many sources, are given as samples of activities used in learning disabilities programs.[1]

## Perception

Many children with learning disabilities live in a warped perceptual world. Although they have no basic impairment in their sensory organs, they cannot interpret sensations in a normal manner. They do not hear, see, feel, or integrate sensory stimuli in their environmental surroundings the way other children do. The abnormality is not in the sensory organ itself, but in perception resulting from stimulation to the sensory organ. Auditory perception takes place in the brain—not in the ear; similarly, visual perception takes place in the brain—not in the eye. There is ample evidence that perceptual disturbances are important factors in the failure to learn, particularly at the early stages of

---

[1] Other techniques are suggested in the following sources: *Perceptual Training Activities Handbook* by Van Witsen (1967); *A Guide to Special Class Programs for Children with Learning Disabilities* by Nash and Pfeffer (1967); *Teaching Devices for Children with Impaired Learning* by Epps, et al.; *The Remediation of Learning Disabilities* by Valett (1967); *Language and Learning Disorders of the Pre-Academic Child* by Bangs (1968); *Psychopathology and Education of the Brain-Injured Child* by Strauss and Lehtinen (1947); *Teaching Educationally Handicapped Children* by Arena (1967); *Learning Disabilities* by Johnson and Myklebust (1967); *Educational Therapy* by Ashlock and Stephen (1966); *Teaching Reading to Individuals with Learning Difficulties* by Ashlock (1969); *Helping Children with Reading Disability* by Edgington (1968); *Teaching Children with Special Learning Needs* by Young (1967); *Auditory Learning* by Zigmond (1968); *Visual Learning* by Buktenica (1968); *Memory* by Hasterok (in press); *Methods for Learning Disorders* by Myers and Hammill (1969); *Aids to Psycholinguistic Teaching* by Bush and Giles (1969); and *Listening Aids* by Russell and Russell (1959).

academic instruction. The widely used term *perceptually handicapped child* stems from the abnormalities such children have with perception.

The perceptual activities suggested in this section are divided into the following categories: visual perception, auditory perception, haptic perception, and cross-modal perception. The teaching strategies are representative of activities that follow from conceptual models of perception and learning disabilities, and many additional teaching activities can be created. The classification of these activities is somewhat arbitrary, since many overlap with other processes and other areas of learning.

## VISUAL PERCEPTION

Numerous studies have established that visual perception is highly related to academic performance, particularly reading. Various authors and studies have found a number of visual perception subskills to be essential. Frostig (1968) identifies *five visual perception functions:* visual-motor coordination, figure-ground perception, perceptual constancy, perception of position in space, and perception of spatial relationships.

In a study of visual discrimination tasks as a predictor of first-grade reading achievement, Barrett (1965) concluded that *three visual discrimination tasks* make the strongest contribution to such a prediction: the ability to read letters and numbers; the ability to copy geometric patterns, and the ability to match printed words. DeHirsch's study (1966) similarly indicated that a number of visual perception tasks significantly contribute to a predictive reading index. They include the Bender *Visuo-Motor Gestalt Test,* word matching, letter matching, and word recognition. It is interesting to note that some of these highly predictive tasks are closer to the category of reading skills than to basic visual perception skills.

The implication of such studies is that direct teaching of visual perception leads to improvement in academic learning. Of course prediction of reading failure does not demonstrate cause and effect, and many of the factors found to be significant are not purely visual in nature. Nevertheless, direct teaching of visual perception skills appears to be a promising approach. Following is a collection of techniques designed to improve visual perception.

1. *Pegboard designs.* Reproduce colored visual geometric patterns to form the design on a pegboard using colored pegs.

2. *Parquetry blocks.* Have the child copy patterns using parquetry blocks.

3. *Block designs.* Using wood or plastic blocks that are all one color, or have faces of different colors, have the child match geometric shapes and build copies of models.

4. *Finding shapes in pictures.* Find all the round objects or designs in a picture. Find all the square objects, etc.

5. *Bead designs.* Copy or reproduce designs with beads on a string, or simply place shapes in varying patterns.

6. *Puzzles.* Have the child put together puzzles that are teacher-made or commercially made. Subjects such as people, animals, forms, numbers, or letters can be cut in pieces to show functional parts.

7. *Classification.* Have the child group or classify geometric shapes of varying sizes and colors. The figures may be cut out of wood or cardboard or be placed on small cards.

8. *Rubber-band designs.* Have the child copy geometric configurations with colored rubber bands stretched between rows of nails on a board.

9. *Worksheets.* Ditto sheets can be purchased (or teacher-made) that are designed to teach visual perception skills. Find the objects or shapes that are different, match the same objects, find objects in varying spacial positions, and separate the shapes and figures from the background. Some publishers put this material into workbooks. The use of an acetate cover is helpful if the workbook is to be re-used.

10. *Matching geometric shapes.* Place shapes on cards and play games requiring the matching of these shapes. Collect different sized jars with lids. Mix the lids and have the child match lids with jars.

11. *Dominoes.* Make a domino-type game by making sets of cards using sandpaper, felt, Contact, or painted dots to be matched.

11. *Playing cards.* A deck of playing cards provides excellent teaching material to match suits, pictures, numbers, and sets.

12. *Letters and numbers.* Visual perception and discrimination of letters is an important reading readiness skill. Games that provide opportunities to match, sort, or name shapes can be adapted to letters and numbers.

13. *Letter bingo.* Bingo cards can be made with letters. As letters are called, the child recognizes and covers up the letters.

14. *Finding missing parts.* Use pictures from magazines and cut off functional parts of the pictures. The child finds and fills in the missing parts from a group of missing parts.

14. *Visual perception of words.* The ability to perceive words is of course highly related to reading. Games of matching, sorting, grouping, tracing, and drawing geometric shapes and letters could be applied to words.

15. *Rate of perception.* Use a tachistoscope or flash cards to reduce the length of time that the child has to recognize pictures, figures, numbers, words.

16. *Far-point visual perception.* Use the overhead projector and a screen for far-point practice in visual perception. Shapes and letters can be cut out of colored transparencies. Overlays of background designs can be placed over shapes for background-foreground practice.

## AUDITORY PERCEPTION

Although more emphasis has been given to visual perception in building readiness skills, we are beginning to fully realize the crucial role auditory perception plays in learning. In order to design teaching strategies for building auditory perception skills, it is necessary to identify the subskills that make up auditory perception and to formulate a sequential hierarchy of these subskills. Messing (1968) has isolated eight categories of auditory perception skills. They are: auditory awareness, auditory focus, auditory figure-background, auditory discrimination, auditory memory, auditory scanning, auditory integration and synthesis, and auditory feedback. Flower (1968) identifies similar auditory processes: auditory sensitivity, auditory attending, auditory discrimination, auditory memory, auditory integration, auditory-visual integration. Flower suggests that such a hierarchy of auditory perception subskills presents certain inherent difficulties for designing both tests and teaching methods.

First, in both testing and teaching, each auditory subskill becomes contaminated with demands of other learning processes. A second difficulty has been that some children who are successful in academic performance fail certain auditory subtests. Third, the relationship between training in an auditory subskill and academic improvement has not yet been clearly established.

What has research shown about the relationship between deficits in auditory perception and academic achievement? DeHirsch's research (1966) showed that two auditory perception tasks made a significant contribution to the predictive reading index: the *Wepman Auditory Discrimination Test* and the *Imitation of Tapped-out Patterns Test.* It can be noted that these tests do not assess auditory perception solely, but also other learning processes such as short-term memory. Dykstra (1966) found that five auditory discrimination measures made a significant contribution to a prediction of reading achievement: (1) discrimination between spoken words which do or do not begin with identical sounds, (2) detection of rhyming elements at the ends of words, (3) identification of the correct pronunciation of words, (4) using auditory clues with context clues to identify strange words, and (5) recognizing similarities and differences in final consonants and rhymes. Again, these tests require other processes besides pure auditory perception. Research with the *Illinois Test of Psycholinguistic Abilities* indicates that reading disability cases do poorly in the subtests of auditory short-term memory, and grammatic closure.

In spite of the lack of clear-cut evidence showing cause-effect relationships and the impreciseness of our knowledge of the subskills that make up auditory perception, authorities do agree that auditory perception is an essential factor in learning and that children should be helped to acquire these skills. Following is a collection of teaching strategies designed to help children improve their auditory perception.

## Auditory Sensitivity to Sounds

1. *Listening for sounds.* Have the children close their eyes and become auditorily sensitive to environmental sounds about them. Sounds like cars, airplanes, animals, outside sounds, sounds in the next room, etc., can be attended to and identified.

2. *Recorded sounds.* Sounds can be placed on tape or records and the child is asked to identify them. Planes, trains, animals, and typewriters are some of the sounds that may be recorded.

3. *Teacher-made sounds.* Have the children close their eyes and identify sounds the teacher makes. Examples of such sounds include dropping a pencil, tearing a piece of paper, using a stapler, bouncing a ball, sharpening a pencil, tapping on a glass, opening a window, snapping the lights, leafing through pages in a book, cutting with scissors, opening a drawer, jingling money, or writing on a blackboard.

4. *Food sounds.* Ask the child to listen for the kind of food that is being eaten, cut, or sliced: celery, apples, carrots.

5. *Shaking sounds.* Place small hard items such as stones, beans, chalk, salt, sand, or rice into small containers or jars with covers. Have the child identify the contents through shaking and listening.

### Auditory Attending

6. *Attending for sound patterns.* Have the child close his eyes or sit facing away from the teacher. Clap hands, play a drum, bounce a ball, etc. Have the child tell how many counts there were or ask him to repeat the patterns made. Rhythmic patterns can be made for the child to repeat. For example: slow, fast, fast.

7. *Sound patterns on two objects* provides a variation on the above suggestion; for example, use a cup and a book to tap out sound patterns.

### Discrimination of Sounds

8. *Near or far.* With eyes closed, the child is to judge what part of the room a sound is coming from, and whether it is near or far.

9. *Loud or soft.* Help the child learn to judge and discriminate between loud and soft sounds.

10. *High and low.* The child learns to judge and discriminate between high and low sounds.

11. *Find the sound.* One child hides a music box or ticking clock and the other children try to find it by locating the sound.

12. *Follow the sound.* The teacher or a child blows a whistle while walking around the room. The child should try to follow the route taken through listening.

13. *Blindman's bluff.* One child in the group says something, like an animal sound, sentence, question, or phrase. The blindfolded child tries to guess who it is.

14. *Auditory figure-background.* To help a child attend to a foreground sound against simultaneous irrelevant environmental noises, have him listen for pertinent auditory stimuli against a background of music.

### Awareness of Phonemes or Letter Sounds

For success at the beginning stages of reading the child must perceive the individual phoneme sounds of the language, and he must learn to discriminate each language sound that represents a letter shape from other sounds. Such abilities are essential for decoding written language.

15. *Initial consonants.* Have the child tell which word begins like *milk.* Say three words like "astronaut, mountain, bicycle." Ask the child to think of words that begin like *Tom.* Find pictures of words that begin like *Tom,* or find pictures of words in magazines that begin with the letter *T.* Find the word that is different at the beginning: "paper, pear, table, past."

16. *Consonant blends, digraphs, endings, vowels.* Similar activities can be devised to help the child learn to auditorily perceive and discriminate other phonic elements.

17. *Rhyming words.* Learning to hear rhyming words helps the child recognize phonograms. Games similar to those for initial consonants can be used with rhyming words. Experience with nursery rhymes and poems that contain rhymes is useful.

18. *Riddle rhymes.* Make up riddles that rhyme. Have the child guess the last rhyming word. For example: "It rhymes with book. You hang your clothes on a _____."

19. Additional activities for the development of auditory perception of letter sounds and words are presented in Chapter 9 under listening skills.

## HAPTIC PERCEPTION: TACTILE AND KINESTHETIC SKILLS

For children who do not learn easily through the visual modality or the auditory modality, haptic perception provides an avenue for learning. The following activities are representative of activities designed to stimulate tactile and kinesthetic perception.

1. *Feeling various textures.* Have the child feel various textures such as smooth wood, metal, sandpaper, felt, flocking, sponge, wet surfaces, foods, etc.

2. *Touch boards.* These boards are made by attaching different materials to small pieces of wood. The child touches the boards without looking and learns to discriminate and match the various surfaces.

3. *Feeling shapes.* Various textures cut in geometric patterns or letters can be placed on boards and felt, discriminated, matched, identified through the tactile perception. These shapes can also be made of plastic, wood, cardboard, clay, etc.

4. *Feeling temperatures.* Fill small jars with water to touch to teach warm, hot, and cold.

5. *Feeling weights.* Fill small cardboard spice containers with beans, rice, etc., to different levels. Have the child match weights through shaking and sensing the weights.

6. *Smelling.* Put materials of distinctive scents in bottles, (cloves, cinnamon, vinegar, etc.). Have the child match the smells.

7. *Stereognosis.* Trace designs, numbers, or letters on the child's palm. Ask him to reproduce or to identify the shape he has felt.

8. *Identifying letters by feel.* Have the child learn to identify shapes, numbers, and letters by feeling them.

9. *Grab bag.* Put various objects in a bag or box. Have the child recognize the object through the sense of touch.

10. *Arranging sizes by feel.* Arrange geometric shapes of varying sizes according to size while blindfolded.

11. *Feel and match.* Match pairs of objects by feeling their shape and texture. Use a variety of textures pasted on pieces of wood, masonite, or plastic.

12. Additional activities for development of kinesthetic perception are included in Chapter 7 under body image and body awareness activities.

## CROSS-MODAL PERCEPTION

For many children the difficulty in learning is due to an inability to transfer information from one perceptual modality to another or an inability to integrate two perceptual modalities. Most academic tasks require such intersensory or cross-modal perception. Below are some activities which require two perceptual modalities to function jointly.

1. *Visual to auditory.* Look at a pattern of dots and dashes and repeat it in a rhythmical form on a drum.

2. *Auditory to visual.* Have the child listen to a rhythmical beat and select the matching visual pattern of dots and dashes from several alternatives.

3. *Auditory to motor-visual.* Have the child listen to a rhythmical beat and transfer it to a visual form by writing out matching dots and dashes.

4. *Auditory-verbal to motor.* Play a game similar to Simon Says. The child listens to commands auditorily and transfers commands to movements of body parts.

5. *Tactile to visual motor.* Have the child feel shapes in a box or under a covering and draw the shapes that are felt on a piece of paper.

6. *Auditory to visual.* Record and play sounds of common objects, pets, household appliances, etc., and ask the child to match the sounds with the appropriate picture from several alternatives.

7. *Beat out names.* Beat the syllables in the rhythm and accent of names of the children in the group. For example: Marilyn McPhergeson.

Drum beat: *Loud*–soft–soft   soft–*loud*–soft–soft

**1**   2   3    4   **1**   2   3

Have the children guess the name being played. Holidays or songs can also be used.

8. *Visual to auditory-verbal.* Have the child look at pictures. Ask: "Which begins with *F*? Which rhymes with *coat*? Which has a short *O* sound?"

9. *Auditory-verbal to visual.* Describe a picture to a child. Then have him choose the picture you were describing from several alternatives.

## Memory

Memory plays a key role in almost all kinds of learning. Memory refers to the ability to store information that has been sensed, perceived, and learned; and memory also refers to the ability to retrieve that information from storage when it is needed. Memory is discussed under a variety of terminologies and subskills: i.e., imagery, retrieval, memory span, auditory memory, visual memory, sequential or serial memory, immediate or short-term memory, and long-term memory. Moreover, it is difficult to discuss, test, or teach memory alone without involving other learning processes.

Because memory plays such a vital role in every aspect of learning, a disability in this function impedes many areas of learning. While there is little research evidence to verify that memory can be improved by practice, Chalfant and Scheffelin (1969) do suggest that it seems possible to expedite the storage and retrieval of specific kinds of information through improving techniques of selective observation, organization of materials, and repetition. The following teaching strategies are representative of activities designed to provide practice in memory tasks. The activities quite obviously overlap those in many other areas of learning.

### AUDITORY MEMORY

1. *Do this.* Place five or six objects in front of the child and give a series of directions to follow. For example: "Put the green block in Jean's lap; place the yellow flower under John's chair; and put the orange ball into Joe's desk." The list can be increased as the child improves in auditory memory.

2. *Following directions.* Give the child several simple tasks to perform. For example: "Draw a big red square on your paper, put a small green circle underneath the square, and draw a black line from the middle of the circle to the upper right-hand corner of the square. Such activities can be taped for use with earphones at a listening center.

3. Help the child hold in mind a list of numbers or single words. Start with two and ask him to repeat them. Gradually add to his list as he performs the task. At first a visual reminder in the form of a picture clue may be helpful.

4. The learning of nursery rhymes, poems, finger plays, etc., may be useful in developing auditory memory.

5. Give a series of numbers and ask the child to answer questions about the series. For example, "Write the fourth one: 3—8—1—9—4." Other directions could include the largest, smallest, closest to five, last, the one nearest your age, etc.

6. Ask the child to watch a television program and remember certain things. For example: "Watch *The Wizard of Oz* tonight and tomorrow tell me all the different lands that Dorothy visited."

7. *Going to the moon.* Update the game of "Grandmother's Trunk" or "Going to New York." Say, "I took a trip to the moon and took my space suit." The next child repeats the statement but adds one item, for example, "helmet." Pictures may be used to help with auditory memory.

## VISUAL MEMORY

8. Expose a collection of objects. Cover and remove one of the objects. Show the collection again, asking the child to identify the missing object.

9. Expose a geometrical design, letters, or numbers. Have the child select the appropriate one from several alternatives or reproduce the design on paper.

10. Expose a short series of shapes, designs, or objects. Have the child place another set of these designs in the identical order from memory. Playing cards, colored blocks, blocks with designs, or Mah-Jongg tiles are among the materials that might be used for such an activity.

11. Tachistoscopic exposure or flash cards can be used for recall of designs, digits, letters, or words that have been seen.

## REFERENCES

Arena, John I., ed. *Teaching Educationally Handicapped Children.* San Rafael, Calif.: Academic Therapy Publications, 1967.

Ashlock, Patrick. *Teaching Reading to Individuals with Learning Difficulties.* Springfield, Ill.: Charles C. Thomas, 1969.

Ashlock, Patrick, and Alberta Stephen. *Educational Therapy in the Elementary School.* Springfield, Ill.: Charles C. Thomas, 1966.

Ayres, Jean A. *Ayres Space Test. Southern California Figure-Ground Visual Perception Test. Southern California Kinesthetic and Tactile Perception Test.* Los Angeles: Western Psychological Services, 1969.

————. "Reading—A Product of Sensory Integrative Process," pp. 77–82 in Helen K. Smith (ed.), *Perception and Reading.* Newark, Del.: International Reading Association, 1968.

Baker, Harry J., and B. Leland. *Detroit Tests of Learning Aptitude.* Indianapolis: Bobbs, Merrill, 1935.

Bangs, Tina E. *Language and Learning Disorders of the Pre-Academic Child.* New York: Appleton-Century-Crofts, 1968.

Barrett, Thomas C. "Visual Discrimination Tasks as Predictors of First-Grade Reading Achievement," *Reading Teacher* 18 (January 1965): 276–282.

Beery, Keith E., and Norman Buktenica. *Developmental Test of Visual-Motor Integration.* Chicago: Follett Publishers, 1967.

Belmont, I., H. G. Birch, and E. Karp. "The Disordering of Intersensory and Intrasensory Integration by Brain Damage," *Journal of Nervous and Mental Diseases* 141 (1965): 410–418.

Bender, Lauretta. *Visual-Motor Gestalt Test and Its Clinical Use.* Research Monograph No. 3. New York: American Orthopsychiatric Association, 1938.

Benton, A. L. *The Revised Benton Visual Retention Test.* New York: Psychological Corporation, 1963.

Birch, Herbert G., and Lillian Belmont. "Auditory-Visual Integration in Normal and Retarded Readers," *American Journal of Orthopsychiatry* 34 (1964): 851–861.

Birch, Herbert G., and A. Lefford. "Intersensory Development in Children," *Monograph of the Society for Research in Child Development* 28 (1963): whole no. 89.

Buktenica, Norman. *Visual Learning.* San Rafael, Calif.: Dimensions Publishing Company, 1968.

Bush, Wilma Jo, and Marion T. Giles. *Aids to Psycholinguistic Teaching.* Columbus, Ohio: Charles E. Merrill, 1969.

Carroll, John B. "Psycholinguistics in the Study of Mental Retardation," pp. 38–53 in Schiefelbusch, Copeland, and Smith (eds.), *Language and Mental Retardation.* New York: Holt, Rinehart, and Winston, 1967.

Chalfant, James C., and Margaret A. Scheffelin. *Central Processing Dysfunction in Children: A Review of Research.* NINDS Monograph No. 9. Bethesda, Md.: U.S. Dept. of Health, Education, and Welfare, 1969.

Charcot, J. M. "New Lectures, 1886," in S. Freud (ed.), *On Aphasia.* New York: International Universities Press, 1953.

Cruickshank, Willam A., et al. *A Teaching Method for Brain Injured and Hyperactive Children.* Syracuse: Syracuse University Press, 1961.

DeHirsch, Katrina, et al. *Predicting Reading Failure.* New York: Harper & Row, 1966.

Durrell, Donald. *Improving Reading Instruction.* New York: Harcourt, Brace & World, 1956.

Dykstra, Robert. "Auditory Discrimination Abilities and Beginning Reading Achievement," *Reading Research Quarterly* Vol. I, No. 1 (Spring 1966): 5–34.

Edgington, Ruth. *Helping Children with Reading Disability.* Chicago: Developmental Learning Materials, 1968.

Eisenberg, Leon. "Psychiatric Implications of Brain Damage in Children," *Psychiatric Quarterly* 31 (1957): 72–92.

Fernald, Grace. *Remedial Techniques in Basic School Subjects.* New York: McGraw-Hill, 1943.

Flower, Richard M. "Auditory Disorders and Reading Disorders," in Flower, Gofman, and Lawson (eds.), *Reading Disorders.* Philadelphia: F. A. Davis 1965.

————. "The Evaluation of Auditory Abilities in the Appraisal of Children with Reading Problems," in Helen K. Smith (ed.), *Perception and Reading.* Newark, Del.: International Reading Association, 1968, pp. 21–24.

Frostig, Marianne. "Corrective Reading in the Classroom," *Reading Teacher* 18 (April 1965): 573–580.

————. "Education for Children with Learning Disabilities," Ch. 10 in H. Myklebust (ed.), *Progress in Learning Disabilities.* New York: Grune & Stratton, 1968.

Frostig, Marianne, et al. *The Marianne Frostig Developmental Test of Visual Perception.* Palo Alto, Calif.: Consulting Psychologists Press, 1964.

Gillingham, A., and B. Stillman. *Remedial Training for Children with Specific Disability in Reading, Spelling, and Penmanship,* 7th ed. Cambridge, Mass.: Educators Publishing Service, 1966.

Goins, Jean T. *Visual Perceptual Abilities and Early Reading Programs.* Supplementary Educational Monographs no. 87. Chicago: University of Chicago Press, 1958.

Graham, F., and B. Kendall. *Memory-for-Designs Test.* Missoula, Mont.: Psychological Test Specialists, 1960.

Hasterok, Gerald. *Memory.* San Rafael, Calif.: Dimensions Publishing Co., in press.

Hochberg, Julian. *Perception.* Englewood Cliffs, N.J.: Prentice-Hall, 1964.

Johnson, Doris, and H. Myklebust. *Learning Disabilities: Educational Principles and Practices.* New York: Grune & Stratton, 1967.

Ketchum, E. G. "Neurological and/or Emotional Factors in Reading Disability," pp. 521–526 in J. Figurel (ed.), *Vistas in Reading.* Newark, Del.: International Reading Association, 1967.

Kimmell, Geraldine M., and Jack Wahl. *The STAP (Screening Test for Auditory Perception).* San Rafael, Calif.: Academic Therapy Publications, 1969.

Kirk, Samuel, James McCarthy, and Winifred Kirk. *Illinois Test of Psycholinguistic Abilities,* rev. ed. Urbana, Ill.: University of Illinois Press, 1968.

Koppitz, Elizabeth. *Bender-Gestalt Test for Young Children.* New York: Grune & Stratton, 1964.

Luria, A. L. *Human Brain and Psychological Process.* New York: Harper & Row, 1966.

McCarthy, Jeanne M. Speech delivered for the Council on Understanding Learning Disabilities, April 1968, Deerfield, Illinois.

Magoun, H. W. "Commentary," pp. 199–201 in F. Darley and C. Millikan (eds.), *Brain Mechanisms Underlying Speech and Language*. New York: Grune & Stratton, 1967.

Messing, Eleanor S. "Auditory Perception: What Is It?" in John I. Arena (ed.), *Successful Programming: Many Points of View*. Fifth Annual Conference Proceedings, Association of Children with Learning Disabilities. San Rafael, Calif.: Academic Therapy Publications, 1969, pp. 439–452.

Meyers, Patricia, and Donald Hammill. *Methods for Learning Disorders*. New York: John Wiley, 1969.

Money, John. "The Laws of Constancy and Learning to Read," pp. 80–97 in *International Approach to Learning Disabilities of Children and Youth*, ACLD Conference. Tulsa, Okla.: Association of Children with Learning Disabilities, 1966.

Money, J., D. Alexander, and H. T. Walker, Jr. *A Standardized Road Map Test of Direction Sense*. Baltimore: Johns Hopkins Press, 1965.

Myklebust, Helmer. "Learning Disorders: Psychoneurological Disturbances in Childhood," *Rehabilitation Literature* 25 (December 1964): 354–360.

Nash, Ralph J., and Judith Pfeffer. *A Guide to a Special Class Program for Children with Learning Disabilities*. Chicago: Chicago Association for Children with Learning Disabilities (Box 4451, Chicago, Ill. 60680), 1967.

Paraskevopoulos, John N., and Samuel A. Kirk. *The Development and Psychometric Characteristics of the Revised Illinois Test of Psycholinguistic Abilities*. Urbana, Ill.: University of Illinois Press, 1969.

Piaget, J. *On the Development of Memory and Identity*. Barre, Mass.: Clark University Press, 1968.

Roswell, Florence, and Jeanne Chall. *Roswell-Chall Auditory Blending Test*. New York: Essay Press, 1963.

Russell, David, and E. Russell. *Listening Aids Through the Grades*. New York: Bureau of Publications, Teachers College, Columbia University, 1959.

Strauss, Alfred, and Laura Lehtinen. *Psychopathology and Education of the Brain-Injured Child*. New York: Grune & Stratton, 1947.

Sutphin, Florence A. *A Perceptual Testing and Training Handbook for First-Grade Teachers*. Winter Haven, Fla.: Winter Haven Lyons Research Foundations, 1964.

Valett, Robert E. *The Remediation of Learning Disabilities*. Palo Alto, Calif.: Fearon Publishers, 1967.

Van Witsen, Betty. *Perceptual Training Activities Handbook*. New York: Teachers College Press, Columbia University, 1967.

Vergason, Glenn A. "Facilitation of Memory in the Retardate," *Exceptional Children* 34 (April 1968): 589–594.

Wechsler, David. *Wechsler Intelligence Scale for Children*. New York: Psychological Corporation, 1949.

Wepman, Joseph. "The Modality Concept," pp. 1–6 in Helen K. Smith (ed.), *Perception and Reading*. Newark, Del.: International Reading Association, 1968.

_____. "The Perceptual Basis for Learning," pp. 25–43 in H. Alan Robinson (ed.), *Meeting Individual Differences in Reading*. Chicago: University of Chicago Press, 1964.

Wiseman, D. E. "A Classroom Procedure for Identifying and Remediating Language Problems," *Mental Retardation* 3 (1965): 20–24.

Young, Milton A. *Teaching Children with Special Learning Needs*. New York: John Day Co., 1967.

Zigmond, Naomi. *Auditory Learning*. San Rafael, Calif.: Dimensions Publishing Co., 1968.

# Chapter 9

# Language

This chapter is divided into four sections: the first examines several theories of language that have implications for learning disabilities; the remaining three sections present teaching strategies in three curricular areas of the language arts. Section two deals with listening and speaking, section three deals with reading, and section four, with the written language areas—writing and spelling.

# THEORY

Language is a wondrous thing—it has been said that language is what makes man Man. It follows that a language deficit may make man less than a man. A language disorder is a non-visible entity. It cannot be seen in the same manner that a crippling defect of the body can be seen. Yet its effects often are more pervasive and insidious than other acute organic defects.

. . . the greatest prevalence of learning disabilities are those in which language is involved. Because the processes of language have remained an enigma, the methods for training by necessity have been intuitive and empirical. They remain largely at this stage today, although perhaps at a sophisticated level of pragmatism. As the psychological and neurological [and linguistic factors] become more specifically identified, our competencies in the area of education and rehabilitation will increase proportionately.

This statement by McGrady (1968) expresses perceptively the idea that language plays a vital role in learning, and that consequently an intimate relationship exists between learning disabilities and deficits in language development.

Language has been recognized as one of man's greatest achievements—more important than all the physical tools invented in the last two thousand years. The acquisition of language is unique to man. Although the lower animals have developed communication systems, only humans have attained the most highly developed system of communication—speech.

Language fulfills several functions for man: it provides man with a means to communicate and socialize with his fellow man; it enables him to transmit the culture from generation to generation; and it becomes a vehicle of thought. Langer (1958) describes these qualities of language well:

Language is . . . the most momentous and at the same time the most mysterious product of the human mind. Between the clearest animal call of love or warning of danger and man's least trivial *word,* there lies a whole day of Creation—or in modern phrase, a whole chapter of evolution. In language we have the free accomplished use of symbolism, the record of articulate conceptual thinking; without language there seems to be nothing like explicit thought whatever.

In spite of our awareness of its importance to mankind, language remains mysterious and relatively little is known about it. How is it acquired by the child? What is the connection between language and the thinking process? What is the interrelationship between symbolic language and other components of human development, such as motor, perceptual, conceptual, and social learnings? What is the relationship between language development and learning disabilities?

Are there universals among the various languages of our world? These questions are among the areas of concern and study for a number of language-related professions, including the fields of linguistics, language pathology, language arts and communications specialties, and psycholinguistics.

## Language and Learning

Many kinds of learning are dependent upon language development and the individual's facility with verbal symbols. The ability to grasp the abstract appears to be highly related to one's mastery of language. Two examples of learning that is limited by language differences or deficiencies appear in research studies of inner-city children and of deaf children.

The language of the inner-city child is significantly different from the standard English spoken by middle-class children. Differences have been noted in vocabulary, dialect, and grammatical structures. While some scholars view nonstandard language as a *deficit* form of English, others view nonstandard language as a different but equal language system.

From the language-deficit viewpoint, the language of the inner-city child is a "restricted code," and this limitation impedes further learning (Bernstein 1964). As a consequence the child is not verbally equipped for the kind of language proficiency required in the classroom. Bloom (1965) observed that the parents of inner-city youngsters are not as likely to provide the kind and amount of verbal "corrective feedback" found in typical middle-class environments.

From the language-difference viewpoint, inner-city children have a fully developed language system that is functionally adequate and structurally systematic. There is a *language difference,* not a language deficiency (Baratz 1969).

Whether the language of the inner-city child is viewed as a *difference* or a *deficit,* there is a mismatch between his language and the language he is expected to have in school. It is estimated that a good beginning reader at age 6 has a speaking vocabulary of 2,500 to 8,000 words; whereas the inner-city child at age 6 has been judged to have a speaking vocabulary of less than 500 words, which is equivalent to that of an average 3-year-old in a more favored environment (Kravitz 1966). In a reading test recently administered to inner-city pupils in a major city, fifth-grade pupils scored at the 18th to 20th percentile, while eighth-grade inner-city pupils scored at the 13th to 16th percentile. The norm for the city as a whole was at about 50th percentile (Black 1967). It should be noted that such tests may be culturally biased in that they reflect middle-class language and values. However, such studies do indicate that one consequence of a language mismatch is that children with such problems fall further and further behind. Two solutions have been proposed. One is to help such youngsters secure a broad oral language base before introducing them to more complex language skills such as reading. The other proposed solution is to change the learning media and materials for the child with different language. Baratz (1969) suggests teaching the inner-city child to read by using his own language as the basis for initial readers. In other words, first teach the child to read, then teach him to read in standard English.

The deaf child is unable to develop speech and language through the avenues of casual hearing or listening. Consequently, his ability to develop concepts is substantially affected. Research reveals that the educational achievement level of the deaf child is three or four years below that of the hearing child. As a result of his deficiency in development of verbal language functions, the intelligence quotient of the average deaf child is about ten points lower than that of the hearing child (Pinter, Eisenson, and Stanton 1945).

The role of language in thinking has been examined by such scholars as Vygotsky (1962), Piaget (1952), and Luria (1961); yet the relationship is still not fully understood. Even so, we do know that as language develops, it plays an increasingly important part in thinking processes. Words become the symbols for objects and classes of objects, and for ideas. Language permits us to speak of things unseen, of the past, and of the future. It is a tool that helps us to learn, retain, recall, and transmit information, and to control our environment.

One of the most dramatic illustrations of the dependency of language on thought is the experience of Helen Keller as she became aware that things have symbolic names that represent them. The impact of this discovery, made at age 7, changed her behavior from that of an intractable, undisciplined animal to that of a language-oriented human being. Her teacher Anne Sullivan described the events (Keller 1961, pp. 273–274):

> I made Helen hold her mug under the spout while I pumped. As the cold water gushed forth, filling the mug, I spelled "w-a-t-e-r" in Helen's free hand. The word coming so close upon the sensation of cold water rushing over her hand seemed to startle her. She dropped the mug and stood as one transfixed. A new light came into her face. She spelled "water" several times. Then she dropped on the ground and asked for its name and pointed to the pump and the trellis and suddenly turning around she asked for my name. . . . All the way back to the house she was highly excited, and learned the name of every object she touched, so that in a few hours she had added thirty new words to her vocabulary.

Helen Keller also described the transformation caused by her own awareness of language as follows (Keller 1961, p. 34):

> As the cool water gushed over one hand she spelled into the other the word *water*, first slowly, then rapidly. I stood still, my whole attention fixed upon the motion of her fingers.
> Suddenly I felt a misty consciousness as of something forgotten—a thrill of returning thought; and somehow the mystery of language was revealed to me. I knew then that "w-a-t-e-r" meant the wonderful, cool something that was flowing over my hand. That living word awakened my soul, gave it light, hope, joy, set it free. . . . I left the well-house eager to learn. Everything had a name, and each name gave birth to a new thought.

Helen Keller had learned that a word can be used to signify objects and to order the events, ideas, and meaning of the world about her. Language had become a tool for her to use.

One other dramatic illustration of the effects of the lack of language development is the case of Victor, the "wild boy of Aveyron" (Itard 1962). Victor was captured in southern France in 1800 at about the age of 12, after living alone as an animal in the forest of Aveyron. He had no concept of language and his behavior was totally uncontrolled and animal-like. Itard, a physician and one of the early workers interested in special education, tried to humanize Victor by teaching him language skills. Although some minimal learning took place after

Itard had worked with him for five years, Victor was never able to develop language skills and did not reach a level of behavior that could be termed "human." Many explanations of Victor's inability to learn have been suggested, but the lack of language acquisition undoubtedly was an important element.

It is interesting to note that much of our knowledge of language development comes through the observation of exceptional children and their language deviations. The balance of this section looks at language from the viewpoints of four different language professionals: the language arts specialist, the language pathologist, the linguist, and the psycholinguist.

## The Language Arts

Within the school setting, the language arts specialist is concerned with all curriculum areas related to language: listening, oral language, reading, writing, and spelling. His responsibilities include materials, methods, and the organization of these curriculum areas for all children in the school. Although his concern is primarily the developmental language arts program of the entire school, the language arts specialist also has rich contributions to make to the understanding of children with language and learning disabilities and to the development of programs for the atypical child. Analysis of the relationship of the various areas of the language arts is one such contribution.

The *language arts* encompass the curriculum activities that utilize language—namely, listening, speaking, reading, and writing. Some writers also add the communication elements of gesturing to this list. An examination of the interrelations of these elements of the language arts has many implications for teaching children with learning disabilities.

For most human beings the acquisition of these skills follows a hierarchy of development: (1) listening, (2) speaking, (3) reading, and (4) writing (Mackintosh 1964). A firm foundation is required at each level before the next skill level can be effectively added or integrated. In the historical development of communication skills, the oral language skills of listening and speaking were developed hundreds of thousands of years before the development of the written skills of reading and writing. The written form of language is relatively recent, and many civilizations even today have only a spoken language and no written form. Kellogg (1967) illustrated the hierarchical relationship between the elements of the language arts in the diagram shown in Figure 9.1.

Since man develops the *oral* language skills of listening and speaking first, they are referred to as the primary language system; reading and writing are referred to as a secondary language system. In reading, we are dealing with a symbol of a symbol. While the spoken word is a symbol of an idea, the written word is a symbol of the spoken word. Helen Keller is said to have considered finger spelling as her primary language system because she learned it first, and braille as a secondary system.

Two of the four elements of the language arts can be categorized as *input* or *receptive* skills while the other two elements are *output* or *expressive* skills. Listening and reading are input or receptive skills, feeding data into the central nervous system. Speaking and writing, which are output or expressive skills, originate data in the brain and send it out.

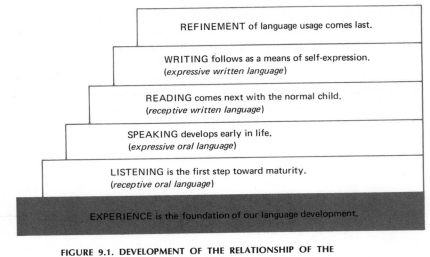

FIGURE 9.1. DEVELOPMENT OF THE RELATIONSHIP OF THE
ELEMENTS OF THE LANGUAGE ARTS
From Ralph E. Kellogg. "Listening," in Pose Lamb (ed.) *Guiding Children's
Language Learning.* Dubuque, Iowa: William C. Brown, 1967, p. 128.

One implication of these categories for teaching is that a large quantity of
input experience and information is necessary before output skills can be effectively executed. This principle has been concisely stated by Dawson (1963)
as *"intake before outgo"* or input precedes output. Language arts specialists
warn against assigning a child to produce output, such as a written theme, before
he has been exposed to adequate input experiences—such as discussions, field
trips, reading, and other media. These experiences will enhance the productivity
of the output, the written composition. The integrating mechanism between the
input and output is the brain or central nervous system. The integrating process
is often referred to as "the black box." The relationship between input and output
skills is diagrammed in Figure 9.2.

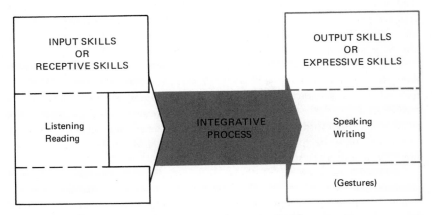

FIGURE 9.2. RELATIONSHIP OF THE FOUR ELEMENTS OF
LANGUAGE ARTS

## THE COMMUNICATION PROCESS

In terms of a communication model, as shown in Figure 9.3, the skills of listening and speaking are described as *decoding* functions whereas speaking and writing are seen as *encoding* functions. In the model, individual A is transmitting an idea to individual B. Individual A must convert his idea into language symbols. He puts it into a coded form, that is, he *encodes* the message into sound symbols (speaking) or visual graphic symbols (writing). Individual B who receives the message must then convert the symbols back into an idea. He *decodes* the sound symbols (listening) or he decodes the visual symbols (reading).

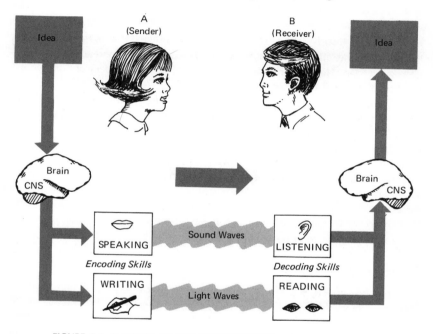

**FIGURE 9.3. A MODEL OF THE COMMUNICATION PROCESS**

The implications of this communication model for language and learning disorders are great. A breakdown could occur anywhere along this process. For example, in the encoding portion of the communication process, the impairment could be in the stage of formulating the idea, in encoding it into spoken and written language symbols, in the memory or sequences of previous symbolic experiences, in the brain signals to the motor mechanism used in speaking or writing. In the decoding portion of the communication process, the impairment could be in the reception and perception of the symbols through the eye or the ear, in the integration of these stimuli in the brain, or in the recall or memory as it affects the ability to translate the sensory images into an idea.

The focus of the language arts specialist, then, is upon the normal language development of the child and the language curriculum of the school. The purpose of analyzing the relationship of various elements of the language arts and communication is to enhance the language arts program and language development in the regular curriculum for all the children in the school. The concern of the language pathologist, however, is that of atypical language development.

## Language Pathology

Language pathology is the study of the causes and treatment of disorders of symbolic verbal behavior (McGrady 1968). Because the experience and education of the language pathologist are likely to be rooted in the field of speech, his areas of expertise include knowledge of developmental speech in the normal child, the kinds and degrees of hearing and speech disorders, the pathology of the ear and speech organs, and the fields of acoustics and phonetics (Hardy 1966). The concern of the speech pathologist is primarily the abnormalities of articulation; however, the concern of the language pathologist is much broader, encompassing disorders of the entire spectrum of communication and verbal behavior.

The language pathologist warns that many children in our schools probably suffer from some form of language disorder. The problem of some children is in receiving symbolic auditory information or in listening; others have difficulty using auditory verbal symbols or speaking; and others have difficulty in reading or writing language. The 3-year-old who does not appear to understand simple directions, the 4-year-old who has not yet learned to speak, or the 10-year-old who cannot read or write may have a language disorder. There is growing evidence that auditory and language deficiencies are extremely important factors in learning difficulties, and these factors have been neglected in comparison to the emphasis given to visual aspects of learning.

### LANGUAGE DISORDERS

Man has developed two forms of communication through language symbols: oral or auditory language and the written language. The chief interest of the language pathologist is in disorders of the oral language—the auditory form of symbols. A number of writers have suggested that a useful way to categorize auditory language development is as *inner language, receptive language,* and *expressive language.* Such an arrangement has been found useful for discussion of language deficits by McCarthy (1964), Schiefelbusch *et al.* (1967), Wood (1959), and Myklebust (1965). A language disorder can occur in any of these developmental stages of auditory language development.

**Inner language disorders.**   The first level of linguistic learning refers to the preverbal ability to internalize and organize experiences, the antecedents of language and speaking. This process has been referred to as "inner speech" by Vygotsky (1962), "pre-operational thought" by Piaget (1952), "inner symbolic manipulation of reality" by Flavell *et al.* (1963), "central language" by Richardson (1967), and "inner language" by Myklebust (1964). A disorder at this level refers to the inability to assimilate experiences. For example, the child may not be able to organize doll furniture or doll families into a meaningful play situation, or he may be unable to associate the sound of a bark with a dog. A disorder at this level is the most severe form of language disturbance.

**Receptive language disorders.** The process of understanding verbal symbols is called *receptive language* (Spradlin 1967), and a disorder of this process is termed receptive aphasia (Kleffner 1964, McGrady 1968). It is thought that language reception is a prerequisite for the development of expressive language.

A child may be deficient in any of the subskills of receptive language. Spradlin (1967) suggests that some children are unable to discriminate between the pitch levels of two tones (tone discrimination), and others cannot discriminate or blend isolated single letter sounds (phonemic discrimination). Another type of receptive language skill which some children lack is the ability to discriminate small word parts within a sentence (morphemic discrimination)—such as the "z" sound difference between "the cows ate grass" and "the cow ate grass."

Some children are unable to understand the meaning of even a single word. Others have difficulty with more complex units of speech such as sentences or longer speech units. A child with receptive language problems may be able to understand single words such as *sit, chair, eat, candy*; but he has difficulty understanding sentences using the words: for example, "Sit on the chair after you eat the candy." Some children understand a word in one context but are unable to relate it to another context. The word *run* may be understood as a method of locomotion; but the child cannot get the meaning when it is used in reference to something in baseball, a faucet, a lady's stocking, or a river. *Echolalia*, the behavior of repeating words or sentences in parrot-like fashion, without understanding the meaning, is another form of receptive aphasia.

**Expressive language disorders.** The process of producing spoken language is called *expressive language* (Spradlin 1967), and a disorder in this process is called *expressive aphasia* (Kleffner 1964, Johnson and Myklebust 1967). Children with this disorder may depend upon pointing and gesturing to make their wants known. The child with an expressive language disorder can understand speech and language when he hears it—he does not have a muscular paralysis that prevents speaking—and he may do well on nonverbal tasks; yet he is poor in the skill of speaking.

There are a number of clinical conditions of expressive language discussed by language pathologists (Johnson and Myklebust 1967). *Dysnomia* refers to a deficiency in remembering and expressing what words sound like. The child may substitute a word like *thing* for every object he cannot remember, or he may attempt to use other expressions to talk around the subject. For example, when asked to list the foods she ate for lunch, one 10-year-old girl used circumlocution in describing a "round red thing that rhymed with potato," but she was unable to remember the word *tomato*. Some children remember the sound of the word, but they cannot at will move or manipulate their speech musculature to make the appropriate sounds, even though they do not have a paralysis. The condition is described as a type of *apraxia*. In another type of expressive aphasia, a child is able to speak single words or short phrases, but he has difficulty in formulating complete sentences. Many of the children in our schools who speak in single words or short phrases are not recognized as having a language disorder.

The language pathologist studies the nature, causes, and treatment of all language disorders in both children and adults. He analyzes normal language development so that he can better understand and treat abnormalities in language function. Another group of scientists, the linguists, study the problem from a different perspective. Linguistics is an intensive study of language itself.

## Linguistics

Linguistics can be defined as the scientific study of the nature and function of human language. Concepts from the field of linguistics are being applied to every area of the language arts. The impact of the application of linguistics on the teaching of listening, speaking, reading, writing, spelling, grammar, and usage may rival the revolution we have recently witnessed in the mathematics curriculum. Linguists are primarily interested in the study of aspects of language itself. Their prime concern is *not* in education or teaching, nor is it necessarily in the application of linguistic findings to the school curriculum. Therefore, educators who wish to incorporate linguistics in educational programs must be knowledgeable in both linguistics and education in order to design and implement workable programs. It seems axiomatic that any professional concerned with language learning or disorders must be well acquainted with the discipline of the science of language.

The linguist uses the methodology and objectivity of the scientist in his investigation and analysis of linguistic phenomena. Early linguists were anthropologists who found that to make an intensive study of a particular culture they needed to understand the language of that culture. The anthropological linguists devised systems such as the International Phonetic Alphabet (IPA) to permit phonetic transcriptions of languages under investigation. Historical and comparative linguists played important roles in the study of language by tracing the historical development of language and by comparing common elements of various languages.

Later, American linguists directed their attention toward the scientific study of American English. Using the tools and technology of earlier linguistic scholars, they developed a framework to describe the structure of the American English language. *Structural linguists* have focused on problems of usage and dialectology. Two groups of linguists concerned with understanding the underlying rules of the American English language are the *structural linguists* and the *generative-transformational linguists.*

Linguistics, then, is the study of the patterns of language systems, the nature of language, its development, its function, and the way it is manipulated. One cannot look at linguistics as a method of teaching, but rather as a scientific approach to the understanding of all language in all its forms.

## LINGUISTICS AND LEARNING

For the teacher of the child with learning disabilities a number of linguistic attitudes and perspectives are pertinent. The linguist urges that teachers develop a fresh attitude toward language. Language should be viewed as a dynamic, living, changing tool, responsive to the needs and circumstances of the people using it, rather than as a static, unchanging, prescribed set of rules. The American branch of the English language, which our children use, has many variations. The linguist encourages a new respect for various dialects and an acceptance of a variety of language forms. A child's own language is, indeed, as close to him as his skin; and it is one of the most important links he has with the outside world. The importance of the child's own language can be appreciated when we realize that it provides one of the few starting points in the educative process. Linguistic science is forcing us to question many of our traditional values and assumptions about language and the teaching of language—assumptions held for so long that they have been placed in the category of principles, truths, and rules.

## LINGUISTIC CONCEPTS

A few basic linguistic concepts and terms are essential for today's teacher of language. Linguists have thought of language as having a number of systems; i.e., *phonology, morphology, syntax,* and *intonation.*

*Phonology* is the system of speech sounds in a language. The smallest unit of sound is a *phoneme.* Different languages and dialects utilize different phonemes. For example, the word *cat* contains three phonemes: k / ae / t. Phoneme recognition is important in learning to read as well as in oral language. The recognition, analysis, and synthesis of phoneme elements in written words, often referred to as *phonics,* is difficult for some children.

*Morphology* is the system of meaning units in a language. The smallest unit of meaning is a *morpheme.* Different languages indicate meaning changes through different morphological forms. In standard English, for example, the word *boy* is one morpheme or meaning unit; and the word *boys* contains two morphemes or meaning units (*boy* plus plurality). The child who does not internalize the morphemic structure of standard English might say, "There are three boy."

*Syntax* refers to the grammar system of language—the way the words are strung together to form sentences. Different languages have developed different syntactic or grammatical systems. In the English language (unlike some other languages), word order is extremely important to convey meaning. Thus, "John pushes a car" has a different meaning from "A car pushes John." A child with a syntactic language disorder may not have learned how to order words in a sentence. Further, in English, we can transform the order of the words—still keeping the same subject—to generate a new meaning: the sentence "Mother is working" can be transformed to generate "Is Mother working?" The child with a syntactic language disorder may be unable to generate such sentence transformations. In one research study (Spradlin 1967), when children with language disorders were asked to repeat the question form of "Is the boy running?" many repeated the simple declarative form, "The boy is running."

Gleason (1965) categorizes different ways of analyzing grammar into three groups: traditional grammar, structural grammar, and generative-transformationalist grammar. Each has different implications for teaching language. Recent research emerging from the generative-transformational approach differentiates two ways of considering the structure of sentences: *surface structure* and *deep structure.* Surface structure refers to the actual string of words that is heard or read, which provides a superficial view of the sentence. Deep structure refers to the underlying basic elements and relationships that are embedded in a sentence, even though these concepts are not actually represented by words. To fully comprehend the language, the listener or reader must understand both the surface structure and the deep structure and be able to relate one to the other.

The *intonation system* refers to the pitch (melody), stress (accent), and juncture (pauses) of a spoken language. The intonation system of each language is different. An example of intonational differences is the difference between the sound of "White House" (where the President of the United States lives) and "white house" (to designate the house where John lives). Children who have been unable to capture the intonation system of English may speak in a monotone without expression.

It is interesting to note that none of the analytic systems of linguistics is developed around the unit of the *word*. The *word* as a unit of language assumes greater importance in written language than in the oral form. In fact, beginning readers are often confused by single words because the oral language does not sound the way the written form looks. One child could not comprehend the meaning when he read the individual words of the sentence, "I want to go to the store." He did not hear each of those individual words as discrete entities when the sentence was spoken orally. Goodman (1968) explains that the linguist's concern is primarily the study of *oral* language. Words are conventional units of written language separated by white space, but they do not really exist separately in speech. This discrepancy proves to be a problem for at least some children who have difficulty bridging the gap between the written language and the auditory form that they know.

## LINGUISTICS AND CHILD DEVELOPMENT

Children, as they learn to understand the verbalizations of others and to respond in a meaningful way, are normally able to internalize these language systems by the time they reach school age (Carroll 1966). As linguists investigate these systems, they try to understand what the child already knows. Such knowledge should be invaluable to the language pathologist and the language arts specialist.

Some linguists have recently focused attention on the mystery of the acquisition of language. The work of the generative-transformationalists (Chomsky 1965) has touched upon topics that also concern specialists in learning disabilities. Two important problems for the generative-transformationalists are: What is it about language that enables a child to learn it, internalize it, and use it? and, What is it about the child that permits him to learn the language? In the words of Noam Chomsky (1965, p. 27):

> What are the initial assumptions concerning the nature of language that the child brings to language learning, and how detailed and specific is the innate scheme (the general definition of "grammar") that gradually becomes more explicit and differentiated as the child learns the language?

In the process of learning a language, the child has a limited number of primary linguistic experiences. At a rather young age he hears speech, and he begins to understand and repeat certain words and sentences. From these definite and limited experiences, he is soon able to understand new sentences that he may never have heard before. He is also able to produce new sentences that he may never have heard. To add to this mystery, children in all cultures have the ability to perform this feat in their native language at about the same chronological and developmental stage. By the time he enters school, the child who has developed along a normal linguistic pattern uses language relatively as well as the adults in his immediate environment. He uses and understands almost all the common sentence patterns. Carroll (1966, p. 577) notes this fascinating characteristic of language learning:

> The process by which children learn their native language is in many respects a mystery. . . . The "average" or "normal" child who is reared in a sufficiently rich linguistic environment has usually mastered all the essential parts of the system by the time he is age six or seven. The fact that he is able to utter and comprehend thousands of sentences that he has never heard before is evidence of this accomplishment.

As the transformational linguist views language acquisition, the child learning a language does not merely learn a set of sentences, but rather he has learned to internalize the total language system in understanding and making new sentences. The task of the linguist is to analyze the process of language learning and producing. Such knowledge should be of great value to the learning disabilities specialist.

Chomsky (1967) suggests that the transition in language learning from the simplest stages of comprehension and expression to the stage at which the child uses a complex mechanism of language is so rapid that accurate notation of the child's language acquistion and development by observation alone is virtually impossible; and the little that can be observed is not very enlightening. In that brief period of transition, the child suddenly learns to use the mechanisms of grammar. Because it is impossible to observe *how* the child normally acquires language, the teacher of language and speech should have an understanding of the nature of language itself or of linguistics. According to Chomsky, the task of learning human language is so complex that some important aspects of language cannot be learned but are innate within the brain. This theory views language learning as similar to learning to walk; rather than being completely acquired, some aspects of spoken language "unfold" or "flower" under appropriate developmental and environmental circumstances.

Several research studies on the acquisition and development of language by children have emerged from the Chomsky and generative-transformational theories of linguistics (Menyuk 1969, Berko 1958, Bellugi and Brown 1964). Research tools to analyze children's language were developed through such studies and they provide valuable data about children who develop language in a normal manner as well as those who develop language in a deviant manner. The information obtained from such work promises to provide important guidelines for teaching children with language disabilities.

The remedial aspect of the field of linguistics is related to another important area of study for the teaching of children with learning disabilities—the field of *psycholinguistics*.

## Psycholinguistics

Psycholinguistics, as the name implies, is a field of study that blends aspects of two disciplines: psychology and linguistics. In a sense these two disciplines view opposite ends of the language or communication process. Whereas the linguist studies the *output* of the process, the language itself, the psychologist is interested in the *input,* the factors causing the speaker to say certain words at a particular time. Psycholinguistics is a field of study that attempts to look at the total picture of the language process, rather than only one facet of it.

Gleason (1965, p. 61) forecast that this cross-fertilization between linguistics and psychology will have important implications for understanding language learning in children. Neither discipline by itself has been able to develop a complete perspective of the language learning process.

> The recent research of child-language specialists has shown that both views were seriously oversimplified. The process of learning a language is far more complex than either had imagined. The educator has erred, basically, in assuming a far too simple notion of language; the linguists underestimated the complexity of the learning process; the layman, of course, failed at both points.

Because psycholinguistics encompasses many points of view, it serves as a discipline that brings together the many segmented fields studying various aspects of language and learning. The goal of psycholinguistics is to develop an understanding and explanation of language processing. Several promising developments in psycholinguistics which are related to learning disabilities are discussed in this section.

## READING AND THE PSYCHOLINGUISTIC PROCESS

One facet of language that has been analyzed within a psycholinguistic framework is the area of reading. Reading and speaking are obviously two vastly different language modes. While reading is a way of receiving or decoding the language of others, speaking is a way of encoding or expressing ideas through language. It is much easier to observe what is happening when the individual speaks than what is happening when the individual reads. Although a child who is reading may be asked comprehension questions, the examiner finds it very difficult to determine from only the responses how the child is processing language as he reads.

Several developments in analyzing the reading process from a psycholinguistic framework seem promising. A psycholinguistic analysis of the errors or miscues in oral reading suggest that the reader's underlying language patterns, including syntax and meaning, play an important role in reading. Goodman (1967, 1969) views reading as a psycholinguistic guessing game, involving an interaction between thought and language ability in anticipating what is to come. That is, the reader must develop skill in selecting the fewest and most productive psycholinguistic cues necessary to provide guesses about the words. Therefore, an analysis of the errors or miscues gives insight into the ongoing psycholinguistic processes of the reader (Burke and Goodman 1970).

Deighton (1968) has observed that, during the reading process, the reader cannot complete the thought until the final word or phrase. For example, in the two phrases "the little white pebble" and "the little understood theory," the word *little* connotes something quite different in each phrase. The reader cannot know the meaning of the word, or sometimes even the pronunciation, until the end of the phrase or sentence. In English the meaning of the beginning is dependent upon the end. The flow of thought in English is not left to right, but in many cases circular. Although the eye goes from left to right, the mind does not. Certain ideas and words must be held until some part of the sentence permits the completion of the thought. For example, "When *Lee* looked at the *note* again, he realized that he should have played a sharp." The meaning of *note* and the gender of *Lee* must be kept in abeyance until the end of the sentence provides the clarification. In the following example, a decision about pronunciation cannot be made until the end of the sentence: "John had *tears* in his shirt."

An interesting study of the psycholinguistic processes underlying reading was made by Beaver (1968). In this study children were given material to read orally and their errors in reading were carefully noted. Psycholinguistic analysis of the errors revealed that many were not phonic or phonological shortcomings. Most of the errors (about four-fifths of his sample) were other kinds of linguistic errors, such as morphological or syntactic errors. Beaver reasoned that the process going on when a person reads is decoding, but also a kind of retroactive encoding. The reader scans the syntactic structure of the sentence, passes the whole back through his own grammar or language rules, and then interprets it within his own grammar or language system. However, his own language system may not correspond to the actual syntactic system of the text. Examples of such errors are:

Text: I am Tiphia, servant *to* Mighty Gwump.
Reader: I am Tiphia, servant *of* Mighty Gwump.

Text: Now he had been *caught.*
Reader: Now he had been *catched.*

Text: Bobby's team *was* the Wildcats.
Reader: Bobby's team *were* the Wildcats.

Text: I *have taken* the book.
Reader: I *has took* the book.

Such studies suggest that not only must the reader decode the words and language of the writer, but he must recode the ideas into his own language pattern to get meaning. The errors are not in decoding the author's language but in recoding it into the reader's linguistic patterns. Any system of teaching reading which is oblivious to underlying psycholinguistic processes is missing an essential element of reading.

A technique called the "cloze procedure" has been used by some reading researchers to discover the psycholinguistic processes underlying the reading act (Rankin 1965, Weaver 1965, Bormuth 1968). The cloze procedure is based on the Gestalt idea of closure—the impulse to complete a structure and make it whole by supplying a missing element. The procedure is applied to the reading process as follows: every "nth" word in a printed passage is omitted and the reader is asked to make closure by supplying the missing words. Because words are deleted at random, both *lexical* words and *structural* words are omitted. In the linguistic framework, lexical words carry primary meaning and are roughly similar to the verbs, nouns, adjectives, and adverbs. The structural words consist of those words which indicate relationships, such as articles, prepositions, conjunctions, and auxiliary verbs. Thus, the reader's closure must bridge gaps in both language and thought; what the reader supplies gives clues to his underlying psycholinguistic processes.

Although this technique has thus far been used by only a small group of reading specialists, it has unexplored possibilities for language research, diagnosis, and instruction (Spache 1968). The procedure has been used successfully as a test of reading comprehension, as a measure of readability or assessment of the difficulty level of a reading selection, and as a method of improving reading. Bormuth (1968, p. 435) described the following steps for the cloze procedure in measuring readability of a reading selection:

1. Passages are selected from the material which is being evaluated.
2. Every fifth word in the passage is deleted and replaced by an underlined blank of a standard length.
3. The tests are duplicated and given, without time limits, to students who have *not* read the passages from which the tests were made.
4. The students are instructed to write in each blank the word they think was deleted.
5. Responses are scored correct when they exactly match the words deleted (minor misspellings are disregarded).

This technique has been reported to be a valid means of measuring the readability level (comprehension difficulty) of passages as well as a reliable measure of reading comprehension. One advantage of the cloze test over the conventional reading test or other "fill-in-the-blank" tests is that the words deleted are randomly selected; therefore, they may represent either lexical words or structural words.

The cloze procedure may have possibilities in probing other psycholinguistic abilities (Hafner 1965). An analysis of why an individual fails to supply the missing words may be used to measure listening ability, to analyze the role of reasoning in reading, to diagnose the student's skills with both structural and lexical linguistic components, to gather information on cognitive styles, and to supply information on the human brain as an information storage and retrieval system.

## ILLINOIS TEST OF PSYCHOLINGUISTIC ABILITIES

One of the standardized testing instruments for assessing underlying psycholinguistic abilities is the *Illinois Test of Psycholinguistic Abilities* (ITPA) (Kirk, McCarthy and Kirk 1968). The purpose of the ITPA is to isolate individual underlying psycholinguistic functions and to evaluate each of them separately. The use and interpretation of the ITPA is discussed in greater detail in Chapter 4.

In summary, the study of the psycholinguistic processes underlying learning is a relatively new but challenging and promising area of study. Psycholinguistics has an important role to play in our understanding of language and learning.

## Summary: Language and Learning

This section has approached learning disabilities from the perspectives of four language-related professions: language arts, language pathology, linguistics, and psycholinguistics. Language plays a vital role in the learning process. Further, language disorders almost always result in a learning disability.

The language arts specialist is concerned with the development of language as it affects academic work. Four elements of language—listening, speaking, reading, and writing—were analyzed and their relationship discussed. The dependency of written language communication skills (reading and writing) upon a sound and firm foundation of oral language development (listening and speaking) was emphasized.

The language pathologist studies the causes and treatment of disorders of symbolic verbal behavior. This subsection discussed the kinds of language disorders that are found in children with learning disabilities.

Linguistics is the scientific study of the nature of language. Several basic linguistic concepts were discussed. Professionals who propose to teach language or treat language disorders should know something about the nature of language —the field of linguistics.

The psycholinguist is interested in the complete communication process— the underlying psychology of language as well as the nature of language itself. Psycholinguists are developing ways of analyzing the thinking processes underlying language.

In spite of the differences within these professions, there is much agreement in their analyses of the language problem. By studying the problems of language and learning from the framework of the other fields, professionals from each can develop unique contributions to the field of learning disabilities.

# TEACHING STRATEGIES: LISTENING AND SPEAKING

The normal sequence of the development of language skills is: (1) listening, (2) speaking, (3) reading, and (4) writing. Spelling and handwriting can be considered as part of writing. Teaching strategies for the development of listening and speaking skills are presented in this section. A discussion of reading is presented in the following section, and the language skills of writing and spelling are presented in the final section of the chapter.

## "Oracy": Listening and Speaking

To parallel the term "literacy" for the skills of reading and writing, the term "oracy" has been coined to refer to the skills of listening and speaking (Wilkinson 1968). Oral language, or oracy, has two contrasting sides: understanding oral language or input, and producing oral language or output. The two functions may be referred to by the language arts specialists as listening and speaking; by the language pathologist, as receptive language and expressive language; and by the psycholinguist, as auditory decoding and verbal encoding. Disorders of these functions are referred to by the language pathologist as receptive aphasia and expressive aphasia. The child with "delayed speech" is one who has not developed language and speech skills at the appropriate chronological stage. This child could have a problem in either or both aspects of oral language —in reception or in expression.

While there is by no means complete agreement, many authorities suggest that development of listening or receptive language skills is a prerequisite and should be taught before the child is taught speaking or expressive language skills. Although it is often impossible to draw a definite line between experiences in listening and speaking, ability to listen and understand is generally considered a basis for speaking (Mackintosh 1964).

## Listening

The input side of oracy, listening, as an element of the language arts and as a specific language skill, has been neglected until recently. While special concern for the instruction of speaking and reading is common, the child is typically expected to acquire the ability to listen without special instruction. The fact is that many children do not acquire functional skills in listening by themselves. According to medical ear specialists, over half the cases referred to them for suspected deafness do not have any defect in hearing acuity or any organic pathology causing their seeming deafness.

The child's ability to listen, it seems, has been taken for granted. We are finally beginning to realize that listening is a basic skill that can be improved through teaching and practice. Compared to the quantity of research in reading, the research and study that has been conducted in listening is miniscule; in fact most of the reports that were available a few years ago were contained in a single bibliographic volume (Duker 1964). One explanation for poor listening skills is that children of today are so bombarded with constant sound that many have actually learned to "tune out" what they do not wish to hear, and many children have become skillful at *not* listening. It is the task of the teacher, particularly the teacher of children with learning disabilities, to help those who have learned not to listen to become auditorily perceptive and to "tune in."

Some children have a learning problem that stems from their inability to comprehend speech. Such a condition is often termed a receptive language disorder, and the child with such a condition may avoid language activities because listening is so painful (Johnson and Myklebust 1967).

Listening differs from hearing, which is a physiological process that does not involve interpretation. One can hear with good auditory acuity a foreign language but be unable to listen to what is being said. In contrast to hearing, listening demands that one select appropriate meanings and organize ideas according to their relationships. In addition, listening calls for evaluation, acceptance or rejection, internalization, and at times appreciation of the ideas expressed. Listening is the foundation of all language growth, and the child with a deficit in listening skills has a handicap in all the communication skills.

## RELATIONSHIP BETWEEN LISTENING AND READING

The two language modes of receiving information and ideas from others are listening and reading. There are many similarities between these two modes of decoding symbolic language. Both require sensory stimulation, one to the eye and one to the ear. Both require the ability to receive, make sense out of, and organize the sensory stimuli. Both need a memory bank of vocabulary to relate the words that are read or heard. Both need a grasp of the various linguistic systems of the language being used, that is, phonology, morphology and syntax. Both require an attentive attitude, for without close attention, half-listening or half-reading results. Finally, both demand the application of specific thinking skills, for comprehension of the ideas being listened to or read. It is not surprising, therefore, that research studies show a high correlation between the receptive language skills of listening and reading and that instruction in listening comprehension is likely to result in improvement in reading comprehension.

There are, however, important differences between listening and reading. The reader can reread and study the material, while the listener can hear the material only once and then it is gone. Of course, the use of a tape recorder modifies that difference somewhat, but a tape recorder can be used in relatively few of the situations that demand careful listening. The reader can regulate his speed, going slower or faster as his purpose and the difficulty of the material dictate, while the listener's speed of listening is set by the speaker. The listener has additional clues of voice, gesture, appearance, and emphasis of the speaker, while the reader cannot derive such supporting information from the printed page. In the listener-speaker combination, there is more opportunity for feedback, questioning, and for a two-way discussion than in reading.

The term *reading* implies comprehension in the reading act; thus, Russell (1957) suggests that the term *auding* be used to refer to comprehension in the listening act. In reading, it is useful to classify skills at the level of decoding skills and at the level of comprehension skills; so too in listening one can speak of a level of decoding or perception of sounds and words and a level of comprehending what is heard, or auding. Table 9.1 illustrates the similarities between the levels of the two receptive language skills of listening and reading.

| Receptive Language Skills | Reading (visual) | Listening (auditory) |
| --- | --- | --- |
| Sensory stimulation | Seeing (eyes) | Hearing (ears) |
| Decoding skills | Visual perception | Auditory perception |
| | Recognition of words in print | Recognition of words and sounds heard |
| Comprehension | Reading | Listening (auding) |

**TABLE 9.1. SIMILARITIES BETWEEN THE LEVELS OF LISTENING AND READING**

When teachers ask children "to listen," they do not mean they should simply *hear,* nor do they mean they should just recognize the words being spoken. When children are directed to listen, they are expected to comprehend, or audit, the communication message being sent. Just as reading is made up of many substrata abilities, so listening contains many component abilities and skills.

The following paragraphs suggest some techniques that have been used to develop, train, and strengthen the subabilities of listening. The optimal sequence of teaching listening or auditory receptive skills has not as yet been clearly specified by research. Therefore, the techniques presented are a collection of methods from authorities in a number of language-related fields.

### Levels of Listening

Listening skills can be categorized into successive levels that require increasingly complex abilities. The following sequence is adapted from Wilt (1964).

1. Auditory perception of non-language sounds.
2. Auditory perception and discrimination of isolated single language sounds.
3. Understanding of words and concepts, and building of a listening vocabulary.
4. Understanding sentences and other linguistic elements of language.
5. Auditory memory.
6. Auding or listening comprehension:
   a. Following directions.
   b. Understanding a sequence of events through listening.
   c. Recalling details.
   d. Getting the main idea.
   e. Making inferences and drawing conclusions.
   f. Critical listening.

Some teaching strategies for each of these levels of listening are suggested below.

**Auditory perception of non-language sounds.** These sounds are the environmental sounds that are around us. Many of the techniques for teaching auditory perception are included in Chapter 8, in *Teaching Strategies: Auditory Perception.* The child is helped to be aware of sounds, to contrast sounds, to locate the direction of sounds, and to associate sounds with objects.

**Auditory perception and discrimination of language sounds.** An important factor in reading readiness is the ability to perceive and recognize the phoneme sounds of our language. Without such a skill, the learning of phonics is impossible.

1. *Initial consonants—auditory recognition.* Use real objects or pictures of objects. Say the name of the object and ask the child to tell which pictures or objects begin with the same sound. The child may group those objects whose names have the same initial sound in one place; he may put all objects whose names begin with that sound in one container or he might paste pictures of these objects on a chart. For example, the initial consonant "m" may be presented with "milk, money, missile, moon, man, monkey."

2. *Sound boxes.* A box, approximately the size of a shoe box, can be used for each sound being taught. Put the letter representing the sound on the front, and collect toys, pictures, and other objects for the children to place in the appropriate box.

3. *Initial consonants—same or different.* Say three words, two of which have the same initial consonant. Ask the child to identify the word that begins with a different sound. For example: car—dog—cat.

4. *Consonant blend bingo.* Make bingo cards with consonant blends and consonant digraphs in the squares. Read words and ask the child to cover the blend that begins each word.

5. *Hear and write.* Read words that begin with initial consonants, consonant blends, or consonant digraphs. Ask the child to listen and write the blend that begins each word.

6. *Substitutions.* Help the child learn to substitute one initial sound for another to make a new word. For example: "Take the end of the word *book* and put in the beginning of the word, *hand,* and get something you hang coats on" (hook).

7. *Auditory blending game.* Have the child identify objects or answer questions when you speak the name of an object by separating the individual phonemes. For example: "p-e-n" or "b-a-ll." "What is your n-ā-m?"

8. *Hearing vowels.* Vowels are more difficult than consonants for many children to hear. Begin by listening for and identifying the short vowels. The use of key words for the child to refer to is helpful. For the short "a" for example, use a picture of an astronaut. After the child recognizes the short vowel, help him to identify the long vowel sound. Then contrast the sound of the short vowel with that of the long vowel. The techniques used for the initial consonants and consonant blends may be adapted for the vowel sounds.

9. *Riddle rhymes.* Make up riddle rhymes and encourage the children to make up others. For example: "I rhyme with *look.* You read me. What am I?"

10. *Awareness of rhyming sounds.* Have the child listen to a series of three words and tell which two of the words rhyme: ball—sit—wall; hit—pie—tie.

11. *Same or different.* Say pairs of words or pairs of nonsense words and ask the child to determine if they are the same or different. For example: tag—tack; big—beg; singing—sinking; shin—chin; lup—lub.

12. *Hearing syllables.* Have the child listen to the pronounciation of multi-syllabic words and determine the number of syllables in each word. Clapping or identifying the vowel sounds heard helps the children determine the number of syllables.

**Understanding of words.** The development of a listening vocabulary is a basic requirement in listening. Children must understand the names of objects, the names of actions, the names of qualities, and the names of more abstract concepts. It is easier to teach what linguists call form class words, those that carry primary lexical meaning (such as nouns, verbs, adjectives, adverbs), than to teach the structure or function words that indicate relationships within sentences. Function words are better taught within the sentence.

13. *Names of objects.* To help a child understand names, use actual objects, such as a ball, pencil, doll. Sometimes exaggeration and gesture is needed to help the child who has a severe receptive disorder understand the meaning of the word that symbolizes the object.

14. *Verb meanings.* It is more difficult to teach the concept of a verb than the name of an object. Verbs such as hop, sit, walk, can be illustrated with the performance of the activity.

15. *Pictures.* Pictures are useful in reinforcing and reviewing the vocabulary that has been taught.

16. *Concepts of attributes.* Words that describe the attributes of objects can be taught by providing contrasting sets of experiences that illustrate the attributes. For example: rough—smooth; pretty—ugly; little—big; hot—cold. Both concrete objects and pictures are useful in teaching attributes.

17. *Development of concepts.* By combining experiences with particular objects, the child is helped to understand the concept beyond the object itself. For example, in learning about the concept of a chair, the child is shown a kitchen chair, an upholstered chair, a folding chair, a lawn chair, a doll chair, and a rocking chair. Through experiences with many objects, the child develops the concept of chair.

18. *Classes of objects.* An even broader classification of objects must be made and labeled with a word. For example, the word *food* refers not to any single type of food but to all foods. Children, therefore, could be taught objects that "are food" and could be asked to remove from a display any objects "that are not food."

**Understanding sentences and other linguistic units.** Individuals are expected to comprehend language within the linguistic structure of the sentence rather than in single words. As the linguists and educators develop methods to help children learn the linguistic systems of the American English language, these methods should also prove useful to the teacher who helps children with language disabilities. Some children with a receptive language difficulty need structured practice in understanding sentences.

19. *Directions.* Simple directions given in sentences can give the child needed experiences in understanding sentences. For example, "Give me the blue truck," or "Put the book on the table" are directions that could be given.

20. *Find the picture.* Line up several pictures. Give a sentence about one picture and ask the child to point to the correct picture. This exercise can be made harder by adding more sentences to describe the picture.

21. *Function words.* Linguists refer to function or structure words as the words that show structural relationship between parts of a sentence and grammatical meaning. They include noun determiners, auxiliary verbal forms, subordinators, prepositions, connectors, and question words. These words cannot be taught in isolation; they must be taught within a sentence or phrase. For example, words such as *on, over, under, behind, in front of, beneath, inside, in,* can be taught by placing objects *in* a box or *under* a chair while saying the entire phrase to convey the meaning.

22. *Riddles.* Have the child listen to the sentence and fill in the word that fits. For example: "I am thinking of a word that tells what you use to go down a snowy hill" (sled).

**Auditory memory.** Not only must the child listen and hear, but he must store the auditory experiences and be able to retrieve them and relate them when he wishes to. Several teaching strategies for improving auditory memory are listed in the section on Teaching Strategies for auditory memory in Chapter 8.

**Auding or listening comprehension.** This skill is similar to what has been called reading comprehension; however, intake is through hearing language rather than reading it. Auding combines listening skills with thinking skills.

23. *Listening for details.* Read a story to the child and ask questions about the story that are detailed in nature: true-false, who, what, when, where, and how questions. In another type of detail exercise, a manual on a subject such as how

to take care of a new pet is read to the child, and the child is asked to list all the things to do.

24. *Sequence of events.* Read a story and ask the child to picture the different events in the order that they happened. The use of a pictorial series, such as a comic strip, to illustrate the events of the story is helpful; the pictures are mixed and the child is asked to place the series in the proper chronological order.

25. *Following directions.* Read directions on making something. Have the materials ready and ask the child to follow the directions step by step.

26. *Getting the main idea.* Read a short but unfamiliar story to the child and ask him to make up a good title for the story. Read a story and ask the child to choose the main idea from three choices.

27. *Making inferences and drawing conclusions.* Read a part of a story that the child does not know. Stop at an exciting point and ask the child to guess what happens next. In another approach, the teacher reads a story that another child started and explains that the author did not know how to finish it. Now that the dog, Red, is in trouble, can the child suggest an ending?

**Critical listening.**   Good listening means not only understanding what is said but also the ability to listen critically, to make judgments and evaluations of what is being said.

28. *Recognizing absurdities.* Tell a short story with a word or phrase that does not fit the story. Ask the child to discover what is funny or foolish about the story. For example: "It rained all night in the middle of the day," or "The sun was shining brightly in the middle of the night."

29. *Listening to advertisements.* Have the child listen to advertisements and determine *how* the advertiser is trying to get the listener to buy the products. The mature child enjoys detecting propaganda techniques.

30. *Correct me.* Use flannel board figures while telling a story. Plan obvious errors through discrepancies between what is said and what is placed on the board. Have the child listen for and correct the mistakes.

Additional suggestions for teaching strategies to develop and improve listening skills can be found in numerous sources. Among them are *Learning Disabilities: Educational Principles and Practices* (Johnson and Myklebust 1967), *Listening Aids Through the Grades* (Russell and Russell 1959), "Let's Teach Listening" (Wilt 1957); *Listening Bibliography* (Duker 1964), and *Language and Learning Disorders of the Pre-Academic Child* (Bangs 1969).

**Listening tests.**   Relatively few listening tests are available to evaluate a child's development in receptive oral language skills—compared to the tests that are available in the field of reading. Among the tests of listening are: *Peabody Picture Vocabulary Test*, the Ammons *Full Range Picture Vocabulary Test, Van Wagenen Listening Vocabulary Scales, Listening Comprehension Test* (a portion of the *Sequential Tests of Educational Progress*), *Brown-Carlsen Listening Comprehension Test, Durrell Listening-Reading Test,* the *Auditory Reception* and *Auditory Memory* tests (subtests of the *Illinois Test of Psycholinguistic Abilities*), and the receptive language portion of the *Northwestern Syntax Screening Test.* Descriptive information concerning these tests can be found in Appendix C.

# Speaking

Oral language, including listening and speaking, is identified as the primary form of language; written language is only a secondary form. In spite of the recognition and acceptance of the primacy of oral language, instructional practices observed in both regular classrooms and remedial work do not always reflect this relationship between oral and written language. Except for the work of speech and language pathologists, emphasis in teaching is too frequently focused on the written forms of communication—reading and writing.

Perhaps one reason for the neglect of oral language in teaching is that there are so many gaps in our knowledge of oral language; i.e., how it develops in the child, what comprises language disorders and delayed language development, and how specifically to go about teaching oral language skills.

Since speaking and language cut across so many disciplines and affect so many aspects of growth and learning, a number of quite diverse perspectives of oral language have evolved. The language pathologist, the language arts specialist, the linguist, the psychologist, the neurologist, and the psycholinguist are all concerned with language behavior. Each discipline has a contribution to make to the formulation of teaching strategies.

## THE DEVELOPMENTAL APPROACH TO LANGUAGE ACQUISITION

A general overview of the child's language development may provide a perspective for viewing language abnormalities. The child's first attempt to use his vocal mechanisms is the birth cry. Through longitudinal and behavioral studies, researchers have observed and categorized the stages that the individual goes through in the short span of time from the birth cry to the full acquisition of speech (McCarthy 1954).

The vocalization of infancy, occurring during the first nine months, is called *babbling*. During this stage the child produces many sounds, those in his native language as well as many sounds that are found in other languages. The child derives pleasure from hearing the sounds he makes and such sound-making gives him the opportunity to use his tongue, larynx, and other vocal apparatus and to respond in an oral manner to those about him. Deaf children have been observed to begin the babbling stages; but because they receive no feedback or satisfaction from hearing the sounds, they soon stop. Some children with language disorders are reported by parents not to have engaged in activities of babbling, gurgling, or blowing of bubbles. Encouragement of such oral play becomes one technique by which the teacher can help these children recapitulate the normal stages toward language acquisition.

By about nine months, the babbling softens and becomes what is called *jargon*. The child retains the phoneme sounds that are used in the language he hears. The rhythm and melody of oral speaking patterns of those about him are reflected in his vocalizations. Although his intonational patterns may be similar to those of adults, he does not yet use words. It is as though the child were pretending to talk. Chinese children, for example, have been observed to have mastery of basic Chinese intonation patterns by 20 months of age, a feat that is very difficult for an English-speaking adult to master. Often, the parents of youngsters who are diagnosed as having language disabilities report that their children had missed this stage of development.

Single words, such as *mama* and *dadda,* normally develop between 12 and 18 months of age. The ability to *imitate* is evident at this stage and the child may well imitate a sound or word that he hears others say or one he himself has produced. Children with language disabilities are frequently reported not to have engaged in verbal imitation and repetition activities.

Two- and three-word sentences follow the use of single words; for example: *Baby eat, Daddy home, Coat off.* Once the child begins to use language, his skill in speech increases at a remarkably rapid pace. Between 18 months, when a baby produces his first two-word utterance, and age 3, many children learn the essentials of English grammar and can produce all linguistic types of sentences (Strickland 1969). The child's oral language development at age 3 appears to be almost abrupt; he has an extensive vocabulary and uses rather complex sentence structures. During this stage, reports become rather hazy—partly because things develop so rapidly and partly because, as observers, we do not understand the underlying mechanism of language acquisition. By the time the child enters school at age six, he is said to have completely captured the grammar of his native language and his understanding vocabulary is estimated to be as high as 24,000 words (Seashore 1948). His speaking vocabulary is, of course, smaller.

As noted in the preceding section of this chapter, on linguistics and child development, it appears to be impossible to observe accurately the child's development in language from the beginning simple stages to the quickly following stage at which he uses a complex mechanism of language (Chomsky 1967). It is in that brief period that the child who is developing normally in language suddenly learns to use the mechanisms of grammar—the syntax of his native language: he is able to formulate sentences.

As our knowledge of normal language acquisition accrues, we are discovering that many children with learning disabilities do not follow a normal developmental language pattern. While language for the normal child seems to be acquired in a relatively natural and easy manner, without a need for the direct teaching of talking, some children have difficulty in acquiring one or several properties of language. Some have difficulty with the phonology of language—in differentiating and producing the appropriate sounds; others have difficulty in remembering words or in structuring morphological rules; still other children have difficulty with grammar or syntax of the language and in putting words together to formulate sentences.

## LISTENING AND SPEAKING

Experiences in listening (the input or receptive side of language) precede speaking (the output or expressive side of language). Listening alone does not produce the ability to speak, but a looping or feedback process must be created in which the child both listens and speaks. The interrelationship of input and output activities provides immediate reinforcement that shapes speaking behavior. For example, teachers have noted that listening to television does not seem to have an impact on the basic language patterns of the viewer. Although the speech on television may be a good model of standard American English, the speech patterns of viewers reflect that of their home and peer group rather than that of television performers.

## STRATEGIES FOR TEACHING SPEAKING

Below are listed a number of activities to improve skills in verbal expression. These techniques are not intended to be inclusive, but merely representative of activities designed to improve the child's skills in speaking.

### Building a Speaking Vocabulary

Throughout their lives, people have a much larger listening vocabulary than speaking vocabulary. The young child is able to understand words long before he is able to produce and use them. A child with a language disorder may be able to recognize words when they are spoken, but he himself cannot initiate the use of those words. Adults with known brain injuries may lose their ability to remember words easily as a result of damage to the language area of the brain. Such a condition is referred to as *dysnomia,* meaning the inability to remember the names of objects. Children may substitute another referent like "thing" or "whatsit" or "that" or a gesture or pantomime for the word they cannot bring to mind. The following are suggested as ways to help the child use words and build an accessible speaking vocabulary.

1. *Naming.* Have the child name common objects in the room or outside (chair, door, table, tree, stone). Have a collection of objects in a box or bag. As each is removed, have the child name them. Have the child name colors, animals, shapes, etc. Use pictures of objects. A collection or a file of good pictures provides excellent teaching material. Pictures can be made more durable and washable by backing them with cardboard and covering them with a self-adhesive transparent material.

2. *Department store.* The game of department store (or hardware store, supermarket, restaurant, shoe store, etc.) gives the child the opportunity to use naming words. One child plays the role of the customer and gives orders to another child who is the clerk. The clerk collects pictures of the items ordered and gives the orders to his customer while naming them.

3. *Rapid naming.* Give the child a specified length of time (one minute) to name all the objects in the room. Keep a record of the number of words named to note improvement. Pictures can be used, having the child name objects in the pictures. Another variation could be related to sports, the outdoors, pets, etc.

4. *Missing words.* Have the child say the word that finishes a riddle. Who delivers the mail? (mailman). I bounce a _____ (ball). Read a story to the children, pausing at certain places leaving out words; the child is to supply the missing word. The use of pictures helps in recall and naming of the object.

5. *Word combinations.* Some words can best be learned as part of a group. When one member of the group is named, the child may be helped to remember the second. For example: paper and pencil, boy and girl, hat and coat, cats and dogs. Series may also be learned in this fashion: days of the week, months of the year.

## Producing Speech Sounds

Some children have difficulty in initiating the motor movements required to produce speech. Such children may be able to remember the words, but cannot activate the appropriate speech musculature although they do not have a paralysis. Such a condition has been referred to as a speech *apraxia*. The techniques of the speech specialist in working with problems of articulation may be helpful in this condition.

6. *Exercising speech muscles and organs.* The child is encouraged to use the various muscles used in speaking for non-speech activities: smiling, chewing, swallowing, whistling, yawning, blowing, laughing, and various tongue movements are exercised.

7. *Feeling vibrations and observing sounds.* As the teacher makes sounds, the child feels the vibrations of the sounds by touching the teacher's face or throat; he observes the mouth movements and shaping during the production of sounds. The use of a mirror is helpful to enable the child to observe himself in producing sounds.

## Learning Linguistic Patterns

8. *Morphological generalizations.* Some children have difficulty learning to internalize and use the morphological structure of the language. For example, one must make generalizations concerning the system of forming plurals, showing past tense, forming possessives. He must also learn the exceptions where the generalizations do not hold true. For example, the phoneme /s/ or /z/ is usually added to a word in English to show plurality: "three cats" or "two dogs." In some cases the sound of /ez/ is added as in "two dresses," or the root word is changed as in "two men." In a few cases the word is not changed as in "four fish." For the child unable to formulate such generalizations, games in making plurals can be helpful. It is interesting to note that the morphemic rules of standard American English do not always hold in dialectical variations. The morphemic generalization in inner-city or ghetto dialect (as well as in certain other languages) is to use the appropriate quantitative adjective but not pluralize the noun: "That cost two dollar."

## Formulating Sentences

Some children are able to use single words or short phrases but are ineffective in generating longer syntactic units or sentences. Linguists hypothesize that children, in acquiring language, must learn to internalize sentence patterns so that they can "generate" new sentences. Some linguists have said that the child becomes a sentence-producing machine. To achieve this state, many skills are required—including the ability to understand language, to remember word sequences, and to formulate complex rules of grammar.

9. *Plan experiences with many kinds of sentences.* Start with the basic kernel sentence and help the child to generate transformations on the kernel sentence. For example, two kernel sentences can be combined in various ways.

Kernel sentence:   The children play games.
Kernel sentence:   The children are tired.

Transformation:   The children who are tired play games.
                  The children who play games are tired.

Sentence pattern variations

| *Statements* | *Questions* |
|---|---|
| Children play games. | Do children play games? |
| Games are played by children. | Are games played by children? |
| Children do not play games. | Don't children play games? |
| Children do play games. | |

10. *Structure words.* These are the function words that show the relationship between parts of the sentence. Words such as *on, in, under, who,* are best taught within the sentence. Close observation reveals that many children have hazy concepts of the meaning of such words. The child can be asked to put blocks *in, on,* or *under* a table or chair, and then to explain what he did. Words such as *yet, but, never, which* often need clarification. The teacher can give a sentence with only the key or class words and then ask the child to add the structure words. For example: "Jack—went—school—sweater."

11. *Substitution to form sentences.* Form new sentences by substituting a single word in an existing kernel sentence. "I took my *coat* off. I took my *boots* off." "The boy is *reading*. The boy is *running*. The boy is *jumping*."

12. *Detective game.* To help the child formulate questions, have him ask questions concerning the location of a hidden object until the object is found.

### Practicing Oral Language Skills

Reading specialists assert that much practice is needed in using and stabilizing newly learned reading skills; they frequently say, "You learn to read by reading." Practice is needed, too, for the child with a deficiency in verbal expression skills. He needs much opportunity in using words and in formulating sentences. For this child, plans must be made to enable him to practice his speaking skills.

13. *Oral language activities.* A number of activities can be used to promote practice in the use of oral language and speaking. These include: conversations; discussions; radio or television broadcasts; show and tell sessions; puppetry; dramatic play; telephoning; choral speaking; reporting; interviewing; telling stories, riddles, or jokes; book reports; and role playing.

Additional suggestions for teaching expressive oral language skills can be found in Johnson and Myklebust (1967), Wood (1964, 1969), Bangs (1968), Herrick and Jacobs (1955, Chapter 6), Dallmann (1966), Dawson (1963), and Anderson (1964).

### Oral Language Tests

There are relatively few standardized measures of expressive oral language development, compared to the quantity of instruments available for evaluation and diagnosis of reading ability. The *Verbal Expression* and *Grammatic Closure* subtests of the *Illinois Test of Psycholinguistic Abilities* provide useful information. Several subtests of the *Wechsler's Intelligence Scale for Children* provide samples of oral expression. Certain subtests of the *Detroit Tests for Learning Aptitude* (such as *Verbal Opposites* and *Free Associations*) add to the picture of the child's speaking abilities. Other assessments of language development are given by the *Houston Test of Language Development,* the *Mecham Verbal Language Development Scale,* and the *Northwestern Syntax Screening Test.* Descriptive information concerning these tests can be found in Appendix C.

DeHirsch (1966) used the *Number of Words Used in a Story* as an informal measure of oral language development. This measure proved to be a significant predictor of reading failure. In this test kindergarten children were asked to tell the story of *The Three Bears,* and the total number of words used by the child constituted the score. Scores ranged from 54 to 594 words, with 226 words marking the critical score level that gave maximum differentiation between the children who later failed in reading in the first grade and those who did not.

## Summary

This section has presented representative teaching strategies for children who have difficulty in oral language. Two dimensions of oral language were discussed and representative teaching strategies for each of the two dimensions, listening and speaking, were suggested.

# TEACHING STRATEGIES: READING

Children with learning disabilities may have difficulties in *any* of the areas of learning and development, but it seems that poor reading skills are the handicap of a preponderance of the children in learning disabilities educational programs. The teaching of reading has historically been the prime responsibility of the schools. The process of learning to read can be divided into two phases: (1) learning word-recognition skills, with emphasis on the beginning stages of learning to read; and (2) learning comprehension skills, with emphasis on the later stages of reading. The concentration in this section is on the first phase of learning to read. The second phase of reading is discussed in Chapter 10.

## The Importance of Reading

It is true, as McLuhan (1964) has so forcefully stated, that in today's world increasing quantities of sensory data and information come to us through non-reading media, and the global environment of television has replaced the world of print in many ways. Even so, it is interesting to note that, in spite of the fact that millions of Americans viewed such events on television as the recent tragic assassinations, the demonstrations in Chicago during the 1968 Democratic convention, and the "moon walk," people were eager to read the newspapers the next day to make the events they viewed coherent and to place them in context. In spite of the new role that non-print media play in providing a message, illiteracy is more debilitating a handicap than ever.

A few generations ago, people managed to get along quite well in the business and social world without the ability to read but this is no longer true. Longer periods of compulsory education, the requirement of diplomas and degrees for jobs, more comprehensive school testing programs, the necessity of filling out application forms and taking licensing examinations—all make life for the non-reader uncomfortable and full of closed doors. Reading teachers have an aphorism: "Children must learn to read so that they can later read to learn." Indeed, reading is the basic tool for all subjects in school, and failure in a school subject is frequently due to inadequate reading skills.

With the increase of automation and computerized technology, there is a demand for trained manpower. Old jobs have become obsolete, and it is predicted that all individuals in every occupational area will have to retrain themselves to prepare for new jobs many times during their work careers. Reading is a key tool for retraining and maintaining employable skills. Recent sociological research revealed that even the crime syndicate has gone through an innovative stage and upgraded personnel requirements. One study of crime organizations concluded that "as criminal jobs become increasingly complex" there will be "no place in the higher levels of organized crime for high-school dropouts" (*Chicago Tribune,* May 15, 1967).

Many of the ills of our society have been related to reading disabilities. The ranks of the unemployed, school dropouts, juvenile delinquents, and criminals tend to have very poor reading skills. Examinations of the problems of our schools, of poverty, of the concerns of troubled parents, as well as of most learning disorders seem to show some association with poor reading. It is not surprising that a large percentage of our current government-sponsored education and poverty programs feature some aspect of reading improvement. The National Advisory Committee on Dyslexia and Related Disorders (1969) concluded that the problem of reading failure was "the most serious educational problem confronting the nation." The U.S. Office of Education has placed the "right to read" as a national goal for the 1970's.

Reading, then, is a skill both basic and essential in today's world, and the teacher of children with learning disabilities should be well informed about the teaching of reading.

## The Development of Reading Skills

The teacher of children with reading problems should have an understanding of developmental reading programs and normal reading growth. The sequence of stages that the child normally goes through in acquiring reading skills is commonly divided as: (1) development of reading readiness; (2) the initial stage in learning to read; (3) rapid development of reading skills; (4) the stage of wide reading; and (5) refinement of reading skills (Harris 1970).

**Stage 1. Development of reading readiness.** This stage begins at birth and continues through the beginning stages of reading. It encompasses the development of language skills of listening and speaking, of motor development, of auditory and visual discrimination, of concept and cognitive thinking, and of the ability to attend to and concentrate on activities. The role of kindergarten has traditionally been to build such reading readiness skills. These skills are sometimes referred to as *prerequisites* of reading.

**Stage 2. Initial stage of learning to read.**   This stage is the start of the formal reading program and has traditionally occurred in first grade; but reading may begin in kindergarten, second grade, or even later. This beginning-to-read stage is the stage of reading that has been the most researched, and the greatest number of innovations and changes has been for children first beginning to read.

Great controversies about the teaching of reading have also revolved about the beginning stage of reading instruction. Chall's (1967) widely reviewed and controversial investigation of differing approaches to beginning reading, reported in *Learning to Read: The Great Debate,* concluded that beginning reading is primarily a decoding process and that code-emphasis methods at this stage produce the best results. Another comprehensive investigation of beginning reading, the Cooperative Research Program in First Grade Reading Instruction (Bond and Dykstra 1967), came to somewhat different conclusions. This large-scale cooperative research, using 20,000 pupils and twenty-seven individual first-grade projects, generated data on the following beginning-to-read methods: basal reading, basal plus phonics, initial teaching alphabet, linguistic, language-experience method, and phonic/linguistic approaches. A major conclusion of this extensive research study was that no one method was so outstanding that it should be used to the exclusion of the others (Bond 1966). Two peripheral findings were: (1) that in almost every instance the experimental population made significantly greater gains than the control population (Stauffer 1966), and (2) that there was greater variation between the teachers within a method than there was between the methods.

A variety of methods are used for the initial stage of reading. Some children begin reading with the language-experience approach; some begin with the first preprimer of the basal reader; some start with a phonics method; and some begin with the new materials or methods, such as linguistics, programed reading, or i.t.a. At this stage, children typically begin to develop a sight vocabulary, start to associate sound with the visual symbol of the letter, and learn to follow a line of print from left to right across a page. Much of the reading at this stage is oral reading and children realize at this stage that reading is merely "talk written down."

**Stage 3. Rapid development of reading skills.**   This phase normally takes place at second and third grades. It is an extension, refinement, and amplification of the previous stage. The child proceeding normally in reading now rapidly develops skills in word-recognition techniques, builds a substantial sight vocabulary, learns to use context clues, and learns the techniques of phonic and structural analysis. The bulk of the phonics program is presented by the end of third grade. This implies that the child developing normally has learned phonic generalizations and makes effective application of them by the end of the primary years. This stage lays the foundation for later reading development.

**Stage 4. Stage of wide reading.** The program of the intermediate grades emphasizes wide reading and extends and enriches the child's reading experiences. The
basic skills of the primary grades are improved and strengthened. Now the child
progressing normally can read for pleasure. Voluntary reading reaches a peak in
these years. Librarians find more enthusiasm for reading among children at this
period than perhaps at any other. This is the age of reading series books. During
this period children discover *Dr. Dolittle* books, the *American Heritage* Series,
*All-of-a-Kind Family* books, the *Bobbsey Twins* and the *Nancy Drew* Series,
or a favorite author like Marguerite Henry or Lois Lenski or Robert McCloskey or
Beverly Cleary. During this stage, too, children share the discovery of a good
book, and a list of children in one classroom are soon waiting to read the new
favorite of one of their classmates. Book clubs are popular at this age and librarians report the middle-graders will want to read a book that has been shown
on television. At this stage children developing normally in reading enjoy reading, but they need help in developing skills in reading factual materials.

**Stage 5. Refinement of reading.** Schools are beginning to realize that reading
development is not completed by the end of elementary school, even for students
who do not have special reading problems. During junior high school and senior
high school years, students need continued guidance for effective reading growth.
In fact, reading skills are never completely perfected; even into college and adult
life one is still developing advanced reading skills. The development of more
advanced comprehension skills, the attainment of study skills, an increase in
reading rate, and the achievement of a flexibility in reading for different purposes
are the responsibility of secondary schools. It is at this point, when longer periods
of concentrated reading are required, that many children begin to fail in reading.
The reading problem at this stage is quite a different one from that of the child
who is unable to learn to decode a graphic symbol at the beginning stage of
reading.

# Reading Methods and Materials

Many innovations have appeared in recent years to help teach
reading. Some of these new approaches use fragments of older methods or
combine elements of several methods; some of the new approaches have modified the sequence of presentation in an attempt to simplify the initial learning
experiences; and some new approaches represent attempts to operationalize
recent learning theories (Wittick 1968). This section reviews the major methods
and materials currently being used in reading instruction. Each of these methods
may be useful for the child with learning disabilities, but the teacher must be
aware of both the attributes of the material and the learning style of the child.

## "DECODING" APPROACHES TO BEGINNING READING

*Decoding* refers to the ability to master the relationship between the sound and
the letter symbol. Many reading authorities speak of this skill as the ability to
"break the code."

The written form of English has an inconsistent phoneme-grapheme relationship, which is the relationship between the letter and its sound equivalent. Some

authorities feel that printed English is difficult for many children to decipher because of the irregular spelling pattern of the English language. The letter "a", for example, is given a different sound in each of the following typical first-grade words: *at, Jane, ball, father, was, saw, are.* Another way to view this complexity is to observe that the phoneme of long "i" has a different spelling pattern in each of the following words: *aisle, aye, I, eye, ice, vie, high, choir, buy, sky, rye, pine, type.* To further complicate the problem of learning to read English, many of the most frequently used sight words in first grade books have irregular spelling patterns. A few of these words are shown in column *A* of Table 9.2, and the way they would be spelled with a dependable phoneme-grapheme relationship, so that readers could "sound them out," is shown in column *B.*

| A. English Spelling | B. Phonic Spelling |
|---|---|
| of | uv |
| laugh | laf |
| was | wuz |
| is | iz |
| come | kum |
| said | sed |
| what | wut |
| from | frum |
| one | wun |
| night | niet |
| know | noe |
| they | thai |

**TABLE 9.2. TYPICAL FIRST-GRADE SIGHT WORDS**

There are two ways to attack this problem of an undependable written form of English: 1) Simplify the initial learning phase by choosing only those words having a consistent sound-symbol spelling relationship. This is the solution of the various phonics approaches and some "linguistic" approaches to reading. 2) Change the written grapheme symbol by modifying the written code or the alphabet. This is the approach of the initial teaching alphabet (i.t.a.), UNIFON, and "words in color." Both of these solutions delay some of the more complex aspects about our written language system for later teaching. In effect, children are kept from learning the "awful truth about spelling" until second grade or later.

The most significant reading programs having special emphasis on decoding are: (a) phonics approaches; (b) linguistic approaches; (c) modified-alphabet approaches, such as the initial teaching alphabet; (d) early letter approaches, and (e) the rebus approach. Children who learn poorly through the auditory modality are likely to have difficulty in learning through decoding approaches.

### Phonics Methods
Phonics systems and phonics books have been on the market for over thirty years. The availability of multi-media has enabled "old wine to be put into new bottles." Old phonics materials are being produced as transparencies, pre-printed carbon masters for duplication, filmstrips, charts, recordings, tapes, and computers. The phonics method is typically synthetic, rather than analytic. First, isolated letters and their sound equivalents are taught; then these individual

elements are blended or synthesized into whole words. Some of the widely used phonics programs are:

*The Economy Program: Phonetic Keys to Reading.* Economy Company.
*Phonovisual Program.* Phonovisual Products, Inc.
*Building Reading Skills.* McCormick-Mathers Publishing Co.
*New Phonics Skilltexts.* Charles E. Merrill Books
*Phonics We Use.* Lyons and Carnahan
*Eye and Ear Fun.* Webster Publishing Company
*Learning About Words Series.* Bureau of Publications, Teachers College, Columbia University
*Speech-to-Print Phonics.* Harcourt Brace & World
*Wordland Series.* Continental Press
*Conquests in Reading.* Webster Publishing Co.
*Individualized Phonics.* Teachers Publishing Corp.
*Remedial Reading Drills* (Hegge, Kirk, Kirk). George Wahr Publishing Company
*Basic Word-Study Skills for Middle Grades.* Ginn & Company
Additional programs are included in Appendix B.

Two recent basal readers that feature an initial phonics approach are: *Basic Reading,* J. B. Lippincott Co., and *Open Court Basic Readers,* Open Court Publishing Co.

Typical exercises in phonics materials are similar to those shown below:

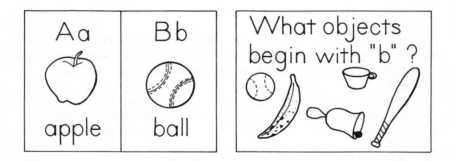

**Teachers of reading and phonics.** Recent studies have revealed that many teachers of reading are not well grounded in phonics and phonic generalizations (Lerner and List 1970). Some teachers do not remember learning phonics when they learned to read, and many teachers have not received phonics instruction in their preservice teacher education. The reader may wish to take the *Foniks Kwiz,* Appendix A, to test his knowledge of phonics. A brief review of phonic generalizations follows the quiz.

### The Linguistic Approach

The linguistic approach to reading of the Bloomfield-Fries (Fries 1963) framework defines learning to read as essentially a decoding process. This view assumes that the child coming to school has already mastered oral language; the child's reading task is learning to break the coded relationship between the written letter and the phoneme sound so that he can respond to the printed marks with the appropriate sounds of speech. Reading, then, within this framework is decoding the phoneme-grapheme relationship. In the linguistic approach, phonology or the sound system of the English language is emphasized, while the linguistic systems of morphology, syntax, and semantics are not emphasized (Lerner 1968).

The developers of this linguistic approach to reading reason that children have already learned to make generalizations about the phonemes or sound elements of oral language, and they should, in a similar way, learn to make generalizations about the written letter symbols that represent speech sounds. Reading is introduced by carefully selecting for the initial reading experiences only those words having a consistent and regular spelling pattern. Words that use a consonant-vowel-consonant (CVC) pattern are presented as whole words, and children are expected to learn the code by making generalizations through minimal contrasts of sounds in the words selected. For example, the child is to make a generalization concerning the short "a" sound by learning words in print such as:

| can | Nan | van |
| fan | Dan | pan |
| man | tan | ran |

These carefully selected, regularly spelled words are then strung together to make sentences. For example: (Bloomfield and Barnhart 1963)

Nan can fan Dan.
Can Dan fan' Nan?
Nan, fan Dan.
Dan, fan Nan.

This linguistic approach differs from the phonics method in that the letters and sound equivalents are not present in isolation to be blended into whole words, but the letters are presented embedded in words that have regular spelling patterns so that the learner can make generalizations about minimal contrast elements (Fries 1965). Some materials based on this linguistic approach are:

*Merrill Linguistic Readers*. Charles E. Merrill Books
*SRA Basic Reading Series*. Science Research Associates
*Visual-Linguistic Basic Reading Series*. Educational Services Press
*The Structural Reading Series*. L. W. Singer, Inc.
*Miami Linguistic Readers*. D. C. Heath & Co.
*Linguistic Readers*. Harper & Row Publishers
*Let's Read*. Clarence L. Barnhart, Inc.

Another linguistic approach to the teaching of reading, emphasizing other linguistic systems, is proposed by Lefevre (1964). This approach involves the development of comprehension in reading by building the skill of "sentence sense." Sentence sense means the ability to translate the secondary written language back into its primary form, spoken English, so that the child will understand the meaning of the sentence. The linguistic tool for accomplishing this is called *intonation*, which consists of pitch, stress, and juncture.

## Modified Alphabets

One procedure for simplifying initial reading instruction is to change the alphabet so that a regular correspondence between sound and symbol can be assured. Modified alphabets in use in the United States have been reviewed by Fry (1965). The modified alphabet approaches described in this section include: (1) the initial teaching alphabet (i.t.a.), (2) the UNIFON sound alphabet, (3) the diacritical marks system (DMS), and (4) words in color (modification of the alphabet through color).

**The initial teaching alphabet (i.t.a.)** The initial teaching alphabet is an attempt to provide a medium that will make spelling as regular as possible. The i.t.a. alphabet consists of 44 characters, each representing a different phoneme. The symbols of the conventional alphabet have been augmented for those phonemes having no letters of their own in traditional orthography, for example, sh, ch, th. Certain letters of the alphabet, such as q and x, have been eliminated because they have sound equivalents represented by other letters. Capital letters or uppercase letters have been eliminated to reduce confusion (Tanyzer–Mazurkiewicz 1967). A sample selection written in i.t.a. is shown here:

"whot ʃhωd wɛɛ næm mɨe
nue bruɹher?" hal ɑskt.
"ɨe nœ a gωd næm,"
maggi sed. "mɨe dog'ꙅ næm
iꙅ ꙅpot. næm yωr bæby ꙅpot."

"ꙅpot iꙅ a gωd næm
for a dog," ted sed.
"it's not a gωd næm
for a bæby," sed hal.

From the book, *Early to Read*-Book 2. Copyright, ©, 1967 by Initial Teaching Alphabet Publications, Inc. Reprinted by permission of Pitman Publishing Corp.

With normal reading growth, the transition to the conventional alphabet (traditional orthography, or t.o.) is planned for the beginning of the second year in the i.t.a. basal series.

**The UNIFON sound alphabet** (1966). This is a 40-phoneme alphabet without lower- and uppercase distinctions which was designed initially to reform spelling. The reader must learn the 40-symbol alphabet, he must learn the sounds for which each symbol stands, and he must learn some rules. Transfer to traditionally spelled words is planned to be accomplished by the sixteenth week of first grade. A sample from a selection printed in UNIFON is shown here:

TŪ MORKⱧT, TŪ MORKⱧT,

TŪ B△ U FAT PⱧG;

HꞶM UGEN, HꞶM UGEN,

DANCⱧↅ U JⱧG.

From *Mother Goose Farm*. Racine, Wis.: Western Publishing Company, Inc. 1968, p. 10.

**Diacritical marking system (DMS)** (Fry 1964).   This modification of the alphabet is designed to regularize orthography for beginning reading instruction by adding marks to regular letters to preserve basic word form. The marks are to be eliminated as the reading habit is established. Material written in DMS appears as follows:

"Lòøk, Bill," såɨd Lindá.

"Hērⱸ cómⱸs Riⱸky.

Hē is̲ âll reₐdy fôr scₕöøl.

Lòøk up and sēⱸ funny Riⱸky."

From Edward Fry "New Alphabet Approaches," in James Kerfoot (ed.), *First Grade Reading Programs*. Newark, Del.: International Reading Assoc., 1965, pp. 72–85.

**Words in color** (Gattegno 1962).   *Words in Color* is an attempt to make initial reading easier and more regular through the use of color, without changing the alphabet or the spelling. A single phoneme sound is always represented by one color regardless of its spelling. The children learn the sound of the "white one," the color of short "a." Whether the spelling is *a, au,* or *ai* as in *pat, laugh,* or *plaid,* it is written in white and pronounced with the short "a." The short "u" as in *up* is yellow, and the short "i" as in *if* is pink, and so on.

### The Early Letter Emphasis Approach

Although this approach does not modify the alphabet, it does emphasize early letter learning. A number of studies show that knowledge of letters has a high correlation to success in learning to read (Barrett 1965). Because of the high predictive value of letter knowledge as a pre-reading skill, a number of readiness and basal reading programs are now teaching letters early.

One program emphasizing letter recognition is the *Distar Reading System* (Engelmann and Bruner 1969). Instead of teaching the letter names, however, it teaches children to identify each letter by the sound it represents. The steps to be followed in this approach include:

1. *Symbol-action games* are used to teach skills such as left-to-right orientation and linear sequence.

2. *Blending* tasks are used to teach children to spell words by sounds (say it slow) and to blend quickly (say it fast).

3. *Rhyming tasks* are used to teach children to recognize the relationship between sounds and words.

The system is a highly structured step-by-step program with emphasis on "code-cracking" skills. Directions for the teacher are precisely specified to meet the educational objectives set for the materials.

### The Rebus Approach

Another attempt to simplify the initial stages of learning to read is through the use of rebus symbols for beginning reading. A rebus is a picture or a symbol of a printed word and it is used in the reading material instead of certain printed words. For example, in the Peabody Rebus Reading Program (Woodcock 1969), the printed word "be" is represented by a picture of a bumblebee. An illustration from the Peabody Reading Program is shown below:

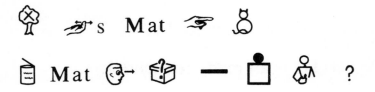

From Peabody Rebus Reading Program, Rebus Reader One. *Red and Blue are on Me.* Circle Pines, Minn.: American Guidance Services, Inc., p. 23.

This selection is to be read as: "Here comes Mat the cat. Can Mat see what is on me?"

## THE LANGUAGE-EXPERIENCE APPROACH

The language-experience method views reading as an integrated extension of the facets of language arts (Lee and Allen 1963). The development of reading skills is interrelated with the development of the skills of listening, speaking, and writing. The raw materials are the experiences and language of the child himself. The child begins by dictating stories to the teacher in his own language. These are written down by the teacher and they then become the basis of the child's first reading experiences. According to Allen (1968), the language-experience approach to reading permits the child to conceptualize the following about written material:

What I can think about, I can talk about.
What I can say, I can write (or someone can write for me).
What I can write, I can read.
I can read what others write for me to read.

There is no predetermined, rigid control over vocabulary, syntax, or content, and the teacher uses the raw materials of the reading matter that the child composes to develop reading skills. This approach to reading has a vitality and immediacy, as well as an element of creativity, that have proved useful both in the beginning-to-read stage with young children and in corrective work with older pupils. Although the interest of the child is high, this approach is initially very dependent on the visual modality and visual memory for words. The emphasis is on reading material that grows out of the child's experiences and the child's natural language in expressing these experiences. A systematic structured system of teaching phonological skills is de-emphasized within this approach.

## MULTI-SENSORY APPROACHES TO READING

Several methods of teaching reading are built upon the premise that stimulation of the several avenues of sensory input reinforces learning. In these methods, kinesthetic and tactile stimulation is emphasized along with the auditory and visual modalities. These methods utilize tracing in teaching and are often referred to as VAKT (visual-auditory-kinesthetic-tactual) methods. The tracing is usually performed by having the child trace a word or letter that has been written on a strip of paper in large cursive and manuscript writing. To teach a word, a strip of about 4 inches by 10 inches could be used. The child traces the word with his finger in contact with the paper. To increase the tactile and kinesthetic sensation, sandpaper letters, sand or clay trays, or finger-paints could be used for tracing activities.

In learning a word in the VAKT technique the child (1) sees the word, (2) hears the teacher say the word, (3) says the word himself, (4) hears himself say the word, (5) feels the muscle movement as he traces the word, (6) feels the tactile surface under his fingertips, (7) sees his hand move as he traces, and (8) hears himself say the word as he traces it (Harris 1970, p. 355).

Two methods of teaching reading which emphasize the tactile and kinesthetic modalities are the Fernald (1943) method and the Gillingham and Stillman (1966) method. Although both of these methods stress tracing, they are quite different in their approach to teaching. In the Fernald method the child learns a word as a total pattern, tracing the entire word, and thereby strengthening his memory and visualization of the entire word. The steps of the Fernald method are described in the next section, on spelling (p. 199). The Gillingham-Stillman method, in contrast, uses the tracing technique to teach individual letters.

The Gillingham-Stillman method is an outgrowth of the Orton theory of reading disability (S. Orton 1937, J. Orton 1966). The Gillingham-Stillman method is a highly structured approach requiring five lessons a week for a minimum of two years. The initial activities are concerned with the learning of individual letter sounds and blending. The child uses a tracing technique to learn single letters and their sound equivalents. These single sounds are later blended into larger groupings and then blended into short words. Simultaneous spelling tasks are also part of this technique; while writing the letters, the child says both the sounds of the letters in sequence and the letter names. The method emphasizes phonics and a highly structured sequence of learning. Independent reading is delayed until the major part of the phonics program has been covered.

## INDIVIDUALIZED READING

The goal of the individualized reading program is to assure that each child within the classroom is reading in books that are suited to his unique needs. No one set of instructional material is likely to be suitable for an entire class or even for all members of a reading group within a class. With this method, each child selects his own interests and level. Further, he has the opportunity to read at the rate that is appropriate for him (Veatch 1959).

An important feature of this method is the individual conference the child has with his teacher. At this conference the child reads aloud and discusses the book with his teacher. Records concerning what the child is reading, his level of performance, and his strengths and weaknesses in reading skills are kept by the teacher from information gathered at the conference. The teacher can then plan activities to build and develop the skills the child is lacking (Miel 1958).

Individualized reading builds upon the child's own interests and enthusiasm. This method has proved to be particularly successful with youngsters who do not do well in a group situation, as it breaks an undesirable lockstep of some reading practices and it promotes an unmeasurable but highly desirable positive attitude toward reading.

**Paperback books programs.**  In addition to reading library books and trade books in individualized reading programs, buying one's own paperback books and membership in paperback book clubs have both proved to be fruitful approaches to individualized reading programs. Fader (1966) described one such program, in which paperback books were used to bring the pleasures of reading to delinquent boys.

## PROGRAMED READING INSTRUCTION

A few programed materials are available for teaching reading. These materials are designed to be self-instructional and self-corrective. The concept behind the programed materials is that the learning process is enhanced because the material is individualized and self-teaching, and provides instant reinforcement. The subject matter is presented in small, discrete, sequential steps or "frames" containing a single question or instruction. The student responds to the question and then checks his answer to see if it is correct before proceeding to the next frame. One widely used programed reading series is the *Sullivan Series of Programmed Reading* for grades 1–6 (Buchanan 1966).

## BASAL READING SERIES

Most basal reading series assume an eclectic approach to the teaching of reading. It is eclectic in that *many* procedures are incorporated to teach readiness, vocabulary, word recognition and perception, comprehension, and enjoyment of literature. A basal reader series consists of an ordered set of books, workbooks, manuals, and other auxiliary materials, designed to present reading skills in a sequential order. The basal program is not meant to be a total reading program, but rather it is to provide a foundation and springboard for the application of reading skills.

The use of a basal reader as an instructional tool has been widely and loudly criticized by many diverse groups, including professors of education, scholars from other academic disciplines, the popular press, parent groups, political observers, and moralists. Critics have scoffed at and satirized the language, phonics presentation, story content, class appeal, pictures, qualities and environment of the characters of the basal reader. In spite of this highly vocal and severe criticism of the basal reader, its acceptance in the classroom had been widespread. Surveys have found the basal reader to be the major tool of reading instruction in ninety to ninety-five percent of the elementary classrooms throughout the country (Austin and Coleman 1963).

The eclectic nature of the basal reader permits changes to occur readily. Modifications are continually being made as publishers respond to the demands of the times and their consumer market. Recent trends in basal readers are: to introduce phonics earlier and to make the teaching of phonics more obvious; to introduce formal reading earlier; to have readiness and kindergarten books introduce more formal aspects of the reading program than they once did—such as letters, sight words; to make stories longer and more sophisticated and to have the stories tell about many ethnic groups and ways of life.

**Multi-racial and urban-centered materials.**   One of the most notable trends at present is the introduction of multi-racial and urban-centered materials. Some of the basal series especially designed for disadvantaged urban multi-racial groups are:

> City Schools Reading Program. Follett Publishing Co.
> The Bank Street Readers. Macmillan Co.
> Multi-media Chandler Reading Program. Chandler Publishing Co.

## BEHAVIOR MODIFICATION APPROACHES TO READING

Recent interest in behavior modification as a technique to teach educational skills has been directed to the teaching of reading. The conceptual framework behind such an approach requires the setting of specified, observable and measurable behavior objectives. The environmental stimuli are then structured so that they will bring about a change in the child's behavior and lead him to the desired objective. A description of case studies in which behavior modification techniques were used to improve reading is presented by Wark (1969) and Haring and Hauch (1969).

## TECHNOLOGICAL INNOVATIONS IN READING

Various kinds of machines are being used to teach reading. The *talking typewriter* developed by O. K. Moore (Johnson 1969) features a typewriter that speaks the name of the letter as the child types it while pictures representing words are flashed on a screen.

*Computer Assisted Instruction* (CAI), is a program that uses a computer to teach initial reading; it was attempted in the Stanford Project, an experiment in Palo Alto, California (Atkinson and Hansen 1966). Wearing earphones, the child observes images on a television screen and touches certain of the screen images with a light-projecting pen. If he touches the right image, a voice says, "Good." If he is incorrect a voice says "No," and then the voice repeats the instruction. If several consecutive mistakes are made, the computer sets up a signal which calls the teacher for more help. The cost of teaching the 100 students for one semester in this project was about one and one half million dollars (Wittick 1968).

*Teaching machines* combine the audio and visual presentation with coordinated tapes and film strips to teach reading. Some of these machines have branch programs; that is, the correct response to a question will trigger the next step of a teaching lesson while an incorrect response will trigger a review or a remedial lesson.

Machines used to improve reading rate include *tachistoscopes* and *accelerating devices*. The tachistoscope exposes numbers, letters, or whole words for short periods of time, ranging from 1/100 to 1½ seconds. The purpose of the short exposure is to increase the speed of visual perception. The accelerating devices provide rate training. There are a number of different types of machines to pace reading. With some, materials are exposed at a predetermined rate on a screen; other machines expose reading material in a book at a predetermined rate. The first regulates eye movement at far-point distance; the latter at near point. The purpose of such devices is to reduce fixations and regressions, develop better attention and concentration, and require more rapid thinking. Films are also available for this purpose. The ability of the reader to transfer skills from a machine-regulated application to reading a book is a controversial topic in the field of reading.

### READING LABORATORIES

Some reading programs, particularly in secondary schools, have developed special-purpose reading laboratory rooms with small carrels to be used by individual students. These individual learning carrels are designed for many types of audiovisual equipment and reading machines, as well as for use of books and workbooks. Individual reading programs that utilize the multi-media approach are developed and designed to meet the requirements of each student. Electrical and mechanical devices, as well as some of the more conventional materials, appear to be well suited to such an approach.

## Learning Disabilities and Reading

The enormous number of reading materials, reading approaches, and reading methods is almost bewildering. The publishers of materials and designers of specific methods exude confidence that their approaches will be able to accomplish what others have failed to do. Cumulative reading research seems to indicate that the most important variable in successful reading programs is not the material, method, or approach, but rather the teacher who is interacting with the child.

To select appropriate reading materials or methods prudently, the learning disabilities specialist must develop competencies in the following: (1) analyzing the nature of the task to be performed with the reading material or method under consideration; (2) analyzing the mental processes and learning styles of the child who is to be helped; and (3) matching the appropriate types of materials to the disabilities and abilities of the child.

## DYSLEXIA

The term *dyslexia* is commonly used in the field of learning disabilities to identify children who have difficulty in learning to read. Since professionals in the field of learning disabilities are so frequently questioned about dyslexia, it seems appropriate to devote a portion of this section on reading to various views of the dyslexic child and to clarify certain questions. What is dyslexia? Have scholars in the field of reading been aware of dyslexia as a factor in reading failure? What theoretical frameworks led some diagnosticians to use the term *dyslexia* and others to prefer the term *reading disability*? (Lerner 1971).

### What is Dyslexia?

Although there may be agreement that dyslexia has something to do with children's difficulty in reading, there are great differences among more precise definitions of dyslexia. A review of the literature reveals that the word *dyslexia* is currently being used in a variety of ways by different authors. Its diverse definitions cover a wide range and include (a) evidence of an etiology of brain damage, (b) the observation of behavioral manifestations of central nervous system dysfunction, (c) the indication of a genetic or inherited cause of the reading problem, (d) the presence of a syndrome of maturational lag, (e) use as a synonym for reading retardation, and (f) use to describe a child who has been unable to learn to read through the regular classroom methods.

The literature consists of two almost entirely separate strands of thought concerning dyslexia. The two views are (1) the medical perspective, and (2) the educational perspective. One group views dyslexia as an inability to read due to brain damage or central nervous system dysfunction. This view is largely medically oriented and much of the research originated in Europe. At the opposite pole, another group of authorities views dyslexia as a reading disability and says that it "simply means there is something wrong with the person's reading" or that dyslexics are "children who are of average or better intelligence who are finding it difficult to learn to read." This view stems largely from educators, psychologists, and reading specialists, and it originated largely in the United States.

The term *dyslexia* has its roots in the term *alexia*, which describes a loss of ability to read because of an injury to the brain, such as a cerebral stroke. The condition of alexia, also called "acquired word blindness," occurs in an adult who had already learned to read. Children who did not learn to read normally were presumed to have brain lesions similar to those found in cases of alexia in adults. Since the condition of adults who lose the ability to read was called *acquired alexia*, children who failed to learn to read were assumed to have *developmental alexia* or *dyslexia*.

## Two Perspectives Concerning Dyslexia: Medical and Educational

The literature on the medical perspective first appeared in England with an article written by a physician (Morgan 1896). Since that time many other investigators have attempted to find medical explanations for poor reading or dyslexia, including Hinshelwood (1917), Schmidt (1918), Orton (1937), Hallgren (1950), Hermann (1961), Critchley (1964), Money (1966), and Johnson and Myklebust (1967). In the past seventy years, over 20,000 books, articles, and papers have been published on the subject; they have sought a common behavior pattern among all dyslexic children and clearcut evidence of a neurological etiology (Eichenwald 1967). The difficulty in finding empirical evidence to support the medical perspective is that it is almost impossible, even at present, to directly examine the brain of the child. Therefore, evidence of dyslexia owing to brain damage or dysfunction is most difficult to establish diagnostically and is necessarily presumptive in nature.

Educators, reading specialists, and psychologists generally have a different view of dyslexia from that of the medically oriented scholars. The early studies of children who could not read (Monroe 1932, Robinson 1946) investigated the causes of reading failure, including the neurological factor; but these investigators concluded that the neurological theories of causation had not been strongly established. Vernon (1957) concluded that the term dyslexia was unacceptable because the condition is not comparable to alexia. Bond and Tinker (1967) also maintained that it is impossible to distinguish dyslexia from a severe reading disability and that "the clinical worker may question the value of the term."

**Implications of the two perspectives of dyslexia.**   What are some of the implications of the differences in these two perspectives? For purposes of discussion the two frameworks will be called the *medical perspective* and the *educational perspective*.

1. While the scholars working within the medical perspective search for a single etiological factor as causal, the scholars in the educational perspective seek a combination of causes, stressing that it is not likely that a single factor can be shown to be causal.

2. The educators are likely to place greater emphasis on the developmental sequence of reading skills, making an intensive search for the child's break with the developmental reading pattern. The medically oriented investigator is likely to place greater emphasis on the language-related areas, such as speech and oral language skills, as well as on other related disabilities, such as arithmetic skills, perception, motor development, and social skills.

3. For the educator, alexia, or the loss of reading skill in the case of an adult, is different from the inability to learn to read in the case of a child. Therefore, the term dyslexia is not generally used among this group. They emphasize the necessity of differentiating "maturational lag" from central nervous system dysfunction.

4. Educators see the diagnosis of dyslexia as lacking operationality in that it does not lead to appropriate teaching strategies. After the diagnosis of dyslexia is made, one must still investigate what reading skills are lacking, how the child best learns, what are the appropriate materials to overcome the problem, and so on. The diagnosis of dyslexia alone provides few clues as to the appropriate treatment and remedial measures.

5. While the medically oriented clinician is likely to focus solely on the disabled child and to emphasize individual treatment, the educator is likely to perceive a broader role and function within the school and to devote a portion of his time and energy to the developmental reading program of the entire school in seeking preventive measures.

In conclusion, there are two strands of thinking concerning dyslexia that have been developed by two separate fields of study: (a) the medical perspective, and (b) the educational perspective. The review of the literature on dyslexia does not lead to conclusive evidence for or against the approach of either discipline. Each researcher and scholar must and should study the reading problem of children in terms of his own training, experience, and framework. Each discipline has built a substantial body of literature, but neither is benefiting sufficiently from the work and foundation that has already been made by the other. If children who cannot read are to be helped, disciplines must forget labels and begin to work together.

The *National Advisory Committee on Dyslexia and Related Reading Disorders* was created by the Secretary of Health, Education and Welfare in 1968 to investigate, clarify, and resolve the controversial issues surrounding dyslexia. The Committee report, released by HEW in August 1969, reported the following information about dyslexia: "In view of these divergencies of opinion the Committee believes that the use of the term 'dyslexia' serves no useful purpose" (National Advisory Committee on Dyslexia and Related Reading Disorders 1969, p. 38). Perhaps more important, however, the Report recommended to the Secretary of the Department of HEW several vital steps to improve the reading of students within our nation who experience difficulty in learning to read. One of the key recommendations was the creation of an Office of Reading Disorders within an appropriate agency of the Department of Health, Education, and Welfare.

## Summary

This section has discussed the skill of reading as it relates to learning disabilities. Reading is a receptive language skill that involves the written form of language. One of the major scholastic difficulties of children with learning disabilities is that they are poor in reading. Reading is a vital skill in our society and it is the basis for further learning both in and out of school.

There is a developmental sequence of reading skills: reading readiness, initial stage of learning to read, rapid development of reading skills, and refinement of reading. Reading can be divided into two major kinds of learning: word recognition and reading comprehension. Alternative approaches to the beginning stages of reading were considered in this section: decoding methods (phonics, linguistics, modified alphabets, the early letter emphasis approach, the Rebus approach), the language-experience approach, multi-sensory approaches, individualized reading programs, programed reading, basal reading series, technological assistance, and reading laboratories.

The issue of dyslexia in learning disabilities and reading was discussed, and two major viewpoints of dyslexia were presented—the medical and educational perspectives.

In addition to the innovations in reading materials and methods described in this chapter, many administrative and organizational modifications in the schools will have an impact on the reading program. Team teaching, nongrading, new types of individualized and group work, use of specialists and consultants, new organizational patterns—all are factors within the school organization which will have a direct impact on the direction of the reading progress of children with learning disabilities.

# TEACHING STRATEGIES: WRITING AND SPELLING

This section deals with learning disabilities in the expressive communication areas of written language; specifically, handwriting, spelling, and written expression.

It is common knowledge that many people dislike writing. Hook (1967) illustrates this disdainful attitude toward writing with the story of the New York City taxicab driver who skillfully guided his cab past a pedestrian. In explaining to his passenger why he was so careful, the cabbie said, "I always try to avoid hittin' 'em because every time ya hit one, ya gotta write out a long report about it."

The written form of language is the highest and most complex form of communication. In the hierarchy of language skills, it is the last to be learned. Prerequisite to writing is a foundation of previous learnings and experiences in listening, speaking, and reading. In addition to an adequate basis of auditory language skills, proficiency in using written language requires many other skills. The ability to keep one idea in mind, to formulate the idea in words and appropriate syntactic patterns, to plan the correct graphic form for each letter and word, to correctly manipulate the writing instrument to produce the letter shapes, to integrate complex eye-hand relationships, and to have sufficient visual and motor memory—all are required for the act of writing.

The three areas of written language discussed in this section are (1) handwriting, (2) spelling, and (3) written expression.

## Handwriting

Handwriting is the most concrete of the communication skills. The child's handwriting can be directly observed, evaluated, and preserved. It differs from the receptive skill of reading in that the measurement of the reading comprehension skill must necessarily be indirect, through the asking of questions; the child must verbalize in some way to let you know what he has read. Handwriting also differs from the expressive skill of speaking in that it provides a permanent record of the output and because it requires visual and motor skills.

Difficulty in handwriting, sometimes referred to as *dysgraphia*, may reflect the underlying presence of many other deficits. Children with handwriting problems may be unable to execute efficiently the motor movements required to write or to copy written letters or forms, they may be unable to transfer the input of visual information to the output of fine motor movement, they may be poor in other visual-motor functions and in activities requiring motor and spatial judgments. Hildreth (1947) has commented on the intricacy of the psychomotor process involved in handwriting.

> Learning to write is not a mechanical, lower-level reflex response, but a thinking process, entailing activity of the cortical nerve areas. Smooth motor coordination of eye and hand, control of arm, hand, and finger muscles are acquired in the process of learning to write and are needed for legible results. Learning to write also requires maturity adequate for accurate perception of the symbol patterns. Writing from memory demands the retention of visual and kinesthetic images of forms, not present to the senses, for future recall. . . . The capacity for graphic representation, such as writing requires, depends on the motor function of the eye and its coordination with eye movements.

Hildreth suggests that some of the underlying shortcomings that interfere with the child's handwriting performance are: (a) poor motor skills, (b) unstable and erratic temperament, (c) faulty visual perception of letters and words, and (d) difficulty in retaining visual impressions. In addition, the child's difficulty may be in cross-modal transfer from the visual to motor modalities. Left-handedness provides an additional obstacle to learning to write. Another cause of poor writing is poor instruction in handwriting skills.

Handwriting of Mike: 10 years old

Handwriting of Allen: 10 years old

FIGURE 9.4. ILLUSTRATIONS OF THE HANDWRITING OF TWO 10-YEAR-OLD BOYS WITH HANDWRITING DISABILITIES. IN BOTH CASES THE BOYS WERE ASKED TO COPY FROM A SAMPLE.

Figure 9.4 illustrates the attempts of two ten-year-old boys with handwriting disorders to copy some writing materials. Difficulties of this type are sometimes referred to as *dysgraphia*.

## CURSIVE VS. MANUSCRIPT WRITING

There is some difference of opinion as to whether writing instruction for children with learning disabilities should begin with manuscript or cursive writing. The developmental handwriting curriculum in most schools begins with manuscript writing (sometimes called *printing*) in first grade; the transfer to cursive writing (sometimes called *script*) is typically made somewhere in the third grade.

The arguments for beginning with cursive writing are that it minimizes spatial judgment problems for the child and that there is a rhythmic continuity and wholeness that is missing from manuscript writing. Further, errors of reversals are virtually eliminated with cursive writing; and by beginning with the cursive form in initial instruction, the need to transfer from one form to another is eliminated. Many children with learning disabilities find it difficult to make the transfer to cursive writing if they have first learned manuscript writing.

The advantages of manuscript writing are: it is easier to learn since it consists of only circles and straight lines; the manuscript letter form is closer to the printed form used in reading; and some educators feel it is not important for a child to transfer to cursive writing at all since the manuscript form is legal, legible, and thought by some to be just as rapid.

Good results have been obtained with instruction in both symbolic forms. Reinforcing the system the child is using in his classroom seems to be a wise strategy, if all other things are equal. For young children, this is likely to be the manuscript form; and for children in the intermediate grades, the cursive form is likely to be used. Samples of manuscript and cursive letters are shown in Figure 9.5.

### The Left-handed Child

The left-handed child presents a special problem in that his natural tendency is to write from right to left on the page. In writing from left to right, the left-hander has difficulty in seeing what he has written because his hand covers it up, and there is a tendency for him to smudge the writing as his left hand moves. To avoid the smudging, some left-handed children begin "hooking" the hand in writing when they begin using cartridge pens.

Left-handedness today is accepted as natural for some children. The child who has not yet stabilized handedness should be encouraged to write with his right hand. However, the child with a strong preference for his left hand should be permitted to write as a "lefty." This does create some special problems in writing, and requires special instruction.

For manuscript writing, the paper should be placed directly in front of the left-handed child, without a slant. However, for cursive writing the top of the paper should be slanted north-northeast, opposite to the slant used by the right-handed child. The pencil should be long, gripped about one inch from the tip, with the eraser pointing to the left shoulder. The position of the hand is curved, with the weight resting on the outside of the little finger, and "hooking" should be avoided. Research shows that left-handers can learn to write just as fast as right-handers.

MANUSCRIPT ALPHABET

ABCDEFGHIJKLMNOPQR
STUVWXYZabcdefghijklm
nopqrstuvwxyz 1 2 3 4 5 6 7 8 9 10

CURSIVE ALPHABET

*Aa Bb Cc Dd Ee Ff*
*Gg Hh Ii Jj Kk Ll*
*Mm Nn Oo Pp Qq Rr*
*Ss Tt Uu Vv Ww Xx*
*Yy Zz 1 2 3 4 5 6 7 8 9 10*

**FIGURE 9.5.**
From the *Sample Manuscript Alphabet,* Grade 3, and the *Sample Cursive Alphabet,* Grade 3. Columbus, Ohio: The Zaner-Bloser Co., 1958.

### Typewriting

Children with severe problems of dysgraphia who do not make progress with clinical instruction or children who write very slowly may find a typewriter a more effective means of written communication. The electric typewriter has proved to be useful for children with severe motor difficulty. Special instruction in typing will be required to help the child learn to use the typewriter. *Typing Our Language* (1969) is one text especially designed to teach typing to the elementary student.

## TEACHING STRATEGIES TO HELP CHILDREN DEVELOP HANDWRITING SKILLS

The following activities are representative of methods that have been useful in helping children learn to write.

1. *Chalkboard activities.* These provide a practice before beginning writing instruction. Circles, lines, geometric shapes, letters, and numbers can be made with large free movements using the muscles of the shoulders, arms, hands, and fingers. See Chapter 7, "chalkboard activities" in the section on fine motor activities, for additional suggestions.

2. *Other materials for writing movement practice.* Fingerpainting, or writing in a clay pan or a sand tray, gives the child practice in writing movements. Put a layer of sand, cornmeal, salt, or non-drying clay on a cookie sheet. Use commercial or homemade fingerpaints for the painting practice. The finger or a pointed stick can be used to practice writing shapes, forms, letters, and numbers. A small wet sponge could be used on a chalkboard to draw shapes.

3. *Position.* To prepare for writing, have the child sit in a comfortable chair, have the table at the proper height, feet flat on the floor, both forearms on the writing surface. The non-writing hand should hold the paper at the top.

4. *Paper.* For manuscript writing, the paper should be placed without a slant, parallel with the lower edge of the desk. For cursive writing, the paper is tilted at an angle approximately sixty degrees from vertical—to the left for right-handed children and to the right for left-handed children. To help the child remember the correct slant, a strip of tape to parallel the top of the paper may be placed at the top of the desk. To keep the paper from sliding, it may be necessary to attach the paper to the desk with masking tape.

5. *Holding the pencil.* Many children with writing disorders do not know how, or are unable, to hold a pencil properly. It should be held between the thumb and middle finger with the index finger riding the pencil. The pencil should be grasped above the sharpened point. A piece of tape or a rubber band can be placed around the pencil to help the child hold it at the right place.

For the child who has difficulty with the grasp, Larson (1968) suggests putting the pencil through a practice golf ball (the kind with many holes). Have the child place his middle finger and thumb around the ball to practice the right grip. Large primary-size pencils, large crayons, and felt-tip pens are useful for the beginning stages of writing. Clay might be placed around the pencil to help the child grasp it. Short pencils should be avoided, as it is impossible to grip them correctly.

6. *Stencils and templates.* Geometric forms (squares, circles, etc.), letters, and numbers can be represented in stencils made from cardboard or plastic. Clip the stencil to the paper to prevent it from moving. Have the child trace the form

with his finger, or with his pencil or crayon, then remove the stencil and show him which figure he has made. The stencil can be made so that the hole creates the shape, or, in reverse, a cutout of the shape itself where the outer edges of the stencil create the shape. Discarded hospital X-ray films and packaged-meat trays have proved to be useful materials for making templates.

7. *Tracing.* Make heavy black figures on white paper and clip a sheet of onion-skin paper over the letters. Have the child trace the forms and letters. Start with diagonal lines and circles, then horizontal and vertical lines, geometric shapes, and finally use letters and numbers. The child may also trace with a crayon or felt-tip pen over a black letter on paper, or he may use a transparent sheet. Another idea is to put letters on transparencies and project the image with an overhead projector onto a chalkboard or a large sheet of paper. The child can then trace over the image.

8. *Drawing between the lines.* Have the child practice making "roads" between double lines in a variety of widths and shapes. Then the child can write letters by going between the double lines of outlined letters. Use arrows and numbers to show direction and sequence of the lines.

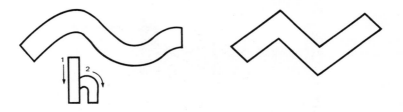

9. *Dot-dot.* Draw a complete figure and then an outline of the same figure using dots. Ask the child to make the figure by connecting the dots.

10. *Tracing with reducing cues.* Write the complete letter or word and have the child trace it; then write the first part of the letter or word and have the child trace your part and then complete the letter. Finally, reduce the cue to only the upstroke and have the child write the entire letter or word.

11. *Lined paper.* Begin by using unlined paper. Later, paper with wide lines may be used to help the child determine placement of letters. Larson (1968) suggests use of specially lined paper that is color-cued to aid in letter placement. Regular lined paper can also be color-cued to help the child in making letters.

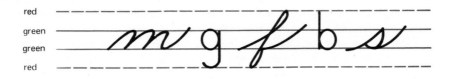

12. *Template lines.* For children who need additional help in stopping at lines, tape can be placed at bottom and top lines. Windows can be cut out of shirt cardboard to give further guidance to the child for spacing letters. Below is a picture of a cardboard with three window slots for 1-line, 2-line, and 3-line letters.

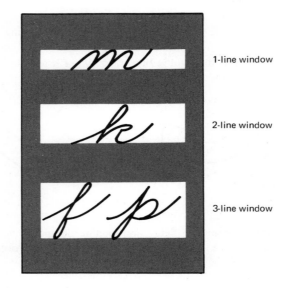

1-line window

2-line window

3-line window

One-line letters are those that fit in a single-line space: a, c, e, i, m, n. Two-line letters are considered to be those with ascenders only: b, d, h, k, l, t. And three-line letters are those with descenders: f, g, j, p, q, z, y.

13. *Letter difficulty.* Larson (1968) suggests teaching the cursive letters in the following order: Beginning letters—m, n, t, i, u, w, r, s, l, e; more difficult letters—x, z, y, j, p, h, b, k, f, g, q; and combinations of letters—me, be, go, it, no, etc.

14. *Auditory reinforcement.* Some children are helped in the motor act of writing by hearing the directions; for example, "down-up-and-around." Care must be taken when using this technique that the child is not distracted by these verbal instructions.

15. *Words and sentences.* After learning to write single letters, instruction should proceed to the writing of words and sentences. Spacing, size, slant are additional factors to be considered.

These activities are representative of handwriting techniques suggested by many authors for helping the child with learning disabilities. Additional suggestions can be obtained in Larson (1968), Academic Therapy Quarterly (1968), Otto and McMenemy (1966), Johnson and Myklebust (1967), and Reger and others (1968).

There are several handwriting scales for evaluating a child's skill, such as *Ayres Measuring Scale for Handwriting* (Educational Testing Service), and the *Freeman Evaluation Scale for Guiding Growth in Handwriting* (Zaner-Bloser).

The goal of handwriting instruction is to help the child develop a useful communication tool. The child should develop a skill in writing legibly and be able to accomplish writing with ease.

## Spelling

Spelling is one curriculum area in which neither creativity nor divergent thinking is encouraged; only one pattern or arrangement of letters can be accepted as correct. The written form or orthography of the English language has an inconsistent pattern; that is, it does not have a complete one-to-one correspondence with the oral or spoken sounds of English. Therefore, spelling is not any easy task, even for youngsters who are not afflicted with learning disabilities. Spelling a word is much more difficult than reading a word. Recognizing a word in print is a decoding task; and in a reading situation there are many clues to aid the reader in word recognition, including context, phonics, structural analysis, and configuration. Reproducing a word, however, is an encoding task; and the opportunity to draw upon peripheral clues is greatly reduced. Many children who are poor in the ability to reproduce words in spelling are skilled in the ability to recognize them in reading. However, the child who is poor in decoding words in reading is almost always poor in spelling as well.

### ENGLISH ORTHOGRAPHY

Examples of the irregular relationship between phonemes (the spoken sound) and graphemes (the written symbol) are easy to cite. George Bernard Shaw, an advocate of spelling reform, is attributed with the suggestion that the word "fish" be spelled *ghoti: gh* as in "cough"; *o* as in "women"; *ti* as in "nation." Following phonic generalizations, the word *natural* could be spelled *pnatchurile*. The many inconsistencies that exist in English spelling are illustrated in the following limericks:*

A king, on assuming his reign,
Exclaimed with a feeling of peign:
"Tho I'm legally heir
No one here seems to ceir
That I haven't been born with a breign."

A merchant addressing a debtor,
Remarked in the course of his lebtor
That he chose to suppose
A man knose what he ose
And the sooner he pays it, the bedtor!

*From the Simplified Spelling Society, quoted in "Strictly Personal: Inglish as it Kud Be Speld," by Sydney J. Harris. *Chicago Daily News,* July 27, 1966.

A young lady crossing the ocean
Grew ill from the ship's dizzy mocean,
She called with a sigh
And a tear in her eigh,
For the doctor to give her a pocean.

And now our brief lesson is through—
I trust you'll agree it was trough;
For it's chiefly designed
To impress on your migned
What wonders our spelling can dough!

Horn (1957) found pupils' spelling of the word "awful" was varied, including: *offul, awful, offel,* and *offle.* Each is an accurate phonetic transcription of the oral sounds of the word. With the orthography of English, a child could conceivably think of the following rules to spell the word "post": *p* as in *psychology; o* as in *Ouija Board; s* as in *sugar;* and *t* as in *themselves.*

## Linguistics and Spelling

In spite of the seemingly numerous exceptions to the rules, recent research in linguistics has indicated that there are predictable spelling patterns and an underlying system of phonological and morphological regularity. Hanna and others (1967) reported that an in-depth analysis of 17,000 words showed that the correct spelling pattern can be predicted for a phoneme sound ninety percent of the time when the main phonological facts of position in syllables, syllable stress, and internal constraints underlying the orthography are taken into consideration. A linguistic approach to the teaching of spelling capitalizes on the underlying regularity that exists between phonological and morphological elements in the oral language and their graphemic representation in orthography.

What is suggested by linguists is that children be helped to discover the underlying linguistic patterns and that words for spelling instruction be selected on the basis of demonstrating the underlying linguistic patterns. Linguists maintain that the spelling curriculum should be organized to encourage such linguistic discovery. When teaching a spelling pattern of the phoneme "oy," for example, the teacher should include in the spelling lesson words like: *boy, joy, Roy,* and *toy,* to help children form a linguistic or phonological generalization.

Similar proposals have been made by authorities in other fields. Durrell (1956), for instance, suggested that spelling programs be merged with phonics instruction. He argues that the phonics and word-analysis skills be practiced, not in the reading class, but during the spelling class. Durrell believes that children make greater progress in spelling through word-analysis practice in reading than through daily instruction in spelling. This view received support in a research study of phonics training and spelling achievement conducted by Cramer (1969).

## Visual Sequential Memory

In addition to phonological generalizations, the ability to spell appears to be related to visual sequential memory. The child who is unable to remember or visualize the letters and order of the letters in words will be poor in spelling.

Many of the techniques that have been successful in teaching spelling have, in effect, been ways to strengthen visual sequential memory. Fernald (1943), for example, developed a tracing technique to teach spelling which reinforced the visual image of the word by using the tactile and kinesthetic modalities. To spell a word correctly, the individual must not only have stored the word in memory, but also be able to retrieve it completely. Unlike recognizing a word in reading, there are no visual clues.

## THE TRADITIONAL APPROACH TO SPELLING

The traditional spelling programs have selected words for spelling instruction on the basis of "frequency-of-use" word lists rather than on the basis of "linguistic patterns." A common core of spelling words that are most frequently used in writing was determined through extensive investigations of the writing done by children and adults. Spelling programs that select words on the basis of their utility in writing use the studies of writing vocabularies conducted by spelling authorities such as Fitzgerald (1951). A relatively small number of words do most of the work. The following estimate of needed spelling words is given by Rinsland (1945):

500 words make up more than 50% of elementary children's writing;
1000 words make up more than 92% of elementary children's writing;
4000 words make up more than 98% of elementary children's writing.

Fitzgerald (1955) suggests that 2,650 words and their repetitions in derivative forms make up about 95 percent of the writing of elementary school children. He recommends a basic list of 3,500 words for children in elementary school. The criteria for word selection in the traditional spelling curriculum, then, are frequency of use, permanency, and utility.

## SPELLING AND LEARNING DISABILITIES

There are many subskills and abilities demanded of the individual in the act of spelling. He must be able, initially, to read the word; he must be knowledgeable and skillful in certain relationships of phonics and structural analysis; he must be able to apply appropriate phonic generalizations; he has to be able to visualize the appearance of the word; and finally, he needs to have the motor facility to write the word. Difficulties in spelling may be due to a deficit in any or a combination of the above skills.

If visual memory is diagnosed as the major problem factor, activities to help the child strengthen and reinforce visual memory are suggested. If a deficit in auditory perception of letter sounds appears to be a factor, or if auditory memory is unable to hold sounds or syllables in mind, the teaching plan would have to take these factors into account. Motor memory is also a factor in spelling, for the speller must remember how the word "felt" when he previously wrote it. In addition, inter-sensory transfer probably plays a crucial role in developing efficient spelling ability. A crossing and integrating of visual, auditory, and kinesthetic modalities are needed before the spelling of a word becomes a subconscious, automatic process.

Some recent work on a behavioral approach to spelling is based on the need to develop inter-sensory transfer for efficient spelling behavior. According to

Personke and Yee (1966):

> No one channel is correct for spelling a particular word each time it is met. Reinforcement of correct responses enlarges the store of the memory drum. The internal inputs, particularly of the immature speller, are subject to constant change. This shifting from one channel to another is perhaps the best indication of the complementarity of the channels.

Using this model, Brothers and Holsclaw (1969) suggest a spelling program designed to fuse five spelling behaviors: (1) copying, (2) proofreading, (3) rewriting, (4) writing from memory consciously, and (5) spelling automatically without conscious thought.

## Diagnosis of Spelling Difficulties

Many survey tests of spelling are available as part of a comprehensive academic achievement battery. These tests yield a grade-level score, but an analysis of the errors made will give greater diagnostic information. A diagnostic test of spelling, the *Gates-Russell Spelling Diagnostic Test* (1937), contains nine subtests and gives information on the following areas: spelling words orally, word pronunciation, giving letter-for-letter sounds, spelling one or more syllables, reversals, methods of word attack and word study, auditory discrimination, and a measure of the effectiveness of visual, kinesthetic, or combined methods of study.

An informal diagnostic test of spelling ability was suggested by Watson (1935) for classroom use. An adaptation of this test can be made for individual diagnosis. The essentials of this method are:

1. Select a list of 30–50 words based on any graded list of the grade level of the child or the class.

2. Administer the spelling test.

3. Score the test and tabulate the results. If used with a class, note the lowest 20 percent.

4. Have the pupils define words they misspelled. Omit words that are not known since they are not in his vocabulary.

5. Have pupils spell any remaining words orally. Keep a record of the spelling, note the syllabication, phonic use, and speech or hearing difficulties.

6. Compare the original spelling to note differences in oral and written responses.

7. Ask the child to study words missed (for about 10 minutes), and to observe his method of study.

8. Analyze errors and incorporate information from the data obtained from other sources.

9. Draw conclusions as to the nature of the spelling problem. Plan educational strategies to overcome the difficulties.

10. Discuss the analysis and teaching plan with the pupil. Provide for pupils to see progress.

## Strategies for Teaching Spelling

1. *Auditory perception and memory of letter sounds*. Provide practice in auditory perception of letter sounds, strengthen knowledge of phonics and structural

analysis, and develop skills in applying phonic generalizations. See Chapter 8 for specific techniques.

2. *Visual perception and memory of letters.* Help the child strengthen visual perception and memory so that he can retain the visual image of the word. Materials should be clear and concise and the child should be helped to focus his attention on the activity. Letting the child use a pocket flashlight might be helpful as an aid in getting him to focus his attention. To develop speed of visual recognition, a tachistoscope can be used to expose material from 1½ seconds to 1/100 second. Flash cards can also be used as an aid in developing speed. See Chapter 8 for specific methods to develop visual perception and memory.

3. *Multi-sensory methods in spelling.* When the child is asked to study his spelling lessons, he is frequently at a loss as to what to do. The following five steps are suggested by Fitzgerald (1955) as a multi-sensory approach that utilizes the visual, auditory, kinesthetic, and tactile modalities.

a. *Meaning and pronunciation.* Have the child look at the word, pronounce it correctly, and use it in a sentence.

b. *Imagery.* Ask the child to "see" the word and say the word. Have him say each syllable of the word, then say the word syllable by syllable. Next, he spells the word orally. Then he traces the word in the air, or over the word itself, with his finger.

c. *Recall.* Ask the child to look at the word and then close his eyes and see the word in his mind's eye. Have him spell the word orally. Ask him to open his eyes to see if he was correct. (If an error is made he should repeat the process.)

d. *Writing the word.* The child writes the word correctly from memory, then checks the spelling against the original to see if it was correct. He should check the writing, too, to make sure every letter is legible.

e. *Mastery.* The child covers the word and writes it. If he is correct, he should cover and write it two more times.

4. *The Fernald-Keller Method* (Fernald 1943). This method is a multi-sensory approach to teaching reading and writing as well as spelling. Very briefly, the following steps are involved:

a. The child is told he is going to learn words in a new way that has proved to be very successful. He is encouraged to select a word that he wishes to learn.

b. The teacher writes his word on a piece of paper, 4 inches by 10 inches, as the child watches and as the teacher says the word.

c. The child traces the word as he says it several times. Then he writes the word on a separate piece of paper as he says it.

d. The word is then written from memory without looking at the original copy. If it is incorrect, the tracing and saying steps are repeated. If the word is correct, it is put in a file box. The words in the file box are used later in stories.

e. At later stages this painstaking tracing method for learning words is not needed. Now the child learns a word by *looking* as the teacher writes it, *saying* it, and *writing* it. At a still later stage, he can learn by only looking at a word in print and writing it. Finally, he learns the word by merely looking at it.

5. *The "Test-Study-Test" vs. the "Study-Test" method.* In teaching spelling to a classroom, there are two common approaches: the "test-study-test" and the "study-test" plans. The test-study-test method uses a pretest, which is usually

given at the beginning of the week. The child then studies only those words that he missed on the pretest. This method is better for older children who have fairly good spelling abilities since there is no need to study words he already knows. The study-test method is better for the young child and the child with poor spelling abilities. Since too many words would be missed on a pretest, this method permits him to study a few well-selected words before the test is given.

6. *Spelling words on the filmstrip projector.* Put spelling words on transparencies. Cut strips to widths to fit into the projector. Push the strip through to show spelling words on the screen. Cover and show quickly for tachistoscopic use. Words can also be written with certain letters left out, to be completed by the child (Lerner and Vaver 1970).

7. *Listening centers and tapes.* Spelling lessons can easily be put on tape. After the child has advanced to a level that would enable him to work by himself, spelling lessons can be completed in a listening laboratory. The use of earphones allows for individualization of instruction, and for many children the earphones provide an aid to block out distracting auditory stimuli.

8. *Programed spelling.* Some of the new materials in spelling are designed as programed materials. The material is given in small steps, immediate reinforcement is provided, and the programs are designed to be self-instructional.

These methods are merely representative of techniques designed to teach spelling. Additional methods can be found in *Building Spelling Skills* (*Academic Therapy Quarterly* 1967), *Corrective and Remedial Teaching* (Otto and McMenemy 1966), *Guiding Language Learning* (Dawson 1963), and *Learning Disabilities* (Johnson and Myklebust 1967).

## Written Expression

Poor facility in expressing thoughts through written language is probably the most prevalent disability of the communication skills. Many adults, as well as children, are unable to communicate effectively and to share ideas through writing. The ability to write down ideas requires many underlying prerequisite skills: facility in oral language, ability to read, some skill in spelling, a legible handwriting, some knowledge of the rules of written usage.

In addition to the preceding requirements, the child must have something to write about. Writing is a means of producing an output of ideas; obviously, there can be little output without an abundance of input. Because a strong relationship exists between the quantity of input experiences and the quality of output in the form of writing, the teacher must provide rich input experiences, such as trips, stories, discussions, and oral language activities. A written assignment that is given without first supplying a receptive buildup (such as, "Write a 500-word theme on Spring") is not likely to yield rich written productions. Writing needs prior sufficient input experiences to create and stimulate ideas the child can write about.

Another possible detriment to writing is the teacher's response to the child's writing, if it takes the form of excessive correction. The child is discouraged from trying if he has attempted to express his ideas and then has his paper returned full of grammatical, spelling, punctuation, and handwriting corrections in red ink with heavy penalties for his mistakes. As one child remarked, "An 'F' looks so much worse in red ink." From the behavior modification viewpoint, the child is receiving negative reinforcement for his behavior. The child soon learns to beat the game by limiting his writing vocabulary to words he knows how to spell, by keeping his sentences simple, by avoiding complex and creative ideas, and by keeping his composition short.

### Strategies for Teaching Written Expression

A number of methods have been used to avoid such discouragement. Teachers may grade only ideas, not the technical form, for some assignments. Or two grades can be given: one for ideas and one for technical skills. For the child who makes errors in many areas, only one skill at a time might be selected for correction, such as capitalization. It is useful to make a differentiation between *personal* writing lessons and *functional* writing lessons. In personal writing, the goal is to develop ideas and express them in written form. The *process* rather than the output itself is important and there is less need for technical perfection. In contrast, the goal of functional writing is learning the form of the output. In this case the final product, such as a business letter, is to be read by another individual and certain standards and forms are essential. By separating the goals of these two types of lessons, different kinds of writing skills can be developed in each.

Dawson (1963) has suggested a developmental sequence in teaching writing:

1. *Composing and dictating to the teacher.* Before the child begins to write by himself, he can develop skills in organizing ideas through language by dictating his composition. The teacher writes his story down; the child gets the idea that thoughts can be expressed in oral language, and thoughts can be written down. These experiences are then permanent, and they can be reviewed by the child and read by other people. He also sees how capital letters, spelling, and punctuation are used to clarify the thoughts he has expressed.

2. *Copying.* The next step in learning to write is to copy the ideas the teacher has put in written form. Now he needs the visual-motor skills and handwriting skills. Copying may be very tiring for some children and it needs close supervision to be of value.

3. *Dictation.* After studying an experience story that the child has written and copied, the teacher helps the child recall the story and then the teacher dictates the entire story or parts of the story for the child to write. At first the child will need to study the story carefully, but later the child will be able to write as the teacher dictates, without previous study.

4. *Rewriting.* Have the child rewrite the story by himself without the dictation by the teacher.

5. *Practice.* Like any other skill, much practice is needed in learning to write. Give the child many experiences in writing. Difficult spelling words can be anticipated and listed on the board, or the child may simply ask for the spelling of difficult words. Fader (1966) found that the assignment of a certain number of pages per week in a personal journal that was uncorrected, and even unread, by the teacher was an excellent technique to provide the needed practice and to improve the quality of writing.

Among the few available tests to measure written language expression are the *Sequential Tests of Educational Progress* (STEP), and the *Picture Story Language Test* (Myklebust 1965).

Additional teaching methods to help children learn to write are suggested by Ferris (1967), "Teaching Children to Write" in *Guiding Children's Language Learning* (Dawson 1963), *They All Want to Write* by Burrows and others (1965) and *From Thoughts to Words* by Glaus (1965).

## Summary

This section has presented teaching strategies for the curriculum areas that involve expressive written language. The skills discussed were handwriting, spelling, and written expression. Expressive written language is the highest and most complex of the language skills. The child with a learning disability in these activities is likely to have underlying deficit areas in which he needs help.

Handwriting is difficult for many children with learning disabilities. This disability may be related to visual-motor disturbances, poor motor development, a deficit in spatial relationships, or a deficit in voluntary motor movement. Teaching strategies that have been useful in helping such children learn handwriting were presented.

Even children who are successful in reading finding spelling difficult to master. Linguistic factors such as the phonological system and visual sequential memory were discussed in relation to spelling. The rationale of the traditional approach to spelling was presented. Many characteristics of the child with learning disabilities combine to make spelling very difficult. Some techniques for teaching spelling were suggested.

Written expression is another troublesome area for the child with learning disabilities. The many elements that have to be integrated and combined for the child to write makes this task difficult. Several ways to develop skills in written expression were suggested.

Written language skills are the last of the language skills to be learned. It is important that the child have a sound foundation in oral language skills as a base for the addition of the most difficult of the language skills.

## REFERENCES

Academic Therapy Quarterly. *Building Handwriting Skills*. San Rafael, Calif.: Academic Therapy Publications 4, Fall 1968.

Academic Therapy Quarterly. *Building Spelling Skills*. San Rafael, Calif.: Academic Therapy Publications 3, Fall 1967.

Allen, Roach Van. "How a Language Experience Program Works," pp. 1–8 in Elaine C. Vilscek (ed.), *Decade of Innovations: Approaches to Beginning Reading*. Newark, Del.: International Reading Association, 1968.

Anderson, Paul S. Chapter 6 in *Language Skills in Elementary Education*. New York: Macmillan, 1964.

Atkinson, Richard C., and Duncan N. Hansen. "Computer-Assisted Instruction in Initial Reading: The Stanford Project," *Reading Research Quarterly* 2 (Fall 1966): 5–26.

Austin, Mary C., and Coleman Morrison. *The First R: The Harvard Report on Reading in Elementary Schools.* New York: Macmillan, 1963.

Austin, Mary C., et al. *The Torch Lighters: Tomorrow's Teachers of Reading.* Cambridge, Mass.: Harvard University Press, 1961.

*Ayres Measuring Scale for Handwriting.* Princeton, N.J.: Cooperative Test Division of Educational Testing Services, 1912.

Bangs, Tina E. *Language and Learning Disorders of the Pre-Academic Child.* New York: Appleton-Century-Crofts, 1968.

Baratz, Joan. "Linguistic and Cultural Factors in Teaching Reading to Ghetto Children," *Elementary English* 46 (February 1969): 199–203.

Barrett, Thomas C. "Visual Discrimination Tasks as Predictors of First Grade Reading Achievement," *Reading Teacher* 18 (January 1965): 276–282.

Beaver, Joseph C. "Transformational Grammar and the Teaching of Reading," *Research in the Teaching of English* 2 (Fall 1968): 161–171.

Bellugi, U., and R. W. Brown, editors. *The Acquisition of Language.* Monographs of the Society for Research in Child Development 29 (1964).

Berko, Jean. "The Child's Learning of English Morphology," *Word* 14 (1958): 150–177.

Bernstein, Basil. "Elaborated and Restricted Codes: Their Social Origins and Some Consequences," *American Anthropologist* 66, Part 2 (1964): 55–69.

Black, Millard H. "To What End?", pp. 25–28 in James K. Kerfoot (ed.), *Reading for the Disadvantaged.* Newark, Del.: International Reading Association, 1967.

Bloom, Benjamin, Allison Davis, and Robert Hess. *Compensatory Education for Cultural Deprivation.* New York: Holt, Rinehart & Winston, 1965.

Bloomfield, Leonard, and Clarence L. Barnhart. *Let's Read,* Part I. Bronxville, N.Y.: C. L. Barnhart, 1963.

Bond, Guy L. "First-Grade Reading Studies: An Overview," *Elementary English* 43 (May 1966): 464–470.

Bond, Guy L., and Robert Dykstra. "The Cooperative Research Program in First-Grade Reading Instruction," *Reading Research Quarterly* 2 (Summer 1967): entire issue.

Bond, Guy L., and Miles A. Tinker. *Reading Difficulties: Their Diagnosis and Correction,* 2nd ed. New York: Appleton-Century-Crofts, 1967.

Bormuth, John R. "The Cloze Readability Procedure," *Elementary English* 45 (April 1968): 429–436.

Brothers, Aileen, and Cora Holsclaw. "Fusing Behaviors into Spelling," *Elementary English* 46 (January 1969): 32–37.

Buchanan, Cynthia. *Programmed Reading.* Sullivan Associates. Manchester, Mo.: Webster Division, McGraw-Hill, 1966.

Burke, Carolyn, and Kenneth Goodman. "What a Child Reads: A Psycholinguistic Analysis," *Elementary English* 47 (January 1970): 121–130.

Burrows, Alvina Treut, et al. *They All Want to Write,* 3rd ed. New York: Holt, Rinehart & Winston, 1965.

Carroll, John. "Some Neglected Relationships in Reading and Language Learning," *Elementary English* 43 (October 1966): 576–579.

Chall, Jeanne. *Learning to Read: The Great Debate.* New York: McGraw-Hill, 1967.

Chomsky, Noam. *Aspects of the Theory of Syntax.* Cambridge, Mass.: MIT Press, 1965.

———. "The General Properties of Language," pp. 73–80 in C. H. Millikan (chairman) and F. L. Darley (ed.), *Brain Mechanisms Underlying Speech and Language.* New York: Grune & Stratton, 1967.

Cramer, Ronald L. "The Influence of Phonic Instructions on Spelling Achievement," *Reading Teacher* 22 (March 1969): 499–503.

Critchley, MacDonald. *Developmental Dyslexia.* Springfield, Ill.: Charles C. Thomas, 1964.

Dallman, Martha. *Teaching the Language Arts in the Elementary School.* Dubuque, Iowa: William C. Brown, 1966.

Dawson, Mildred, et al. *Guiding Language Learning.* New York: Harcourt, Brace & World, 1963.

De Hirsch, Katrina, et al. *Predicting Reading Failure.* New York: Harper & Row, 1966.

Deighton, Lee C. "Flow of Thought Through an English Sentence," pp. 73–76 in Mildred Dawson (ed.), *Developing Comprehension Including Critical Reading.* Newark, Del.: International Reading Association, 1968.

Duker, Sam. *Listening Bibliography.* New York: The Scarecrow Press, 1964.

Durrell, Donald. *Improving Reading Instruction.* New York: Harcourt, Brace & World, 1956.

Eichenwald, Heinz F. "The Pathology of Reading Disorders: Psychophysiological Factors," in M. Johnson and R. Kress (eds.), *Corrective Reading in the Elementary Classroom*. Newark, Del.: International Reading Association, 1967.

Engelmann, Siegfried, and Elaine C. Bruner. *Distar Reading I and II: An Instructional System*. Chicago: Science Research Associates, 1969.

Fader, Daniel N., and M. Schaevitz. *Hooked on Books*. New York: Berkley Publishing Co., 1966.

Fernald, Grace. *Remedial Techniques in Basic School Subjects*. New York: McGraw-Hill, 1943.

Ferris, Donald R. "Teaching Children to Write," Chapter 6 in Pose Lamb (ed.), *Guiding Children's Language Learning*. Dubuque, Iowa: William C. Brown, 1967.

Fitzgerald, James A. *A Basic Life Spelling Vocabulary*. Milwaukee: Bruce Publishing Co., 1951.

————. "Children's Experiences in Spelling," Chapter 11 in V. Herrick and L. Jacobs (eds.), *Children and the Language Arts*. Englewood Cliffs, N.J.: Prentice-Hall, 1955.

Flavell, J. H., D. R. Beach, and J. M. Chinsky. "Spontaneous Verbal Rehearsal in a Memory Task as a Function of Age," *Child Development* 37 (1963): 283–300.

*Freeman Evaluation Scale for Guiding Growth in Handwriting*. Columbus, Ohio: Zaner-Bloser, 1958.

Fries, Charles C. *Linguistics and Reading*. New York: Holt, Rinehart & Winston, 1963.

————. "Linguistic Approaches," in James Kerfoot (ed.), *First Grade Reading Programs*. Newark, Del.: International Reading Association, 1965.

Fry, Edward. "A Diacritical Marking System to Aid Beginning Reading Instruction," *Elementary English* 41, May 1964.

————. "New Alphabet Approaches," pp. 72–95 in James Kerfoot (ed.), *First Grade Reading Programs*. Newark, Del.: International Reading Association, 1965.

*Gates-Russell Spelling Diagnostic Test*. New York: Teachers College, Columbia University, 1937.

Gattegno, Caleb. *Words in Color*. Chicago: Learning Materials, Inc., Encyclopaedia Britannica, 1962.

Gillingham, Anna, and Bessie W. Stillman. *Remedial Training for Children with Specific Difficulty in Reading, Spelling, and Penmanship*, 7th ed. Cambridge, Mass.: Educators Publishing Service, 1966.

Glaus, Marlene. *From Thoughts to Words*. Champaign, Ill.: National Council of Teachers of English, 1965.

Gleason, H. A., Jr. *Linguistics and English Grammar*. New York: Holt, Rinehart & Winston, 1965.

Goodman, Kenneth S. "Reading: A Psycholinguistic Guessing Game," *Journal of the Reading Specialist* 6 (May 1967): 126-135.

————. "Analysis of Oral Reading Miscues," *Reading Research Quarterly* 5 (Fall 1969): 9–30.

————. "Words and Morphemes in Reading," pp. 25–33 in K. Goodman and J. Fleming (eds.), *Psycholinguistics and the Teaching of Reading*. Newark, Del.: International Reading Association, 1969.

Hafner, Lawrence E. "Implications of Cloze," pp. 151–158 in E. Thurston and L. Hafner (eds.), *Philosophical and Sociological Bases of Reading*. Milwaukee: National Reading Conference, 1965.

Hallgren, B. "Specific Dyslexia: A Clinical and Genetic Study," *Acta Psychiatrica Neurologica*, Supplement 65 (1950): 1–287.

Hanna, Paul R., et al. "A Summary: Linguistic Cues for Spelling Improvement," *Elementary English* 44 (December 1967): 862–865.

Hardy, Miriam P. "Communication and Communication Disorders," pp. 129–136 in W. Cruickshank (ed.), *Teacher of the Brain-Injured Child*. Syracuse: Syracuse University Press, 1966.

Haring, Norris G., and Mary Ann Hauch. "Improving Learning Conditions in the Establishment of Reading Skills with Disabled Readers," *Exceptional Children* 35 (January 1969): 341–352.

Harris, Albert. *How to Increase Reading Ability*, 5th ed. New York: David McKay, 1970.

Hermann, Knud. *Reading Disability: A Medical Study of Word-Blindness and Related Handicaps*. Springfield, Ill.: Charles C. Thomas, 1959.

Herrick, Virgil E., and Leland B. Jacobs (eds.). *Children and the Language Arts*. Englewood Cliffs, N.J.: Prentice-Hall, 1955.

Hildreth, Gertrude. Chapters 19–21 in *Learning the Three R's*. Minneapolis: Educational Test Bureau, 1947.

Hinshelwood, James. *Congenital Word-Blindness*. London: H. K. Lewis, 1917.

Hook, J. N. "So What Good Is English?" Distinguished Lecture for National Council of Teachers of English, 1967.

Horn, Ernst. "Phonetics and Spelling," *Elementary School Journal* 57 (May 1957): 424–432.

Itard, J. M. *The Wild Boy of Aveyron*. New York: Appleton-Century-Crofts, 1962.

Johnson, Doris, and Helmer Myklebust. *Learning Disabilities: Educational Principles and Practices*. New York: Grune & Stratton, 1967.

Johnson, Dorothy K. "The O. K. Moore Typewriter Procedure," pp. 511–516 in A. R. Binter et al. (eds.), *Readings on Reading*. Scranton, Pa.: International Textbook Co., 1969.

Keller, Helen. *The Story of My Life*. New York: Dell, 1961.

Kellogg, Ralph E. "Listening," pp. 117–136 in Pose Lamb (ed.), *Guiding Children's Language Learning*. Dubuque, Iowa: William C. Brown, 1967.

Kirk, Samuel A., James P. McCarthy, and Winifred D. Kirk. *The Illinois Test of Psycholinguistic Abilities*, rev. ed. Urbana, Ill.: University of Illinois Press, 1968.

Kleffner, Frank R. "Teaching Aphasic Children," pp. 330–337 in J. Magary and J. Eichorn (eds.), *The Exceptional Child*. New York: Holt, Rinehart & Winston, 1964.

Kravitz, Ida. "The Disadvantaged Child: Some Implications for Teaching of Reading," pp. 13–26 in *The Culturally Deprived Reader*. Newark, Del.: International Reading Association, 1966.

Langer, Suzanne K. *Philosophy in a New Key*. New York: Mentor Books, New American Library, 1958.

Larson, Charlotte. "Teaching Beginning Writing," *Academic Therapy Quarterly* 4 (Fall 1968): 61–66.

Lee, Dorris M., and Roach Van Allen. *Learning to Read Through Experience*, 2nd ed. New York: Appleton-Century-Crofts, 1963.

Lefevre, Carl. *Linguistics and the Teaching of Reading*. New York: McGraw-Hill, 1964.

Lerner, Janet W. "A Global Theory of Reading—and Linguistics," *Reading Teacher* 21 (February 1968): 416–421.

———. "A New Focus for Reading Research—The Decision-Making Process," *Elementary English* 44 (March 1967): 236–242.

———. "A Thorn by Any Name: Dyslexia or Reading Disability," *Elementary English* 48, January 1971.

Lerner, Janet W., and Lynne List. "The Phonics Knowledge of Prospective Teachers, Experienced Teachers, and Elementary Pupils," *Illinois School Research* 7 (Fall 1970): 39–42.

Lerner, Janet W., and Gerald A. Vaver. "Filmstrips in Learning," *Academic Therapy Quarterly* 4 (Summer 1970): 320–325.

Luria, A. R. *Speech and the Regulation of Behavior*. New York: Liveright, 1961.

Mackintosh, Helen K., editor. *Children and Oral Language*. Joint publication of the Association for Childhood Education International, Association for Supervision and Curriculum Development, International Reading Association, National Council of Teachers of English, 1964.

McCarthy, Dorothea. "Language Development in Children," in Leonard Carmichael (ed.), *A Manual of Child Psychology*. New York: John Wiley & Sons, 1954.

McCarthy, J. "Research of the Linguistic Problems of the Mentally Retarded," *Mental Retardation Abstracts* 2 (1964): 90–96.

McGrady, Harold J. "Language Pathology and Learning Disabilities, pp. 199–233 in H. Myklebust (ed.), *Progress in Learning Disorders*, vol. I. New York: Grune & Stratton, 1968.

McLuhan, Marshall. *Understanding Media: The Extensions of Man*, 2nd ed. New York: Signet, New American Library, 1964.

Menyuk, Paula. *Sentences Children Use*. Cambridge, Mass.: MIT Press, 1969.

Miel, Alice. *Individualized Reading Practices*. New York: Columbia University, 1958.

Money, John, editor. *The Disabled Reader: Education of the Dyslexic Child*. Baltimore: Johns Hopkins Press, 1966.

Monroe, Marion. *Children Who Cannot Read*. Chicago: University of Chicago Press, 1932.

Morgan, W. P. "A Case of Congenital Word-Blindness," *British Medical Journal* 2 (November 1896): 1378.

Myklebust, Helmer. *Picture Story Language Test. The Development and Disorders of Written Language*, Vol. 1. New York: Grune & Stratton, 1965.

———. *The Psychology of Deafness*, 2nd ed. New York: Grune & Stratton, 1964.

National Advisory Committee on Dyslexia and Related Disorders. *Report to the Secretary of the Department of Health, Education and Welfare*, August 1969.

Orton, June L. "The Orton-Gillingham Approach," pp. 119–146 in John Money (ed.), *The Disabled Reader.* Baltimore: Johns Hopkins Press, 1966.

Orton, Samuel T. *Reading, Writing and Speech Problems in Children.* New York: W. W. Norton, 1937.

Otto, Wayne, and Richard A. McMenemy. *Corrective and Remedial Teaching: Principles and Practices.* Boston: Houghton Mifflin, 1966.

Personke, Carl, and Albert H. Yee. "A Model for the Analysis of Spelling Behavior," *Elementary English* 43 (March 1966): 278–284.

Piaget, J. *The Origins of Intelligence in Children.* M. Cook, trans. New York: International University Press, 1952.

Pinter, Rudolph, Jon Eisenson, and Mildred Stanton. Chapter 5 in *The Psychology of the Physically Handicapped.* New York: Appleton-Century-Crofts, 1945.

Rankin, Earl F., Jr. "The Cloze Procedure—A Survey of Research," pp. 133–150 in E. Thurston and L. Hafner (eds.), *The Philosophical and Sociological Bases of Reading,* fourteenth yearbook of the National Reading Conference. Milwaukee: National Reading Conference, 1965.

Reger, Roger, W. Schroeder, and K. Uschold. *Special Education.* New York: Oxford University Press, 1968.

Richardson, Sylvia O. "Language Training for Mentally Retarded Children," pp. 146–161 in R. Schiefelbusch et al. (eds.), *Language and Mental Retardation.* New York: Holt, Rinehart & Winston, 1967.

Rinsland, Henry D. *A Basic Vocabulary of Elementary School Children.* New York: Macmillan, 1945.

Robinson, Helen M. *Why Pupils Fail in Reading.* Chicago: University of Chicago, 1946.

Russell, David H., and Elizabeth F. Russell. *Listening Aids Through the Grades.* New York: Teachers College, Columbia University, 1959.

Schiefelbusch, Richard, Ross H. Copeland, and James O. Smith. *Language and Mental Retardation.* New York: Holt, Rinehart & Winston, 1967.

Schmitt, Clara. "Developmental Alexia," *Elementary School Journal* 18 (May 1918): 680–700, 757–769.

Seashore, Robert H. "The Importance of Vocabulary in Learning Language Skills," *Elementary English* 25 (March 1948): 137–152.

*Sequential Tests of Educational Progress.* Princeton, N.Y.: Cooperative Test Division, Educational Testing Service.

Spache, George. "Contributions of Allied Fields to the Teaching of Reading," pp. 237–290 in H. Robinson (ed.), *Innovations and Change in Reading Instruction.* Chicago: University of Chicago Press, 1968.

Spradlin, Joseph. "Procedures for Evaluating Processes Associated with Receptive and Expressive Language," pp. 118–136 in R. Schiefelbusch, R. Copeland, and J. Smith (eds.), *Language and Mental Retardation.* New York: Holt, Rinehart & Winston, 1967.

Stauffer, Russell G. "The Verdict: Speculative Controversy," *Reading Teacher* 19 (May 1966): 563.

Strickland, Ruth. "Building on What We Know," pp. 55–62 in J. Allen Figurel (ed.), *Reading and Realism.* Newark, Del.: International Reading Association, 1969.

Tanyzer, Harold J., and Albert J. Mazurkiewicz. *Early-to-Read i/t/a Program Book 2.* New York: i/t/a Publications, 1967.

*Typing Our Language: Elementary Typewriting.* Chicago: Scott-Foresman, 1969.

*UNIFON Reading Program.* Racine, Wis.: Western Publishing Educational Services, 1966.

Veatch, Jeanette. *Individualize Your Reading Program.* New York: G. P. Putnam & Sons, 1959.

Vernon, M. *Backwardness in Reading.* London: Cambridge University Press, 1957.

Vygotsky, L. S. *Thought and Language.* Cambridge, Mass.: MIT Press, 1962.

Wark, David M. "Case Studies in Behavior Modification," pp. 217–228 in G. Schick and M. May (eds.), *The Psychology of Reading Behavior.* Milwaukee: National Reading Conference, 1969.

Watson, A. E. *Experimental Studies in the Psychology and Teaching of Spelling.* Contributions to Education, no. 638. New York: Teachers College, Columbia University, 1935.

Weaver, Wendel W. "Theoretical Aspects of the Cloze Procedure," pp. 115–132 in E. Thurson and L. Hafner (eds.), *The Philosophical and Sociological Bases of Reading.* Fourteenth yearbook of the National Reading Conference. Milwaukee: National Reading Conference, 1965.

Wilkinson, Andrew. "Oracy in English Teaching," *Elementary English* 45 (October 1968): 743–748.

Wilt, Miriam E. "Let's Teach Listening." Creative Ways in Teaching the Language Arts, Leaflet 4. Champaign, Ill.: National Council of Teachers of English, 1957.

———. "The Teaching of Listening and Why," in V. Anderson *et al.* (eds.), *Readings in the Language Arts*. New York: Macmillan, 1964.

Wittick, Mildred Letton. "Innovations in Reading Instruction: for Beginners," pp. 72–125 in H. Robinson (ed.), *Innovation and Change in Reading Instruction*, 67th yearbook of the National Society for the Study of Education, pt. 2. Chicago: University of Chicago Press, 1968.

Wood, Nancy. *Delayed Speech and Language Development*. Englewood Cliffs, N.J.: Prentice-Hall, 1964.

———. *Language Disorders in Children*. Chicago: National Society for Crippled Children and Adults, 1959.

———. *Verbal Learning*. San Rafael, Calif.: Dimensions Publishing Co., 1969.

Woodcock, Richard W., and Charlotte R. Clark. *Peabody Rebus Reading Program*. Circle Pines, Minn.: American Guidance Service, 1969.

# Chapter 10

# Cognitive Skills

# THEORY

In this chapter, the discussion concerns the acquisition of cognitive skills—specifically: (a) concept development, (b) mental processes, (c) developmental imbalances, and (d) language as a cognitive process.

At the apex of man's developmental hierarchy is the acquisition of cognitive skills—the ability to conceptualize, to use abstractions, and to think creatively and critically. The other stages of development (motor development, perception, memory, and language), discussed in previous chapters, provide the base for the development of the cognitive skills.

A disturbance in the thinking process no doubt is an important factor for many children with learning disabilities. Further, a disturbance or inadequate development at the lower levels of the hierarchy is likely to adversely affect the development of the higher cognitive abilities. In discussing the development of cognitive structures in children with learning problems, Gardner (1966, pp. 145–146) states:

> It is known that even mild brain damage may have severe effects upon concept formation. . . . Impairments of the capacity to categorize and abstract effectively are sometimes among the most easily observed sequelae of brain damage. . . .
>
> In the school situation, the combination of difficulties affecting concept formation may have some traumatic effects. It may be difficult for even the mildly brain-damaged child to understand, and especially to remember relationships among superficially dissimilar ideas. He may adopt a piecemeal approach to concept formation in which some abstract relationships (in which a capacity for concrete association can be substituted for true abstraction) with remarkable ease but fail to grasp other relationships that appear superficially to be equally simple.

## Concept Development

In spite of the obvious importance of the development of cognitive abilities to learning, the teacher of children with learning disabilities has less help in the form of tests, diagnostic instruments, and teaching materials for this area than for the other levels of learning. The learning of concepts is now regarded as an important objective in all areas of education. Contributing to this field are such eminent scholars as Bruner (1956, 1966), Guilford (1960), Flavell (1963), Hunt (1961), and Skinner (1953). All agree to the general statement that the learning of concepts is an important objective. The difficulty comes in operationalizing the goal of concept development into methods of learning and teaching.

Klausmeier and Miller (1968) point out three reasons for this difficulty:

1. Concepts have not been clearly defined. As a result teachers and others do not know precisely what to teach as concepts.

2. Learning theorists have not come up with a clear explanation of concept learning. The course of concept learning cannot be predicted or controlled well, based on learning theory.

3. The considerable knowledge from empirical research about concept learning has not been translated into instructional guidelines.

## WHAT ARE CONCEPTS?

Concepts are commonly explained as the thinking process, ideas, cognition, or abstractions. A typical illustration of a concept is a *chair, dog,* or *man.* These terms refer to an idea, an abstraction, or a symbol of concrete experiences. A person's experiences may have included exposure to a specific rocking chair, an upholstered chair, and a baby's high chair; but the concept *chair* symbolizes a set of attributes about "chairness"; the person makes an inference about new experiences with chairs, such as a lawn chair, that he observes for the first time. The symbol itself does not have an empirical reference point. The Greeks searched for an understanding of concepts which Plato, in the *Republic,* equated with knowing the "essence" of things.

Although it is possible to form concepts without words, language plays an important role in concept development; and a child's language disorder is likely to be reflected in faulty conceptual abilities.

At a higher level of conceptualization, the ideas are still further removed from concrete referents. The concept *chair* is part of a higher concept of *furniture.* Concepts even more removed from the sensory world are ideas such as *democracy, loyalty, fairness,* or *freedom.* A "generalization" is broader than a concept and is formed by relating at least two concepts. The following statement may be considered a generalization: "Man makes adaptations to his environment."

## FAULTY CONCEPTIONS

What happens when concepts have not been well built? What are the consequences to learning if concepts are meager, lacking in preciseness, inaccurate, or isolated strands?

Children may have learning problems at any of the levels of conceptualization. Some children confuse one attribute of an object with the concept of the object. For example, one child could not understand the circular concept of the roundness of a plate. When told that the plate was round and asked to feel the circle along its edges, the child said, "That's not round; that's a dish." Some children confuse the concept of an object with its name. When one child was asked if the moon could be called by another name, such as "cow," he responded, "No, because the moon doesn't give milk."

Multiple meanings of words also cause confusion. The confusion of multiple meanings in our language is well-illustrated by Smith (1963) who gave as an example the many meanings of the word, "note": (1) In music, *note* means the elliptical character in a certain position on the music staff. (2) In arithmetic or business, a *note* might mean a written promise to pay. (3) In English or study hall a *note* might refer to an informal written communication. (4) In social studies a *note* might refer to a formal communique between the heads of two nations. (5) In science one might be able to *note* results of an experiment, meaning to observe it. (6) In English class, the selection in literature might discuss an individual who was a person of great *note* in the community. (7) In any lesson, the student could be asked to make *note* of an examination date, meaning to remember it. (8) The teacher could make a *note* in the margin of the paper, meaning to make a remark. (9) In material on England, paper money may be called a *bank note*. The child who could not hold the various concepts of this word in mind would have trouble understanding many areas of the curriculum.

The following serves to illustrate the consequences of the misunderstanding of a symbol with multiple concepts: A nine-year-old girl came home from school in tears with a medical form from the school nurse that advised the parents to take their daughter for an eye examination. The child sobbed that the cause of her anguish was not that she needed eye-glasses, but that the blank next to the word *SEX* on the examination form had been filled in by the nurse with an "F." That symbol "F" conveyed the concept of a grade, and the girl feared she had failed sex.

A further confusion in school learning is related to the fact that important concepts are presented as technical terms in school subjects: *plateau, continental divide, density of population, pollution, the law of gravity, monopoly.* Problems in reading in the content areas are frequently due not to the difficulty of the words, but to the concentration and compactness of the presentation of the concepts.

If the pupil fails to read a word he does not know, it may change the meaning of the entire passage. A high school student thought the school was using pornographic material because the people described in the following passage were nude: "The pilgrims did not wear gaudy clothes." Since the boy did not know the meaning of the word *gaudy,* he simply eliminated it from the sentence. Another high school student, misinterpreting a concept because of a word with multiple meanings, filled in an exercise in the following manner. "One swallow does not make a (drunk)."

An implication for teaching to remedy this confusion between concepts and words and faulty conceptualizations is that children need experiences that will equip them for building appropriate concepts. A first step in building a concept is that of having primary experiences. A further aid to concept development is helping children develop the skill of drawing conclusions from the experiences. A more advanced stage is learning to classify, summarize, and generalize conclusions from several experiences.

## A Theory of Mental Processes

Ideas concerning intellectual functioning have changed in the last fifty years, since the appearance of Spearman's (1927) work studying and measuring the intellect. The view of intelligence as a global or general entity proved useful for the early scholars, but today a more fruitful approach appears to be to view intelligence as consisting of many subskills of mental functioning.

Instead of a single "g" factor of global intelligence, there are many elements or components of intelligence. Guilford (1967), for example, suggests that there are as many as 120 different factors of intellectual ability, of which about 80 are known. Until recently the tests available to the school psychologists have been too global to yield the specific information required for making effective teaching plans. As testing instruments are becoming available to measure the subfactors, the diagnostician is able to compare performance in various abilities. Some theories of learning disabilities see learning disability related to a disparity of these various subfactors which make up the intellect.

## STRUCTURE OF MENTAL PROCESSES

One attempt to show the multifaceted nature of the intellect is Guilford's three-dimensional model of the structure of the intellect, shown in Figure 10.1. Guilford (1967) classified intellectual abilities into three categories, each of which cuts across the others: (a) operations, (b) content, and (c) products.

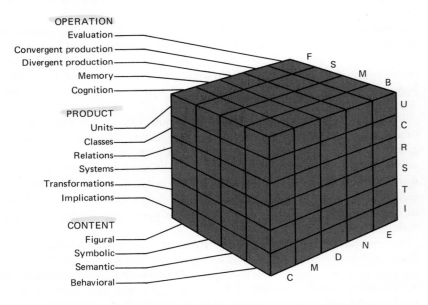

**FIGURE 10.1. GUILFORD MODEL OF THE STRUCTURE OF THE INTELLECT.**
From *The Nature of Human Intelligence* by J. P. Guilford, p. 63. Copyright © 1967 by McGraw-Hill Book Company. Used with permission of McGraw-Hill Book Company.

**Operations.** These are the processes involved in thinking. It refers to what the individual does. The Guilford model has five categories of operations: cognition, memory, convergent thinking, divergent thinking, and evaluation.

a) *Cognition* refers to ways of understanding or comprehension. The group of cognitive abilities has to do with discovery and recognition of information.

b) *Memory* refers to the operations of retention and reproduction of information.

c) *Convergent thinking* is the bringing together of known facts or associations which result in one definite, predictable outcome. The conclusion is determined by the given information and there is a recognition of the best of the conventional conclusions.

d) *Divergent thinking* is the utilization of knowledge in new ways to produce one or many novel solutions or a variety of ideas. This ability may be referred to as creative thinking.

e) *Evaluation* requires the establishment of a value system against which to weigh various alternative actions or results. The ability is sometimes called critical thinking.

**Content.**   Content can be of various types: figural, semantic, symbolic, behavioral. This is a completely different way of classifying abilities and it cuts across operations. Content is concerned with the nature of the material or information. Information that is concrete, that can be seen, heard or felt is called "figural." Information in the abstract form of symbols (such as letters, numbers, or words) is "symbolic" content. "Semantic" content refers to the ideas or meanings that the symbols represent. "Behavioral" content refers to information about the behavior of ourselves and others—including thoughts, desires, feelings, and intentions.

**Products.**   This term refers to the levels of intellectual activities: units, classes, relations, systems, transformations, implications. This third classification is concerned with the products of information; the form of the relationships or groupings of information. Each level of activity is more complex, requiring a higher degree of mental functioning and a more sophisticated way of relating information.

Figure 10.1 shows Guilford's three-dimensional model of the structure of the intellect. When the three cross-classifications are combined, the intersection of a certain kind of *operation*, a certain kind of *content*, and a certain kind of *product*, is represented by a single cell. There are 120 separate cells in the structure of the intellect as represented in the model.

## IMPLICATIONS FOR LEARNING DISABILITIES

The implications of this or a comparable model of the structure of the intellect for the field of learning disabilities are significant. A multi-dimensional approach to intelligence identifies many more abilities (and consequent disabilities) than we had been cognizant of. Further, such approaches imply that some of these discrete abilities may function or dysfunction somewhat apart from the others. While the *Stanford-Binet Intelligence Scale* yielded one global score of general intelligence, the *Wechsler Intelligence Scale for Children* was designed to yield two scores  (verbal and performance scores), and the *Illinois Test of Psycholinguistic Abilities* provides information on twelve areas of mental functioning. Guilford, however, hypothesizes that there are 120 separate cells or areas. As diagnostic tools become available to identify these areas of mental functioning, we can expect that methods of teaching to build these areas will be generated. It can be predicted that such models of mental processes will have a significant impact on both diagnosis and teaching in the field of learning disabilities.

# Developmental Imbalances

Some theorists of learning disabilities focus on the many component parts of the intellect contributing to the learning process; they hypothesize that an uneven development among the various skills has a positive relationship to learning disturbances. According to Gallagher (1966), an observed key difference between children who have special learning problems and children without learning problems is that children who find learning difficult exhibit a large disparity in the developmental patterns of intelligence subskills, that are important to school success. The normal child without a learning disorder exhibits a relatively uniform pattern among subskills, with small differences between his best and worst performances in various mental abilities.

Similarly, the school-age mentally retarded child also shows a relatively consistent pattern, although he exhibits a low level of ability over *all* areas of abilities and skills in comparison to the norm for his chronological age. Neither the normal child nor the mentally retarded child shows substantial variations among the various mental abilities; however, the child with learning disabilities exhibits significant differences in abilities among various mental factors.

To illustrate such a characteristic, a first-grade child with developmental imbalances may show the general language development of a 6-year-old while his perceptual-motor skills may be at a 2- or 3-year-old level.

Gallagher (1966, p. 28) defines developmental imbalances as follows:

> Children with developmental imbalances are those who reveal a developmental disparity in psychological processes related to education of such a degree (often four years or more) as to require the instructional programming of developmental tasks appropriate to the nature and level of the deviant developmental process.

To determine abilities or strengths and weaknesses of a child, it is necessary to break down general intellectual functioning into its various contributing component parts and to measure the functioning level of each. A profile of the subskill scores obtained on a diagnostic test designed for this purpose can indicate if a child with a learning problem has developmental imbalances. Although we lack evidence to show how much disparity in pattern represents a range within normal limits, Gallagher suggests that a deviation of four years or more between the best and worst skills is beyond the normal range.

The *Illinois Test for Psycholinguistic Abilities* (Kirk, McCarthy, and Kirk, 1968), previously discussed in Chapter 4, is one test designed to show a patterning of abilities for diagnostic interpretation. Figure 10.2 shows a profile obtained on a student as a result of his performance on the ITPA. The composite score of the child's Psycholinguistic Abilities Age (PLA) was 5 years 9 months. The figure shows his performance in the twelve subtests expressed in scaled scores. The mean or average scaled score was 35. The profile shows that some scores were more than one standard deviation above the mean score while some scores were more than one standard deviation below the mean score. The performance of this student on the ITPA shows a disparity of 4 standard deviations between the high score on the Verbal Expression subtest and the low score on the Manual Expression subtest. Similarly, when these scores are translated into age-scores (not shown on the graph), these reveal a disparity of over five years between the

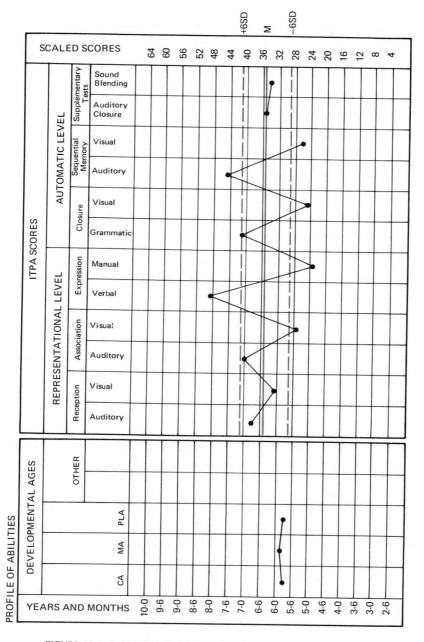

**FIGURE 10.2. A PROFILE OF SCALED SCORES FOR A CHILD WITH A VISUAL CHANNEL DISABILITY.**
From Samuel A. Kirk and Winifred D. Kirk. *Psycholinguistic Learning Disabilities: Diagnosis and Remediation.* Urbana, Illinois: University of Illinois Press, 1971.

high and low scores. The gap between scores higher than one standard deviation above the mean and scores lower than one standard deviation below the mean suggests this child has a significant developmental imbalance, as does the disparity of more than five years between high and low age scores. Further analysis reveals that these intraindividual differences are statistically significant. In addition, such a profile of performance in component abilities permits the location of specific abilities and disabilities which can aid in both diagnosis and the planning of teaching strategies. For example, in the case shown in Figure 10.2, the subject performed substantially better on the auditory-vocal subtests than on the visual-motor subtests, suggesting strength in the auditory-vocal channels and a deficit in the visual-motor channel functions.

## Language as a Cognitive Process

Language cannot be separated from cognitive and thinking processes. Cognition has been defined as the process by which the sensory input is transformed, reduced, elaborated, stored, recovered, and used (Neisser 1967, p. 4). Within such an approach, both the receptive language skills of listening and reading and the expressive language skills of speaking and writing can be viewed as elements of cognition. Language becomes a vehicle for thinking by helping to organize and assimilate input data and by helping to formulate and develop the output. At the same time, the development of cognitive strategies strengthen and enhance language development.

Because of the commonality in the thinking processes underlying all areas of language, the improvement of language skill in one area is likely to result in the improvement of language in other areas. For example, improvement in the skill of listening is likely to produce a concomitant improvement in the area of reading comprehension. Further, many children with severe basic language disabilities, such as severely delayed language acquisition, have been observed to deteriorate in all areas of intellectual function as they get older. The absence of functional language seems to adversely affect nonverbal cognitive abilities.

There is a need for researchers to clarify the relationship between the cognitive process and language development. Some scholars working in the language area of reading are examining the reading process as a cognitive skill.

### MODELS OF READING COMPREHENSION

Reading is often defined as a thinking process (Stauffer 1969). Because there is such a close relationship between the cognitive process and reading comprehension, recent attempts to develop theories and models of reading comprehension closely parallel recent developments in theories of intelligence. Just as theories of the intellect have shifted from the global concept to the concept of underlying abilities, so views of reading comprehension have similarly evolved and model builders now recognize that there are many contributing subabilities or subskills that comprise reading comprehension.

Smith (1963), for example, stresses that "comprehension," as such, cannot be taught because it is a blanket term covering an entire composite of thought-getting processes in reading. It is necessary to determine specific comprehension

**TABLE 10.1. SPACHE'S APPLICATION OF THE GUILFORD MODEL TO READING COMPREHENSION**

| | Unit | Class | Relations | Systems | Transformations | Implications |
|---|---|---|---|---|---|---|
| Cognition (recognition of information) | Recognition that word has meaning | Recognition of sentence as complete thought | Recognition of paragraph meaning (literal idea of paragraph) | Recognition of types of relationships within structure of paragraph | Underline key words of paragraph | Recognize that there are implications in author's main idea |
| Memory (retention of information) | Recall specific word meanings | Recall of thoughts of sentence (reverberations) | Comprehend main idea as summation of sentences (reverberation) | Summarize facts of paragraph in own words with due attention to structure | Combine recall with own associations | Choose possible implications from given alternates |
| Divergent Production (logical, creative ideas) | Meaning from context by inference | Selecting implied meaning of sentence | Choosing implied main idea | Analyze author's reasons for structure | Construct rebus of paragraph: offer new titles for paragraph | Amplify author's implications and ideas in free association |
| Convergent Production (conclusions, inductive thinking) | Meaning from structure of context, (i.e. appositive sentence) | Combining ideas into literal meaning of sentence | Evolving main idea as extension of topic sentence | Categorize structure of paragraph; outline it | Choose among alternate titles or statements of main idea | Suggest future applications of author's ideas |
| Evaluation (critical thinking) | Acceptance or rejection of author's diction | Acceptance or rejection of meaning of sentence, as fact-opinion | Acceptance or rejection of main idea as fact or opinion; check author's sources; compare with own experiences and beliefs | Look for fallacies in logic, appeals to reader's emotions, overgeneralizations, omissions, distortions | Identify author's viewpoint and purpose; compare with other viewpoints; explore the ultimate outcomes of acceptance of author's viewpoint | Check author's background as basis for viewpoint; react to author's value judgments; examine author's basic assumptions and inferences from these |

From George D. Spache. *Toward Better Reading*. Champaign, Ill.: Garrard Publishing Co., 1963, p. 67. Copyright 1963 by George D. Spache.

skills and to distinguish one from another in terms of the thinking functions involved.

Several reading scholars have viewed reading comprehension within models of cognition. Guilford (1960) suggests that reading is one of the most complex cognitive achievements, involving many intellectual functions; he sees reading in terms of the Guilford three-dimensional model of the structure of the intellect discussed earlier in this chapter. While not all of the cells have relevance for reading, Spache (1963) generates many subskills of reading comprehension by applying the Guilford model to reading.

| | | | | | | | | What Is Read | | |
|---|---|---|---|---|---|---|---|---|---|---|
| Thinking Abilities | Main Ideas | Supporting Details | Sequences | Conclusions | Predictions | Interpretations | Implications | Comparisons and Contrasts | Parts and Wholes | Causes and Effects |
| Recognizes | | | | | | | | | | |
| Reproduces | | | | | | | | | | |
| Distinguishes | | | | | | | | | | |
| Concludes | | | | | | | | | | |
| Summarizes | | | | | | | | | | |
| Generalizes | | | | | | | | | | |
| Anticipates | | | | | | | | | | |
| Relates | | | | | | | | | | |
| Analyzes | | | | | | | | | | |
| Synthesizes | | | | | | | | | | |
| Classifies | | | | | | | | | | |
| Organizes | | | | | | | | | | |
| Infers | | | | | | | | | | |

**TABLE 10.2. COMPREHENSION SKILLS GRID: THINKING SKILLS AND READING COMPREHENSION SKILLS**
From Robert Emans. "Identifying Significant Reading Skills: In Grades Four Through Eight," in H. Alan Robinson, (ed.), *Reading: Seventy-Five Years of Progress*. Chicago: University of Chicago Press, p. 39. Copyright © 1966 by the University of Chicago.

In Table 10.1, Spache presents a hypothetical description of the operation of the basic intellectual processes that occur in reading. In this table, the *unit* is considered to be the word, the *class* is the sentence, *relations* are the interrelations of sentences, and *systems* are the arrangements of sentences we call paragraphs. Finally, *transformations* are the manipulations of paragraphs, and *implications* represent inferential reactions to paragraphs.

Emans (1966) has attempted to illustrate the interrelationship between reading comprehension and cognitive skills with another two-dimensional grid (Table 10.2). Barrett developed a taxonomy of cognitive skills of reading comprehension in which he identified some thirty separate skills (Clymer 1968). Another approach to discovering the underlying skills that contribute to reading comprehension is the model developed by Holmes (1965) in his Substrata Model of Reading. The Holmes theory holds that reading ability is composed of organized systems and that these systems, in turn, have contributing subsystems and abilities. The research within this framework attempted to measure the amount that each of the many subskills and substrata systems contribute to the ability to read.

## OTHER CLASSIFICATIONS OF READING COMPREHENSION

Other reading specialists have delineated the multifaceted nature of reading comprehension by specifying individual tasks that appear to be required for comprehension. Typical of many such lists that have been developed is that of Fareed (1969):

1. Noting clearly stated facts and important details.
2. Grasping the main ideas.
3. Following a sequence of events or steps.
4. Drawing inferences and reaching conclusions.
5. Organizing ideas and relationships.
6. Applying what is read to solve problems and verify statements.
7. Evaluating material for bias, relevancy, and consistency.

These comprehension skills, as well as teaching strategies to help children learn these skills, are discussed in greater detail later in this chapter.

Another way to categorize thought-getting in reading is in terms of depth of understanding of the material. These levels have been referred to as: (1) literal comprehension; (2) interpretation; (3) critical reading; (4) assimilation; and (5) creative reading. Each level requires increasingly complex cognitive functioning. (Andresen and Robinson 1967.)

*Literal* comprehension refers to the skills at the bottom of the reading comprehension ladder. It is the ability to recognize and understand the direct, stated ideas of the author. It is sometimes referred to as "reading the lines" of print.

The *interpretation* level refers to the kind of reading needed to gather not only the meanings directly stated by the text, but also the meanings that are implied. The reader must think of more than the words and symbols themselves to supply the meanings intended. This level of reading has also been referred to as "reading between the lines."

The *critical* level is the third level of reading and it refers to the kind of reading that requires personal judgment and evaluation. At this level, the reader forms generalizations, draws conclusions, compares, analyzes and applies ideas gained in reading. This level is often referred to as "reading beyond the lines."

At the *assimilation* level the reader must understand, interpret, and evaluate the author's ideas; but in addition, he identifies with the material and adds thoughts from his own experiences and imagination. The reader integrates the thinking of the author with his own. In some respects the reader has changed as a result of the reading experience.

The *creative* level of reading is considered the highest of mental processes, involving the development of new thoughts, fresh ideas, and imaginative insights as a result of the reading experience.

There are times when effective reading requires the reader to perform at all of these levels when reading a single selection. Such an occasion is aptly described by Adler (1956, p. 14) in *How to Read A Book*:

> When [people] are in love and are reading a love letter, they read for all they are worth. They read every word three ways: they read the whole in terms of the parts, and each part in terms of the whole; they grow sensitive to context and ambiguity, to insinuation and implication; they perceive the color of words, the order of phrases, and the weight

of sentences. They may even take punctuation into account. Then, if never before or after, they read.

The models and views of reading comprehension discussed in this section help to identify and organize the elements of reading comprehension. In the second section of this chapter reading comprehension is discussed further by examining the implications for children with learning disabilities and reviewing teaching approaches. In this context, however, the focus is that reading at the higher levels is closely related to the thinking or cognitive processes. Good teaching of reading necessitates the development of thinking during the reading process; and further, training in the thinking processes facilitates reading comprehension.

## Summary

This section has discussed cognitive skills from four points of view: concept development, mental processes, developmental imbalances, and language as a cognitive process.

A concept is an abstraction or a symbol of concrete experiences. When concepts are meager, or inaccurate, the child is not able to receive the idea or to communicate it to others. Such children need help in concept development.

The trend today is to view intelligence as being composed of many subabilities of mental processing rather than as a single global factor. The model of these substructures of the intellect and their relationship as formulated by Guilford was discussed.

Developmental imbalance refers to a discrepancy in the maturation and development of the various subabilities of the intellect. Children with learning disabilities are often found to have extreme discrepancies in the development of these various subfactors.

Language and cognitive development are interdependent. One language area, reading, can be viewed as a thinking process. As such, reading implies the development of cognitive skills. Several models relating reading comprehension to cognitive development were presented.

Many children with learning disabilities have disturbances with higher mental processes. This is the area of disability that teachers find the most baffling and the most difficult to overcome. As theorists and researchers learn more about cognitive functioning, our understanding of learning disabilities in this vital area also develops.

# TEACHING STRATEGIES

Cognitive abilities are needed in every area of the school curriculum as well as in most other areas of learning. In spite of the obvious importance of cognitive skills, the guidelines for implementing the teaching of thinking skills are still rather hazy. Theories of cognitive development are still in the process of formulation and modification; the dimensions and components of cognition have not as yet been precisely defined; nor have the relationships among these components been operationally determined. As a consequence, the development of curricula and teaching strategies to promote cognitive skills along the lines of theoretical cognitive models is still in its infant stages. Even so, current models of cognitive development do suggest certain desirable goals and some means of reaching these goals.

The child who has a deficit in cognition is likely to perform poorly in many school subjects. In this section, only two areas of functioning will be considered in relation to cognitive skills: (1) arithmetic, as a school subject requiring quantitative thinking; and (2) reading comprehension, as a school subject requiring a language-type of thinking. These two areas of functioning provide a useful vehicle for the discussion of cognitive skills. Arithmetic and reading are basic school subjects which children with learning disabilities frequently fail, and these subjects represent two sectors of cognitive functioning—nonverbal and verbal.

This section (1) contrasts two views of teaching cognitive skills; (2) discusses arithmetic as a cognitive skill and presents strategies for teaching arithmetic; and (3) discusses reading comprehension and presents some strategies to teach reading comprehension.

# Theories of Teaching Cognition

It is helpful to identify two contrasting theories on cognitive learning. They are (a) the stimulus-response approach, and (b) the hypothesis-testing approach. Each theory leads to quite different methods of teaching.

## THE STIMULUS-RESPONSE THEORY OF LEARNING

In the stimulus-response framework, learning proceeds as a result of conditioned and mechanical connections between environmental events and the response of an individual to those events. Associations are formed as a function of external stimulus conditions. An assumption of this view is that cognitive learning of complex processes is similar to the learning of simple skills. Further, this view assumes that explanations of simpler kinds of learning provide adequate explanations of concept learning and cognition. Basically, the sequence to be considered in teaching is (a) stimulation, (b) response, and (c) reward. By manipulating and structuring the stimulation and reward, the teacher can achieve certain desired responses or behaviors on the part of the subject. Structure, overlearning, reinforcement, and drill are important elements of this approach. The beginning work within this approach to learning is generally attributed to Skinner (1953).

A program to teach the cognitive skills within the stimulus-response framework must specify precisely what skill is to be learned, and then design a program to stimulate and reward the desired response. One teaching method that results from this theory of learning is behavior modification, which is described in greater detail in Chapter 11. Another outgrowth of this view is programed instruction.

**Programed instruction.** The development of programed instructional materials has evolved from the stimulus-response theory of learning. These materials are designed to teach many areas of the curriculum, including reading and arithmetic. The essential principles of programed instruction are:

1. To break down the subject to be taught to an ordered sequence of steps or stimulus items.

2. To provide a means for the students to respond in a specified way to each item or stimulus and to record that response.

3. To reinforce the student's response so that he has immediate knowledge of the results.

4. To make each sequential step very small to assure the student will make few errors and practice mostly correct responses.

5. To move the student step by step, from what he knows to what he is supposed to learn.

The program must identify as precisely as possible the objectives set for the student. Further, a successful program must ascertain continually that the student going through the program is learning each task identified by the program.

In summary, the stimulus-response approach to cognitive learning postulates that the educator can design teaching materials and manipulate the environment in such a fashion that specific cognitive skills will be learned. Examples of materials designed from this point of view include: *Distar* programs in reading, arithmetic and language by Engelmann and others (Science Research Associates), *Write and See* by Skinner and others (Lyons and Carnahan), and *Programmed Reading* by Sullivan Associates (McGraw-Hill). Reported research studies based on the stimulus-response theory of teaching reading include the "Stanford Computor-Assisted Instruction" (Atkinson and Hanson 1966), "Programed Tutoring" by Ellson and others (1965).

## THE HYPOTHESIS-TESTING THEORY OF LEARNING

In contrast to the stimulus-response view of cognitive learning is the hypothesis-testing theory. This view presumes cognitive learning to be a highly active process of "seeking" behavior rather than a passive process of "responding" behavior. In this view, cognitive learning can be approached as a kind of decision-making process. The individual observes data, proposes his own problems, constructs hypotheses to solve the problems, seeks to reaffirm his hypotheses, and finally formulates his own generalizations. Curriculum plans that have evolved from such a viewpoint have been referred to as the "inquiry method," "discovery-learning," "creativity approaches," and "problem-solving techniques." One curriculum designer who works from this theory is Suchman (1960).

The hypothesis-testing approach to the teaching of cognitive skills in the area of reading has been suggested by Stauffer (1969). He believes that children need to be taught to read in such a way that the child is free to develop cognitive and thinking skills. The child, not the teacher, must gather the data, make predictions, propose the problems, and ask questions, and finally find solutions. Teachers' questions about the content are used as an occasional testing device, rather than as a conditioning mechanism.

Reading comprehension is approached as a process of inquiry (Stauffer 1967). The task of the teacher is to set up an environment that is conducive to the thinking process while the child is reading. The student is helped to (1) raise questions, (2) build hypotheses, (3) read and process data, and (4) test findings to determine validity. While the teacher plays an important guiding role, the initiative and structure is set by the student.

Henderson (1969, pp. 89–90) has contrasted the hypothesis-testing and the stimulus-response approaches to teaching cognitive skills. The following differences are emphasized:

1. In the stimulus-response approach, the responsible agent is the teacher (or the material); but in the hypothesis-testing approach, the responsible agent is the student. In the first, what the teacher (or material) does to the pupil is significant; while in the latter, what the student does to the material is significant.

2. In the hypothesis-testing approach, the student takes the initiative, selecting what is to be acted upon. In the stimulus-response approach, the teacher selects the material to be acted upon.

3. The hypothesis-testing approach analyzes the thinking and cognitive skills while the stimulus-response approach analyzes the content to be learned. Teaching that evolves from the hypothesis-testing framework implies the selection and exercise of cognitive skills, not a mastery of particular content.

In this discussion, the two approaches to teaching cognition—the stimulus-response approach and the hypothesis-testing approach—have been presented as diametrically opposed extremes. Probably there is a role to be played by each approach. Individuals undoubtedly acquire some learning according to stimulus-response principles and some according to hypothesis-testing principles. Individuals are both passive responders and active searchers. Teaching methods, therefore, should reflect both kinds of learning.

## Quantitative Thinking: Arithmetic

Arithmetic has been called a universal language. It is a symbolic language that enables human beings to think about, record, and communicate ideas concerning the elements and the relationships of quantity. The field of mathematics includes counting, measurement, arithmetic, calculations, geometry, and algebra. The focus of the "new mathematics" is on helping children gain insight into the structure and application of our number system.

### ARITHMETIC AND LEARNING DISABILITIES

A learning disability in the area of arithmetic comprehension and related conceptual disturbances in learning about quantitative elements has been referred to as "dyscalculia" (Cohn 1961). Not all children with learning disabilities have difficulty with number concepts. In fact, many children with severe reading disability have been observed to be strong in arithmetic skills. Nevertheless, arithmetic is a school subject that very frequently is a problem area for children with learning disabilities.

Kaliski (1967) has noted that many of the symptoms that identify children with learning disabilities can be related to arithmetic difficulties. Disturbances in spacial relationships, visual perception abnormalities, perseveration, difficulty with symbols, and cognitive disturbances all have obvious implications for number learning. Some of the characteristics of children identified as dyscalculic are discussed in the following subsections. It must be remembered, however, that each child is unique and not all children with an arithmetic disability possess all of the deficiencies described.

For some children, difficulty with numerical relationships begins at an early age. The ability to count, to understand the one-to-one correspondence, to match, to sort, and to compare are dependent upon the child's experiences in manipulating objects. The child with a short attention span, with poor perception, or with poor motor development may not have had appropriate experiences with activities of manipulation—experiences that would prepare him to build understandings of space, form, order, time, distance, and quantity.

A child's early concepts of quantity are evidenced in his early language in such phrases as, "all gone," "that's all," "more," "big," and "little" (Johnson and Myklebust 1967). The young child plays with pots and pans and with boxes that fit into each other; he puts objects into containers. All these activities aid the development of a sense of space, sequence, and order. The child with an arithmetic learning disability may have missed these essential experiences as an infant. Parents often report that children with such disorders had not enjoyed or engaged in play with blocks, puzzles, models, or construction-type toys (Johnson and Myklebust 1967).

### Disturbances of Spatial Relationships

Concepts of spatial relationships are normally acquired at the preschool level. Kaliski (1967) reports that the child with an arithmetic disability often confuses spatial relationships such as: up-down, over-under, top-bottom, high-low, near-far, front-back, beginning-end, and across. Strauss and Lehtinen (1947) found that a disturbance in spatial perception interferes with the visualization of the entire number system. The child may be unable to perceive distances between numbers, and he may not know if the number 3 is closer to 4 or 6.

### Disturbances of Visual-Perception and Visual-Motor Association

Children with arithmetic disabilities have been observed to have difficulty with activities that require visual perception and visual-motor association. Strauss (1951) noted that some brain-injured children are unable to count objects in a series by pointing to each of them and saying, "One, two, three, four, five." Such children must first learn to count by grasping and physically manipulating objects. Grasping the objects appears to be an earlier development in the neuro-motor and perceptual developmental hierarchy than pointing to objects.

Many children with a basic arithmetic disability are unable to see objects in groups or sets—an ability that enables others to quickly identify the number of objects in a group. Even when adding a group or set of three with a set of four objects, some children with an arithmetic disability must begin by counting the objects one by one to determine the total number in the sets.

Some children are unable to visually perceive a geometric shape as an entire entity. For these children, a square may not appear as a square shape but as four unrelated lines, as a hexagon, or even as a circle.

Other children have difficulty in learning to visually perceive number symbols. Strauss (1951) noted that some children confuse the vertical stroke on the number *1* and the number *4*, or they may confuse the upper half of the number *2* and portions of the number *3*.

Children with poor arithmetic abilities frequently perform inadequately in visual-motor tasks. Because they cannot capture the gestalt of a shape and because they have a disturbance in perceiving spatial relationships and in making spatial judgments, they may not be able to copy geometric forms, shapes, numbers, or letters adequately. Consequently, such children are likely to be very poor in handwriting skills as well as arithmetic.

## Other Characteristics of the Child with an Arithmetic Disability

Children with poor number sense have been observed to have an inaccurate or imprecise notion of body image. These children may be unable to understand the basic relationship of the body parts. When asked to draw a picture of a human figure, the child may draw the body parts as completely unrelated or misplaced, or with stick legs coming from the head, or with no body at all.

In addition, the child with an arithmetic disability often has a poor sense of direction and time. He becomes lost easily and cannot find his way to a friend's house or home from school. Such a child often forgets if it is morning or afternoon and he may go home during the recess period thinking the school day has ended. He has difficulty estimating the time span of an hour, a minute, several hours, or a week; and he cannot guess how long a task will take.

An understanding of the underlying number system is important to success in mathematics, but of equal importance is the development of skills in the computational operations of arithmetic. For efficient work in arithmetic, these computational skills of adding, subtracting, multiplying, and dividing must become automatic. Often the child with a severe memory deficit understands the underlying number system, but he is unable to remember the number facts. Such a child may find it necessary to do repeated addition each time he comes to a multiplication problem.

Scores on social maturity and social perception have been found to be low among many children with poor arithmetic abilities. Johnson and Myklebust (1967) describe a research project that showed that the mean social quotient of a group of dyscalculic children was substantially below their mean verbal intelligence quotient. Further, the performance scores on an intelligence test for this group were far below the scores obtained on the verbal portions of the test.

Finally, it has been noted that some children with an arithmetic disability have good verbal and auditory abilities. Such youngsters are highly verbal and may even be excellent readers. However, the problems of other children with an arithmetic disability are compounded by handicaps in reading. The child who cannot read and understand the arithmetic problem will obviously be unable to perform the mathematical tasks required.

In their summary of a study of research on the basic cognitive processes underlying the attainment of quantitative concepts, Chalfant and Scheffelin (1969, Chap. 10) grouped factors related to a quantitative disability into five categories: (1) intelligence, (2) spatial ability, (3) verbal ability, (4) problem-solving ability, and (5) neurophysiological correlates. The child's arithmetic disability may be due to a verbal, spatial, perceptual, or memory deficiency. If so, it may be necessary to provide special remedial procedures to ameliorate the basic disorder in the learning processes.

## MODERN MATH

In most schools today, the arithmetic curriculum follows a modern mathematics program. The modern mathematics curriculum assumes an hypothesis-testing approach to learning. The goal of the "modern math" program is to help the child develop an understanding of the basic structure of our number system rather than rote performance and rote learning of isolated skills and facts. The emphasis is on teaching the *why,* as well as the *how,* of arithmetic. The mathematics program leads pupils to knowledge through the processes of *discovery* and *exploration;* the program emphasizes the comprehension, formulation, and practical application of new concepts and skills.

These goals appear to be desirable ones for the child with learning disabilities. However, the question to be asked is, "How does the modern mathematics approach affect children with a learning disability in numbers and mathematics?" It is difficult to answer this question at present because little research is available to clarify the issue. According to Otto and McMenemy (1966), virtually nothing has been written on remedial methods for teaching the new mathematics. Indeed, the problems faced by children who have failed after exposure to the modern mathematics curriculum seem similar to those faced by children who failed in the old mathematics programs.

## TEACHING THE CHILD WITH ARITHMETIC DISABILITIES

Before deciding on the techniques to teach arithmetic, the teacher must understand the *child* as well as the *subject matter* of arithmetic. In addition to knowing whether the child is successful at certain levels and certain operations in arithmetic, it is necessary to probe into the strengths and weaknesses of learning which the child brings to the arithmetic situation. How do the child's adaptations of his deficiencies affect his approach? What other tasks does he approach in this way? How far back is it necessary to go to insure a firm foundation in number concepts? What techniques appear to be most appropriate?

Chalfant and Schefflin (1969, Chap. 10) suggest that it is useful to investigate the following areas in assessing psychological and neurological correlates to learning disabilities in quantitative thinking:

1. Determine if the child has *comprehension of number structure and arithmetic operations.* Is he able to understand the meaning of spoken numbers? Can he read and write numbers? Can he do basic arithmetic operations? Can he tell which is larger and which is smaller?

2. Determine his skills in *spatial orientation.* Has he established a left-right directionality. Does he show evidence of spatial disorientation?

3. Does he have difficulty with *finger localization?* Can he name or designate the fingers of each hand in response to oral command? Can he name or designate fingers that are touched when his eyes are closed?

4. To what extent does *language ability* affect or contribute to problems in arithmetic?

Freidus (1966) stresses the importance of checking far enough back into the child's previously acquired number learnings to insure readiness for what he now needs to learn. Time and effort invested in building a firm foundation can prevent many of the difficulties that children experience as they try to move on to more advanced and more abstract arithmetic processes. Freidus (1966, pp.116–120) suggests consideration of the following levels in assessing the child's development of number concepts:

1. Sets and Matching: (concept of the "same" and grouping of objects).
2. Relationship concepts: (comparing and relating objects).
3. Measuring and Pairing: (estimating, fitting objects, one-to-one correspondence).
4. Counting (matching numerals to objects).
5. Sequential values: (arranging like objects in order by quantitative differences).
6. Relationships of parts-to-whole and parts to each other: (experimentation with self-correcting materials to discover numerical relationships).
7. Operations: (manipulation of number facts without reference to concrete objects—number facts up to ten).
8. The Decimal System: (learning of the system of numeration and notation beyond ten and upon the base ten).

### Teaching Strategies

The following paragraphs present a collection of techniques and methods for teaching the child with an arithmetic disability.

1. *Workspace.* A large table with equipment that can help in performing number tasks is helpful. Counting materials, an abacus, beans, sticks, play money, rulers, measuring instruments are among the items the child might use when he needed them.

2. *Matching and sorting.* A first step in the development of number concepts is the ability to focus upon and recognize a single object or shape. Have the child search through a collection of assorted objects to find a particular type of object. For example, he might look in a box of colored beads or blocks for a red one, search through a collection of various kinds of nuts for all the almonds, choose the forks from a box of silverware, look in a box of buttons for the oval ones, sort a bagful of cardboard shapes to pick out the circles, or look in a container of nuts and bolts for the square pieces.

3. *Puzzles, peg boards, formboards.* These are useful to help the child focus on shapes and spatial relations. For the child who has difficulty finding and fitting the missing piece, auditory cues and verbalization may be helpful. Discuss the shape he is seeking and ask him to feel the edges for tactile cues.

4. *Relationship concepts of size and length.* Have the child compare and contrast objects of different size, so that he formulates concepts of smaller, bigger, taller, shorter. Make cardboard objects such as circles, trees, houses, etc., or collect objects like washers, paper clips, screws, etc. Have the child arrange them by size. Have the child estimate the size of objects by asking him to guess whether certain objects would fit into certain spaces.

5. *Pairing and one-to-one correspondence.* To provide a foundation for counting, the child must have a concept of one-to-one relationships. Activities designed to match or align one object with another are useful. Have the child arrange a row of pegs to match a prearranged row in a pegboard. Have the child set a table and place one cookie on each dish. Have him plan the allocation of materials to the group so that each person receives one object.

6. *Counting* Some children learn to count verbally, but without attaining the concept that each number corresponds to one object. Such children are helped by making a strong motor and tactile response along with the counting. Visual stimuli or pointing to the object may not be enough because such children will count erratically, skipping objects or saying two numbers for one object. Motor activities to help such a child establish the counting principle include placing a peg in a hole, clipping clothespins on a line, and stringing beads onto a pipe cleaner. The auditory modality can be used to reinforce visual counting by having the child close his eyes and listen to the counts of a drum beat. He may make a mark for each sound and then count the marks. Have the child establish the counting principle through motor activities; e.g.; clap three times; jump four times; tap on the table two times.

7. *Recognition of sets of objects.* Cards with colored discs, domino games, playing cards, concrete objects, felt boards, magnetic boards, mathematics work-books—all provide excellent materials for developing concepts of sets.

8. *Serial order and relationships.* As the child learns to count, ask him to tell the number that comes after 6, or before 5, or between 2 and 4. Also, ask him to indicate the first, last or third of a series of objects. Other measured quantities can be arranged by other dimensions, such as size, weight, intensity, color, volume, pitch of sound, etc.

9. *Visual recognition of numbers.* The child must learn to recognize the printed numbers, 7, 8, 3, and the words *seven, eight, three;* and he must learn to inte-grate the written forms with the spoken symbol. For the child who confuses one number with another, color cues may be used: make the top of the 3 green and the bottom red. Have the child match the correct number with the correct set of objects; felt, cardboard, sandpaper symbols, and sets of objects can be used.

10. *Number lines.* Number lines and number blocks to walk on are helpful in understanding the symbols and their relationships to each other. 0 1 2 3 4 5 6

11. *Measuring.* Pouring sand, water, or beans from a container of one shape or size to a different container helps the child develop concepts of measurement. Estimating quantities, the use of measuring cups, and the introduction of fractions can be emphasized in such activities.

12. *Rate of perception.* The use of a tachistoscope or flashcards is a way to increase the rate of recognition of sets of objects, of number symbols, and of answers to number facts. A teacher-made tachistoscope can be improvised by putting information on transparencies, then cutting the transparencies into strips and inserting them in a filmstrip projector. By covering the lens with a sheet of cardboard and exposing the material for a short period of time, the teacher uses the projector as a tachistoscope (Lerner and Vaver, 1970).

13. *Playing cards.* A deck of ordinary playing cards becomes a versatile tool for teaching number concepts. Arranging suits in sequential order by number, matching sets, adding and subtracting the individual cards, and quick recognition of the number in a set are some activities to be accomplished with a deck of cards.

14. *Puzzle cards of combinations.* Make cardboard cards on which problems of addition, subtraction, multiplication, and division are worked. Cut each card in two so that the problem is on one part and the answer is on the other. Each card must be cut uniquely, so that when the student tries to assemble the puzzle, he will find that only the correct answer will fit.

15. *Tap out combinations.* Tap out combinations of numbers on a table or have the child tap out the combinations. This reinforces the number learning with the kinesthetic and auditory modality.

16. *Reinforcement of auditory expression.* Some children find it helpful to talk aloud as they relate the number sequences and facts.

17. *Counting cups.* Make a set of containers, such as cups, with a numeral to designate each container. Have the child fill the container with the correct number of objects, using items such as bottle caps, chips, buttons, screws, or washers.

18. *Number stamp.* Using a stamp pad and a stamp (the eraser on the end of a pencil will serve very well), the child can make his own set of numerals with matching dots. Two children can play the classic card game, "War," with one standard deck of cards and one deck made with stamped dots; the first child to recognize and claim matching cards can take them.

19. *Parking lot.* Draw a parking lot on a poster, numbering parking spaces with dots instead of numerals. Paint numerals on small cars and have the child park the car in the correct parking space.

20. *Basic computational skills.* A child's learning disability in arithmetic should be evaluated with reference to underlying deficits in learning processes. Thus, a teaching program should give prime consideration to such deficit areas as verbal, spatial, perceptual, or memory factors. In addition, however, the teaching plan must also consider basic computational skills that the child is lacking. These include addition, subtraction, multiplication, division, fractions, decimals and percentages.

There are fifty-six basic number facts to be mastered in each mode of arithmetic computation (addition, subtraction, multiplication, and division), if the facts involving the 1's $(3 + 1 = 4)$ and doubles $(3 \times 3 = 9)$ are not included (Otto and McMenemy 1966). Examples of number facts are: $3 + 4 = 7$; $9 - 5 = 4$; $3 \times 7 = 21$; $18 \div 6 = 3$. In the computational skill of addition, for example, there are eighty-one separate facts involved in the span from $1 + 1 = 2$ to $9 + 9 = 18$. According to Otto and McMenemy, few pupils have trouble with the 1's $(5 + 1 = 6)$ or with the doubles $(2 + 2 = 4)$. Therefore, if these facts are omitted, there are fifty-six basic addition facts to be mastered. Similarly with the other calculation processes, without the 1's and doubles there are fifty-six facts to be mastered in each of the other compution areas—subtraction, multiplication, and division.

To learn fractions, as well as other computational skills, the child with an arithmetic disability requires much experience with concrete and manipulative materials before moving to the abstract and symbolic level of numbers. Objects and materials that can be physically taken apart and put back together help the child to visually observe the relationship of the fractional parts of the whole.

21. *Other areas related to arithmetic.* Children with arithmetic disabilities are likely to have difficulty with concepts in related areas. Specific lessons and plans will be needed to develop concepts of time and of directions, map reading, reading of graphs and charts, and the concepts of money.

22. *Directions in space.* This activity is designed to help the child understand the concepts of north, east, south, and west on a map. Draw a large circle on the floor. Place the directions N., S., E., W. on the appropriate spots on the circle. The child in the center of the circle is asked to turn in different directions in response to the teacher.

23. *Time.* Time is a difficult dimension for many children with learning disabilities to grasp. Such children may require planned remediation to learn to tell time. Real clocks or teacher-made clocks are needed to teach this skill. A teacher-made clock can be created by using a paper plate and cardboard hands attached with a paper fastener. A sequence for teaching time might be to teach: (1) the hour (1:00 o'clock); (2) the half-hour (4:30 o'clock); (3) the quarter hour (7:15 o'clock); (4) five-minute intervals (2:25 o'clock); (5) before and after the hour; (6) minute intervals; and (7) seconds. Use television schedules of programs or classroom activities and relate them to clock time.

24. *Money.* The use of real money and lifelike situations is an effective way to teach number facts to some children: playing store; making change; ordering a meal from a restaurant menu, then adding up the cost and paying for it. All these situations provide concrete and meaningful practice for learning arithmetic.

25. *Measurement.* Actual containers and measurement objects should be used to introduce the idea of measurement. Containers for pints, quarts, half-gallons, gallons, pounds, and half-pounds provide the opportunity to teach measurement and to demonstrate relationships of measurement.

Many of the materials for teaching arithmetic concepts and skills have to be teacher made. However, some commercial materials are useful. Among them are the Cuisenaire Rods (Cuisenaire Company), Stern *Structural Arithmetic Program* (Houghton Mifflin), Montessori materials, various materials from other commercial firms (Teaching Resources, Developmental Learning Materials). Additional materials for teaching arithmetic are listed in Appendix B. As with all teaching materials, a measure of caution is required in their use. Materials should be considered to be tools that are useful when they are appropriate to the child, his disability, the diagnosis, and the teaching plan. The materials, themselves, should not be permitted to direct the teaching program.

Additional suggestions for teaching strategies in arithmetic can be found in *Teaching Children with Special Learning Needs* (Young 1967), *The Remediation of Learning Disabilities* (Valett 1967), "Arithmetic and the Brain-injured Child" (Kaliski 1967), "The Needs of Teachers for Special Information on Number Concepts," (Freidus 1966), *Corrective and Remedial Teaching* (Otto and McMenemy 1966), *Learning Disabilities* (Johnson and Myklebust 1967), *A Guide to a Special Class Program for Children with Learning Disabilities* (Nash and Pfeffer), *Psychopathology and Education of the Brain-injured Child* (Strauss and Lehtinen 1947), "Teaching Aids for Elementary School Arithmetic," (Clary 1966), *Academic Therapy Quarterly* (Fall 1970), *PLUS* (Educational Services), *Conceptual Learning* (Engelmann 1969).

# Verbal Thinking: Reading Comprehension

Thorndike (1917) likened the cognitive process used in mathematics to that of reading comprehension. Although mathematics is considered a nonverbal operation while reading is considered a verbal one, both were ascertained to have similar underlying cognitive processes. (Thorndike 1917, p. 329).

> . . . understanding a paragraph is like solving a problem in mathematics. It consists in selecting the right elements of the situation and putting them together in the right relations, and also with the right amount of weight or influence or force for each. . . . all under the influence of the right mental set or purpose or demand.

Learning to read can be viewed as a two-stage process: (1) the decoding stage, and (2) the meaning-getting stage. In the initial phase of learning to read, learning to decode the printed symbols is very important. The child must learn to decode words by associating sound with the printed or graphic equivalent. This stage of reading was discussed in Chapter 9. In the later stage of learning to read, the emphasis shifts to the skills of obtaining meaning from the printed page, reading comprehension. Getting meaning is the heart of the reading act. Decoding and recognizing words are valuable only as they make comprehension possible.

There is a parallel between reading comprehension skills and cognitive or thinking skills. Stauffer (1969), for example, defines reading as cognitive functioning. Moreover, there is a similarity between the comprehension skills needed for reading and the comprehension skills needed for listening to oral language. In both of these modes of verbal comprehension, the skill depends upon the individual's capacity to use and understand language, his familiarity with the content of the material, and his ability to attend to and actively interact with the ideas and concepts of the writer or speaker. It is not surprising, therefore, to find that practice in listening skills results in improvement in reading.

Stauffer (1970) views reading comprehension as something akin to problem solving. As in problem solving, the reader must employ concepts, develop hypotheses, test them out, and modify his concepts. In this way, reading comprehension is a mode of inquiry, and methods that employ discovery techniques should be used in the teaching of reading.

## READING COMPREHENSION AND LEARNING DISABILITIES

For many children with learning disabilities who have difficulty in reading, the problem is not in decoding words but in understanding the meaning of what is read. The difficulty may be associated with language disability, with poor attending capacity, or with a deficit in cognitive and conceptual functioning. In one recent study (Serafica and Sigel 1970), a difference in cognitive styles was noted between good readers and disabled readers. These researchers detected a dysfunction in cognition in the poor readers, particularly in their ability to reach a conceptual synthesis and in their skills of categorization.

Most of the attention and debate concerning reading methods have been directed to the decoding stage of reading; yet the problems related to teaching reading comprehension are far more important. Disabilities with the comprehension area of reading affect many more children than disabilities in decoding. Further, reading comprehension is much more difficult to teach.

Reading comprehension skills can be taught. It is necessary to determine what specific comprehension skills a child lacks and then plan learning experiences to develop abilities in those specific skills. The posing of appropriate questions is an important technique in helping a child develop comprehension skills. Comprehension cannot be taught as a single unitary skill; instead, specific subskills must be identified in designing a teaching plan. Fareed (1969) has identified some reading comprehension skills; these skills and some teaching strategies are described in the following paragraphs.

## Comprehension Skills

1. *Noting clearly stated facts and important details of a selection.* This skill is considered one of the easiest comprehension skills. Most of the questions asked on reading tests and by teachers are questions of detail. For example: "What color was Jane's new dress?" "What is the largest city in Montana?" "In what year was the treaty signed?" This skill requires memory; if the detail can be related to a main idea, it is easier to remember.

2. *Grasping the main idea.* This skill entails the reader's ability to get the nucleus of the idea presented or to capture the core of the information. It is much harder than finding details, and many children are unable to see through the details to get the central thought of a selection. Ways to help a child develop this skill include asking him to select the best title of a selection from several alternatives, having him make up a title for a selection, or asking him to state in one sentence what a short selection was about.

3. *Following a sequence of events or steps.* This skill is one of organizing—being able to see the steps of a process or the events in a story. Seeing such order is important to thinking, understanding language, and reading. To provide practice with this skill, the teacher can give the events in scrambled order and ask the child to sort them into the correct order. The ability to follow printed directions is closely allied to this skill, and the reader proceeds step by step to carry out some project. The Boy Scout Handbook, model plane directions, a cookbook, or directions for playing a game provide practical material to teach this skill.

4. *Drawing inferences and reaching conclusions.* This skill requires great emphasis upon thoughtful reading and interpretation. Here the reader must go beyond the lines and the facts that are given in order to reach a conclusion. Questions such as "What does the author mean?" or "Can you predict or anticipate what will happen next?" are questions geared to encourage such thinking. If the reader can do this, it shows that he is thinking along with the author.

5. *Organizing ideas.* This skill refers to the ability to see interrelationships among the ideas of a reading selection. It involves sensing cause and effect, comparing and contrasting relationships, and seeing the author's general plan of structuring the material. Studying the table of contents, looking at topic headings, and outlining are techniques to help the student see how the ideas are organized.

6. *Applying what is read to solve problems and verify statements.* If reading is to be a functional skill, the material must be adapted to new situations and integrated with previous experiences. The ability to transfer and integrate the knowledge and skills gained in reading is a difficult skill for many children to acquire. Information gained through reading a story about a boy in Mexico might be applied to a lesson in social studies. Or a problem can be formulated and the answer found through reading a selection.

7. *Evaluating materials for bias, relevancy and consistency.* This skill is sometimes referred to as critical reading. The ability to make judgments about the

author's bias, to compare several sources of information, to detect propaganda techniques, and to determine the logic of an argument or approach are all included in this skill. Even children who are able readers are likely to need help with this comprehension skill. Children enjoy the critical examination of advertisements for the detection of propaganda techniques. The comparing of editorials on the same subject or of two news reports of a single event provides good material for developing this skill.

8. *The Directed Reading-Thinking Activity Plan.* Stauffer (1969) urges that the cognitive processes in reading are best taught through the directed reading-thinking activity (D-R-T-A). Pointing to the many similarities between reading and thinking, he concludes that reading should be taught as a thinking activity. Both reading and thinking require a context to be read or thought about, both embody the dynamics of discovery, and both entail a systematic examination of ideas.

> Reading, like thinking is in continual change. At every turning of a page, or even a phrase, the reader has to take into account the context —its parts, its problems, its perplexities. From these he must be able to follow the threads of a plot that point the way toward the plot end. Or, he must follow the course of ideas in nonfiction that lead to an outcome or solution. He must assess what he finds, weigh it, accept or reject it, or alter his objectives.
>
> It is apparent, therefore, that both reading and thinking start with a state of doubt or of desire. It is apparent also that the process of reconstruction goes on as inquiry or discovery, until the doubt is resolved, the perplexity settled, or the pleasure attained (Stauffer 1969, p. 38).

Within such an approach, teaching reading becomes a way of teaching thinking. Important questions the teacher asks in directing the process are: "What do you think?" "Why do you think so?" and "Can you prove it?" The emphasis in the D-R-T-A is on pupil thinking. The goals are to teach pupils: (1) to examine, (2) to hypothesize, (3) to find proof, (4) to suspend judgment, and (5) to make decisions.

## Materials for Teaching Reading Comprehension

Some materials that are designed to help the child develop comprehension skills are listed in Appendix B. A few of the commonly used materials include:

*Standard Test Lessons in Reading* by W. A. McCall & L. M. Crabbs (Teachers College Press, Columbia University), grades 2–12.

*Gates-Peardon Practice Reading Exercises* (Teachers College Press, Columbia University), grades 3–6.

*E D L Study Skills Library* (Educational Developmental Laboratories), grades 4–9.

*Barnell Loft Specific Skill Series* (Dexter & Westbrook, Ltd.), grades 1–6.

*New Practice Readers* (Webster Division; McGraw-Hill), grades 2–8.

*Effective Reading* (Globe Book Co.), grades 4–8.

*Reading for Meaning Series* (J. B. Lippincott Co.), grades 4–12.

*Reader's Digest Reading Skill Builders* Reader's Digest Services, Inc.), grades 1–8.

*Study Exercises for Developing Reading Skills* (Laidlaw Brothers), grades 4–8.

*Developmental Reading Text-Workbooks* (Bobbs-Merril Co.), grades 1–6.

Additional materials for teaching reading comprehension are listed in Appendix B, part 3.

# Summary

This section has discussed the cognitive skills in quantitative thinking and reading comprehension. Two areas of the curriculum, arithmetic and reading comprehension, were selected as vehicles for a discussion of cognitive skills.

The discussion of arithmetic reviewed the characteristics of children who have a learning disability in arithmetic, then presented a sequence of basic number understandings and suggested some teaching strategies useful for teaching children with a disability in this area of functioning.

The discussion of reading comprehension analyzed the role of comprehension in reading and learning to read, then discussed children with a learning disability in this area and presented some ways of teaching reading comprehension.

## REFERENCES

*Academic Therapy Quarterly* 6 Fall 1970 (entire issue). Academic Therapy Publications.

Adler, Mortimer J. *How to Read a Book.* New York: Simon & Schuster, 1956.

Andresen, Oliver, and H. Alan Robinson. "Developing Competence in Reading Comprehension," pp. 102–110 in Marion D. Jenkinson (ed.), *Reading Instruction: An International Forum.* Newark, Del.: International Reading Association, 1967.

Atkinson, Richard C., and Duncan N. Hansen. "Computer-Assisted Instruction in Initial Reading: The Stanford Project," *Reading Research Quarterly* 2 (Fall 1966): 5–26.

Bruner, J. S. *Toward A Theory of Instruction.* Cambridge, Mass.: Harvard University Press, 1966.

Bruner, J. S., J. J. Goodnow, and G. A. Austin. *A Study of Thinking.* New York: Wiley, 1956.

Chalfant, James C., and Margaret A. Scheffelin. *Central Processing Dysfunction in Children: A Review of Research.* NINDS Monograph No. 9. Bethesda, Md.: U.S. Department of Health, Education and Welfare, 1969.

Clary, Robert C. "Teaching Aids for Elementary School Arithmetic," *Arithmetic Teacher* 13 (February 1966): 135–136.

Clymer, Theodore. "The Barrett Taxonomy—Cognitive and Affective Dimensions of Reading Comprehension," pp. 19–23 in Helen M. Robinson (ed.), *Innovation and Change in Reading Instruction.* Sixty-seventh Yearbook of the National Society for the Study of Education, Part II. Chicago: University of Chicago Press, 1968.

Cohn, Robert. "Dyscalculia," *Archives of Neurology* 4 (1961): 301–307.

*Cuisenaire Rods.* Mt. Vernon, N.Y.: Cuisenaire Company of America.

*Developmental Learning Materials.* Chicago, Ill.

Ellson, D. G., Larry Barber, T. L. Engle, and Leonard Kampwerth. "Programmed Tutoring: A Teaching Aid and a Research Tool," *Reading Research Quarterly* 1 (Fall 1965): 77–127.

Emans, Robert. "Identifying Significant Reading Skills: In Grades Four Through Eight," in H. Alan Robinson (ed.), *Reading: Seventy-five Years of Progress.* Chicago: University of Chicago Press, 1966, p. 39.

Engelmann, Siegfried. *Conceptual Learning.* San Rafael, Calif.: Dimensions, 1969.

Engelmann, Siegfried, and Elaine Bruner. *Distar Reading I and II.* Chicago: Science Research Associates, 1969.

Engelmann, Siegfried, and Doug Carnine. *Distar Arithmetic I and II.* Chicago: Science Research Associates, 1970.

Engelmann, Siegfried, Jean Osborn, and Therese Engelmann. *Distar Language I and II.* Chicago: Science Research Associates, 1970.

Fareed, Ahmed. "Interpretive Responses in Reading History and Biology." Ph.D. dissertation, University of Chicago (March 1969).

Flavell, John H. *The Developmental Psychology of Jean Piaget.* Princeton, N.J.: Van Nostrand, 1963.

Freidus, Elizabeth S. "The Needs of Teachers for Special Information on Number Concepts,"
    chapter 7 in William M. Cruickshank (ed.), *The Teacher of Brain-Injured Chil-
    dren: A Discussion for the Bases of Competency.* Syracuse, N.Y.: Syracuse
    University Press, 1966.

Gallagher, James. "Children with Developmental Imbalances: A Psychoeducational Defini-
    tion," chapter 2 in William Cruickshank (ed.), *The Teacher of Brain-Injured
    Children.* Syracuse, N.Y.: Syracuse University Press, 1966.

Gardner, Riley W. "The Needs of Teachers for Specialized Information on the Develop-
    ment of Cognitive Structures," pp. 137–150 in William Cruickshank (ed.),
    *The Teacher of Brain-Injured Children.* Syracuse, N.Y.: Syracuse University
    Press, 1966.

Guilford, J. P. "Frontiers in Thinking That Teachers Should Know About," *Reading Teacher*
    13 (February 1960): 176–182.

———. *The Nature of Human Intelligence.* New York: McGraw-Hill Book Company, 1967.

Henderson, Edmund H. "Do We Apply What We Know About Comprehension?" pp. 85–96
    in Nila B. Smith (ed.), *Current Issues in Reading.* Newark, Del.: International
    Reading Association, 1969.

Holmes, Jack A. "Basic Assumptions Underlying the Substrata-Factor Theory," *Reading
    Research Quarterly* 1 (Fall 1965): 5–23.

Hunt, J. McV. *Intelligence and Experience.* New York: Ronald Press, 1961.

Johnson, Doris, and H. Myklebust. *Learning Disabilities: Educational Principles and Prac-
    tices.* New York: Grune & Stratton, 1967.

Kaliski, Lotte. "Arithmetic and the Brain-Injured Child," pp. 458–466 in Edward Frierson
    and Walter Barbe (eds.), *Educating Children with Learning Disabilities: Selected
    Readings.* New York: Appleton-Century-Crofts, 1967.

Kirk, Samuel A., James J. McCarthy, and Winifred D. Kirk. *Illinois Test of Psycholinguistic
    Abilities,* rev. ed. Urbana, Ill.: University of Illinois Press, 1968.

Kirk, Samuel A., and Winifred D. Kirk. *Psycholinguistic Learning Disabilities: Diagnosis
    and Remediation.* Urbana, Ill.: University of Illinois Press, 1971.

Klausmeier, Herbert J., and Gerald Miller. "Concept Learning," pp. 1–14 in Russell G.
    Stauffer (ed.), *Reading and Concept Attainment.* Newark, Del.: International
    Reading Association, 1968.

Lerner, Janet W., and Gerald A. Vaver. "Filmstrips in Learning," *Academic Therapy Quar-
    terly* 5 (Summer 1970): 320–324.

Montessori, Maria. *The Montessori Method.* Translated by Anne E. George. Cambridge,
    Mass.: Bentley, 1964.

Neisser, U. *Cognitive Psychology.* New York: Appleton-Century-Crofts, 1967.

Otto, Wayne, and R. McMenemy, *Corrective and Remedial Teaching: Principles and Prac-
    tices.* Boston: Houghton Mifflin Co., 1966.

Plato. *The Republic.* B. Jowett, trans. New York: Modern Library.

*PLUS* (arithmetic ideas). Stevensville, Mich.: Educational Services, Inc.

Serafica, Felicisma C., and Irving E. Sigel. "Styles of Categorization and Reading Disability,"
    *Journal of Reading Behavior* 2 (Spring 1970): 105–115.

Skinner, B. F. *Science and Human Behavior.* New York: Macmillan, 1953.

Skinner, B. F., *et al. Write and See.* Chicago: Lyons & Carnahan, 1968.

Smith, Nila B. *Reading Instruction for Today's Children.* New York: Prentice-Hall, 1963.

Spache, George, *Toward Better Reading.* Champaign, Ill.: Garrard, 1963.

Spearman, C. *The Abilities of Man.* New York: Macmillan, 1927.

Stauffer, Russell G. "Reading As Experience in Inquiry," *Educational Leadership* 24 (Feb-
    ruary 1967): 407–412.

———. *Directing Reading Maturity as a Cognitive Process.* New York: Harper & Row, 1969.

———. "Reading as Cognitive Functioning," pp. 124–147 in Harry Singer and Robert
    Ruddell (eds.), *Theoretical Models and Processes of Reading.* Newark, Del.:
    International Reading Association, 1970.

Stern, Catharine. *Structural Arithmetic Program.* Boston: Houghton Mifflin, 1952.

Strauss, A. A. "The Education of the Brain-Injured Child," *American Journal of Mental
    Deficiency* 56 (January 1951): 712–718.

Strauss, A. A., and L. Lehtinen. *Psychopathology and Education of the Brain-Injured Child.*
    New York: Grune & Stratton, 1947.

Suchman, J. Richard. "Inquiry Training in the Elementary School," *Science Teacher* 27
    (1960): 42–47.

Sullivan Associates. *Programmed Reading.* St. Louis: Webster-McGraw-Hill, 1969.

Teaching Resources program and materials. Boston: Educational Services of the *New York Times,* Teaching Resources Corp.

Thorndike, Edward L. "Reading as Reasoning: A Study of Mistakes in Paragraph Reading," *Journal of Educational Psychology* 8 (June 1917): 323–332.

Valett, Robert E. *The Remediation of Learning Disabilities.* Palo Alto, Calif.: Fearon, 1967.

Young, Milton A. *Teaching Children with Special Learning Needs.* New York: John Day, 1967.

# Chapter 11

# Maturational, Psychological and Social Factors

# THEORY

This chapter discusses children with learning disabilities from these perspectives: (a) maturational, (b) psychological, and (c) social. The chapter concludes with suggested teaching strategies for helping children overcome social deficits.

## The Maturational Point of View

An understanding of the developmental process of the normal child is important as a basis for understanding the child with learning disabilities. Theories of maturation of normal children have been developed and these provide a framework for viewing children with learning problems. This section discusses a number of theories of maturation and their implications.

### THE DEVELOPMENTAL STAGES OF LOGICAL THINKING: PIAGET

The child's ability to think and learn changes with his age, that is, he passes through a number of maturational or developmental stages. The quantity, quality, depth, and breadth of the learning that occurs is a function of the stage during which it takes place. Piaget (Flavell 1963) provides a schematic description of the normal child's stages of development.

1. The child's first two years of life are called the *sensorimotor* period. During this time the child learns through his senses and movements and by interacting with the physical environment. By moving, touching, hitting, biting, and so on, and by physically manipulating objects, he learns about the properties of space, time, location, permanance, and causality. A discussion of sensorimotor learnings was presented in Chapter 7.

2. Piaget calls the next five years of life, ages 2 to 7, the *preoperational* stage. During this stage the child makes intuitive judgments about relationships. He also begins to think with symbols. Language now becomes increasingly important and the child learns to use symbols to represent the concrete world. He begins to learn about the properties and attributes of the world about him. His thinking is dominated largely by the world of perception. The subject of perception was the concern of Chapter 8.

3. The period occurring between ages 7 to 11 is called the *concrete operations* stage. The child is now able to think through relationships, to perceive consequences of acts, and to group entities in a logical fashion. He is better able to systematize and organize his thoughts. His thoughts, however, are shaped in

large measure by experiences he has had and dependent upon concrete objects that he has manipulated or understood through the senses.

4. The fourth stage, that of *formal operations,* commences at about age 11 and reflects a major transition in the thinking process. At this stage, instead of observations directing thought, thought now directs observations. The child now has the capacity to work with abstractions, theories, and logical relationships without having to refer to the concrete. The formal operations period provides a generalized orientation toward problem-solving activity.

The transition from one level to the next involves maturation. According to Piaget, the stages are sequential and hierarchal, and it is essential that a child be given opportunities to stabilize behavior and thought at each stage of development. However, frequently the school curriculum requires the child to develop abstract and logical conceptualizations in a given area without enabling him to go through preliminary levels of understanding. Attempts to teach abstract, logical concepts divorced from any real experiential understanding on the part of the child may lead to inadequate and shaky learning. The teacher may think the child is learning true concept development, but he may instead be learning only surface verbal responses.

Illustrations of young children who have surface verbal skills without an in-depth understanding of concepts are frequently amusing. One first-grade youngster, who was being exposed to "modern math" in school, watched his mother unpack the oranges from a grocery bag and remarked, "I see you have a set of objects equivalent to the numeral six." Several hours later the same youngster was observed doing his arithmetic homework with his shoes and socks off. His simple explanation was that the answer was "eleven" and he had run out of fingers. One wonders if he truly had captured the concept of numbers and sets.

Another kindergarten child explained with seemingly verbal proficiency the scientific technicalities of a space ship being shot into orbit. His seemingly precocious explanation ended with: "and now for the blast-off . . . 10—3—8—5—6—1!"

The maturation of the cognitive ability to categorize objects was apparent when each of three children, ages 7, 9, and 11, was asked to pack clothes for a trip in two suitcases. The 11-year-old was adult like in her thinking, packing day clothes in one case and night clothes in another. The 7-year-old had no organizational arrangement and proceeded to randomly stuff one suitcase with as much as it would hold and then to stuff the second with the remainder. The 9-year-old girl made an organizational plan that called for clothes above the waist to go in one suitcase and clothes below the waist to go in the second. The top parts of pajamas and a two-piece bathing suit were placed in one suitcase and the bottoms in the other. Each child had categorized in a manner appropriate to his maturational stage.

Schools sometimes neglect the need for prelogical experiences and learnings in their attempts to meet the current trend to teach abstract concepts and logical thinking in the primary grades. In instituting a modern mathematics program in one district's kindergarten, the teachers were advised that an understanding of the one-to-one correspondence was a higher and more important cognitive level than other kinds of number learning. Serial learnings of numbers taught through games like "Ten Little Indians" and other counting experiences were unfortunately dropped from the kindergarten curriculum because these activities did not develop "logical thinking."

## MATURATIONAL LAG

An early researcher of the concept of maturational lag, or a slowness in certain specialized aspects of neurological development, was Bender (1957). This point of view acknowledges that each individual has a preset rate of development and maturation of the various factors of human growth, including intelligence. Children who show discrepancies among various subabilities do not necessarily suffer from central nervous system dysfunction or brain damage; rather, the discrepancies show that various abilities are maturing at different rates. Proponents of the maturational-lag viewpoint hypothesize that children with learning disorders are not so different from children without them. It is more a matter of *timing* than an actual difference in abilities. They assume a temporary developmental lag in the maturation of certain skills and abilities.

The concept of maturational lag, according to Ames (1968), leads to a belief that the majority of learning disabilities need not occur; but they are actually created because children are pushed by society into attempting performances before they are ready. The educator compounds the distortion by introducing experiences beyond the readiness or capacity of the child at a given stage of development. Ames (1968, pp. 72–73) concludes that:

> The outstanding cause of school difficulty in our experience is immaturity. The majority of children experiencing learning problems as seen by our clinical service have been overplaced in school. This presents a serious hazard since overplacement or lack of readiness not only aggravates learning problems when they exist, but causes problems in cases where there is potential for good performance. Many children's normal or superior intelligence has led to great academic expectations on the part of parents and schools; however, they have been immature for the work of the grade in which age placed them. Thus, instead of being often labeled "underachievers," these children actually performed remarkably well considering that too much was being expected of them. . . . In final summary, it may be suspected that we create a high percentage of the learning problems encountered in the elementary schools.

This view receives support from the findings of a study conducted by Silver and Hagin (1966). A study was made in 1962 of children who had been patients at Bellevue Hospital Mental Hygiene Clinic and had been diagnosed and treated for reading disabilities in 1949–1951. When they were called back for a follow-up evaluation in 1962, they were young adults of 16–24 years of age. At this time, they did not show difficulty in spatial orientation of symbols, auditory discrimination, or left-right discrimination, although they had manifested such problems as children. Through the process of maturation, many of these problems had apparently disappeared.

In an extensive study aimed at finding factors that best predicted reading failure in kindergarten children, deHirsch (1966) found that tests that were most sensitive to differences in maturation were the ones that best predicted reading and spelling achievement in second grade. Of the tests grouped under the category,

"Maturation-Sensitive Tests," 76 percent were significantly correlated with grade achievement, compared to only 17 percent of the "Non-maturation-Sensitive Tests." DeHirsch contended that the data generated by the study supported the theory that maturational status is the crucial factor in forecasting subsequent reading achievement.

Wepman (1967) also supports a maturational-lag point of view, contending that a diagnosis of brain injury from observation of behavior is untenable and that a more useful concept is failure of neural development or *agenesis*. He states that there is greater evidence to support the concept of cerebral agenesis, or a lag in neural development for the majority of non-physically handicapped children with learning disorders, than there is for the concept of neurological damage.

## Primary Reading Retardation

A closely related view is taken by Rabinovitch (1962), a physician whose work at the North Hawthorne Center in Northville, Michigan, led to a categorization of three kinds of diagnostic groupings of reading retardation. They are: (1) brain injury with resultant reading retardation; (2) secondary reading retardation (cases with exogenous causative factors such as emotional problems, lack of opportunity); and (3) primary reading retardation (no definite brain damage suggested in the history or in the neurological examination). The concept of primary reading retardation can be compared to the theories of maturational lag, or a lag in neural development. Primary reading retardation involves severe impairment of capacity to learn to read, where there is no evident brain damage or other causative factors.

Another view of the impact of maturation on the child with learning disabilities is proposed by Kirk (1967), who sets forth the hypothesis that during the growing stages the child normally tends to perform in those functions that are comfortable for him while avoiding activities and functions that are uncomfortable for him. Since certain processes have lagged in maturation and are not functioning adequately for the child with learning disabilities, he avoids and withdraws from activities that require that process. As a result, that function fails to develop and the deficit area is thereby intensified and exaggerated. The purpose of remedial teaching is to build and develop these deficit areas so the child can reverse this behavior and development.

In summary, the maturational point of view expresses the belief that all individuals have a natural development and time for the maturation of various skills. What is sometimes thought to be a learning problem in a child may be merely a lag in the maturation of certain processes. It is important for those who have the responsibility of providing the educational environment for the child to be aware of the child's stage of maturation and of any lags in maturation that may be present. It has been noted, ironically, that with all our attempts to be "scientific" about decisions made in education, one of the most important— when to teach a child to read—is based on the science of *astrology*. The star under which the child is born, his birth date, is the key determining factor of this crucial decision because this determines when he begins formal school learning.

# Psychological Views of Learning Disabilities

## EMOTIONAL STATUS: THE PSYCHODYNAMIC VIEW

Psychic development, personality structure, and ego functioning have important implications for understanding the child with learning problems. Among the scholars who have concentrated on the psychological and emotional aspects of learning disabilities are Giffin (1968), Rappaport (1966), and Eisenberg (1967). While the previous views of the child with learning disorders emphasized the sensory-motor, perceptual, language, or cognitive learnings of the child, those professionals who view the child from a personality or psychiatric perspective ask the question: "How does the child with learning disabilities *feel?*" (Giffin 1968).

Rappaport (1966) contrasts the ego development of the normal child with that of the child with learning disabilities. The normal child, who has a central nervous system that is intact and maturing in an even and normal manner, has the opportunity to develop important basic ego functions. The normally developing child has hundreds of opportunities to be pleased with himself, and he has the satisfaction of knowing he is pleasing those about him. His relationship with his parents is mutually satisfying because his accomplishments stimulate their normal parental responses of approval and encouragement.

The normal child, as a result of both his inner feelings about his accomplishments and his awareness that those in his environment approve of him, develops feelings of self-worth and prideful identity. His feelings about his experiences in the world are positive for he establishes healthy identifications with his mother, father, and other key figures in his life. Ego functions, such as frustration tolerance and consideration for others, are developed in a normal manner. He learns to interact successfully with other people in his environment.

In contrast, the personality development of the child with learning disabilities does not follow such a pattern, according to Rappaport (1966). Ego functions are adversely affected if the central nervous system is not intact and is not maturing in a normal and even manner. A disturbance in such functions as motility and perception leads to an inadequate development of ego functions. The child's attempts at mastery of tasks lead to feelings of frustration, rather than feelings of accomplishment. Instead of building up self-esteem, his activities produce an attitude of self-derision. The child's responses and activities do not stimulate his parent's normal responses of pride; instead they cause the parents to experience feelings of anxiety and frustration, and finally result in rejection or overprotection.

For the learning-disabled child, then, the feelings within himself and the feedback from the outside environment mold a concept of an insecure and threatening world and a concept of himself as an inept person without identity. Such a child does not receive the normal satisfaction of recognition, achievement, or affection.

The battering of the child's developing personality continues and increases when the child enters school. Giffin (1968) suspects that the pupil who manifests learning problems when beginning academic work in school probably has been handicapped by learning disabilities in his preschool life. The school may be a place where he is to face a situation that makes no allowances for his shortcomings and where those directing the learning are unable to comprehend his difficulties.

Ironically, the characteristic inconsistency and unpredictability of the child with learning disabilities may account for an occasional academic breakthrough when he performs well, and such random moments of achievement may serve to make matters worse for the child. Now the school may be convinced that "he could do it if he just tried harder." His failure now may be viewed purely on terms of his behavior and poor attitude. Eisenberg (1967) notes that increased impatience and an attitude of blame on the part of the teacher intensifies the child's anxiety, frustration, and confusion, which brings disastrous consequences to the ego.

There appears to be no common characteristic of personality development for children with learning disabilities. Each child has his own unique way of handling his feelings, his deficiencies, and his environment. As Eisenberg (1967, p. 171) puts it: "The patient is a psychobiological entity, subject both to biological and to social influences in manifesting a psychological continuity of his own." Gardner's The Child's Book About Brain Injury (1966) is designed to help a child understand himself.

In summary, the child's feelings must be taken into consideration in an analysis of the child with learning disabilities. The psychological and emotional status of the child has an impact on the learning process. The important question from the psychological and emotional point of view are: "How does the child feel?" "Are the child's needs being satisfied?" and "What is the child's emotional status?" Emotional well-being and a favorable attitude are essential prerequisites before effective learning can take place.

## PARENTS OF CHILDREN WITH LEARNING DISABILITIES

Help of a psychiatric or psychological nature is often needed by the parents of children with learning disabilities. Giffin (1968) indicated that psychiatrists are becoming increasingly aware that the presence of a handicapping problem must be faced by both the child and other members of his family. In addition to an honest acceptance of the problem, there must be recognition that improvement is often a slow process. Giffin has found that the reaction of parents is often one of denial, followed by anger, then by a search for other diagnoses. Sometimes parents also need help of a psychotherapeutic nature in accepting the problem, in developing empathy for their child, and in providing a beneficial home environment. Guidance counselors and social workers play important roles in providing such help.

Parent groups that meet to discuss common problems are also useful in providing supportive help. Further, such parent groups have been useful in alerting the community, school personnel, other professionals in the community, and legislative bodies to the plight of their children.

Barsch (1967, pp. 150–151) conducted a seven-year experiment in group counseling of parents of brain-damaged children. The following conclusions were reached as a result of the study:

1. A counseling technique to help parents develop experimental approaches to behavior organization in the brain-injured child is ego-strengthening, supportive, and practically helpful.

2. These parents experience a homogeneity of anxieties stemming from apprehension regarding the psychological and educational development of their children. Only on a secondary basis do they appear to concern themselves with factors in physical development.

3. A selection process is necessary to determine whether the needs of a particular parent might best be served in a group or individual counseling setting, or whether referral for psychotherapy might be more profitable.

4. The parent of the brain-injured child must be considered an integral part of the organization of the child's behavior.

5. Parents can be taught to perceive their children differently and learn to deal with their child's problems more effectively.

6. Comments of the mothers consistently reflect changed response patterns in relation to problems represented by their children; they learn to apply a technique. There is some restoration of feelings of competency and self-worth.

7. The mothers learn to recognize their unique responsibility in developing organized response patterns in their children.

8. The number of mothers (10) selected for each group on an arbitrary basis has proven an effective and workable figure.

Although this study was specifically designed for parents of brain-damaged children, it appears to have applicability for effective counseling of parents of children with learning disabilities.

## BEHAVIOR MODIFICATION: THE APPROACH OF BEHAVIORAL PSYCHOLOGY

The study of the behavior of the child, in contrast to the study of his emotional status, is the concern of a group of scholars called behavioral psychologists. By applying the concepts and procedures of behavior-modification theories, the behavior and learning patterns of the child can be changed and shaped. This approach to studying human behavior is an outgrowth of the concept of operant conditioning developed by learning theorists such as Skinner (1953, 1963). Briefly, behavior modification is a method of modifying human activity—academic as well as social learning activities (Krasner and Ullman 1965).

Behavior modification procedures require the investigator to (1) carefully observe and tabulate the occurrence of the events that precede the behavior of interest and the events that follow the behavior of interest; and (2) manipulate those events to effect a desired change in the subject's behavior. The event preceding the behavior interest is called the *antecedent event* or *stimulus;* while the event immediately following the behavior in question is called the *subsequent event* or *reinforcement.* For example, when John is asked to read, he begins to disturb others in the classroom by hitting them. The stimulus or antecedent event that precedes John's hitting behavior is the request that John read. When Betty reads five pages, she receives two tokens which are exchangeable for toys. The subsequent event or reinforcement following reading behavior is the receipt of the tokens.

The investigator working in this tradition observes the effects of various reinforcements or rewards on the individual behavior of a particular child. He then analyzes the observations to determine patterns of response to rewards. Finally, he attempts to construct a reward system that will promote the desired behavior.

Research suggests that reinforcements that are positive and immediate are most effective in promoting the desired behavior. Examples of positive reinforcers include candy, tokens, points earned, praise, flashing lights, or simply the satisfaction of knowing that the answer is correct. For example, in teaching reading, the desired behavior could be having the child say the sound equivalent of the letter "a" every time a stimulus card with the letter "a" is shown. Each time he responds correctly, the child may immediately receive a positive reinforcement such as a piece of candy, some frosted cereal, stars, points, or money.

The behavior-modification approach requires that the teacher determine a behavioral goal to be accomplished by the child. This goal must be specific rather than broad; moreover, evidence of learning should be observable instead of only being inferred. For example, the goal of teaching a child to be sociable is too broad and too difficult to observe; however, the behavior of saying "thank you" when the child is offered food is specific and observable.

Unlike some other theories of learning disabilities, the teacher using behavior-modification techniques does not seek to discover the underlying causes of inappropriate behavior; rather he tries to change the behavior by manipulating the environment of the learner. For example, the hyperkinetic child might be encouraged to modify his hyperactive behavior if he receives a positive reinforcement for a behavior of sitting quietly for a period of five minutes. The highly distractable child could be encouraged to modify his behavior by receiving a positive reinforcement for reading a certain number of words, or pages or reading for a certain period of time.

Within this approach, the behaviors that interfere with learning a task are first identified; then plans are made to manipulate the environment to shape a desired behavior. As an illustration, Marion's hyperactivity and constant movement in the room during the reading lesson interfered with her learning to read. A desired behavior was to have Marion remain in her seat during the lesson. This behavior was shaped through a system of positive reinforcements. Each time Marion remained in her seat for a period of five minutes during the reading lesson, she was reinforced with a small piece of candy. As her attentive behavior was shaped by the candy reinforcer, she stayed in her seat for longer periods of time and her ability to attend improved.

A few studies using the behavior-modification approach to teach children with learning disabilities have been reported; they indicate that the technique was successful in modifying the behavior of children with learning disabilities and contributed to their academic learning (Lovitt 1967, Lovitt and others 1968, Haring and Hauck 1969). Precise and accurate data describing the child's performance must be collected to form the basis for making decisions and planning a method of modifying behavior. Lovitt and others (1968) have evolved the following basic decisions that must be made if a behavior modification framework is to be effective:

1. Discover a consequence or reinforcement event that will accelerate a child's rate of performance on a specific task.

2. Change the program of instructional materials so that the correct performance is facilitated.

3. When the child's performance is accurate, increase the reinforcer; and when the child makes an error decrease the reinforcer.

4. Eventually, have the child make his own instructional decisions, such as corrections and establishment of reinforcement values.

### A Hierarchy of Behavioral Levels

A goal of the behavior-modification approach is to gradually reduce the need for immediate extrinsic reinforcers so that the individual can eventually achieve such behavior without outside motivation. Hewett (1967, 1968) developed a seven-level hierarchy of behavior that reflects the dependency upon outside reinforcers. As the individual moves from level to level, he moves from complete dependency on immediate extrinsic reinforcement to complete independence and self-motivation in learning situations.

At the *primary* level the child will modify his behavior only to receive the primary reinforcement that gratifies basic desires. For example, he will learn appropriate behaviors to receive candy reinforcements. At the *acceptance* level the teacher is able to communicate complete acceptance of the child and the child will now work on a one-to-one basis without the need for constant direct reinforcement. At the *order* level, the teacher is able to hold the child for more appropriate behavior and the child will accept certain conditions for learning, including structure, routine, and definite limits in the learning situation. In the *exploratory* level of the behavioral hierarchy, the child is ready to investigate the world about him through motor activity, sensory and perceptual exploration, and concrete experiences. At the *relationship* level of this hierarchy the child is concerned with the teacher's approval and recognition; and this interpersonal relationship takes on value as a social reinforcer. At the *mastery* level the child is finally ready for academic learning. He now learns the basic skills of reading, writing, and arithmetic. Finally, at the *achievement* level he consistently reflects self-motivating behavior. The child at this level is achieving up to his potential, he is eager for new learning experiences, and he no longer needs outside reinforcers to motive his learning.

While this hierarchy has been used extensively to view the emotionally disturbed child, many applications can be made to the child with learning disabilities.

## Social Development

The learning of social skills, though not strictly in the realm of academic achievement is nevertheless a vital area of learning. Some authorities see the child who is unable to make appropriate judgments concerning his social environment or who is unable to perform social activities in keeping with his chronological age and intelligence as a child handicapped by a deficiency in social perception (Johnson and Myklebust 1967). These authors hypothesize that a child's deficit in social perception is a function of neurological dysfunction that can be related to certain areas of the brain. Such children may be average or even high in areas of learning such as verbal intelligence, but they have difficulty in the basic social demands of every-day life.

## CHARACTERISTICS OF THE CHILD WITH A SOCIAL DISABILITY

What are the observable characteristics related to a deficit in social perception of the child with learning disabilities? Such a child has been described, in general (1) as performing poorly in independent activities expected of children of his chronological age, (2) as poor in judging moods and attitudes of people he is with, (3) as insensitive to the general atmosphere of a social situation, and (4) as continually doing or saying the inappropriate thing. Strauss and Lehtenin (1947) observed an emotional shallowness in the brain-injured children enrolled in their schools. They characterized such children's depth of feeling as shallow and fleeting, lacking the enduring quality of a normal emotion. Benton (1962) noted a lack of affective bonds between the brain-injured child and other people. Baer (1961) reported that these children frequently have impaired interpersonal relations. Lewis (1960) stated that the mechanism that organizes behavior and enables the child to perceive social situations and develop awareness of social attitudes fails to operate properly. All of these writers viewed the social deficits as part of a syndrome of many other characteristics. Johnson and Myklebust (1967), however, suggest that the socially imperceptive child may have a wholly separate learning disability. These authors see the child with such a handicap as having characteristics that are different from those of other types of learning disabilities. Consequently, children with a social disability require a different kind of therapy.

These youngsters often go unrecognized as children with a learning disability for their deficits may not prevent them from using verbal language with fluency or from learning to read or write. Further, at present there are few formal procedures for identifying these children. There is some evidence that the social quotient as measured by the *Vineland Social Maturity Scale* (Doll 1953) is likely to be substantially lower than the verbal ability measured by intelligence test performance (Johnson and Myklebust 1967). Other traits that appear to correlate with a social disability are poor self-perception and immature concepts of body image. The *Goodenough-Harris Drawing Test* (Harris 1963) yields indications of the child's development in these areas.

An illustration of the behavior of the child with poor social perception is Sally, a 13-year-old with high average intelligence, who was rejected from a summer camp program because she failed the intake interview. When asked by the camp counselor why she would be attending camp, Sally replied that her parents wanted to go to Europe and that was the only way to get rid of her. With such a response, the interviewer decided that Sally was not a good candidate for the camp. In contrast, Sally's younger brother, at age 9, was a socially perceptive youngster whose answer to the interviewer was, "I want to go to camp because it's healthy and I love the great outdoors."

A deficit of social skills implies a lack of sensitivity to people and a poor perception of social situations, thus the deficit affects almost every area of the child's life. This is probably the most debilitating learning problem the child can have.

# TEACHING STRATEGIES: SOCIAL SKILLS

The activities presented in this section represent ways that have been used to help children develop social skills. The activities are divided into the following categories: (a) body image and self-perception; (b) sensitivity to other people; (c) social situations; and (d) social maturity. While the normal child is able to learn many of these skills by himself merely through daily living and observation, the child with a deficit in social skills needs conscious effort and direct and specific teaching to learn about the world, its social nuances, and its silent language.

## Body Image and Self-Perception

1. See Chapter 7, the section on body image, for suggested motor activities for the development of concepts of body image.

2. Have the child locate parts of the body on a doll, on another child, and finally on himself. Discuss the function of each part of the body.

3. Make a cardboard man with movable limbs. Put the man in various positions and have the child duplicate the positions. For example, put the left leg and right arm out.

4. Make a puzzle from a picture of a person, and have the child assemble the pieces. Cut the puzzle so that each major part is easily identifiable.

5. Have the child complete a partially drawn figure or tell what is missing in an incomplete picture.

6. Help the child put together a scrapbook about himself. Include pictures of him at different stages of growth, pictures of his family and his pets, a list of his likes and dislikes, anecdotes of his past, accounts of trips, awards he has won, and so on.

## Sensitivity to Other People

The concept that the spoken language is but one means of communication and that people "talk" to each other without the use of words was presented by Hall in *The Silent Language* (1961). The child with a social deficit, however, needs help in learning how to decode the communication messages involved in this "silent language." For example, these children often fail to understand the meaning implied in facial expression and gesture.

7. Draw pictures of faces or collect pictures of faces and have the child ascertain if the face conveys the emotion of happiness or sadness. Other emotions to be shown include anger, surprise, pain, love, etc. Dimitrovsky (1964) suggests pictures that can be used for such an activity.

8. Discuss the meanings of various gestures, such as waving good-bye, shaking a finger for "no," shrugging a shoulder, turning away, tapping of a finger or foot in impatience, outstretched arms in gestures of welcome.

9. Find pictures, short filmed sequences, or story situations where the social implications of gesture, space, and time are presented.

10. Help the child learn to recognize implications in human voice beyond the words themselves. Have a child listen to a voice on a tape recorder to determine the mood of the speaker and to decipher the communication beyond the words.

## Social Situations

Children with disabilities in this area have been called "children with social imperceptions" or "social cripples" by professionals; while members of their peer group may label them "weirdos," "queers," or "out of it." Such children appear unable to make the appropriate response in social situations without direct teaching.

11. Read or tell the child an incomplete story that involves social judgment. Have the child anticipate the ending or supply the completion of the story. A short film of a social situation provides an opportunity to critically discuss the activities of the people in the film. For example, discuss the consequences of a child's rudeness when an acquaintance tries to begin a conversation; or of a child's making a face when asked by his mother's friend if he likes her new dress; or of hitting someone at a party; and so on.

12. A series of pictures can be arranged to tell a story involving a social situation. Have the child arrange the pictures and explain the story. Comics, readiness books, beginning readers, and magazine advertising all provide good source materials for such activities. These series can also be pictures on transparencies.

13. Use transparency overlays on an overhead projector to create a fairly complex social situation. Discuss the social situation as it develops. Start with a basic simple form and add additional concepts with each transparency overlay. The complete picture might show activities on a school playground, for example.

14. Space and directional concepts are often imprecise. Specific activities to help a child read maps, to practice following directions to reach specific places, and to estimate distances are helpful.

15. Time concepts are often faulty. Learning to tell time; discussing appropriate activities for morning, afternoon, and evening; estimating time needed to accomplish various activities may all be helpful.

16. Help the child learn to differentiate between real and make-believe situations. What could happen in real life and what could happen only in the world of make-believe?

## Social Maturity

Social development involves growing from immaturity to maturity. At the time of birth the human infant, among all species of animal life, is perhaps the most dependent upon others for his sheer survival. The road from complete dependency to relative independency is the long and gradual growth toward social maturity.

Behavior can be observed and recorded which indicates a level of social growth. Areas of social maturity include the recognition of rights and responsibilities of self and others, making friends, cooperating with a group, following procedures agreed upon by others, making moral and ethical judgments, gaining independence in going places, etc. The *Vineland Social Maturity Scale* (1953) is an instrument designed to measure social maturity. The scale is a standardized developmental schedule extending from birth to adulthood. Social maturation is divided into six categories: (1) self-help; (2) locomotion; (3) occupation; (4) communication; (5) self-direction; and (6) socialization. The scale indicates for example, that a 6-year-old should be able to go to school alone; a 10-year-old should be able to get about his home town freely; a 12-year-old should begin to buy some of his own articles for personal use; a 15-year-old should be able to manage an allowance; and an 18-year-old should be able to make arrangements for a trip to a distant point.

17. *Anticipating consequences of social acts.* Help the child learn what to expect if he breaks rules in games. Role playing, creative play, stories, and discussions help the child to see what happens if rules of the game or rules of manners are broken.

18. *Establishing independence.* Encourage the child to go places by himself. Make simple maps with directions to follow, talk about the various steps to take in getting to the desired location. Use a walking map, if necessary. Plan activities so that he makes simple purchases by himself. Plan activities that provide opportunities to talk to other people, ask directions, interview others, etc.

19. *Ethical judgments.* Help the child learn cultural mores and learn to make value judgments. The *Unfinished Stories For Use in the Classroom* (National Education Association 1968) provides good material for discussing judgments of right and wrong.

20. *Planning and implementing.* Have the child make plans for a trip, activity, party, picnic, meeting, etc. Then help him to successfully implement the plan to gain a feeling of independence and maturity.

21. The *"Weekend Problem."* As a consequence of a disability in social perception, some children have difficulty in making friends. Parents frequently complain of a "weekend problem" when their child appears to have nothing to do. Without companions and friends, summers and vacations often prove to be difficult periods for such youngsters. The initiative and cooperation of parent groups and community organizations will be needed to help develop solutions to such problems.

## Summary

This final chapter of Part III discussed theories of maturational, psychological, and social abnormalities of children with learning disabilities. Representative teaching strategies to help children learn social skills were suggested.

The maturation theories describe the normal developmental patterns of children and emphasize that each stage of development requires stabilization before the subsequent stage can be successfully added. The development of abstract thinking is one of the last stages to evolve and it must build upon many other previous learnings. A maturational lag in a specific area of development may be the cause of poor academic achievement in some cases of learning disabilities.

Two psychological theories were reviewed. The first, a psychodynamic approach, analyzed the emotions and feelings of the child with learning disabilities. This view suggests that a child's failures at home and school result in poor ego development. In turn, this has further implications for a worsened learning situation. The second psychological theory, a behavioral view, discussed an approach to helping the child learn by modifying his behavior through contingency rein-forcements.

Problems in social perception were discussed in the last section of the chapter. Characteristics of the child with a social disability were reviewed and teaching strategies for improvement of social perception were suggested.

## Review of Part III

The purpose of Part III, within the plan of this book, was to review the many approaches, frameworks, and theories of children with learning disabilities. An additional purpose was to describe representative teaching strategies that evolve from each of the theories or approaches. Each of these theories concentrates on an in-depth analysis of one aspect of the child. It is essential to understand as fully as possible each of these elements, since each of the views has an important contribution to make. Still, the problem of integrating the many views and factors remains a difficult one. The child is more than a sum of many different parts; therefore, to most effectively help a child, a comprehensive and integrative view is needed. The problem is that each of the factors must be understood separately, yet the interrelationships of the many factors must also be clarified and seen as a whole.

The problem of implementing a workable teaching program in an institutional setting is discussed in Part IV.

## REFERENCES

Ames, Louise Bates. "Learning Disabilities: The Developmental Point of View," pp. 39–76 in Helmer Myklebust (ed.), *Progress in Learning Disabilities,* Vol. 1. New York: Grune & Stratton, 1968.

Baer, Paul E. "Problems in the Differential Diagnosis of Brain-Damage and Childhood Schizophrenia," *American Journal of Orthopsychiatry* 31 (1961): 728–737.

Barsch, Ray. "Counseling the Parent of the Brain-Damaged Child," pp. 145–151 in E. Frierson and W. Barbe (eds.), *Educating Children with Learning Disabilities.* New York: Appleton-Century-Crofts, 1967.

Bender, Loretta. "Specific Reading Disability as a Maturational Lag," *Bulletin of the Orton Society* 7 (1957): 9–18.

Benton, A. L. "Behavioral Indices of Brain Injury in School Children," *Child Development* 33 (1962): 199–208.

deHirsch, Katrina, Jeanette J. Jansky, and William S. Langford, *Predicting Reading Failure.* New York: Harper & Row, 1966.

Dimitrovsky, L. "The Ability to Identify the Emotional Meanings of Vocal Expressions at Successive Age Levels," pp. 69–89 in J. R. Davitz (ed.), *The Communication of Emotional Meaning.* New York: McGraw-Hill, 1964.

Doll, E. *The Measurement of Social Competence: Manual for the Vineland Social Maturity Scale.* Minneapolis: Educational Test Bureau, 1953.

Eisenberg, Leon. "Psychiatric Implications of Brain Damage in Children," pp. 171–187 in Edward Frierson and W. Barbe (eds.), *Educating Children with Learning Disabilities.* New York: Appleton-Century-Crofts, 1967.

Flavell, John H. *The Developmental Psychology of Jean Piaget.* Princeton, N.J.: Van Nostrand, 1963.

Gardner, Richard A. *The Child's Book About Brain Injury.* New York: New York Association for Brain-Injured Children, 1966.

Giffin, Mary. "The Role of Child Psychiatry in Learning Disabilities," pp. 75–98 in H. Myklebust (ed.), *Progress in Learning Disabilities,* Vol. 1. New York: Grune & Stratton, 1968.

Hall, Edward T. *The Silent Language*. Greenwich, Conn.: Primier Book, Fawcett, 1961.

Haring, Norris G., and Mary Ann Hauck, "Improving Learning Conditions in the Establishment of Reading Skills with Disabled Readers," *Exceptional Children* 35 (January 1969): 341–352.

Harris, Dale. *Children's Drawings as Measures of Intellectual Maturity*. New York: Harcourt, Brace & World, 1963.

Hewett, Frank M. "A Hierarchy of Educational Tasks for Children with Learning Disorders," pp. 342–352 in E. C. Frierson and W. B. Barbe (eds.), *Educating Children with Learning Disabilities: Selected Readings*. New York: Appleton-Century-Crofts, 1967.

———. *The Emotionally Disturbed Child in the Classroom*. Boston: Allyn & Bacon, 1968.

Johnson, Doris, and H. Myklebust. *Learning Disabilities: Educational Principles and Practices*. New York: Grune & Stratton, 1967.

Kirk, Samuel A. "Amelioration of Mental Abilities Through Psychodiagnostic and Remedial Procedures," in George A. Jervis (ed.), *Mental Retardation*. Springfield, Ill.: Charles A. Thomas, 1967.

Krasner, Leonard, and Leonard Ullman (eds.) *Research in Behavior Modification: New Developments and Implications*. New York: Holt, Rinehart & Winston, 1965.

Lewis, R. S., A. Strauss, and L. Lehtinen. *The Other Child*. 2nd ed. New York: Grune & Stratton, 1960.

Lovitt, Thomas C. "Assessment of Children with Learning Disabilities," *Exceptional Children* 34 (December 1967): 233–239.

Lovitt, Thomas C., Harold P. Kunzelmann, Patricia A. Nolen, and William J. Hulten. "The Dimensions of Classroom Data," *Journal of Learning Disabilities* 1 (December 1968): 710–721.

Rabinovitch, Ralph D. "Dyslexia: Psychiatric Considerations," chapter 5 in John Money (ed.), *Reading Disability: Progress and Research Needs in Dyslexia*. Baltimore: Johns Hopkins, 1962.

Rappaport, Sheldon R. "Personality Factors Teachers Need for Relationship Structure," pp. 45–56 in W. Cruickshank (ed.), *The Teacher of Brain-Injured Children: A Discussion of the Bases of Competency*. Syracuse, N.Y.: Syracuse University Press, 1966.

Silver, Archie A., and Rosa A. Hagin, "Maturation of Perceptual Functions in Children with Specific Reading Disabilities," *The Reading Teacher* 19 (January 1966): 253–259.

Skinner, B. F. *Science and Human Behavior*. New York: Macmillan, 1953.

———. "Operant Behavior," *American Psychologist* 18 (1963): 503–515.

Strauss, Alfred A., and Laura Lehtinen. *Psychopathology and Education of Brain-Injured Children*. New York: Grune & Stratton, 1947.

Unfinished Stories for Use in the Classroom. Stock No. 381–11766. Washington, D.C.: National Education Association, 1968.

Wepman, Joseph M. "Neurological Approaches to Mental Retardation," chapter 7 in Richard L. Schiefelbusch, Ross H. Copeland, and James O. Smith (eds.), *Language and Mental Retardation*. New York: Holt, Rinehart & Winston, 1967.

# IV

# ORGANIZATIONAL PATTERNS

# Chapter 12

# Facilities and Programs for Teaching Children with Learning Disabilities

The implementation of a program for children with learning disabilities generally takes place within some organizational setting, such as a school, clinic, hospital, or child guidance center. Many variations of organizational patterns are possible to provide the facilities for serving these children. Both the pattern selected and the organization itself will have a direct and strong impact on the teacher, the child, and the success of the program.

There are many organizational factors that affect the direction of a learning disabilities program, including the administration of the institution, the working and personal relationship among staff members, the goals and ambitions of the organization, and the role and status of the learning disabilities specialist within the organization. This final chapter considers the variety of organizational settings and programs that have been developed to cope with children who find learning difficult.

A variety of organizational patterns and placement facilities have been developed for diagnosing and treating children with learning disabilities. As a particular child progresses in his learning, changes in his setting may be necessary; new patterns may prove to be better suited to his new educational needs. Therefore, flexible arrangements and numerous variations within any organizational facility are needed to provide for the different and changing educational needs of children.

Factors to be considered in placement include the child's educational level, his behavior, his ability to maintain himself in groups, his chronological age, the individualization of instruction offered in the regular classroom of his school, and his level of schooling (primary, intermediate, secondary).

Among the public school settings developed for educating children with learning disabilities are the residential school, special day schools, self-contained classrooms, itinerant special teachers, and resource teachers. Other settings for helping the child with learning disabilities include private schools, community agencies, child guidance clinics, hospital clinics, university clinics, and private clinics. Recently, innovative, experimental, and cooperative projects have been attempted within many of these settings. This chapter discusses (1) the numerous organization patterns and facilities, and (2) some representative innovative, experimental, and ongoing programs in various parts of the country.

# Organizational Settings

## The Residential School

The residential school provides full-time placement for children away from their homes. Relatively few children have handicaps severe enough to warrant such placement. However, if the community lacks adequate alternative facilities, if the behavioral manifestations are extremely severe, and if the emotional reaction among other members of the family is debilitating, residential placement on a twenty-four-hour basis may be the only solution for both the child and his family.

Although residential schools are the oldest provision for dealing with exceptional children, there are many disadvantages to them. Removal of the child from his home and neighborhood, emphasis on the handicap, rigidity of institutional life, and lack of opportunity for normal social experiences are among the shortcomings of the residential school. As the public and private schools and other community agencies develop more services, the need decreases for residential placement for most children with learning disabilities.

## The Special Day School

The special day school is a separate school facility established specifically for children with a special handicap—in this case, learning disabilities. These schools are usually private and, historically, have been established when the public was either unaware of or unwilling to recognize the learning problem. Some children attend the special school full time; others attend for a half-day and may attend the public school for the balance of the school day.

The disadvantages of such programs include the high expense to parents, the traveling distance required, and the lack of opportunity to be with normal children for some portion of the school day. These schools served well, however, as pilot programs for later classes in public schools.

## Special Classes

The designation of special classrooms within the public school was one of the first approaches of the public school system to the education of children with learning disabilities. Classes were established that contained six to ten children who had been diagnosed as having brain damage, perceptual handicaps, minimal brain dysfunction, or other related labels. A wide variety of materials and environmental arrangements were available to the teacher. Often the classes were begun with one or two children, and additional pupils were enrolled one at a time to permit the establishment of classroom routine before each new child was added to the class.

Cruickshank's (1961) detailed description of special classes for brain-injured and hyperactive children became a prototype for many self-contained special classes. The classroom researched by Cruickshank had specially equipped rooms designed to reduce environmental distractions, and the teaching techniques were highly structured and exacting.

One of the first special classes to be established in the Illinois public schools was located in Joliet, Illinois. The state of New York and the city of Chicago provided special self-contained special classes for neurologically impaired children. Oakland, Michigan organized one of the early public school programs with special classes in their Perceptual Development Program. In many of the early special-class public school programs, criteria for admittance included medical evidence of a neurological abnormality.

The goal of special classes is to help children organize themselves for increased independent learning so that they will be able to eventually return to normal classes. Usually the children begin the transition by attending a selected subject within the regular classroom and gradually they increase participation until they attend regular classes on a full-time basis. If the transition is to be effective, a good working relationship must be maintained between the teacher of the class and the teacher of the regular classes.

## The Itinerant Teacher

For those children whose handicap is not severe enough to warrant a special class, the itinerant teacher can provide teaching services. The itinerant learning disabilities teacher travels to several schools, serving children in many classrooms by providing educational treatment. Children are scheduled to leave their regular classroom at a specified time for work with the itinerant teacher. They may come individually or in small groups of two to five children. Sessions may be held daily or several times per week, and the sessions generally last from thirty minutes to an hour. Care must be taken in scheduling. For example, if the pupil enjoys physical education, the teacher should avoid pre-empting this period for the teaching session. In addition, the classroom teacher should be consulted about the optimum time for the child to leave the classroom. If the learning disabilities teacher intends to work on reading, the regular classroom reading time may provide a convenient time for scheduling the special therapy session. Some schools use a revolving time arrangement schedule so that the child misses a different subject each time he works with the itinerant teacher.

The rooms used by the itinerant teacher should be pleasant and have an abundant supply of materials. Since the child often has a short attention span, it is wise to plan for a number of different activities during the teaching session; and these should provide for a change of pace.

## The Resource Teacher

The current trend in the field of learning disabilities is toward the development of resource rooms for children with learning disabilities. This room is served by a highly trained professional who is capable of diagnosing the child, of planning a teaching program on the basis of this diagnosis, and of implementing the teaching plan. The position of the resource teacher may include many responsibilities. In addition to diagnosing and teaching, the resource teacher may be a consultant, aiding the classroom teacher in interpreting the diagnostic findings and in operationalizing the diagnosis in terms of teaching methods, approaches, and materials. He may help the classroom teacher plan the classroom instruction for the child with learning disabilities. Moreover, the resource teacher may be responsible for in-service sessions, demonstration lessons, and continuous evaluation of the progress of the children.

The learning disabilities resource teacher may also serve as a liaison between the school's various specialists, such as the psychologist, speech teacher, physical education teacher, nurse, and administrators, as well as non-school personnel, such as the parents, physicians, and representatives of community agencies. These duties require a person who not only is an expert in the field of learning disabilities but also has the capacity to work well with other professionals by gaining their confidence and respect. The successful resource teacher must have that extra spark of enthusiasm needed for work with children who find learning difficult, and he must be able to transmit this enthusiasm and spirit to others. Dynamic human relations and an understanding of the entire school organization is required of the person serving in the role of resource teacher.

### The Secondary School Program

Most of the help for children with learning disabilities has been at the elementary levels, but junior and senior high schools are beginning to provide services for the pupil with learning disabilities. The problems increase at the high school level. The high school staff member is likely to be primarily interested in the subject area in which he is a specialist. His concern and perspective tend to be content oriented rather than child oriented. Consequently, it becomes more difficult to convince the high school staff that accommodations are needed and that flexibility is required to help these students. Scheduling, too, becomes a difficult problem because students cannot easily miss scheduled classes. Free periods, a second English period, release from music or art classes have provided the needed time in some secondary programs.

Further difficulties at the secondary school level are due to the increased frustration and emotional problems that accompany the learning disabilities of a student who has reached the high school level. High school students generally need direct help in finding ways to attack their content subjects.

In some high school programs students attend their regular classes, which may be modified, but they also report to a "resource room" for several periods a week. Diagnosis and planning of programs may be made by a multidisciplinary team consisting of the school psychologist, social worker, guidance counselor and the learning disabilities teacher. However, the implementation and teaching is the responsibility of the learning disabilities specialist. Many students participating in such a program may have been previously diagnosed as having other kinds of exceptionality or other causes of school failure.

### The Diagnostic-Remedial Specialist

This title has been used by Kirk (1969) to describe the complex role and responsibilities of the learning disabilities specialist. This individual is highly trained in the diagnostic-teaching process and is knowledgeable in the field of learning disabilities and other related areas. He serves as the responsible agent for the child, and pulls together the findings of other specialists—diagnosing and assessing the child, planning the teaching procedures, and implementing the teaching.

## Representative Ongoing Programs

This section describes a number of ongoing programs for children with learning disabilities which have been implemented in various parts of the country. The wide diversity among the programs illustrates that there are many ways to help these children. Differences in programs are due to institutional variations, personnel available, and theoretical perspectives of the program developers.

Diagnostic and treatment services for children with learning disabilities are offered not only in school settings, but also by child guidance clinics, hospital clinics, and university clinics. In such nonschool settings, children usually report for therapy sessions after school, on Saturdays, or during summers. In some cases children are released from school for therapy sessions at the agencies. Such settings often have the advantage of having a staff of diverse professionals who can provide interdisciplinary services. Medical specialists, social workers, or guidance counselors are often available at such centers.

## Hospital Settings

Clinics for children with learning disabilities are located in some hospital settings. Whitsell and Whitsell (1968) describe one such clinic at the University of California Medical Center, Department of Pediatrics, in San Francisco. This hospital clinic accepts children between the ages of 5 and 16, providing, among other services, a treatment facility for children who are having difficulty in learning school subjects. In addition, the clinic assists in the evaluation of children brought to the Hospital Child Study Unit who are encountering school and learning problems. After an interdisciplinary diagnosis is made, the child reports to the clinic two or three times per week for instruction individually or in small groups of not more than five.

The reporters of this hospital program conclude that the hospital environment has advantages for medical personnel, clinical teachers, the child, and the community. Medical students, interns, and residents, help in the diagnosis; they communicate freely with teachers; and they become aware of the problems encountered in the instructional situations. The clinical teachers interact daily with the medical staff and thereby gain confidence in their roles as members of an interdisciplinary team. Whitsell and Whitsell also suggest that the medical setting provides a better understanding and appreciation of the problem by the child and his parents. In addition to an indirect psychotherapeutic benefit, the hospital setting provides auxiliary services the child may need. The advantage to the community is that this type of clinic provides a facility for training medical students, physicians, nurses, social workers, psychologists, and other paramedical personnel.

## Community Mental Health Centers and Child Guidance Centers

Mental health centers and child guidance clinics are other settings for programs for children with learning disabilities. A description of one such program, the Child Guidance Center in Marathon County, Wisconsin, is reported by Kline and others (1968). In this center children receive therapy for one-hour sessions, four to five times per week. The program makes extensive use of nonprofessional volunteers who work on a part-time basis. Orientation courses, periods of observation, and consultation with an orthopsychiatric team help train these nonprofessionals to provide the educational therapy.

## School Programs

Individual schools and school districts have developed innovative organizational arrangements for helping children with learning disabilities. Like the children themselves, each school environment is unique. Therefore, a pattern or structure that has been successful in one school environment cannot completely be adapted to another without modification:

Some school systems have implemented a plan that calls for the division of diagnostic and teaching responsibilities between two or more staff members. The *psychoeducational diagnostician* provides the diagnosis through testing and consultation with other professionals who examine the child, and then he develops a broad teaching plan from the diagnosis. The *educational therapist* implements that plan and does the actual teaching. Continuous communication is required between these persons because plans must be modified as additional information is acquired through the teaching process.

Jacobson (1969) describes such a program in Skokie, Illinois, in which responsibilities are divided between a *diagnostic teacher* and a *remedial teacher*. The diagnostic teacher is responsible for: (1) screening the school population to identify children with learning disabilities; (2) giving diagnostic tests to identify and diagnose children with learning disabilities; (3) requesting special services, such as psychological or medical aid, when necessary; (4) evaluating the child; and (5) formulating educational prescriptions or a teaching plan. The duties of the remedial teacher are to implement the educational prescription by teaching the child. The remedial teacher meets the child several times per week in a small group or individually.

This program was originated to overcome the shortage of trained learning disabilities teachers. The educational prescriptions are designed to be sufficiently clear and detailed to be carried out by faculty who are not learning disabilities specialists but are classroom teachers by training and experience. Another feature of this program is a card file consisting of number-coded cards categorized by academic subjects and psychological correlates to learning. Remedial plans usually include references to numbered-coded file cards that will provide the teacher with specific activities relevant to the skill he is planning to teach. In this way, the remedial teacher learns while teaching.

The *psychoeducational diagnostician* is the heart of the learning disabilities program in Schaumberg Township, Illinois (McCarthy 1969). A primary aim of the person in this role is to bridge the gap between diagnosis and teaching—between the psychologist who has never taught and the teacher who does not understand psychological jargon. The duties of the psychoeducational diagnostician in this program include providing intensive diagnosis, clinical teaching, and consultation with the classroom teacher. In addition, this school system developed an early identification screening program, self-contained classrooms, itinerant teaching programs, and resource rooms.

The *master teacher* serves in a liaison role for the schools in the Las Cruces, New Mexico area (New Mexico State University 1970). Within the Regional Resource Center for the Improvement of the Education of Handicapped Children, which is a project of New Mexico State University at Las Cruces and the public schools, the master teacher is responsible for helping classroom teachers in regular and special classrooms to implement teaching prescriptions that have been formulated by the diagnostic-prescription team at the Regional Resource Center. The following stages of implementation concern the master teacher:

1. A child is recommended by the public school principal and the Regional Resource Center staff.

2. The public school teacher agrees to attempt to implement individual recommended prescriptions.

3. An assessment of the child is made by the staff at the Regional Resource Center, and a master teacher is assigned to the case.

4. Teacher conferences are held every four weeks to evaluate progress and provide the next set of educational objectives to be carried out in the succeeding four-week span.

5. The master teacher demonstrates within the classroom the first step of each four-week teaching plan agreed upon at the conference.

A *placement specialist* is used in a public school program in Memphis, Tennessee (Perry and Morris 1969). The responsibility of the placement specialist is to translate technical and clinical information into workable terms. This specialist formulates a psychoeducational profile from information derived from psychologists and others; and he interprets it to parents, administrators, and special class teachers. He also helps make appropriate placement for pupils, and he aids the special teacher in implementing the findings of the diagnosis.

Many schools have a *multiplan* arrangement that utilizes several organizational settings within a single school. Thus the self-contained classroom, the itinerant teacher, and the resource room could all be found within a school or district. The severity of the child's problem would determine the appropriate placement. Such arrangements also have the advantage of providing alternative placement facilities as the child progresses and his needs change. In a report of the learning disabilities programs in Ohio, Serio and Todd (1969) indicate that three types of approaches are available in some school districts in the state of Ohio. They are described as: (1) adjustments within the regular classroom, (2) supplementary instruction in addition to the regular classroom, and (3) special classes.

### The Area Learning Center

The area regional learning center provides a team approach to attacking the problems involved in the diagnosis, prescriptions, materials, and followup (Huizinga and Smalligan 1968). In one such program in Grand Rapids, Michigan, a classroom teacher may call upon the area learning center for help. The child in question is observed and tested by the consultant, who also provides the classroom teacher with information about the child's problem and with suggestions for teaching him within the classroom. If further diagnosis is deemed necessary, the child is brought to the learning center where further testing is done by the team staff which includes reading experts, psychologists, psychiatrists, pediatricians, and others. An educational plan is made and a conference is held with the classroom teacher.

A good example of an area clinic is the Public School Reading Clinic of the St. Louis public schools, described by Stubblefield (1966). Each of the seven well-equipped clinics in St. Louis services the schools in the administrative district in which it is located. The staff of each clinic includes four full-time teachers and a secretary; part-time services of a physician, nurse, and a social worker are also available to the clinic. Students are excused from their home schools to attend a session at the clinic that lasts for about an hour, and students then return to their home schools. The St. Louis clinics also fulfill an important function as a teacher training institution because classroom teachers work in the clinics for a period of time and then return to their positions in the classroom.

Gold (1969) describes a Regional Learning Disability Center in Binghamton, New York. Fifteen public and two private school districts, located in three counties, established a diagnostic and treatment center under Title III. Pupils referred to the area center were screened with informal tests to determine eligibility for the program. In addition to diagnostic and treatment facilities for children in the cooperating school districts, the Center housed a professional library, developed a curriculum resource center, sponsored in-service training programs, offered consultation services to school districts, and developed research papers to provide schools with information.

The operation of a learning disabilities area learning center for 29 elementary schools of Waterford, Michigan, is described by Heckerl and Webb (1969). A multidisciplinary staff at the school district's Learning Improvement Center first identifies and then diagnoses children in the district who are likely to benefit from a learning disabilities program. Educational procedures are subsequently planned for children accepted into the program. Groups limited to six children meet four times a week with a teacher from the Learning Improvement Center for forty-five-minute sessions. The Center also provides supportive help and special materials for the classroom teacher to use with the child in the regular classroom; it provides in-service training sessions for the classroom teachers in the district; it offers a clinical training session for teachers; and it offers an educational program for children during the summer.

## Summer Programs

Schools, as well as camps, provide special programs during the summer for children with learning disabilities. Rochford and others (1969) describe one summer program in Erie County, New York. In this four-week summer session, children received instruction in academic areas, perceptual skills, art, physical education, and swimming. Sabatino and Hayden (1970) describe a six-week summer program in La Plata, Maryland, which emphasized unisensory perceptual training. The use of language cues as a technique of strengthening perceptual deficits was another feature of this program.

The summer season provides an ideal opportunity to develop sensorimotor and perceptual-motor skills such as those described by Kephart (1960), which evolved at the Achievement Center for Children at Purdue University and a camp in Ft. Collins, Colorado. Some summer programs for the child with learning disabilities have combined camping and academic activities. Stetler and Turner (1969) describe a combined camping-academic program in Monmouth County, New Jersey. An integrated camping and academic summer program located at a children's camp served as a teacher-training practicum for Northeastern Illinois State College (Lerner et al. 1971).

Educators who have had experience with summer programs underscore the importance of creating an atmosphere that is very different from that of the academic year so that the child does not feel penalized by attending school during the summer months. Moreover, summer programs provide a practical way to lengthen the school year.

## Cooperative School District Arrangements

Many small school districts have found it advantageous to merge their efforts in building programs for children with learning disabilities. One such cooperative enterprise combined the efforts of six school systems, public and parochial, from three counties in Kentucky (Pollack 1969). Four multidisciplinary teams were organized—each composed of a psychologist, a psychometrist, a psychiatric social worker, and an educational specialist; these teams served four geographical areas in the three-county region. The teams assumed responsibility for conferring and consulting, as well as for the evaluation and treatment of children with learning disabilities.

## The Interdisciplinary Team for Both Diagnosis and Therapy

An underlying aim of many programs for children with learning disabilities is the integration of professional skills of contributing disciplines. An interdisciplinary team approach to both diagnosing and treating learning difficulties has been a goal of the Pupil Appraisal Center of North Texas at the North Texas State University (Landreth and others 1969). The developers of this team approach found that children are likely to have a complex, multifaceted cluster of learning disabilities rather than a single difficulty in isolation. They therefore concluded that a multifaceted diagnosis as well as a multifaceted therapeutic teaching arrangement was necessary.

In actual practice, team approaches are often interdisciplinary in name only; certain team members or disciplines are not accorded equal status in diagnosis, and the teamwork is not carried through in therapy. As a result, the teaching is isolated, scattered, and without interdisciplinary contact. To assure that the work of the members of the team in both diagnosis and therapy is unified and integrated the Pupil Appraisal Center developers caution that the following elements are essential:

1. Members of the team should have a commitment to the belief that learning disabilities do not occur in isolation. Because there are many factors involved in the learning problem, each discipline has an essential contribution to make.

2. Team cohesiveness requires freedom from professional prejudices. Interdisciplinary rivalries can easily be transformed into personality conflicts that prevent interdisciplinary cooperation.

3. Familiarity among the team members as to their colleagues' ideas, perspectives, and ways of talking about their fields is important in the formation of a successful team. Without such familiarity and frequent communication, common perceptions cannot be established; and without common perceptions, effective communication is not possible.

4. Sufficient time, free from other pressures, is needed by team members with diverse backgrounds to develop quality interaction.

5. Personal acceptance of each other's professional competencies is necessary for effective team functioning. The freedom to admit errors or inadequacies without fear of losing professional or personal status may lead to higher levels of group processes.

6. Physical proximity is conducive to an effective team relationship. A physical facility that provides team members the opportunity for frequent face-to-face contact strongly reinforces communication.

This review of ongoing programs suggests that many organizational and administrative patterns and settings have proved useful for helping children with learning disabilities. We appear to be on the threshold of organizational innovation in all areas of education and this condition will no doubt have its impact on programs for children with learning disabilities. The entire organization must be geared to the problems of children with learning disabilities. The mere employment of a learning disabilities specialist is only the beginning of the task. The structure of the organization and the patterns of administrative behavior have a direct and strong impact on the direction of the learning disabilities program. No one arrangement will be found to be best for all children and for all organizations. Each new organizational innovation and experimental program adds to our knowledge of the complex problem of helping children with learning disabilities.

## The Role of the Learning Disabilities Specialist

The teacher of children with learning disabilities plays many roles. Among the jobs he may be expected to perform either as an individual or as part of a team, are the following: (1) setting up programs for identifying, diagnosing and instructing children with learning disabilities; (2) finding or screening the children within the school who are handicapped by learning disabilities; (3) consulting with professionals from contributing disciplines and interpreting their reports; (4) testing and diagnosing individual children; (5) planning prescriptive educational programs; (6) implementing the educational plan through teaching, and creating or locating appropriate materials and methods; (7) interviewing and consulting with parents; (8) helping the classroom teacher and other school personnel to understand the child, and providing teachers with ways to help the child; and (9), perhaps most important, helping the child to understand himself and to gain the hope and confidence necessary to cope with his handicap and start to overcome it.

The specialist in learning disabilities is an expert in helping the child find the elusive key to learning. The normal pathways for learning are not open to this child; new roads to learning must be found and some avenues must be cleared so that linguistic, academic, and behavioral goals can be reached.

## Summary

Many variations of organizational patterns and facilities are possible to provide the facilities for helping children with learning disabilities. These are the basic plans in school programs: (1) self-contained classrooms provide a separate classroom setting for children with learning disabilities. Typically six to ten children are taught within such a setting in a public school. (2) The itinerant teacher travels to several schools and teaches children individually or in small groups. The children are released from their regular classrooms for teaching sessions with the itinerant teacher. (3) The resource room is located within one school and is the center for servicing the children with learning disabilities within that school. It contains a variety of teaching materials and equipment. The specialist who is responsible for the resource room is likely to have many responsibilities, including diagnosing children, planning teaching programs, implementing teaching programs, and consulting with classroom teachers. The professional in this role assumes responsibility for the child; he is the person who coordinates the efforts of others and follows through.

As programs for children with learning disabilities develop, there will probably continue to be a wide diversity in programs that are dedicated to helping these children. Private schools, hospitals, community health centers, and public schools all have developed excellent programs and their experiences contribute to our knowledge. Interdisciplinary teams for diagnosis and treatment are found in many of these settings. The trend in the field of learning disabilities at present is toward the development of learning disabilities specialists who are competent in the complete diagnostic-teaching process.

## REFERENCES

Cruickshank, William M., et al. A Teaching Method for Brain-Injured and Hyperactive Children. Syracuse, N.Y.: Syracuse University Press, 1961.

Gold, Laurence. "The Implementation of a Regional Learning Disability Center for the Treatment of Pupils Who Manifest the Dyslexic Syndrome," pp. 82–94 in George D. Spache (ed.), Reading Disability and Perception. Newark, Del.: International Reading Association, 1969.

Heckerl, John R., and Susan M. Webb. "An Educational Approach to the Treatment of Children with Learning Disabilities," Journal of Learning Disabilities 2 (April 1969): 199–204.

Huizinga, Raleigh J., and Donald H. Smalligan, "The Area Learning Center—A Regional Program for School Children with Learning Disabilities," Journal of Learning Disabilities (September 1968): 502–506.

Jacobson, Anita M. "Systemwide Identification and Instructional Practices," pp. 103–112 in J. Arena (ed.), Successful Programing: Many Points of View. Association of Children with Learning Disabilities. San Rafael, Calif.: Academic Therapy Publications, 1969.

Kephart, Newell C. The Slow Learner in the Classroom. Columbus, Ohio: Merrill, 1960.

Kirk, Samuel A. "Learning Disabilities: The View from Here," pp. 21–26 in J. Arena (ed.), Progress in Parent Information: Professional Growth and Public Policy. Association for Children with Learning Disabilities. San Rafael, Calif.: Academic Therapy Publications, 1969.

Kline, Carl L., et al. "The Treatment of Specific Dyslexia in a Community Mental Health Center," Journal of Learning Disabilities 1 (August 1968), 456–466.

Landreth, Gary L., Willard S. Jacquet, and Louise Allen. "A Team Approach to Disabilities," Journal of Learning Disabilities 2 (February 1969): 24–29.

Lerner, Janet W., Dorothy Bernstein, Lillian Stevenson, and Anne Rubin. "Bridging the Gap in Teacher Training: A Camping-Academic Program for Children with School Learning Disorders." Academic Therapy Quarterly VI (Summer 1971): 367–374.

McCarthy, Jeanne McRae. "Providing Services in the Public Schools for Children with Learning Disabilities," pp. 43–52 in John Arena (ed.), Management of the Child with Learning Disabilities. San Rafael, Calif.: Academic Therapy Publications, 1969.

New Mexico State University, Las Cruces, N.M. Regional Resource Center. Job Specifications, description for Master Teacher, 1970.

Perry, Harold W., and Thann E. Morris. "The Role of the Educational Diagnostician," pp. 128–130 in J. Arena (ed.), Successful Programing: Many Points of View. Association for Children with Learning Disabilities. San Rafael, Calif.: Academic Therapy Publications, 1969.

Pollack, John S. "Opportunities for Learning Disabilities, Title III, ESEA," pp. 149–152 in J. Arena (ed.), Successful Programing: Many Points of View. San Rafael, Calif.: Academic Therapy Publications, 1969.

Rochford, Timothy, Wendy Schroder, and Roger Reger. "A Summer Program for Children with Learning Disabilities," pp. 333—339 in J. Arena (ed.), Successful Programing: Many Points of View. San Rafael, Calif.: Academic Therapy Publications, 1969.

Sabatino, David A., and David L. Hayden. "Prescriptive Teaching in a Summer Learning Disabilities Program," *Journal of Learning Disabilities* 3 (April 1970): 220–227.

Serio, Martha, and Joseph H. Todd. "Operations of Programs in Ohio," pp. 377–379 in J. Arena (ed.), *Successful Programing: Many Points of View*. San Rafael, Calif.: Academic Therapy Publications, 1969.

Stetler, Margaret, and Dolores Turner. "Summer Workshops and Recreation Programs for the Learning Disabled," pp. 340–355 in John I. Arena (ed.), *Successful Programing*. San Rafael, Calif.: Academic Therapy Publication, 1969.

Stubblefield, Caroline. "The Public School Reading Clinic as a Training Center," pp. 16–23 in *Some Administrative Problems of Reading Clinics*. Newark, Del.: International Reading Association, 1965.

Whitsell, Alice J., and Leon J. Whitsell. "Remedial Reading in a Medical Center," *The Reading Teacher* 21 (May 1968): 707–711.

# APPENDICES

# APPENDIX A
# PHONICS

This appendix has two sections. The first part is a short phonics quiz to assess the teacher's knowledge of this subject area. The second part is a brief review of some phonic generalizations.

## ə fŏn' ĭks kwĭz (A Phonics Quiz)

The purpose of the phonics quiz is to give teachers the opportunity to evaluate their knowledge of phonics, structural or morphemic analysis, and phonic generalizations. Even among advocates of conflicting approaches to the teaching of reading, there is agreement that skills in word recognition and phonics are essential for effective reading. And all reading authorities agree that teachers of reading and language arts have the responsibility to help children acquire the skills that will enable them to unlock unknown words. Without phonics, most children cannot become self-reliant, discriminating, efficient readers.

In spite of this strong and united stand taken by the reading experts, many teachers and prospective teachers are not knowledgeable in this content area (Lerner and List 1970). *The Torch Lighters* (Austin 1961), an intensive and broad study, supported by the Carnegie Corporation, of tomorrow's teachers of reading revealed that many prospective teachers do not know techniques or generalizations of phonics. A major recommendation resulting from the study was that college instructors take responsibility in making certain that their students who will be teaching reading master the principles of phonics. Phonics and structural or morphemic analysis, then, should be part of the content area for the teacher of reading, language arts, and English.

It should be noted that recent research on the utility of phonic generalizations reveals that these rules have many exceptions. In fact, some are applicable less than half the time. Therefore certain generalizations may have a limited utility value (Clymer 1963, Emans 1967, Bailey 1967, Burmeister 1968, Lerner 1969, Winkley 1966). Nevertheless, these generalizations do provide a helpful start in analyzing unknown words.

Although knowledge of rules and facts concerning phonics is part of the content area for the teacher, this is not presented as a recommended way to teach phonics to a child. The strategies selected to teach a child the skill of unlocking words will depend upon many factors.

To check your knowledge of phonics, select the correct answer for each of the following 50 questions. Compare your choices with the correct answers printed at the end of the Phonics Quiz. Score two points for each correct answer. Check the table below the answers for your rating and classification.

### CHOOSE THE CORRECT ANSWER
### CONSONANTS

1. Which of the following words ends with a consonant sound?
   a) piano   b) baby   c) relay   d) pencil   e) below

2. A combination of 2 or 3 consonants pronounced so that each letter keeps its own identity is called a
   a) silent consonant   b) consonant digraph   c) diphthong
   d) schwa   e) consonant blend

3. A word with a consonant digraph is
   a) stop   b) blue   c) bend   d) stripe   e) none of the above

4. A word with a consonant blend is
   a) chair   b) ties   c) thing   d) strict   e) where

5. A soft "c" is in the word
   a) city   b) cat   c) chair   d) Chicago   e) none of the above

6. A soft "g" is in the word
   a) great   b) go   c) ghost   d) rig   e) none of the above

7. A hard "c" is sounded in pronouncing which of the following nonsense words?
   a) cadur   b) ceiter   c) cymling   d) ciblent   e) chodly

8. A hard "g" would be likely to be found in which of the following nonsense words?
   a) gyfing   b) gesturn   c) gailing   d) gimber   e) geit

9. A *voiced* consonant digraph is in the word
   a) think   b) ship   c) whip   d) the   e) photo

10. An *unvoiced* consonant digraph is in the word
    a) those   b) thirteen   c) that   d) bridge   e) these

### VOWELS

11. Which of the following words contains a long vowel sound?
    a) paste   b) stem   c) urge   d) ball   e) off

12. Which of the following words contain a short vowel sound?
    a) treat   b) start   c) slip   d) paw   e) father

13. If "tife" were a word, the letter "i" would probably sound like the "i" in
    a) if   b) beautiful   c) find   d) ceiling   e) sing
    Why?

14. If "aik" were a word, the letter "a" would probably sound like the "a" in
      a) pack  b) ball  c) about  d) boat  e) cake
      Why?

15. If "ne" were a word, the letter "e" would probably sound like the "e" in
      a) fed  b) seat  c) batter  d) friend  e) weight
      Why?

16. A vowel sound represented by the alphabet letter name of that vowel is a
      a) short vowel  b) long vowel  c) diphthong  d) digraph
      e) schwa

17. An example of the schwa sound is found in
      a) cotton  b) phoneme  c) stopping  d) preview  e) grouping

18. A diphthong is in the word
      a) coat  b) boy  c) battle  d) retarded  e) slow

19. Which of the following words contains a vowel digraph?
      a) toil  b) amazing  c) happy  d) cape  e) coat

## SYLLABLES

Indicate the correct way to divide the following nonsense words into syllables:

20. l i d b e r
      a) li–dber  b) lidb–er  c) lid–ber  d) none of the above
      Why?

21. s e f u m
      a) se–fum  b) sef–um  c) s–efum  d) sefu–m  e) none
      Why?

22. s k e b l e
      a) skeb–le  b) ske–ble  c) sk–eble  d) none of these
      Why?

23. g o p h u l
      a) gop–hul  b) go–phul  c) goph–ul  d) none
      Why?

24. r e p a i n l y
      a) rep–ain–ly  b) re–pai–nly  c) re–pain–ly
      d) none of the above
      Why?

25. How many syllables are in the word "barked"?
      a) one  b) two  c) three  d) four  e) five

26. How many syllables are in the word "generalizations"?
      a) four  b) five  c) six  d) seven  e) eight

27. A word with an open syllable is
      a) pike  b) go  c) bend  d) butter  e) if

28. A word with a closed syllable is
>  a) throw   b) see   c) why   d) cow   e) win

## ACCENT

29. If "trigler" were word, which syllable would probably be accented?
>  a) trig   b) ler   c) neither   d) both
>  Why?

30. If "tronition" were a word, which syllable would probably be accented?
>  a) tro   b) ni   c) tion   d) none
>  Why?

31. If "pretaineringly" were a word, which syllable would probably be accented?
>  a) pre   b) tain   c) er   d) ing   e) ly
>  Why?

## SOUND OF LETTER "Y"

32. If "gly" were a word, the letter "y" would probably sound like
>  a) the "e" in *eel*   b) the "e" in *pet*   c) the "i" in *isle*
>  d) the "i" in *if*   e) the "y" in *happy*
>  Why?

33. If "agby" were a word, the letter "y" would probably sound like
>  a) the "e" in *eel*   b) the "e" in *egg*   c) the "i" in *ice*
>  d) the "i" in *if*   e) the "y" in *cry*
>  Why?

## SILENT LETTERS

34. *No* silent letters are found in which of the following nonsense words?
>  a) knip   b) gine   c) camb   d) wron   e) shan

35. *No* silent letters are in
>  a) nade   b) fruting   c) kettin   d) foat   e) pnam

## TERMINOLOGY

36. A printed symbol made up of two letters representing one single phoneme or speech sound is a
>  a) schwa   b) consonant blend   c) phonetics
>  d) digraph   e) diphthong

37. The smallest sound bearing unit or a basic sound of speech is a
>  a) phoneme   b) morpheme   c) grapheme
>  d) silent consonant   e) schwa

38. A study of all the speech sounds in language and how these sounds are produced is
   a) phonics   b) semantics   c) orthography   d) etymology
   e) phonetics

39. The application of speech sounds applied to the teaching of reading letters or groups of letters is called
   a) phonics   b) phonemics   c) orthography   d) etymology
   e) phonetics

40. The study of the nature and function of human language utilizing the methodology and objectivity of the scientist is
   a) phonetics   b) phonology   c) linguistics   d) morphology
   e) semantics

41. The approach to beginning reading which selects words that have a consistent sound-symbol relationship (CVC) is the
   a) basal reader approach   b) phonics approach
   c) linguistics approach   d) language-experience approach
   e) initial teaching alphabet approach

42. The approach to beginning reading which uses a more simple, reliable alphabet to make the decoding of English phonemes less complex is the
   a) basal reader approach   b) phonetic approach
   c) linguistic approach   d) language-experience approach
   e) initial teaching alphabet approach

43. A *phonic element* is similar to which word in linguistic terminology?
   a) syntax   b) phoneme   c) morpheme
   d) grapheme   e) intonation

44. The study of structural analysis is similar to what element of linguistics?
   a) syntax   b) phonology   c) morphology
   d) graphology   e) intonation

## THE UTILITY OF PHONIC GENERALIZATIONS

In examining both words that are exceptions to the rules and words that conform to the rules, researchers have found a varying percent of utility to the generalizations in items 45–48. How frequently does each hold true?

45. When there are two vowels side by side, the long sound of the first one is heard and the second is usually silent.
   a) 25%   b) 45%   c) 75%   d) 90%   e) 100% of the time

46. When there are two vowels, one of which is final e, the first vowel is long and the e is silent.
   a) 30%   b) 60%   c) 75%   d) 90%   e) 100%

47. When a vowel is in the middle of a one-syllable word, the vowel is short.
   a) 30%   b) 50%   c) 70%   d) 90%   e) 100%

48. When a word begins with *kn*, the *k* is silent.
   a) 30%   b) 50%   c) 70%   d) 90%   e) 100%

49. The first American educator to advocate the teaching of phonics as an aid to word recognition and pronunciation was

    a) Noah Webster in The *American Blueback Spelling Book,* 1790

    b) William McGuffey in *McGuffey's Readers,* 1879

    c) Leonard Bloomfield, *Language,* 1933

    d) Rudolph Flesch in *Why Johnny Can't Read,* 1955

    e) Charles Fries, *Linguistics and Reading,* 1963

50. Most reading authorities agree that

    a) the sight word method is the best way to teach reading

    b) the phonics method is the best way to teach reading

    c) structural or morphemic analysis is the best way to teach reading

    d) there is no *one* best way to teach reading

Read the following nonsense words applying phonic generalizations to determine their appropriate pronunciations.

| | |
|---|---|
| bongtrike | crangle |
| plignel | magsletting |
| abcealter | phister |
| conborvement | flabinstate |
| gingabution | craipthrusher |
| recentively | wonaprint |
| fudder | knidderflicing |
| gentropher | |

## ANSWERS TO PHONICS QUIZ

1. d
2. e
3. e
4. d
5. a
6. e
7. a
8. c
9. d
10. b
11. a
12. c
13. c: long vowel with silent "e"
14. e: with 2 vowels, first is long, second is silent
15. b: one-syllable ending in vowel is long
16. b
17. a

18. b
19. e
20. c: divide between 2 consonants
21. a: vowel, consonant, vowel
22. b: words ending in "le"–consonant precedes the "le"
23. b: consonant digraphs are not divided
24. c: prefix and suffix are separate syllables
25. a
26. c
27. b
28. e
29. a: accent first of two syllables
30. b: accent syllables before "tion" ending
31. b: accent syllable with two adjacent vowels
32. c: "y" at end of one syllable word has a long "i" sound
33. a: "y" at end of a multi-syllable word has long "e" sound
34. e

35. b
36. d
37. a
38. e
39. a
40. c
41. c
42. e
43. b
44. c
45. b
46. b
47. c
48. e
49. a
50. d

**RATING SCALE**

| Score | Rating |
|---|---|
| 92–100 | EXCELLENT Congratulations! You do know your phonics. |
| 84–92 | GOOD A Brief refresher will help, though. |
| 76–84 | FAIR Study with your favorite third grader. |
| 68–76 | POOR You could be a case of "the blind leading the blind." |

# A Review of Common Phonic Generalizations

## CONSONANTS

Consonants are the letters in the alphabet that are not vowels. Consonant speech sounds are formed by modifying or altering or obstructing the stream of vocal sound with the organs of speech. These obstructions may be stops, fricatives, or resonants. Consonant sounds are relatively consistent and have a regular grapheme-phoneme relationship. They include: b, d, f, h, j, k, l, m, n, p, r, s, t, v, w, y (initial position).

### Consonants "c" and "g"

Hard "c" pronounced like "k" when followed by a, o, u. (cup, cat).
Soft "c" pronounced like "s" when followed by i, e, y. (city, cent).
Hard "g" when followed by *a, o, u,* (go, gay).
Soft "g" when followed by *i, e, y,* sounds like "j" (gentle, gyp).

### Consonant Blends

A combination of two or three consonant letters blended in such a way that each letter in the blend keeps its own identity: bl, sl, cl, fl, gl, pl, br, cr, dr, fr, gr, pr, tr, sc, sk, sl, sw, sn, sp, sm, spl, spr, str, scr, ng, nk, tw, dw.

### Consonant Digraphs

A combination of two consonant letters representing one phoneme or speech sound that is not a blend of the two letters: sh, ch, wh, ck, ph, gh, th.

### Silent Consonants

Silent consonants are those consonants which, when combined with specific other letters, are not pronounced. In the examples below, the silent consonants are the ones enclosed in parentheses, and the letters shown with them are the specific letters that cause them to be silent in combination. (There are exceptions, however.)

| | |
|---|---|
| i(gh) | sight, bright |
| m(b) | comb, lamb |
| (w)r | wren, wrong |
| (l)k | talk, walk |
| (k)n | knew, knife |
| s(t) | listen, hasten |
| f(t) | often, soften |

## VOWELS

The vowels of the alphabet are the letters *a, e, i, o, u,* and sometimes *y*. The vowel speech sounds are produced in the resonance chamber formed by the stream of air passing through in the oral cavity.

**Short vowels: a, e, i, o, u, (sometimes y)**   A single vowel in a medial position usually has the short vowel sound: consonant, vowel, consonant (CVC). A diacritical mark called a "breve" ˘ may indicate the short vowel: păt, sad, led, sit, pot, cup, gyp.

**Long vowels: a, e, i, o, u, (sometimes y)**   The long vowel sounds the same as the alphabet letter name of the vowel. It is indicated with the diacritical mark called a macron: ¯ gō, cake, eel, ice, no, uniform, cry.

### Double Vowels: Vowel Digraph

Frequently, when two vowels are adjacent, the first vowel has the long sound while the second is silent. Recent research has shown this generalization to hold true about 45% of the time. tie, coat, rain, eat, pay.

### Final "e"

In words with a vowel-consonant-e pattern (VCe), the vowel frequently has the long sound while the "e" is silent. Research has shown this generalization to hold true about 60% of the time. make, Pete, slide, hope, cube.

### Vowels Modified by "r"

Vowels followed by the letter "r" are neither long nor short, but the sound is modified by the letter "r." This holds true about 85% of the time. star, her, stir, horn, fur.

### Diphthongs

Two adjacent printed symbols representing two vowels, each of which contributes to a blended speech sound. joy, toil, cow, house, few.

### Schwa Sound

This is the vowel sound in an unaccented syllable and is indicated with the symbol ə. balloon, eaten, beautify, button, circus.

## SYLLABICATION

### Number of Syllables

There are as many syllables in a word as there are vowel sounds heard. bruise (1 syllable), beautiful (3 syllables)

### Two Consonants (VC–CV)

If the initial vowel is followed by two consonants, divide the word between the two consonants. This rule holds true about 80% of the time. con-tact, let-ter, mar-ket

### Single Consonant (V–CV)

If the initial vowel is followed by one consonant, the consonant usually begins the second syllable. There are many exceptions to this rule. The generalization holds true about 50% of the time. mo-tor, na-tion, stu-dent

### Consonant-Le (C-le) Endings

If a word ends in "le," the consonant preceding the "le" begins the last syllable. This generalization holds true about 95% of the time. ta-ble, pur-ple, han-dle

### Consonant Blends and Consonant Digraphs

Consonant blends and digraphs are not divided in separating a word into syllables. This holds true 100% of the time. teach-er, graph-ic, de-scribe

### Prefixes and Suffixes

Prefixes and suffixes usually form a separate syllable. re-plac-ing, dis-appoint-ment

### Suffix "ed"

If the suffix "ed" is preceded by "d" or "t," it does form a separate syllable and is pronounced "ed." If the suffix "ed" is not preceded by a "d" or "t," it does not form a separate syllable; it is pronounced like "t." When it follows an unvoiced consonant and it is pronounced like "d" when it follows a voiced consonant. sanded (ed), patted (ed), asked (t), pushed (t), tamed (d), crazed (d)

### Open and Closed Syllables

Syllables that end with a consonant are closed syllables and the vowel is short. can-vass

Syllables that end with a vowel are open syllables and the vowel is long. ba-by

### The "y" Sound in One-Syllable Words and Multisyllable Words

When the "y" is the final sound in a one-syllable word, it usually has the sound of a long "i." cry, my, ply

When the "y" is the final sound of a multisyllable word, it usually has the long "e" sound. funny, lady

## ACCENT

When there is no other clue in a two-syllable word, the accent frequently falls on the first syllable. This generalization is true about 80% of the time. pen'cil, sau'cer

In inflected or derived forms of words, the primary accent usually falls on or within the root word. fix'es, un touched'

Two vowels together in the last syllable of a word gives a clue to an accented final syllable. re main', re peal'

If two identical consonants are in a word, the syllable before the double consonant is usually accented. big'ger, hal'low ed

The primary accent usually falls on the syllable preceding these suffixes: ion, ity, ic, ical, ian, ial, ious. at ten' tion, hys ter' ical, bar bar' ian, bil' ious

# REFERENCES

Austin, Mary C. *The Torch Lighters: Tomorrow's Teachers of Reading.* Cambridge, Mass.: Harvard University Press, 1961.

Bailey, Mildred H. "The Utility of Phonic Generalizations in Grades One Through Six," *Reading Teacher* 20 (1967): 413–418.

Burmeister, Lou E. "Usefulness of Phonic Generalizations," *Reading Teacher* 21 (1968): 349–356.

Clymer, Theodore L. "The Utility of Phonic Generalizations in the Primary Grades," *Reading Teacher* 16 (1963): 252–258.

Emans, Robert. "When Two Vowels Go Walking and Other Such Things," *Reading Teacher* 21 (1967): 262–269.

Lerner, Janet W. "The Utility of Phonic Generalizations—A Modification," *The Journal of the Reading Specialist* 8 (March 1969): 117–118.

Lerner, Janet W. and Lynne List. The Phonics Knowledge of Prospective Teachers, Experienced Teachers, and Elementary Pupils," *Illinois School Research* 7 (Fall 1970): 39–42.

Winkley, Carol K. "Which Accent Generalizations are Worth Teaching?" *Reading Teacher* 20 (1966): 219–224.

# APPENDIX B
# MATERIALS

Many commercial materials are available on the market which may prove useful in planning teaching programs for children with learning disabilities. The materials should be viewed as tools to be used as and when needed to teach a particular child. The learning disabilities specialist, not the author of the set of materials, should direct the program and make the decisions concerning the focus and direction of the teaching process. Some of the commercial materials that are available are listed in this appendix. Since new items are constantly being introduced, this listing cannot be complete. The listing of materials in this section does not imply recommendation. The lists are meant to serve as a convenient reference of materials for educators as they implement learning disabilities programs. The items should be carefully evaluated or catalog descriptions should be examined before materials are selected. The complete names and addresses of publishers and companies that manufacture this material are included in Appendix D.

The materials are divided into the following categories:

Materials for teaching readiness, perception, language, and number concepts.

Materials for teaching beginning reading, phonics, word analysis, and decoding.

Materials for teaching reading comprehension and reading improvement.

Multimedia equipment and machines for teaching.

Films about children with learning disabilities.

## MATERIALS FOR TEACHING READINESS, PERCEPTION, LANGUAGE, AND NUMBER CONCEPTS

*Academic Games Development Program.* Motivational Research. Games for Learning.

*Auditory Discrimination Training.* Learning Through Seeing, Inc. A program for pre-reading and beginning reading.

*Children's World.* Holt, Rinehart and Winston, Inc. A kit of multisensory materials for early childhood and readiness.

*Concept Builders with Write and See.* New Century.

*Dandy Dog's Early Learning Program.* American Book Company. A readiness program.

*Detect.* Science Research Associates. A sensorimotor approach to visual discrimination.

*Developing Learning Readiness Program.* Webster. A motor and perceptual development program.

*Distar Language I and II.* Science Research Associates. (Preschool and primary) Highly structured program designed to teach basic language concepts and build vocabulary.

*Early Childhood Discovery Materials.* Macmillan. Readiness program.

*Experimental Development Program.* Benefic Press. A readiness program.

*The Fitzhugh PLUS program.* Allied Education Council. Perceptual training, spatial organization books, for reading and arithmetic.

*The Frostig Program for the Development of Visual Perception.* Follett. Workbooks for training visual perception.

*I Can Do It.* Mafex Associates. Visual-motor activity exercises.

*Inquisitive.* Science Research Associates. Games for exploring numbers and space.

*Learning Aids for Young Children in Accordance with Montessori.* Teaching Aids. Materials and equipment for readiness, perception, motor development.

*Matric Games Package.* Appleton-Century-Crofts. Games for Readiness.

*Michigan Successive Discrimination Program.* Ann Arbor Press. Symbol tracking, visual tracking, word tracking.

*Montessori-type Teaching Aids.* Educational Teaching Aids. Materials patterned after the Montessori program.

*Peabody Language Developmental Kits.* American Guidance Service. Kits of puppets, pictures, lessons plans to develop oral language skills.

*Try Experiences for Young Children.* Noble and Noble. Visual-perceptual tasks.

## Publishers and Manufacturers of Materials, Games, Aids, and Equipment for Teaching Readiness, Perception, Numbers, Language

*Beckely-Cardy.* Mathematics aids and games, reading aids and games.

*Continental Press.* Preprinted masters for liquid duplication. Readiness, perceptual, visual-motor material.

*Creative Playthings, Inc.* Variety of toys and games for perception, motor activities, art activities.

*Developmental Learning Materials.* A variety of manipulatable materials for the development of perception, motor coordination, number concepts, handwriting.

*Garrard Publishing Co.* Dolch Teaching Aids. Teaching aids and games for phonics, reading, and arithmetic.

*J. L. Hammet Co.* A variety of art activities and aids for reading and arithmetic.

*Ideal School Supply Co.* Reading aids, mathematics aids.

*Instructo Corp.* Instructo Aids to Education. Materials for early childhood. Transparencies, flannel board visual aids, mathematics aids.

*Kenworthy Educational Service.* Games, phonic games.

*Milton Bradley Company.* Reading games, arithmetic games.

*F. A. Owen Publishing Co.* Instructor teaching aids. Language arts, mathematics, early learning.

*J. A. Preston Corp.* Material for motor assessment and teaching. Eye-hand coordination, perception.

*Teachers Publishing Corp.* Reading aids and games.

*Teaching Resources.* A variety of programs for visuomotor, perceptual-motor, eye-hand coordination.

## Materials Designed to Teach Arithmetic Concepts

*Benefic Press.* "Math Lab." A kit of boxed cards with activities to teach mathematics concepts. (P–Jr. High)

*Continental Press.* "Arithmetic Step by Step." (Kit A) Boxed preprinted duplicating masters for 10 units in arithmetic. (readiness–3)

*Developmental Learning Materials.* "The Sensorithmetic Program." Teaching basic number and arithmetic concepts through the use of sensory reinforcement materials.

*Distar Arithmetic I and II.* Science Research Associates. (K-2) Highly structured program to teach basic number concepts.

*The Economy Co.* "Count down." Use of pacers (audio-tape player) and pacetapes (tape recordings), books for an individualized mathematics program. (1–3).

*Educational Services, Inc.* "Plus." Teacher's handbook of games, ideas and activities to teach arithmetic.

*Educational Teaching Aids Division.* A. Daigger & Co. Mathematics materials. Manipulatable and concrete materials to teach number concepts.

*EduKaid.* Equipment and materials for teaching arithmetic.

*General Learning Corp.* "Judy" mathematics material. Concrete materials to enhance the teaching of number concepts.

*Teaching Resources.* Number relationships, time concepts. Games and manipulative materials.

## MATERIALS FOR TEACHING BEGINNING READING, PHONICS, WORD ANALYSIS AND DECODING

*Conquests in Reading.* Webster. (4–6) Review of phonics and word attack skills.

*Decoding for Reading.* Macmillan. Audiovisual program for older nonreaders.

*Developmental and Remedial Reading Materials.* Educator's Publishing Service.

*Distar Reading I and II.* Science Research Associates. (K–2). Highly structured program to teach beginning reading. Emphasis on cracking the code.

*Durrell-Murphy Phonics Practice Program.* Harcourt, Brace & World. Self-directing phonics picture cards.

*First Experiences with Consonants. First Experiences with Vowels.* Instructo Corp. Materials to teach consonants and vowels.

*Get Set Games.* Houghton Mifflin. Games to teach decoding skills.

*Ginn Word Enrichment Program.* Ginn. Seven workbooks for word recognition skills.

*Intersensory Reading Method.* Book-Lab, Inc. Beginning phonics: books, cards, materials.

*i/t/a Early-to-Read Program* revised. Initial Teaching Alphabet. Uses i/t/a as a medium for beginning reading.

*The Landon Phonics Program.* Chandler. A phonics series.

*Language Experiences in Reading Program.* Encyclopaedia Britannica Education Corp. Language experience approach to beginning reading.

*Lift-Off to Reading.* Science Research Associates. A programed beginning reading approach.

*Macmillan Reading Spectrum.* Macmillan. Six levels of word analysis. (4–6)

*Magic World of Dr. Spello.* Webster Division, McGraw-Hill. Phonics and spelling book. (4–8).

*Merrill Linguistic Readers.* Merrill. A linguistic-approach basal reader.

*Michigan Language Program.* Learning Research Associates. Individualized program for beginning reading books for listening, reading words, word attack and comprehension.

*Mott Basic Language Skills Program.* Allied Education Council. Reading program for adolescents. Levels 1–3, levels 4–6. Text-workbooks.

*Open Court Correlated Language Arts Program.* Open Court Publishing Co. Basal reader series stressing phonics.

*The Palo Alto Reading Program: Sequential Steps in Reading.* Harcourt Brace & World. A programed and linguistic approach to beginning reading.

*Peabody Rebus Reading Program.* American Guidance Service. The use of rebus pictures for teaching beginning reading.

*Phonetic Keys to Reading.* Economy Company. A phonic approach to beginning reading. Books, cards, charts. (1–4)

*Phonics Skill Builders.* McCormick-Mathers. Set of 6 workbooks for teaching phonics skills. (1–6)

*Phonics We Use.* Lyons and Carnahan. A series of phonics workbooks. (1–8)

*The Phonovisual Method.* Phonovisual Products. A series of books, charts, manuals, and cards for teaching phonics. (primary)

*Programmed Reading.* McGraw Hill. Twenty-one books of programmed instruction in reading.

*The Reading Experience and Development Series* (READ). American Book Co.

*Reading Helper Books.* Book-Lab, Inc. Five activities books for beginning reading. (K–2)

*Reading in High Gear.* Science Research Associates. A programed reading program for adolescent non-readers.

*Reading with Phonics.* Lippincott. Workbooks and phonics cards for teaching phonics skills. (primary)

*Remedial Reading Drills* (Hegge, Kirk, Kirk). George Wahr Publishing Co. Exercises to develop skills in phonics and word recognition. (1–3)

*Speech-to-Print Phonics.* Harcourt, Brace & World. Cards and manual for developing phonics skills.

*SRA Reading Program.* Science Research Associates. A basal reading series with a linguistic emphasis. (1–6)

*Structural Reading Program.* L. W. Singer Co. A structured basal program with emphasis on phonics. (pre-reading–2)

*Sullivan Remedial Reading Program.* Behavioral Research Laboratories. Series of programed workbooks.

*Weekly Reading Practice Books.* American Guidance Service. Beginning Reading phonics program.

*Wenkart Phonics Readers.* Wenkhart Publishing Co. A set of readers with a phonics emphasis.

*Word Attack Series.* Teaching College Press. Three workbooks to teach word-analysis skills.

*Wordland series.* Continental Press. A phonics program on preprinted ditto masters.

*Words in Color.* Zerox Education Division. Use of color to teach initial reading.

*Write and See.* Appleton-Century-Crofts, New Century Publications. Self-correcting phonics materials with re-appearing ink process. (1–4)

# MATERIALS FOR TEACHING READING COMPREHENSION AND READING IMPROVEMENT

*Barnell-Loft Specific Skill series.* Dexter & Westbrook, Ltd. Exercise books designed for practice in specific reading comprehension skills: locating the answer, following directions, using the context, getting the facts, working with sound, drawing conclusions, getting the main idea. (1–6)

*Basic Reading Skills for Junior High School Use.* Scott, Foresman. Workbook for developing reading skills. Designed for remedial reading pupils at junior high level.

*Be a Better Reader.* Prentice-Hall. Reading improvement in the content areas. (junior high)

*Be a Better Reader, Foundations.* Prentice-Hall. Designed for practice in reading in content areas. (4–6)

*Developing Reading Efficiency.* Burgess. A workbook for junior high level containing lessons for a variety of reading skills.

*Developmental Reading Text-Workbooks.* Bobbs-Merrill Co. Six workbooks to give training and practice in several reading skills. (K–6)

*Diagnostic Reading Workbooks Series.* Charles E. Merrill. Workbooks designed for developmental or remedial programs in reading. (K–6)

*Effective Reading.* Globe Book Co. Exercises and materials for levels 4–8.

*Gaining Independence in Reading.* Charles E. Merrill. Three hard-covered textbooks. (grades 4 and up)

*Gates-Peardon Reading Exercises.* Teachers College Press. Reading exercises to develop the ability to read for general significance, to predict outcomes, to understand directions, to note details. (3–6)

*Improve Your Reading Ability.* Charles E. Merrill. Text-workbook for development of comprehension skills and rate. Intermediate difficulty level.

*Macmillan Reading Spectrum, Reading Comprehension.* Six workbooks for improvement of reading comprehension. (3–8)

*McCall-Crabbs Standard Test Lessons in Reading.* Teachers College Press. Paperback booklets with short reading selections and comprehension questions. (3–7)

*New Goals in Reading, Reading Essentials series.* Steck-Vaughn. Reading workbooks. (3–4)

*New Practice Readers.* Webster Division, McGraw-Hill. Reading selections and questions designed to improve comprehension skills in reading. (2–8)

*Reading Improvement Material.* Reader's Digest Services. Workbooks for reading improvement at advanced levels. (7–10)

*Reading for Meaning Series.* J. B. Lippincott. A series of workbooks designed to improve comprehension skills: vocabulary, central thought, details, organization, summarization. (4–6) and (7–9)

*Reading Skills Builders.* Reader's Digest Services. Magazine format with short reading selections and accompanying comprehension questions. (1–8)

*The Reading Skills Lab Program.* Houghton Mifflin. Nine workbooks for teaching specific comprehension skills. (4–6)

*Reading Skilltext series.* Charles E. Merrill. Reading comprehension workbooks. (1–6)

*Reading Success Series.* My Weekly Reader. Six booklets of high interest level to teach basic reading skills.

• *Reading for Understanding.* Science Research Associates. Boxed multilevel selections graduated in difficulty. Designed to develop comprehension skills. (5–12)

*Reading-Thinking Skills.* Continental Press. Preprinted masters for liquid duplicating. (PP–6)

*SRA Reading Laboratory.* Science Research Associates. Boxed materials consisting of multilevel and color-cued reading matter with questions and answer keys. Materials for improving rate as well as comprehension is included. (1–12)

*Step up Your Reading Power*. Webster Division, McGraw-Hill. Five workbooks designed for remedial reading students to improve reading comprehension.

*Study Skills Library*. Educational Developmental Laboratories, Division of McGraw-Hill. Reading skills focusing on content subjects. Material is boxed by subject area and difficulty level. (4–9)

*Study Type Reading Exercises*. Teachers College Press. Reading exercises at the secondary level. (high school)

*The Thinking Box*. Benefic Press. Designed to develop critical thinking skills. Boxed material, individualized to teach 12 thinking skills. (upper intermediate to junior high)

# MULTIMEDIA EQUIPMENT AND MACHINES FOR TEACHING

*Audio-Visual Research*. Reading rateometer. AVR Eye-Span Trainer, AVR Flash-tachment. Machines for improvement of reading rate.

*Bell and Howell*. Language Master. An audio-tape system for teaching language, phonics, vocabulary.

*Benefic Press*. Reading multimedia kits. A multimedia reading program for adolescents.

*Borg-Warner Educational Systems*. System 80. An individualized audiovisual programed approach to teaching beginning reading.

*Bowmar*. Coordinated Books, photographs, sound filmstrips, records for the readiness level.

*Bowmar*. Reading Incentive Program. Books, records, filmstrips. Junior high school interest level.

*Craig Corp*. Craig Reader: machines for reading-rate improvement. Multitrack recording tape equipment.

*Educational Developmental Laboratories*. Audiovisual reading improvement equipment. Tapes and workbooks for listening skills.

*Educational Projections Corp*. Self-instructional reading readiness program. Film lessons for reading readiness. Multichoice viewer.

*Electronic Future, Inc*. Wireless Reading Systems, Audio Flashcard system.

*General Learning Corp*. Phono-viewer system. Combination filmslide record units. Designed to be self-instructional for young children.

*Hoffman Information Systems*. Audiovisual reading improvement program.

*Imperial International Learning*. Audiovisual equipment. Spelling, reading, speech, and mathematics programs.

*Keystone View Co*. Overhead projector, tachistoscope.

*Litton Instructional Materials, Inc*. Group Tutorial System.

*Perceptual Development Laboratories*. Reading-rate improvement equipment.

*Psychotechnics*. Remedial reading filmstrips, tachistoscope, reading laboratories, shadow-scope reading pacer.

*Readers Digest*. Young Pegasus Packet. Related storybook and games for readiness.

*Reading Institute.* Hand tachistoscope, manually operated.

*Rheem Califone.* Multimedia reading program, tape lessons, books, manuals.

*Scholastic Magazine.* Multimedia kit of posters, records, paperbacks for reading improvement. (Reading levels, 2–4; interest, junior high)

*Science Research Associates.* Reading accelerator, pacer for improvement of reading rate.

*Teaching Technology Corp.* Multimedia reading program, filmstrips, tapes, records, magnetic cords, manuals, books.

*Viking Press.* Viking Sound Filmstrips. Coordinated record, filmstrip and user's guide for presentation of literature to children.

## Films About Children With Learning Disabilities

Following are some films that are useful for teacher training or community education. They present theories, diagnosis, and teaching strategies for children with learning disabilities.

*Anyone Can.* 16mm. 30 min. Sound/Color. 16 min. Teacher training guide for a program of motor development. California Association for Neurologically Handicapped Children, 6742 Will Rogers Street, Los Angeles, Calif. 96045 or Bradley Wright Films, 309 N. Duane Avenue, San Gabriel, Calif. 91775

*Bright Boy: Bad Scholar.* 16mm. Sound/Black and white. 28 min. Illustrates the diagnosis and treatment of children with learning disabilities. McGraw-Hill, Tex-Film Division, 330 W. 42nd Street, New York, N.Y. 10001

*A Filmed Demonstration of the ITPA.* 16 mm. Sound/Black and white. 43 min. A demonstration of the administration of the various subtests of the revised *Illinois Test of Psycholinguistic Abilities.* Samuel A. Kirk and Winifred D. Kirk, University of Illinois Press, Urbana, Ill. 61801

*Help in Auditory Perception.* 16mm. Sound/Black and white. 36 min. Overview of problems in auditory perception, and description of materials and tasks assigned to students for independent study. New York State Education Department, Division for Handicapped Children, Special Education Instructional Materials Center, 800 North Pearl Street, Albany, N.Y. 12204.

*Help in Visual Perception.* 16mm. Sound/Black and white. 30 min. Presents the activities involved in increasing visual memory in a child whose "eyes play tricks" on him. New York State Education Department, Division for Handicapped Children, Special Education Instructional Materials Center, 800 North Pearl Street, Albany, N.Y. 12204

*Motor Development I.* 16mm. Sound/Black and white. 51 min. Deals with the early development of motor sequences in children. N.C. Kephart, Film Coordinator, Special Education Section, Purdue University, SCAX. Lafayette, Ind. 47907

*Motor Development II.* 16mm. Sound/Black and white. 50 min. Continuation of Motor Development I showing examples of differentiation, mostly abnormal, with comparisons in movement. (same source as Motor Development I)

*Movement Exploration.* 16mm. Sound/Color. 22 min. Demonstrates the techniques of various motor skills. Documental Films, 3217 Trout Gulch Rd., Aptos, Calif. 95003

*A Movigenic Curriculum.* 16mm. Sound/Black and white. 41 min. Explains an experimental motor curriculum. Shows exercise for various areas of motor development. Ray Barsch. Bureau of Audio Visual Instruction, 1327 University Ave., P.O. Box 2093, Madison, Wisc. 53701

*Public School Program for Learning Disabilities.* 16mm. Sound/Color. 16 min. Film of a self-contained classroom of young children with various neurological learning disorders. Office of Educational Service Region of Cook County, Chicago Civic Center, Room 407, Clark & Washington Sts., Chicago, Ill. 60602

*The Sensitoric Readiness Program.* 22 min. 16mm. Sound/Black and white. Illustrates the academic implications of training in motor skills. Pathway School Resource Center, Box 181, Norristown, Pa. 19404

*Thursday's Child.* 32 min. Sound/color. Presents three major areas: 1) characteristics (especially sensory-motor problems), 2) diagnostic evaluation, and 3) educational programming. Swank Motion Pictures, Inc. 201 South Jefferson Avenue, St. Louis, Missouri 63166.

*Visual Perception and Failure to Learn.* 16mm. Sound/Black and white. 20 min. Uses the Frostig Test of Visual Perception to demonstrate the relationship between disabilities in visual perception and various difficulties in learning and behavior. Churchill Films, 662 North Robertson Blvd., Los Angeles, Calif. 90069

*Why Billy Couldn't Learn.* 40 min. Sound/Color. 16mm. Demonstrates problems, diagnosis, and education of children with neurological handicap. California Association for Neurologically Handicapped Children, 6742 Will Rogers St., Los Angeles, Calif. 96405

# APPENDIX C
# SOME FORMAL TESTS THAT
# ARE USEFUL IN DIAGNOSIS

The purpose of this appendix is to list in alphabetical order some tests that are useful in formulating a diagnosis. This list includes tests that have been mentioned elsewhere in this book, as well as tests not discussed in this book. The descriptive material about each test is brief and it is not designed to be evaluative. Since tests are frequently revised and new forms or manuals are frequently issued, it is desirable to obtain a current catalog from the publisher before placing an order. Detailed descriptions and critical evaluations of tests can be obtained from the *Mental Measurements Yearbook*, O. K. Buros, Editor, Gryphon Press (See Appendix D for address). This book is available in reference libraries.

*Ammons Full-Range Picture Vocabulary Test*. Psychological Test Specialists. Forms A and B. Preschool to Adult. An individually administered test of receptive language vocabulary.

*Bender-Gestalt Test*. Western Psychological Services. An individually administered test of a child's performance in copying designs. The Koppitz Scoring (The *Bender Gestalt Test for Young Children*: E. Koppitz. N.Y.: Grune & Stratton, 1963) provides a developmental scoring system for young children to age 10.

*Benton Visual Retention Test*, Revised. Psychological Corp. Individually administered test of ability to draw designs from memory.

*Botel Reading Inventory*. Follett. Grade levels 1–12. A group of tests to determine a variety of reading skills.

*Brown-Carlsen Listening Comprehension Test*. Harcourt, Brace & World. Grades 9–13. A test designed for group use to determine ability to understand spoken English. A receptive language test.

*California Achievement Tests*. California Test Bureau. Levels 1–college. A battery of group tests to assess several areas of academic achievement. Also *California Reading Tests* (levels 1–college).

*Detroit Tests of Learning Aptitude*. Bobbs Merril. Ages 4–adult. An individual test of mental functioning. There are nineteen subtests measuring various elements of mental processing. In addition to an overall mental age score, each subtest yields a separate mental age score, allowing a flexible choice of tests for diagnostic purposes.

*Developmental Test of Visual-Motor Integration*. Follett. Ages 5–20. A visual-motor test of the subject's abilities in copying designs.

*Diagnostic Tests and Self-Help in Arithmetic*. California Test Bureau. Test designed to determine a diagnosis of arithmetic difficulties.

*Durrell Analysis of Reading Difficulty*. Harcourt, Brace, & World. A battery of diagnostic tests designed to help in the analysis and evaluation of specific reading difficulties.

*Durrell Reading-Listening Series*. Harcourt, Brace & World. Primary (grades 1–3.5); intermediate (grades 3.5–6); advanced (grades 7–9). Group tests of listening and reading ability. Permits a comparison of these two language skills.

*Frostig Developmental Test of Visual Perception.* Consulting Psychologists Press. Ages 4–9. This test measures skill in five areas of visual perception.

*Gates-MacGinitie Reading Tests.* Teachers College Press. Five forms (for grades 1–9). A general test of silent reading designed for group administration.

*Gates-McKillop Reading Diagnostic Tests.* Teachers College Press. Battery of tests for individual administration, designed to give diagnostic information about a child's reading skills.

*Gilmore Oral Reading Test.* Harcourt Brace & World. Grades 1–8. An oral reading test, individually administered. Gives information about word accuracy, rate, and comprehension.

*Goodenough-Harris Drawing Test.* Harcourt Brace & World. Provides a score of nonverbal intelligence obtained through an objective scoring of a child's drawing of a human figure.

*Gray Oral Reading Tests.* Bobbs-Merrill. An individually administered oral reading test. Combines rate and accuracy to obtain grade level score. Comprehension questions available but not scored.

*Harris Tests of Lateral Dominance,* Psychological Corp. Tests to show right or left preference with hand, eye, foot.

*Heath Railwalking Test.* A quick test of balance and motor ability while walking across a rail or balance beam. (See C. Goetzinger, "A Reevaluation of the Heath Railwalking Test," *Journal of Educational Research* 54, 1060, pp. 187–191; S. Heath, "Railwalking performance as related to mental age and etiologocal type among the mentally retarded," *American Journal of Psychology* 55: 240, April 1942; H. G. Seashore, "The development of a beam walking test and its use in measuring development of balance in children," *American Association for Health, Physical Education and Recreation, Research Quarterly* 18, 246, December 1947.)

*Houston Test of Language Development.* Houston Press. Part I (18 months–36 months); Part 2 (3–6 years). Assesses several areas of general language development.

*Illinois Test of Psycholinguistic Abilities, Revised.* University of Illinois Press. Individually administered test containing twelve subtests of dimensions of mental processes. Scores obtained on subtests can be used for diagnostic purposes.

*Iowa Every-Pupil Tests of Basic Skills.* Houghton Mifflin. Ages 3–9. Group tests of several academic areas: reading, arithmetic, language, workstudy skills.

*Keystone Visual Survey Service for Schools.* Keystone View Co. Individually administered visual screening device to determine the need for further referral for a visual examination.

*Lincoln-Oseretsky Motor Development Scale.* Western Psychological Services. Ages 6–14. Individual tests of a variety of motor skills.

*McCullough Word Analysis Tests.* Ginn. Grades 4–8. Group tests of word analysis skills.

*Mecham Verbal Language Development Scale.* American Guidance Service. An evaluation of language development obtained through an interview with an informant, usually a parent.

*Metropolitan Achievement Tests.* Harcourt, Brace & World. Grades 5–8. Battery of tests. Group administration. Measures several areas of academic achievement: reading, spelling, arithmetic.

*Monroe Reading Aptitude Tests.* Houghton Mifflin. Ages 6–9. Group-administered test to measure readiness for reading. Non-reading test that assesses several areas of mental functioning.

*Nebraska Test of Learning Aptitude.* Marshall A. Hiskey. An individual test of intellectual potential. Used widely with the deaf or hard-of-hearing.

*Northwestern Syntax Screening Test.* Northwestern University Press. Ages 3–7. Individually administered test of receptive and expressive syntactiç linguistic abilities.

*Ortho-rater.* Bausch & Lomb. Individual visual screening test.

*Peabody Individual Achievement Test.* Pre-school to adult level. Contains five individually administered subtests: mathematics, reading recognition, reading comprehension, spelling, general information. American Guidance Services, Inc.

*Peabody Picture Vocabulary Test.* American Guidance Services. Ages 2–8. In individually administered test of receptive language vocabulary.

*Picture Story Language Test.* Grune & Stratton. An individually administered test of the child's achievement in written language.

*Purdue Perceptual Motor Survey.* Charles E. Merrill. Ages 4–10. A series of tests for assessing motor development and motor skills.

*Roswell-Chall Auditory Blending Test.* Essay Press. Individually administered short tests to assess ability to hear and blend sounds to say the word.

*Roswell-Chall Diagnostic Reading Test.* Essay Press. Individually administered short test to assess child's phonic abilities.

*Screening Test of Auditory Perception* (STAP). Academic Therapy Publications. Group and individual test of auditory perception. Assesses ability to differentiate vowel sounds, initial consonants, and blends; to recognize and remember rhymes and rhythmic patterns; to discriminate same or different pairs of words.

*Screening Tests for Identifying Children with Specific Language Disability.* Educator's Publishing Service. Grades 1–4. Battery of tests designed to screen for children likely to have difficulty in language-related subjects.

*Sequential Tests of Educational Progress.* Educational Testing Service. Grades 4–12. A battery of achievement tests. Includes tests of reading comprehension and listening comprehension.

*Slosson Intelligence Test.* Slosson Educational Publications. A short individual screening test of intelligence, for use by teachers and other professional persons for a quick estimate of mental ability.

*Southern California Test Battery for Assessment of Dysfunction.* Western Psychological Services. Ages 3–10. A battery containing the following separate tests: *Southern California Kinesthesia and Tactile Perception Tests; Southern California Figure-Ground Visual Perception Test; Southern California Motor Accuracy Test; Southern California Perceptual-Motor Tests;* and the *Ayers Space Test.*

*Spache Diagnostic Reading Scales.* California Test Bureau. Grade 1 and up. Individually administered battery of tests to diagnose reading difficulties.

*SRA Achievement Scales.* Science Research Associates. Grades 1–9. Group tests of several areas of academic achievement, including reading.

*SRA Primary Mental Abilities Tests.* Science Research Associates. Grades K–adult. Group intelligence test designed to measure several subabilities of mental functioning. MA and IQ scores for verbal meaning, number facility, reasoning, perceptual speed, and spatial relations.

*Stanford Achievement Test.* Harcourt Brace & World. Group tests of academic achievement, including reading.

*Stanford-Binet Intelligence Scale, Revised, 3rd edition.* Houghton Mifflin. Ages 2–adult. Individual test of general intelligence. Yields MA and IQ scores. To be administered by trained psychological examiners.

*Stanford Diagnostic Arithmetic Test.* Harcourt, Brace & World. Group test to diagnose nature of arithmetic difficulties.

*Stanford Diagnostic Reading Test.* Harcourt, Brace & World. Grades 2.5–8.5. Group test to diagnose nature of reading difficulties. Measures performance in comprehension, vocabulary, syllabication, auditory skills, phonetic analysis, and reading rate.

*Templin-Darley Tests of Articulation.* University of Iowa Bureau of Research and Service. Individual test of the articulation of speech sounds.

*Valett Developmental Survey of Basic Learning Abilities.* Fearon Publishers. Ages 2–7. A survey of skill development in several areas of growth.

*Van Wagenen Listening Vocabulary Scales.* Van Wagenen Psycho-educational Research Laboratories. Grades 2–6. A listening or receptive language test of words.

*Vineland Social Maturity Scale.* American Guidance Service. Birth–adult. Individual measure of social maturity and independence. Information derived by interview with an informant, usually a parent.

*Wechsler Adult Intelligence Scale.* Psychological Corp. Ages 16–adult. An individual intelligence test for subjects over age 15. Yields verbal, performance, and full-scale scores. To be administered by trained psychological examiners.

*Wechsler Intelligence Scale for Children* (WISC). Psychological Corp. Ages 5–15. Individual intelligence test that yields verbal and performance scores as well as full-scale MA and IQ scores. To be administered by trained psychological examiners.

*Wechsler Preschool and Primary Scale of Intelligence* (WPSI). Psychological Corp. Ages 4–6.5. Individual intelligence test similar to the WISC for preschool children. Yields verbal, performance and full-scale scores. To be administered by trained psychological examiners.

*Wepman Test of Auditory Discrimination.* Language Research Associates. Ages 5–9. Individual test of auditory discrimination of phoneme sounds.

*Wide Range Achievement Test,* Revised Edition (1965). Guidance Associates. Ages 5–adult. A brief individual test of word recognition, spelling, and arithmetic computation.

# APPENDIX D
# DIRECTORY OF
# PUBLISHERS

The following list contains, in alphabetical order, the names and addresses of the publishers and manufacturers of materials mentioned elsewhere in this book. The list also includes some entries of producers of materials that were not mentioned. The purpose of the listing is to serve as a convenient directory for the reader. The rapidity of changes in names and addresses makes it inevitable that some of the entries below will become out of date during the life of this textbook.

Academic Therapy Publications. 1543 Fifth Ave., San Rafael, Calif. 94901.

Allied Education Council. P.O. Box 78, Galien, Mich. 49113.

Allyn & Bacon, 470 Atlantic Ave., Boston, Mass 02210.

American Book Co., A Division of Litton Educational Publishers, Inc. 450 W. 33 St., New York, N.Y. 10001.

American Education Publications. A Xerox Company. 55 High St., Middletown, Conn. 06457.

American Guidance Associates. 1526 Gilpin Ave., Wilmington, Del.

American Guidance Service, Inc. (AGS). Publishers' Building, Circle Pines, Minn. 55014.

Ann Arbor Publishers. Campus Village Arcade, 611 Church St., Ann Arbor, Mich. 48104.

Appleton-Century-Crofts. 440 Park Avenue South, New York, N.Y. 10016.

Arrow Book Club. (Scholastic Book Services). 50 West 44th St., New York, N.Y. 10036.

Audio-visual Research. 1509 Eighth Street, S.E., Waseca, Minn. 56093.

Bantam Books, Inc., 666 Fifth Ave., New York, N.Y. 10019.

Barnell-Loft. See Dexter & Westbrook, Ltd.

Basic Books, Inc. 404 Park Avenue South, New York, N.Y. 10016.

Bausch & Lomb Optical Co. Rochester, N.Y. 14602.

Beckley-Cardy. 1900 N. Narragansett, Chicago, Ill. 60639.

Behavioral Research Laboratories. P.O. Box 577, Palo Alto, Calif. 94302.

Bell and Howell. 7100 McCormick Rd., Chicago, Ill. 60645.

Benefic Press. 10300 W. Roosevelt Rd., Westchester, Ill. 60153.

Bobbs-Merrill Co. 4300 W. 62nd St., Indianapolis, Ind. 46268.

Book-Lab, Inc. 1449–37th St., Brooklyn, N.Y. 11218.

Borg-Warner Educational Systems, A Division of Borg-Warner Corp. 7450 N. Natchez Ave., Niles, Ill. 60648.

Bowmar Publishing. 622 Rodier Dr., Glendale, Calif. 91201.

William C. Brown Co., Publishers. 135 S. Locust St., Dubuque, Iowa 52001.

Burgess Publishing Co. 426 S. 6th St., Minneapolis, Minn. 55415.

California Test Bureau, A Division of McGraw-Hill Book Co. Del Monte Research Park, Monterey, Calif. 93940.

Cenco Center. 2600 S. Kostner Ave., Chicago, Ill. 60623.

Chandler Publishing Co. 124 Spear St., San Francisco, Calif. 94105.

Consulting Psychologists Press. 577 College Avenue, Palo Alto, Calif. 94306.

Continental Press, Inc. Elizabethtown, Pa. 17022.

Council for Exceptional Children. Jefferson Plaza Office Bldg. One, Suite 900, 1411 S. Jefferson Davis Hgwy., Arlington, Va. 22202.

Craig Corp. 3410 S. LaCienga Blvd., Los Angeles, Calif. 90016.

Creative Playthings, Inc. Edinburg Rd., Cranbury, N.J. 08540.

Creative Visuals, Inc. P.O. Box 310, Big Spring, Texas 79720.

Cuisenaire Company of America, Inc. 12 Church St., New Rochelle, N.Y. 10850.

Developmental Learning Materials. 3505 N. Ashland Ave., Chicago, Ill. 60657.

Dexter & Westbrook, Ltd. (Barnell-Loft.) 111 South Centre Ave., Rockville Centre, N.Y. 11571.

Dick Blick Co. P.O. Box 1269, Galesburg, Ill. 61405.

Dimensions Publishing Co. Box 4221, San Rafael, Calif. 94903.

Economy Company. 1901 N. Walnut Ave., Oklahoma City, Okla. 73105.

Educational Activities, Inc. 1937 Grand Ave., Baldwin, N.Y. 11520.

Educational Development Laboratories, A Division of McGraw-Hill. 284 Pulaski St., Huntington, N.Y. 11744.

Educational Projections Corp. Box 1187, Jackson, Miss. 39205.

Educational Service, Inc. P.O. Box 219, Stevensville, Mich. 49127.

Educational Teaching Aids Division, A. Daigger & Co. 159 W. Kinzie St., Chicago, Ill. 60610.

Educational Testing Service. Princeton, N.J. 08540.

Educator's Publishing Service. 75 Moulton St., Cambridge, Mass. 02138.

Edukaid of Ridgewood. 1250 E. Ridgewood Ave., Ridgewood, N.J. 07450.

Electronic Future, Inc. 57 Dodge Ave., North Haven, Conn. 06473.

Encyclopaedia Britannica Educational Corp. 425 N. Michigan Ave., Chicago, Ill. 60611.

Essay Press. Box 5, Planetarium Station, New York, N.Y. 10024.

Fearon Publishers. 2165 Park Blvd., Palo Alto, Calif. 94306.

Field Educational Publications, Inc. 609 Mission St., San Francisco, Calif. 94105.

Follett Educational Corp. 1010 W. Washington Blvd., Chicago, Ill. 60607.

Garrard Publishing Co. 1607 N. Market St., Champaign, Ill. 61820.

General Learning Corp. 250 James St., Morristown, N.J. 07960.

Ginn & Company. 125 Second Ave., Waltham, Mass. 02154.

Globe Book Co., Inc. 175 Fifth Ave., New York, N.Y. 10010.

Grune & Stratton. 757 Third Ave., New York, N.Y. 10017.

Gryphon Press. 220 Montgomery St., Highland Park, N.J. 08904.

Guidance Associates. 1526 Gilpin Ave., Wilmington, Del. 19800.

E. M. Hale & Co. 1201 S. Hastings Way, Eau Claire, Wisc. 54701.

C. S. Hammond & Co. 515 Valley St., Maplewood, N.J. 07040.

Harcourt, Brace & Jovanovich, Inc. 757 Third Ave., New York, N.Y. 10017.

Harper & Row Publishers, Inc. 49 E. 33rd St., New York, N.Y. 10016.

Harr Wagner. See Field Educational Publications.

D. C. Heath & Co. 125 Spring St., Lexington, Mass. 02173.

Marshall S. Hiskey. 5640 Baldwin, Lincoln, Neb. 68507.

Hoffman Information Systems, Inc. 5632 Peck Rd., Arcadia, Calif. 91006.

Holt, Rinehart & Winston, Inc. 383 Madison Ave., New York, N.Y. 10017

Houghton Mifflin Co. 110 Tremont St., Boston, Mass. 02107.

Houston Press. University of Houston, Houston, Texas 77000.

Ideal School Supply Co. 11000 South Lavergre, Oak Lawn, Ill. 60453.

Imperial Productions, Inc. 247 W. Court St., Kankakee, Ill. 60901.

Initial Teaching Alphabet Publications, Inc. 6 E. 43 St., New York, N.Y. 10017.

Inland Book Distributors. 642 Factory Rd., Addison, Ill. 60101.

Instructo Corp. 200 Cedar Hollow Rd., Paoli, Pa. 19301.

The Instructor Publications. 7 Bank St., Danville, N.Y. 14437.

International Reading Association. Six Tyre Ave., Newark, Del. 19711.

Journal of Learning Disabilities. 5 N. Wabash Ave., Chicago, Ill. 60602.

Judy Manufacturing Co. 310 N. Second St., Minneapolis, Minn. 55401.

Kenworthy Educational Service. P.O. Box 3031, 138 Allen St., Buffalo, N.Y. 14205.

Keystone View Co. Meadville, Pa. 16335.

Laidlaw Brothers, A Div. of Doubleday and Co. Thatcher & Madison Sts., River Forest, Ill. 60305.

Language Research Associates. Box 95, 950 E. 59th St., Chicago, Ill. 60637.

Learning Research Associates. 1501 Broadway, New York, N.Y. 10036.

Learning Through Seeing, Inc. 8138 Foothill Blvd., Sunland, Calif. 91040.

J. B. Lippincott Co. E. Washington Square, Philadelphia, Pa. 19105.

Litton Instructional Materials, Inc. 1695 W. Crescent Ave., Anaheim, Calif. 92801.

Lyons and Carnaham Educational Publishers. 407 E. 25th St., Chicago, Ill. 60616.

The Macmillan Company. 866 Third Ave., New York, N.Y. 10022.

Mafex Associates, Inc. 111 Barron Ave., Johnstown, Pa. 15906.

McCormick-Mathers Publishing Co. 450 W. 33 St., New York, N.Y. 10001.

McGraw-Hill Book Co. 330 W. 42nd St., New York, N.Y. 10036.

David McKay Co., Inc. 750 Third Ave., New York, N.Y. 10017.

Charles E. Merrill. 1300 Alum Creek Dr., Columbus, Ohio 43216.

Milton Bradley Company. 74 Park St., Springfield, Mass. 01101.

Motivational Research, Inc. P.O. Box 140, McLean, Va. 22101.

National Council of Teachers of English. 508 S. 6th St., Champaign, Ill. 61820.

National Education Association. 1201 Sixteenth Street, N.W., Washington, D.C. 20036.

National Reading Conference. Inc. Reading Center, Marquette University, Milwaukee, Wisc. 53233.

New Century. 440 Park Avenue South, New York, N.Y. 10016.

Noble and Noble Publishers, Inc. 750 Third Ave., New York, N.Y. 10017.

Northwestern University Press. 1735 Benson Ave., Evanston, Ill. 60201.

Open Court Publishing Co. Box 599, LaSalle, Ill. 61301.

F. A. Owen Publishing Co. 7 Bank St., Dansville, N.Y. 14437.

Peek Publications. P.O. Box 11065, Palo Alto, Calif. 94306.

Perceptual Development Laboratories. 6767 Southwest Ave., St. Louis, Mo. 63143.

Phonovisual Products. Box 5625, Washington, D.C. 20016.

Portal Press (subsidiary of John Wiley & Sons, Inc.). 605 Third Ave., New York, N.Y. 10016.

Prentice-Hall, Inc. Englewood Cliffs, N.J. 07632.

J. A. Preston Corp. 71 Fifth Ave., New York, N.Y. 10003.

The Psychological Corp. 304 E. 45th St., New York, N.Y. 10017.

Psychological Test Specialists. Box 1441, Missoula, Mont. 59801.

Psychotechnics. 1900 Pickwick Ave., Glenview, Ill. 60025.

Rand McNally & Company. P.O. Box 7600, Chicago, Ill. 60680.

Random House. 201 E. 50 St., New York, N.Y. 10022.

Reader's Digest Services, Educational Division. Pleasantville, N.Y. 10570.

Reading Institute, Inc. 116 Newbury St., Boston, Mass. 02116.

The Reading Newsreport. 111 W. 42nd St., New York, N.Y. 10036.

Remedial Education Center. 2138 Bancroft Place N.W., Washington, D.C. 20008.

Rheem Califone. 5922 Bancroft St., Los Angeles, Calif. 90016.

Scholastic Magazine and Book Services. 50 West 44th St., New York, N.Y. 10036.

Scott, Foresman & Co. 1900 East Lake Ave., Glenview, Ill. 60025.

Silver Burdett Co., A Division of General Learning Corp. Park Ave. & Columbia Rd., Morristown, N.J. 07960.

Simon and Schuster, Inc. 630 Fifth Ave., New York, N.Y. 10020.

The L. W. Singer Co., A Division of Random House. 201 E. 50 St., New York, N.Y. 10022.

Slosson Educational Publications. 140 Pine St., East Aurora, N.Y. 14052.

Society for Visual Education, Inc. 1345 Diversey Parkway, Chicago, Ill. 60614.

Special Child Publications, Inc. 4635 Union Bay Place N.E., Seattle, Wash. 98105.

Steck-Vaughn Co. P.O. Box 2028, Austin, Texas 78767.

C. H. Stoelting Co. 424 N. Homan Ave., Chicago, Ill. 60624.

Systems for Education, Inc. 612 N. Michigan Ave., Chicago, Ill. 60611.

Teachers College Press, Teachers College, Columbia University, 525 W. 120th St., New York, N.Y. 10027.

Teachers Publishing Corp. 22 W. Putnam Ave., Greenwich, Conn. 06830.

Teaching Aids. 159 W. Kinzie St., Chicago, Ill. 60610.

Teacher Resources. 100 Boylston St., Boston, Mass. 02116.

Teaching Technology Corp. 5520 Cleon Ave., North Hollywood, Calif. 91601.

Charles C. Thomas Publishers. 301–327 E. Lawrence Ave., Springfield, Ill. 62703.

3M Company, Visual Products Division. 2501 Hudson Rd., Bldg. 220–10 W., St. Paul, Minn. 55119.

Tweedy Transparencies. 207 Hollywood Ave., East Orange, N.J. 07018.

University of Chicago Press. 5750 Ellis Ave., Chicago, Ill. 60637.

University of Illinois Press. Urbana, Ill. 61801.

University of Iowa, Bureau of Research. Iowa City, Iowa 52240.

Viking Press. 625 Madison Ave., New York, N.Y. 10022.

Visual Needs, Inc. 135 State St., Rochester, N.Y. 14614.

George Wahr Publishing Co. 316 State St., Ann Arbor, Mich. 41808.

Webster Division, McGraw-Hill. Manchester Rd., Manchester, Mo. 63011.

Weekly Reader Paperback Book Club. American Education Publications, a Xerox Co. 55 High St., Middletown, Conn. 06457.

Wenkart Publishing Co. 4 Shady Hill Square, Cambridge, Mass. 02138.

Western Psychological Services, A Division of Manson Western Corp. 12031 Wilshire Blvd., Los Angeles, Calif. 90025.

Western Publishing Education Services. 1220 Mound Ave., Racine, Wisc. 53404.

Winter Haven Lions Research Foundation, Inc. Box. 1112, Winter Haven, Fla. 33880.

Xerox Education Division. 600 Madison Ave., New York, N.Y. 10022.

Zaner-Bloser Co. 612 North Park St., Columbus, Ohio 43215.

# APPENDIX E
# GLOSSARY

**Agnosia.** The inability to obtain information through one of the input channels or senses, despite the fact that the receiving organ itself is not impaired. The medical term is associated with a neurological abnormality of the central nervous system.

**Alexia.** The loss of ability to read because of some brain damage, such as a cerebral stroke. The term also refers to the complete failure to *acquire* reading skills as well as to a partial or complete loss of these skills through damage.

**Anomia.** Difficulty in recalling or remembering words or the names of objects.

**Aphasia.** Impairment of the ability to use or understand oral language. It is usually associated with an injury or abnormality of the speech centers of the brain. Several classifications are used, including expressive and receptive, congenital, and acquired aphasia.

**Apraxia.** Difficulty in motor output or in performing purposeful motor movements. This medical term reflects an abnormality of the central nervous system.

**Auding.** A level of auditory reception that involves comprehension as well as hearing and listening.

**Auditory blending.** The ability to synthesize the phonemes of a word, when they are pronounced with separations between phonemes, so that the word can be recognized as a whole.

**Auditory perception.** The ability to interpret or organize the sensory data received through the ear.

**Basal reader approach.** A method of teaching reading in which instruction is given through the use of a series of basal readers. Sequence of skills, content, vocabulary, and activities are determined by the authors of the series. Teacher's manuals and children's activity books accompany the basal reading series.

**Behavior modification.** A technique of changing human behavior based on the theory of operant behavior and conditioning. Careful observation of events preceding and following the behavior in question is required. The environment is manipulated to reinforce the desired responses, thereby bringing about the desired change in behavior.

**Bibliotherapy.** The use of reading, particularly the use of characters in books with whom the child identifies, for therapeutic purposes.

**Binocular difficulties.** A visual impairment due to the inability of the two eyes to function together.

**Body image.** An awareness of one's own body and the relationship of the body parts to each other and to the outside environment.

**Brain-injured child.** A child who before, during, or after birth has received an injury to or suffered an infection of the brain. As a result of such organic impairment, there are disturbances which prevent or impede the normal learning process.

**Cerebral dominance.** The control of activities by the brain, with one hemisphere usually considered consistently dominant over the other. In most individuals, the left side of the brain controls language function, and the left side is considered the dominant hemisphere.

**Clinical teaching.** An approach to teaching that attempts to tailor-make learning experiences for the unique needs of a particular child. Consideration is given to the child's individualistic ways of learning and processing information.

**Closure.** The ability to recognize a whole or Gestalt, especially when one or more parts of the whole are missing or when the continuity is interrupted by gaps.

**Cloze procedure.** A technique used in testing, teaching reading comprehension, and determination of readability. It involves deletion of words from the text and leaving blank spaces. Measurement is made by rating the number of blanks which can be correctly filled.

**Cognition.** The act or process of knowing; the various thinking skills and processes are considered cognitive skills.

**Concept.** An abstract idea generalized from particular instances.

**Conceptual disorders.** A disturbance in the thinking process and in cognitive activities, or a disturbance in the ability to formulate concepts.

**Content words** (class words or lexical words.) Words in a language that have referential meaning, as opposed to words or morphemes with relational value (function or structure words). Content words are roughly similar to verbs, nouns, adjectives, and adverbs.

**Cross-modality perception.** The neurological process of converting information received through one input modality to another system within the brain. The process is also referred to as "intersensory transfer," "intermodal transfer," and "transducing."

**Developmental imbalance.** A disparity in the developmental patterns of intellectual skills.

**Developmental reading.** The pattern and sequence of normal reading growth and development in a child in the learning-to-read process.

**Dyscalculia.** Lack of ability to perform mathematical functions, usually associated with neurological dysfunction or brain damage.

**Dysgraphia.** Extremely poor handwriting or the inability to perform the motor movements required for handwriting. The condition is often associated with neurological dysfunction.

**Dyslexia.** A disorder of children who, despite conventional classroom experience, fail to attain the skills of reading. The term is frequently used when neurological dysfunction is suspected as the cause of the reading disability.

**Dysnomia.** See *Anomia*.

**Echolalia.** The parrot-like repetition of words or phrases or sentences spoken by another person, without understanding the meaning of the language.

**Educational therapist.** A teacher who teaches or treats a child who has difficulty in learning. Specialized materials and methods are used.

**Electroencephalograph.** An instrument for graphically recording and measuring electrical energy generated by the cerebral cortex during brain functioning. It is often abbreviated as EEG.

**Endogenous.** A condition or defect based on hereditary or genetic factors is labeled an endogenous condition.

**Etiology.** The cause or origin of a condition.

**Exogenous.** A condition or defect resulting from other than heredity or genetic factors (such as environment or trauma) is labeled as exogenous condition.

**Expressive language skills.** Skills required to produce language for communication with other individuals. Speaking and writing are expressive language skills.

**Figure-ground distortion.** An inability to focus on an object itself without having the background or setting interfere with perception.

**Figure-ground perception.** The ability to attend to one aspect of the visual field while perceiving it in relation to the rest of the field.

**Function words.** See *Structure words.*

**Grapheme.** A written language symbol that represents an oral language code.

**Homologous.** This term refers to body structures which have the same origin in different species; e.g., the arm of a man and the wing of a bird. It is also used to refer to crawling by moving the two arms together and then the two legs together.

**Hyperkinesis.** Constant and excessive movement and motor activity.

**Hypokinesis.** The absence of a normal amount of bodily movement and motor activity. Extreme lack of movement or listlessness.

**Impulsivity.** The behavioral characteristic of acting upon impulse without consideration of the consequences of an action.

**Individualized reading.** The method of teaching reading that utilizes the child's interest; learning is structured through the child's own reading selections, using a variety of books. The teacher acts as a consultant, aid, and counselor.

**Innate response system.** The unlearned motor responses that the child has within him at birth.

**Inner language.** The process of internalizing and organizing experiences without the use of linguistic symbols.

**Integrative learning.** The type of learning in which all modality systems function simultaneously, working together as a unit. Also the process of incorporating input stimuli with previously learned information.

**Interneurosensory learning.** Learning that results from the interrelated function of two or more systems in combination.

**Intonation system.** The linguistic system within any particular language that has to do with the pitch (melody), stress (accent), and juncture (pauses) of the spoken language.

**Intraneurosensory learning.** Learning that takes place predominantly through one sense modality.

**Itinerant teacher.** A teacher who moves about a school district to several schools and schedules children for teaching periods. Children leave their regular classrooms to work with the itinerant teacher.

**Language arts.** School curricular activities that utilize language, namely: listening, speaking, reading, writing, handwriting, and spelling.

**Language-experience approach to reading.** A method of teaching reading and other language skills, based on the experiences of children. The method frequently involves the generation of experienced-based materials that are dictated by the child, written down by the teacher, then used in class as the material for teaching reading.

**Language pathology.** The study of the causes and treatment of disorders of symbolic behavior.

**Lateral confusion.** See *Mixed laterality.*

**Laterality.** Involves the awareness of the two sides of one's body and the ability to identify them as left or right correctly.

**Learning disabilities.** (Based on definition provided by the National Advisory Committee on Handicapped Children, U.S. Dept. of Health, Education, and Welfare, 1968.) A learning disability refers to one or more significant deficits in essential learning processes requiring special educational techniques for its remediation. Children with learning disabilities generally demonstrate a discrepancy between expected and actual achievement in one or more areas, such as spoken, read, or written language, mathematics, and spatial orientation. The learning disability referred to is not primarily the result of sensory, motor, intellectual, or emotional handicap, or lack of opportunity to learn. Deficits are to be defined in terms of accepted diagnostic procedures in education and psychology. Essential learning processes are those currently referred to in behavioral science as perception, integration, and expression, either verbal or nonverbal. Special education techniques for remediation require educational planning based on the diagnostic procedures and findings.

**Lexical words.** See *Structure words.*

**Linguistics.** The scientific study of the nature and function of human language.

**Maturational lag.** A slowness in certain specialized aspects of neurological development.

**Memory.** The ability to store and retrieve upon demand previously experienced sensations and perceptions, even when the stimulus that originally evoked them is no longer present. Also referred to as "imagery" and "recall."

**Minimal brain dysfunction.** A mild or minimal neurological abnormality which causes learning difficulties in the child with near-average intelligence.

**Mixed laterality or lateral confusion.** Tendency to perform some acts with a right side preference and others with a left, or the shifting from right to left for certain activities.

**Modality.** The pathways through which an individual receives information and thereby learns. The "modality concept" postulates that some individuals learn better through one modality than through another. For example, a child may receive data better through the visual modality than through his auditory modality.

**Morpheme.** The smallest meaning-bearing unit in a language.

**Morphology.** The linguistic system of meaning units in any particular language.

**Ocular pursuit.** Eye movement that is the result of visually following a moving target.

**Oracy.** The communication skills of oral language: listening and speaking.

**Perception.** The process of organizing or interpreting the raw data obtained through the senses.

**Perception of position.** The perception of the size and movement of an object in relation to the observer.

**Perception of spatial relationship.** The perception of the positions of two or more objects in relation to each other.

**Perceptual constancy.** The ability to accurately perceive the invariant properties of objects—such as shape, position, size, etc.—in spite of the variability of the impression these objects make on the senses of the observer.

**Perceptual disorder.** A disturbance in the awareness of objects, relations, or qualities, involving the interpretation of sensory stimulation.

**Perceptually handicapped.** A term applied to the person who has difficulty in learning because of a disturbance in his perception of sensory stimuli.

**Perceptual-motor.** A term describing the interaction of the various channels of perception with motor activity. The channels of perception include visual, auditory, tactual, and kinesthetic.

**Perceptual-motor match.** The process of comparing and collating the input data received through the motor system and the input data received through perception.

**Perseveration.** The tendency to continue an activity once it has been started and to be unable to modify or stop the activity even though it is acknowledged to have become inappropriate.

**Phoneme.** The smallest unit of sound in any particular language.

**Phonetics.** A study of all the speech sounds in language and how these sounds are produced.

**Phonics.** The application of portions of phonetics to the teaching of reading, particularly the teaching of reading in English. The establishment of the sound (or phoneme) of the language with the equivalent written symbol (or grapheme).

**Phonology.** The linguistic system of speech sounds in a particular language.

**Primary reading retardation.** The capacity to learn to read is impaired and no definite brain damage is suggested in the history or neurological examination. Further, there is no evidence of secondary reading retardation (that due to exogenous causes such as emotional disturbances or lack of opportunity). The problem seems to reflect a lack of neurological organization.

**Programed reading.** A method of teaching reading that uses programed self-instructional and self-corrective materials.

**Psychoeducational diagnostician.** A specialist who diagnoses and evaluates a child who is having difficulty in learning. A variety of psychological and educational testing instruments are used.

**Psycholinguistics.** The field of study that blends aspects of two disciplines—psychology and linguistics—to examine the total picture of the language process.

**Readability level.** An indication of the difficulty of reading material in terms of the grade level at which it might be expected to be read successfully.

**Receptive language.** Language that is spoken or written by others and received by the individual. The receptive language skills are listening and reading.

**Resource teacher.** A specialist who works with children with learning disabilities and acts as a consultant to other teachers, providing materials and methods to help children who are having difficulty within the regular classroom. The resource teacher may work from a centralized resource room within a school where appropriate materials are housed.

**Semi-autonomous systems concept of brain function.** A theory of brain function which suggests that at times a given modality functions semi-independently and at other times the modality functions in a supplementary way with another modality system; at still other times, all the modality systems function together as a unit.

**Sensory-motor.** A term applied to the combination of the input of sensations and the output of motor activity. The motor activity reflects what is happening to the sensory organs such as the visual, auditory, tactual, and kinesthetic sensations.

**Social perception.** The ability to interpret stimuli in the social environment and appropriately relate such interpretations to the social situation.

**Soft neurological signs.** Neurological abnormalities that are mild or slight and difficult to detect, as contrasted with the gross or obvious neurological abnormalities.

**Strauss Syndrome.** A collection of behavioral characteristics describing the child who has difficulty in learning.

**Strephosymbolia.** Perception of visual stimuli, especially words, in reversed or twisted order. The condition may be explained as "twisted symbols."

**Structure words** (function words). Linguistic referents for words of a sentence that show the relationship between parts of the sentence as opposed to content words. Structure words include these elements of traditional grammar: prepositions, conjunctions, modal and auxiliary verbs, and articles.

**Syntax.** The grammar system of a language. The linguistic rules of word order and the function of words in a sentence.

**Tachistoscope.** A machine that exposes written material for a short period of time. Practice with such machines is designed to improve rate and span of visual perception of words.

**Tactile perception.** The ability to interpret and give meaning to sensory stimuli that are experienced through the sense of touch.

**Task analysis.** The technique of carefully examining a particular task to discover the elements it comprises and the processes required to perform it.

**Trial lessons.** A diagnostic technique to discover how a child best learns. Short lessons are given through the visual, auditory, tactual, and combination approaches. Evaluations of the child's performance on each provides information concerning his learning style.

**Visual-motor coordination.** The ability to coordinate vision with the movements of the body or parts of the body.

**Visual perception.** The identification, organization, and interpretation of sensory data received by the individual through the eye.

# INDEX